Also by Garrett Epps

The Shad Treatment

The Floating Island: A Tale of Washington

To an Unknown God: Religious Freedom on Trial

DEMOCRACY REBORN

DEMOCRACY
REBORN

The Fourteenth Amendment
and the Fight for Equal Rights
in Post–Civil War America

GARRETT EPPS

A JOHN MACRAE BOOK
Henry Holt and Company · New York

Henry Holt and Company, LLC
Publishers since 1866
175 Fifth Avenue
New York, New York 10010
www.henryholt.com

Henry Holt® and ® are registered trademarks
of Henry Holt and Company, LLC.

"Revolution is the Pod" by Emily Dickinson reprinted by
permission of the publishers and the Trustees of Amherst
College from *The Poems of Emily Dickinson: Variorum Edition,*
Ralph W. Franklin, ed., Cambridge, Mass.: The Belknap Press
of Harvard University Press, Copyright © 1998 by the President
and Fellows of Harvard College. Copyright © 1951, 1955, 1979,
1983 by the President and Fellows of Harvard College.

Distributed in Canada by H. B. Fenn and Company Ltd.

Library of Congress Cataloging-in-Publication Data
Epps, Garrett.
  Democracy reborn : the Fourteenth Amendment and the fight for equal
rights in post–Civil War America / Garrett Epps.—1st ed.
    p. cm.
  "A John Macrae book."
  Includes bibliographical references and index.
  ISBN-13: 978-0-8050-7130-6
  ISBN-10: 0-8050-7130-X
  1. United States. Constitution. 14th Amendment.   2. African Americans—
Civil rights—History.   3. Civil rights—United States—History.   4. Equality
before the law—United States. I. Title.

KF4757.E67 2006   2006043379

Henry Holt books are available for special promotions and
premiums. For details contact: Director, Special Markets.

First Edition 2006

Designed by Victoria Hartman
Printed in the United States of America
    1   3   5   7   9   10   8   6   4   2

For the muse

Gratitude is riches

The youthful elements which constitute the people of the new world cannot submit to rules which are not of their own making; they must throw off the fetters which bind them to an old decrepit order of things. They resolve to enter the great family of nations as an independent member. And in the colony of free humanity, whose mother-country is the world, they establish *the Republic of equal rights, where the title of manhood is the title to citizenship.*

—Carl Schurz (1859)

Revolution is the Pod
Systems rattle from
When the Winds of Will are stirred
Excellent is Bloom

But except its Russet Base
Every Summer be
The Entomber of itself,
So of Liberty—

Left inactive on the Stalk
All its Purple fled
Revolution shakes it for
Test if it be dead.

—Emily Dickinson (1865)

· CONTENTS ·

DEMOCRACY REBORN

PHILADELPHIA 1787:
RED SKY AT MORNING

From his vantage point in Paris, Thomas Jefferson had hailed the makeup of the Constitutional Convention of 1787 in characteristic hyperbole. "It really is an assembly of demi-gods," he wrote to John Adams.

Perhaps. But by August 1787, the demigods were feeling tired and distinctly mortal. Since May 25, they had spent day after day in the small assembly room of the Pennsylvania statehouse, dressed in wool and broadcloth finery amid the humid swelter of Philadelphia—the new nation's cosmopolis, to be sure, but still in summer something of a fever port. To make the room even hotter, they had barred the windows, lest the revolutionary plan they were hatching—to scrap the entire American political system and replace it with a powerful national government—leak out before their work was completed. Day after day, they had marched through agonizing problems. Would the new government have no executive, multiple executives, or only one? That dilemma was solved by creating a powerful presidency custom-tailored for the convention's presiding officer, George Washington. Would there be a new system of federal courts? That one they finessed, by creating a Supreme Court and leaving the question of lower courts to the discretion of future Congresses. How would the new Congress be selected? The large and small states had compromised on this, creating a House apportioned by population and a Senate in which each state would be equal. Who could veto laws passed by Congress? They lodged this power solely in the president, just as the British reposed it in their king. What powers would Congress have? Nationalist delegates like James Madison wanted the Constitution to state that Congress would have the power to "legislate in all cases to which the separate States are incompetent, or in which the harmony of the United States may be interrupted by the exercise of individual Legislation [and] to negate all laws passed by the several States." But delegates jealous of the powers of the states had forced a retreat, giving Congress a set of enumerated powers that were designed to keep it out of local matters.

What we know about what went on in that small hot room is mostly revealed in handwritten notes taken by Madison, the strongest advocate of a powerful new national government. Many delegates took lengthy leaves of absence during the summer, drawn away by their own business affairs or the deliberations of the Continental Congress, meeting in New York. Not Madison. Day after day this earnest, brilliant little man was in his seat, scribbling in his odd abbreviated style what each delegate had to say about each part of the proposed new government. Night after night, while other delegates relaxed amid the pleasures of a city known for fine wine, sophisticated conversation, and beautiful women, Madison stayed at his desk, revising his notes and reviewing the historical record of federal republics, beginning with the Amphictionic League of ancient Greece and moving forward to the contemporaneous Dutch Republic. Madison's gifts to the new country include the plan of both the Constitution and the Bill of Rights; but even set against those triumphs, his handwritten notes represent an important legacy to the future.

Those notes spark many feelings in Americans today. There is exhilaration and pride, to be sure. These fifty-five men, who came from states with radically different interests and wildly divergent social systems, were patient, practical, and often eloquent. They were willing to listen to those who differed with them and to change their most profound ideas if the arguments on the other side seemed good—or the disagreement so profound that it might threaten the convention with failure.

The debates, however, also spark dismay and even shame. The demigods did not see how inequality of wealth and status, of sex and race, would poison the new republic they were building. A reader feels compassion, too, for men who were racing against chaos in the new country to build a structure for a future they could only dimly foresee. And finally, from time to time, there is puzzlement. Because amid the true debate—the cut and thrust of brilliant minds with differing views—there were repeated moments of reticence, when important questions about the future were floated by one speaker or another, only to fall dead without any response in the still dusty air of the hall. Such a moment came on September 12, after the convention had, with great labor, produced an all-but-final draft of the document to be adopted. Without warning, George Mason of Virginia (who would eventually refuse to sign the Constitution because he viewed it as a blueprint for "monarchy, or a tyrannical aristocracy") popped up to suggest that the convention should now produce a Bill of Rights. "It would give great quiet to the people," Madison records Mason saying, "and with the aid of the State declarations, a bill might be prepared in a few hours."

Like marathon runners hearing that the finish line might be moved a couple of miles farther back, the convention received this idea in sullen silence. Not a single state delegation voted to proceed with drafting a Bill of Rights. It was a mistake; the lack of a Bill of Rights outraged many Americans, and came close to dooming the new Constitution to rejection.

But of all the lost voices of Philadelphia 1787, the one that should most haunt modern ears is that of Gouverneur Morris of New York, who rose on August 8 to say what many of the delegates knew in their heart, but deeply wished not to acknowledge or discuss.

Crowded as the delegates were in the small meeting room in the

East Wing, there was something huge in it with them—an ill omen that no one truly wanted to acknowledge. As Philadelphia spring turned to summer, most of those present had come to realize that the infant republic carried within it the seeds of its own destruction, flaws that might strangle the child in the cradle, or destroy it years or even decades later.

When the delegates gathered, they had expected friction between the large powerful states like Virginia and New York on the one hand and the small states like New Jersey and Georgia on the other. That divide surfaced quickly and shaped the schemes for electing Congress and the president. But another less expected division appeared in Philadelphia—one that never went away again. On June 30, Madison noted that "the States were divided into different interests not by their difference of size, but by other circumstances; the most material of which resulted partly from climate, but principally from their having or not having slaves. These two causes concurred in forming the great division of interests in the U[nited] States. It did not lie between the large & small States; it lay between the Northern and the Southern. . . ."

The divide was not as simple as we might imagine today. There was no gulf between "slave states" and "free states" because in 1787 there was only one free state—Massachusetts, where a court decision had effectively throttled the institution in 1783. (Vermont, which had abolished slavery in 1777, was still an independent republic and would not join the Union until 1791.) There were slaves in all the other states—twenty thousand of them in New York alone. But there was a difference between North and South—the difference of climate Madison referred to. Slavery in the North was an embarrassment; worse than that, it was unprofitable. But in the plantations of the South, soil and rainfall favored the cultivation of cash crops for sale abroad—tobacco, rice, indigo and, more recently, cotton. Those crops could only be grown profitably with slave labor, and the planters who ruled the Southern states found that embarrassment lessened as profits increased. They were wed to slavery and zealous to protect it from any new government created in Philadelphia. The men sent by the South—led by Charles Pinckney and his cousin, General Charles Cotesworth Pinckney, both of South Carolina—wanted a federal government that would have no power over slavery. More than that, the new government must be pledged to *protect* slavery as well. "S[outh] Carolina & Georgia cannot do without slaves," General Pinckney explained to the convention. Over and over during the weary months of constitution-making, the Southerners made their position clear: if they did not get protection and support for slave property, the South would not join the new Republic and the convention's program would fail.

The prospect of disunion was terrifying to all the delegates, Northern and Southern. Gouverneur Morris on July 5 had set out starkly what he saw as the stakes; they were not just national survival but perhaps the very lives of those present and their families. Disunion meant civil war and blood running in the streets. "This country must be united. If persuasion does not unite it, the sword will," he warned. "The scenes of horror attending civil commotion cannot be described, and the conclusion of them will be worse than the term of their continuance. The stronger party will then make traitors of the weaker; and the Gallows & Halter will finish the work of the sword."

But Southerners vowed they would risk disunion rather than give up the protections they sought. Northerners believed them; and so, link by link, they forged the multiple chains that would tie slavery to the federal government. Congress could control interstate and foreign commerce, but it would not be allowed to bar the import of slaves until 1808. Northern states were required to return runaway slaves to their Southern masters, even if slavery became illegal in the North. If the Southern states faced a slave revolt, the federal government was required to furnish troops to crush it. Congress could tax imports (which the people of the North depended on) but not *exports*—the cash crops that fueled the slave economy.

Many of the Northern delegates were embarrassed by the bargain they felt forced to strike. But the discomfort did not break out into the open until the convention tackled the issue of apportionment. The new House of Representatives would be chosen "by the People of the several states." But power in the House was to be distributed according to population. Here the power of the slave states became more than embarrassing; it began to seem onerous. Led by the Pinckneys, Southern delegates at first insisted that every slave be counted in the state's population for apportionment; these human chattels, who could not vote or marry or enter into contracts or testify in court, were nonetheless entitled to *representation* in Congress—representation that their white masters would supply, gaining power in the federal government as a reward for their maintenance of a slave system. With a great show of magnanimity, the South at last consented to abandon the idea of full representation for its slaves. Instead, it would "compromise" at something called "the federal ratio," which had once been proposed by the Continental Congress for the apportionment of taxes. For each slave, the state would receive credit for three-fifths of a free citizen. As a result, one white voter in the South might have the same power as two or even three in the North.

Nor was that the end of it. Madison had proposed that the people elect the president; but the Southern interests feared being outvoted in those elections, too, and they supported another "compromise"— the president would be chosen by "electors," and each state would have the same number of electors as it had members of Congress. Thus the slaves who boosted Southern power in the House would also give it a heightened voice in the choice of the president as well.

On August 8, the "three-fifths compromise" finally pushed Gouverneur Morris over the edge of parliamentary politeness. Morris had warned the convention of the consequences of disunion, an apocalyptic vision of civil war and summary execution. Now he looked at the alternative—union on Southern terms—and he did not like that much better.

In 1787, Morris was a veteran revolutionary, though still only thirty-five. Born in New York, he had been selected as a delegate to the convention from Pennsylvania, where he had moved only ten years earlier. His figure was unforgettable. Well over six feet tall (his political enemies called him "the Tall Boy"), he was the only delegate who could match the convention's president, George Washington, in physical stature. His appearance was unforgettable, not only because of the good looks that attracted women to him throughout his life, but because a carriage accident had led to the amputation of his left leg seven years earlier. He would hoist himself aloft on a wooden leg and teeter above his colleagues as he spoke. Morris rose often—only Madison and James Wilson of Pennsylvania spoke more often than he did during the deliberations. And when he spoke, the members took notice—though not a few, no doubt, did so with as much disquiet as fascination. Because Morris not only spoke often, he spoke well, and, unlike many more practical politicians, he said what was on his mind.

One recent biographer, Richard Brookhiser, has called Morris "the rake who wrote the Constitution." Rake he was, both as a young man and in the years after Philadelphia, when he scandalized Paris with his affair with Adèle de Flahaut, a married woman who was also the mistress of the Revolutionary diplomat Talleyrand. As for the Constitution, he might better be called its "editor"—true authorship, if it lies anywhere, goes to Madison—but Morris's agile pen smoothed out the final version before adoption, adding, among other things, the felicitous words "We the People of the United States." Morris's constitutional effectiveness stemmed from his politics, which are even more worthy of note than his amours: he was that rarest and most useful of figures, a conservative who genuinely embraced radical change.

During the years before Independence, Morris had repeatedly sought to slow the momentum toward revolution. But once the colonies were in the fight, he single-mindedly pursued victory. He was not a soldier (he was once nominated for a commission in the New York militia, but was repulsed at the idea that his unit would be commanded by a mechanic, far below him in social status). He was, instead, a decisive, even ruthless, man of affairs. Beginning in 1778, he began to work with the Revolution's financier, Robert Morris (no relation), to bring stability to the colonial economy and to raise much-needed funds to pay soldiers and purchase matériel. As a member of the Continental Congress, he spent the terrible winter of 1778 at camp with Washington at Valley Forge. Though his first response was characteristically worldly ("there are no fine Women here," he mournfully wrote a friend), the ordeal of the Continental army convinced him that an army moves on its nation's pocketbook as much as on its stomach; the very survival of the Revolutionary cause depended on convincing the members of the Congress, and the skittish state governments they represented, to tax themselves in order to pay and supply the troops in the field. Morris was one of the first strong advocates of a national currency; he suggested that it take its name from the popular Spanish dollar. In early 1783, when the Continental army threatened Congress with revolt if the troops were not paid, Morris was in the background, endorsing, if not helping plan, the confrontation. He viewed it as the only way to convince the nation to "give to the Government that power without which Government is but a Name."

August 8 displayed Morris's conservative radicalism at its finest. On that day, he moved to rescind the three-fifths compromise and to base representation in Congress only on the number of "free inhabitants" in a state.

Madison meticulously noted Morris's explanation, which cut to the heart of the dilemma confronting the delegates. Morris "never would concur in upholding domestic slavery. It was a nefarious institution. It was the curse of heaven on the States where it prevailed." States that relied on slavery, he said, were poor, unhappy, barren, ignorant, and uneducated, a picture that must have nettled the Pinckneys (and perhaps the slave-owning Madison himself). "Upon what principle is it that the slaves shall be computed in the representation?" Morris asked. That proposal "comes to this: that an inhabitant of Georgia and [South Carolina] who goes to the Coast of Africa, and in defiance of the most sacred laws of humanity tears away his fellow creatures from their dearest connections & damns them to the most cruel bondages, shall have more votes in a Gov[ernment] instituted for protection of the rights of mankind, than the Citizen of P[ennsylvania] or N[ew] Jersey who views with a laudable horror, so nefarious a practice."

This was a fool's bargain, Morris warned. "What is the proposed compensation to the Northern States for a sacrifice of every principle of right, of every impulse of humanity[?] They are to bind themselves to march their militia for the defence of the S[outhern] States; for their defence ag[ainst] those very slaves of whom they complain." Then he said plainly what many delegates must have been thinking: not only did slavery risk calling down God's judgment on those who maintained it, but the institution had now warped the new Constitution almost beyond redemption. "He would sooner submit himself to a tax for paying for all the negroes in the U[nited] States, than saddle posterity with such a Constitution."

Even more than two centuries later, Morris's words are compelling; but after he spoke them, an eerie calm returned. In future years, words such as Morris's would earn Northern leaders challenges to a duel, or blows of the bastinado; but on this occasion the Southern delegates found them unworthy of any but the most dismissive reply. "Mr. [Charles] Pinckney [of South Carolina] considered the fisheries & the Western frontier more burdensome to the U.S. than the slaves," Madison noted. "He thought this could be demonstrated if the occasion were a proper one." Then Morris's motion was put to a vote; it failed ten states to one, and was lost forever.

The problem of slavery and its political power was rarely mentioned again; and on September 10, when Morris sat down at the head of the "committee on stile" to put the Constitution into final form, he did not object to any of the provisions he had excoriated the month before. Between disunion and "the curse of heaven," he, like most other delegates, opted for the curse.

When the delegates finally signed the Constitution on September 17, the aged Benjamin Franklin rose to rejoice in the convention's success. On the back of the president's ceremonial chair in the hall, he pointed out, craftsmen had painted a sun half-hidden by the horizon. "Painters," Franklin said, "had found it difficult to distinguish in their art a rising from a setting sun." But with the adoption of the new draft Constitution, "I have the happiness to know that it is a rising and not a setting Sun."

The old man was right. The Constitution, after much suspense, was ratified, and the United States took its place on the world stage as a full-grown republic, capable of growth, change, and self-defense. But we now know that Franklin's rising sun was ascending into any sailor's nightmare, an angry red morning sky. What historian Leonard Richards called "Morris's Prophecy" proved prescient indeed. The "curse of heaven" troubled the new union from its inception, and the storms came more often and more violently as its history progressed. To most Americans, the Framers of the Constitution are more than demigods. They are "the Founding Fathers." They predicted America's rise to world dominance and political stability; they found the "brilliant solution" that led to "the miracle at Philadelphia"; like Einstein or Prometheus, they "split the atom of sovereignty": like God in the six days of Creation, they brought a new world into being.

But demigods are not gods, and the Constitution of 1787 was neither divine nor eternal. The compromises the Framers made brought the government into being; but they doomed it as well. The political power the Framers gave to the slave states grew and grew in importance as the eighteenth century turned into the nineteenth. By early in the federal period, many Northerners began to complain that the slave South would, under the new rules, always outvote the free North. Within a few years, they had coined a term to describe the problem. The nation, they said at first hesitantly and then more insistently with each passing year, was not ruled by "we the people." It was ruled by something they called "the slave interest," or "the slavocracy," or, most commonly, "the Slave Power." With its constitutional privileges, the Slave Power ruled Washington, and whether the issue was taxation, war, or westward expansion, this protected interest was able to shape national policy to its will. Because the federal government had limited powers, the slave states were able to impose strict control on their own populations. No voices challenging slavery were permitted, and whoever lost Southern elections, slavery always won. Because the structure of the federal government was built around the three-fifths compromise, the South had congressional and electoral votes to bargain for Northern support. By the 1830s, many Northern voices had begun to suggest that Morris had been right all along—the Union with slavery at its heart was more dangerous to free Northern society than no Union at all.

Then, after years of threats, crises, and cobbled-together compromises, the nation was obliged to fight yet another, far bloodier, revolutionary war. The Constitution of 1787 died at Fort Sumter. And when the guns fell silent in 1865, the Union was still in grave danger.

Those who gathered in Washington after Appomattox knew that victory depended on taming the Slave Power, on making sure it did not survive the death of slavery itself. A few small adjustments would not save the nation. What was needed was a renovation of the Framers' house. That renovation appears today toward the end of the Constitution under the bland heading "Amendment XIV." At more than four hundred words, the Fourteenth Amendment is the longest amendment ever ratified, and it has, over time, changed almost every detail of our national life. Scholars have called it "the second Constitution." This second Constitution was not perfect, to be sure; like the first, it was marred by compromise and expediency, as the first had been. But it did produce—in words Gouverneur Morris wrote into the final text of the Constitution—"a more perfect union" than the old one.

Even though Americans still revere the demigods of 1787, few of us know the names or the stories of the sages of 1865. The leaders whose work is detailed in this book, though, belong in our historical memory alongside Madison, Franklin, and Morris. It is they, not the Philadelphia Framers, who planted democracy's seeds in the Constitution.

Who are the most important of this group? President Andrew Johnson, to begin with, more or less forced constitutional change on the country through his obstinate refusal to acknowledge that the Civil War had changed anything. Johnson's adamant opposition to reform energized his enemies in Congress, who came together to frame the Fourteenth Amendment. Senator Charles Sumner of Massachusetts, and Representative Thaddeus Stevens of Pennsylvania, spoke for the new constitutional vision that came directly out of American antislavery and abolitionism, and their experience with the Slave Power shaped the amendment's final text, directly and indirectly. Senator William Pitt Fessenden of Maine, a less intense, more intellectual antislavery voice, spoke in the cool, rational tones of Framers like Madison and Morris. Senator Lyman Trumbull of Illinois had already learned how to create constitutional change, as the principal author of the Thirteenth Amendment outlawing slavery. Representative John Armour Bingham of Ohio drew his inspiration from a stubborn, dissenting Presbyterianism; he insisted that America's destiny was to create a republic of equal citizens modeled directly on the kingdom of God.

Not all the important players held political office. The black abolitionist Frederick Douglass was active outside Congress, opposing some of the compromises that white members of Congress thought expedient. The German-American soldier, diplomat, and politician Carl Schurz insisted that the new American republic must include immigrants and their children on equal terms with other Americans. The utopian crusader Robert Dale Owen, American voice of socialism, birth control, divorce, and spiritualism, was a profound ideological force and produced a draft that led directly to the amendment's final text. The feminist leaders Susan B. Anthony and Elizabeth Cady Stanton, who could not vote or serve in Congress, nonetheless shaped the debate about the new meaning of freedom.

These "Re-Framers" were not demigods. Most were practical, sometimes rather prosy men in frock coats who bear an uncomfortable resemblance to politicians in the early twenty-first century. By turns prescient, bold, altruistic, blind, timorous, and self-seeking, they nonetheless saved the nation as surely as did the men of 1787. We live in the house they redesigned.

· 1 ·

THE BRAVE TAILOR

On May 23 and 24, 1865, Washington, D.C., was the scene of the most powerful military display in the history of the New World: the Grand Review of the Armies of the Potomac and the West. These two armed behemoths, commanded by George G. Meade and William Tecumseh Sherman, respectively, had destroyed the Confederacy. Now they had assembled to parade in triumph in front of their commander in chief.

Abraham Lincoln had been dead more than a month. The Grand Review was to follow the same route his catafalque had taken on April 19, before his body, in a flag-draped casket, was loaded on a train for the final trip to Springfield.

But today was not a day for mourning. Thousands thronged downtown Washington—one estimate suggests the population of the city increased by nearly 50 percent during the Review's two days—to watch what remained of the mighty armies that had saved the Union.

It was a celebration, though a subdued and somber one. As historian Shelby Foote explains, for every two living Union soldiers stepping in cadence before the reviewing stand, the ghost of another—killed by bullets or cannon, disease or accident—marched unseen by their side.

In December 1863, one British newspaper correspondent had described wintertime Washington as "a great, scrambling, slack-baked embryo of a city basking in the December sun like an alligator on the mud-bank of a bayou in July." The years of fighting since then had brought little in the way of civic improvement. In 1865, the city was a throbbing but shabby agglomeration of 120,000 permanent residents, augmented by an unknown number—as many as 30,000 by some estimates—of former slaves who had fled there during and after the fighting, and who now lived precariously in makeshift shelters and shacks in the city's side streets and alleys. Carriages and horses thronged the cobblestones of Pennsylvania Avenue; on the side streets, chickens, ducks, and pigs wandered freely over oceans of mud. The railroad canal that ran from Capitol Hill to Georgetown was a reeking mass of filth, so noisome that residents forced to go near it tied handkerchiefs across their faces.

As for the magnificent structures of government—the Capitol, the Treasury, the White House—they were surrounded by cheap hotels, seedy gambling houses and brothels, pawnshops, and secondhand clothing stores, or simply by vacant lots waiting for future use. The marble buildings reminded visitors of the ruins of a vanished civilization rather than the triumphant monuments of a rising power. Henry Adams, whose life was spent in and out of the capital, wrote that his first impressions of it were of the Post Office and the Patent Office facing each other across an unruly waste "like white Greek temples in the abandoned gravel pits of a deserted Syrian city." Not much had happened since Adams's boyhood to make the place seem more finished.

In front of the White House, carpenters had erected a reviewing stand, sheltered from the sun by an awning, for the president, Lieutenant General Ulysses S. Grant, the Cabinet, and the diplomatic corps. Other stands were reserved for members of Congress and for the army's officers and their families. A philanthropist from Boston had also paid to erect a fourth stand, for the wounded soldiers who were still in hospitals but well enough to see the show. Further down Pennsylvania Avenue, toward the Capitol, ordinary citizens—more than had ever appeared in those streets before—sat in bleachers, or stood for hours in the brilliant sun to watch the greatest army in America's history—in some ways the greatest army that had ever existed on the earth—march past.

For two days—in all, thirteen solid hours at any one point on the route—the armies paced past. Meade's Army of the Potomac was natty in new fitted uniforms and rakish kepis. The infantry marched twenty abreast, the cavalry rode twelve across. The mounted troops alone, on the first day, took an hour to pass the reviewing stand (ever the showman, the young Major General George Armstrong Custer somehow managed to spook his horse just as it appeared before the reviewing stand, so that the rider appeared to the crowd in all his glory, dashing madly down the street, yellow hair flying, and bringing the stallion under control before leading his division past the president).

After the horsemen came the infantry, 160 regiments, five hours of ranks of twenty, each unit bearing its unit guidons, tired, tattered flags that had been through the country's greatest battles and showed it. Following each regiment came its mule-drawn ambulances carrying stretchers still stained with the blood of the wounded and the dead. Even more stirring was the sight the next day, when Sherman's Army of the West took its place in the review. Unlike the eastern soldiers, Sherman's men knew few fancy drill maneuvers; their uniforms were so faded by wind and weather that one onlooker almost could not tell whether they were Union blue or Confederate gray—though no one would have doubted which side they were on once they sighted the presidential reviewing stand and burst into the popular new patriotic song, "Marching Through Georgia":

> *Hurrah! Hurrah! We bring the Jubilee!*
> *Hurrah! Hurrah! The flag that makes you free!*

The assembled crowds loved Sherman's men, who marched with a loose stride but kept their eyes rigidly forward. "The column was compact," Sherman wrote proudly in his memoirs, "and the glittering muskets looked like a solid mass of steel, moving with the regularity of a pendulum."

One of the thousands of onlookers in front of the White House that day was Walt Whitman. Whitman had come to Washington early in the war and had stayed as a self-appointed hospital visitor and volunteer nurse for the thousands of wounded and dying who had flowed back from the battlefields of Virginia to lie, often thirsty or in pain, in the city's makeshift hospitals (which sometimes, when the butchery was particularly intense, included the Rotunda of the Capitol). To support himself, the poet had found a day job, as the pardon clerk in the attorney general's office, copying documents attached to the applications from defeated Southerners for restoration of their civil rights.

The job was so appropriate—it put Whitman in the very epicenter of the political and constitutional earthquake that would consume the nation for the next few years—that one should not be surprised that Whitman had found it. For nearly twenty years before the war, Whitman had striven to be the spirit of America—more than its conscience or even its voice, he had sought to embody the entire country within himself, with all its contradictions, to contain the American multitudes, white and black, Northern and Southern, male and female. In some ways, his greatest disappointment was the publication of the first edition of his masterwork, *Leaves of Grass*. The book had sold respectably, and the critics had been rhapsodic. But Whitman had wanted more, as his biographer, David S. Reynolds, has written. He had hoped—he had expected—that *Leaves* would by itself heal the country.

In such hubris—and in the suffering it brings—poets find their share of greatness. After two decades as a poet and journalist, Whitman had refined his spirit until, in 1865, he was like a powerful instrument that can detect tiny tremors, inaudible sounds, and insignificant disturbances and piece them together into a prophecy of what is to come. Whitman was impressed by the review; in "Spirit Whose Work Is Done" he recalled seeing

those slanted bayonets, whole forests of them appearing in the
  distance, approach and pass on, returning homeward,
Moving with steady motion, swaying to and fro to the right and
  left,
Evenly rising and falling while the steps keep time.

But of all the awe-inspiring sights he saw during the review, the one that impressed him most was the new president, Andrew Johnson of Tennessee. "I saw the President several times," he wrote his mother the day after the review, "stood close by him, & took a good look at him—& like his expression much—he is very plain & substantial—it seemed wonderful that just that plain middling-sized ordinary man, dressed in black, without the least badge or ornament, should be the master of all these myriads of soldiers, the best that ever trod the earth, with forty or fifty Major-Generals, around him or riding by, with their broad yellow-satin belts around their waists— and of all the artillery & cavalry—to say nothing of all the Forts & Ships, &c., &c."

Whitman had detected what was truly new in the review. For though the armies' grim cannons and repeating rifles were destructive in a way that past generations could not have imagined, there was nothing new about military power and triumph. But Andrew Johnson, on those May days when he stood before the White House in immaculate black broadcloth, was something new to Americans of his time, though he would be more than familiar in ours. Andrew Johnson was the first modern American president.

No president in our history—not Washington, or Jefferson, or Andrew Jackson, or even Lincoln himself—had ever held in his hands such power as Johnson possessed in May 1865. Today Americans are used to the idea that the nation's leader holds the keys of life and death for millions. But in 1865, the modern presidency was something new. Some presidents, like Washington and Jackson, had won the office through their martial prowess. But as chief magistrate, they had cut, by today's standards, rather modest figures. Except in time of war, presidents had almost no standing military to command. They had few sources of information that they did not share with everyone else, and they were heavily dependent on Congress to fund and approve the things they wanted to do. Presidents walked the streets of Washington like everyone else, often without any escort, and their fellow citizens were used to seeing them engaged in mortal occupations.

Lincoln had changed all that, without really meaning to. He was to all appearances a simple republican figure, unhandsome and awkward, usually dressed in ill-fitting clothes. He would often go riding in the street, or would take Mary Todd Lincoln for a solitary drive in a carriage. (Whitman, who came to love the martyred president and spent much of the rest of his life reciting a popular lecture on his greatness, had often seen Lincoln walking or riding, and while the two never spoke, they would exchange smiles and nods of recognition, neighbors passing in the street.) When Lincoln was curious about the news, he would pick up his hat and stroll to the War Department, at Seventeenth and G Streets NW, to get the latest information from a telegraph clerk.

But the outward simplicity was deceptive. Lincoln had transformed the office. By the time of his death, he was commander in chief of a quarter-million-man army. The telegraph office, so inconveniently located, put him in touch with his officials and commanders all over the country. And he commanded, for the first time, a fearsome "national security" apparatus, too—military provost marshals who monitored what citizens did and said, not only along the battlefront but in cities well behind the lines. A suggestion from a federal official would lead within hours to the arrest of a suspected spy or traitor, who might be held without charge until the president relented.

Despite his ongoing headaches with Congress, Lincoln had mastered and subdued that unruly institution, too. In his first days in office, he had on his own authority expanded the army, committed the public credit to pay for the war, ordered a naval blockade of the Confederacy, and suspended habeas corpus nationwide. Explaining these actions, he sounded a distinctly modern note, portraying the president as an official charged with immediate action and uniquely in touch with public opinion: "These measures, whether strictly legal or not, were ventured upon, under what appeared to be a popular demand, and a public necessity; trusting, then as now, that Congress would readily ratify them." Congress had grumbled, but it had ratified. The executive now dominated the government, and the nation, in a way that none of the Founders—or even the politicians of 1860—could ever have imagined.

In fact, Lincoln's death had completed the process. Now the office was defined by the remembered greatness of a martyr; Booth's bullet marked the first time an assassin had successfully targeted a president. It also brought to view a truth that every president since then has understood: the president of the United States is now so important that strangers believe they can save the world simply by killing him.

What made the president so potent was death, death on an unprecedented scale—a holocaust that consumed the lives of 620,000 men in uniform. The North lost 360,000, the South 260,000, by official count, and that count is woefully incomplete. Many blue- and gray-clad bodies were never found or counted, and many civilians died during the four years of fighting, either from stray bullets or ordnance or from disease, starvation, and private "irregular" violence that flared up in the wake of the advancing armies. The war—not yet called "the Civil War," it was known to Northerners as "the Rebellion" and to Southerners as "the war for Southern independence" or "the Revolution"—had spread death and destruction on a scale not seen on the North American continent since the beginning of time.

And it was not just lives that had disappeared. Americans attending the grand review might easily have been searching for the country they had known—the loose federation of local communities over which the government in Washington had genially presided like a distant, absentminded uncle. Their new nation was a bustling, centralized military-industrial machine. The federal government supervised railroad construction, local road-building, and a host of other projects; interstate corporations, gigantic by antebellum standards, were growing fat on the federal cash spent for arms, uniforms, rations, and rolling stock. Even that cash was new: for the first time in history, the United States had a national currency, the famous "greenbacks," paper money backed by nothing but a promise, each dollar bill imprinted with the imposing dome of Salmon P. Chase, the Treasury secretary who had printed it; and Americans had learned an unfamiliar word to describe what happens when the government prints money to pay for its needs—"inflation."

For the first time, Americans paid a tax on their income—3 percent for those who made between $600 and $10,000 a year, and 5 percent for the wealthy who made more than $10,000. For the first time, federal officials arrived in local communities to draft men into the army, willingly or otherwise. And for the first time, U.S. Army provost marshals could appear anywhere—in private homes, in public meetings, even sometimes in churches—to arrest ordinary citizens deemed disloyal in word or deed and take them to military prisons to await trial by special military tribunals.

Even "We the People" were different. Despite the massive losses on the battlefield, the territory of the United States housed 4 million more people in 1865 than it had at the time of the 1860 census, for a total of a whopping 35.7 million. Most of the increase came from immigration, foreigners from Germany and Ireland. Some 350,000 immigrants fought under the Stars and Stripes between 1861 and 1865, 20 percent of the army's total strength for those four terrible years.

And they were not the only new citizens to don Union blue; by the time of Lee's surrender in April 1865, one active-duty American soldier in every four was of African descent: either Northern free blacks or escaped Southern slaves, earning on the battlefield a de facto citizenship that the Supreme Court had closed to them as recently as 1857. Northern and Southern whites alike, most of whom were neither abolitionists nor particularly racially enlightened, found the sight of proud black regiments (unthinkable as late as 1862) profoundly new and unsettling, a mark of the strange new country that was rising from the ashes of the old.

Such were the office and the country Andrew Johnson had inherited. His tragedy—and the tragedy of the nation—is that he never understood the unique opportunities and perils of the power he wielded. In 1865, Andrew Johnson was fifty-six years old, a handsome, strong-looking man who appeared to be in his prime. Six feet tall, broad in the shoulder, with an imposing head and jutting brows, he looked the part of president far more than had Lincoln, with his overlong telescoping limbs and ill-fitting clothes. Johnson customarily dressed in black, wearing an impeccably fitted full frock coat and vest matched with black doeskin trousers. He took pride in his clothes; by trade, he was a tailor.

He and Lincoln shared many similarities. Both were sons of the upper South—Lincoln had been born in Kentucky, Johnson in North Carolina. Both came from humble origins. Lincoln's father had been a farmer, Johnson's a bank porter and roustabout. Neither had been formally educated—Lincoln had only a few years of elementary school, Johnson had no schooling at all. Both had achieved prosperity by hard work and sheer determination; both loved the Union with an almost religious devotion, and both had risked their lives to preserve it.

But there were profound differences that were, in 1865, less easy to discern. Character, modern political commentators like to say, is the essential quality to seek in a president. Issues change, unexpected crises appear; what is inside a leader determines the nation's fate. And yet even today, in the twenty-first century, we do not understand the wellsprings of character—why the office strengthens one president and destroys another. Foremost among the enigmas of our history must surely be the transcendent qualities Lincoln displayed during the nation's greatest crisis. Uneducated, politically inexperienced, provincial, awkward, disorganized, Lincoln in 1861 had few if any traits promising greatness as a chief executive. Yet he rose to the challenge as few men could have. Faced with discouragement—the long delays, the repeated bloody defeats—he was determined. Faced with opposition, ridicule, and disloyalty, he was forebearant. Faced with the unexpected, he did not hesitate to compromise and discard his own plans if change would suit the greater good. He had, it seems, no personal vanity at all, and cheerfully joined hands with politicians who had ridiculed him behind his back. Seemingly passive, he had an unparalleled sense of where history was moving. He had the confidence to wait, even though his friends and his enemies urged precipitate action, until the moment was ripe.

Johnson's character, the nation would learn over the next year, was in many ways the opposite of Lincoln's. His long solitary struggle had made him self-confident and even vainglorious. He judged the world around him by his own story and people by their allegiance to him. He never forgot, and rarely forgave, a political slight. He was impulsive, and in the heat of the moment was given to making promises he could not keep. Once committed to a course, however, he was inflexible, and those who differed with him, even slightly, became his enemies.

Biographers try to illuminate Johnson's singular character by telling his story: the boyhood of poverty in North Carolina; the apprenticeship at age nine, which seemed to him barely one step above slavery; the escape at fifteen, and the long trek by foot first to South Carolina and eventually across the Smoky Mountains to the East Tennessee hill country, where slavery was little practiced; the marriage to Eliza McCardle; the steady rise in business and politics—from penniless tailor's boy to prosperous businessman and urban landowner; and service as mayor, state legislator, congressman, governor, and finally senator: The war years, when Johnson was the only Southern senator to remain in Congress. Service—at considerable danger—as Lincoln's military governor in Union-held Tennessee. Finally, the nomination for vice president at a time when Lincoln despaired of reelection and sought a Southerner, and a lifelong Democrat, to give a facade of national unity to the Republican Party, which had renamed itself in 1864 the National Union Party.

Such a success story would swell the self-assurance of any mortal. It was far more glorious, in its early stages, than Lincoln's, who underwent bankruptcy and repeated political eclipse before catching the antislavery updraft in 1860. Johnson's years as a political rebel had trained him to rely only on himself and had given him an unshakeable and idiosyncratic set of political principles. He was an orthodox Jacksonian, emotionally bound to a vision of democracy by and for white men, committed to the welfare of the landless, the poor, and the working class from which he had sprung.

Class resentment is probably the dominant motif of Johnson's early life. He was a runaway apprentice, as much subject to recapture and return as a fugitive slave. To escape that fate, Johnson walked from North Carolina to Tennessee. He arrived there in 1825, at the age of seventeen, and finished learning the tailor's trade there. Eventually he moved his entire family to Tennessee and supported them by a flourishing business as a master tailor. Over the years, he also bought up real estate around town, then turned his attention to politics.

When he bought his family their first real house, the neighbors raised their eyebrows at the upstarts. One family in particular complained that a calf the Johnsons were raising bellowed too much during the day. Years later, the neighboring family went bankrupt. The well-to-do Johnson appeared at the auction and ostentatiously bought the property. One acquaintance in the crowd asked him what he would do with it, and Johnson replied in a loud voice, "I want it, by God, for a calf pasture."

He revered the Union and the Constitution as the Founders had written it in 1787. States' rights, free trade, limited government spending, and hard money were absolutes. Until well after war began, he took the most extreme pro-slavery position available: not only could the federal government not abolish slavery, he argued, but neither could a state government. The institution was sacred and no government could touch it. He himself owned nearly a dozen slaves; in later years he boasted that he had never sold a slave, although property records in Greeneville suggest otherwise. But he hated the "Slave Power"—the aristocrats in the plantation regions—as much as any Northerner, and sought throughout his career to do away with the political bonus these slavemasters received through extra legislative representation, in both the state and federal legislatures, for their slaves. For black Southerners he had nothing but contempt. A proposal to strike the word *white* from voting rolls, he wrote during the

1850s, "would place every splay-footed, bandy-shanked, hump-backed, thick-lipped, flat-nosed, wooly headed, ebon-colored negro in the country upon an equality with the poor white man." Time and war had not softened this view, and after he became president he was quoted in a Missouri newspaper as saying, "This is a country for white men, and by God, as long as I am President, it shall be a government for white men."

Like many other Southern slave owners, Johnson was at the same time convinced that he understood black people in a way that Northerners never could. His "understanding" included the idea that blacks were inferior, that their destiny was to serve whites, and that their "true" white friends were those who urged them to accept that status without hoping for more. Even by the standards of the time, it was a relatively unfriendly message, but Johnson thought it was not only benevolent but almost divine. He had a fondness for comparing himself to biblical figures, and one of his most famous moments before taking office was the "Moses speech," delivered on October 24, 1864.

The audience was a crowd of black Tennesseans who thronged the streets in front of the statehouse in Nashville. It was a "serenade"—an evening visit at which the crowd shouted for a speech from Johnson, the military governor. Newspaper accounts describe the dark street, lit only by flaring torches and transparent lanterns. The crowd was packed shoulder to shoulder, receding into the darkness as far as the eye could see. Johnson was stirred by the moment to claim for himself a place in history as important as that of Lincoln. Lincoln's Emancipation Proclamation had freed only the slaves behind Confederate lines; now, on his own authority, Johnson impulsively "freed" the people of Tennessee, black and white: "I, too, without reference to the President or any other person, have a proclamation to make; and, standing here upon the steps of the Capitol, with the past history of the State to witness, the present condition to guide, and its future to encourage me, I, Andrew Johnson, do hereby proclaim freedom, full, broad, and unconditional, to every man in Tennessee!"

Johnson then delivered a full-throated Radical speech, advocating destruction of the planter class and redistribution of their land to the freed slaves. From now on, these proud planters would play no role in ruling the South: "Loyal men, from this day forward, are to be the controllers of Tennessee's grand and sublime destiny, and Rebels must be dumb."

Turning to the subject of his black audience, Johnson coyly said that he was "almost induced to wish that, as in the days of old, a Moses might arise who would lead them safely to their promised land of freedom and happiness."

The crowd, which had had long experience in taking hints from white men, began to shout, "You are our Moses!"

Johnson feigned reluctance, saying that "in due time your leader will come forth; your Moses will be revealed to you."

"We want no Moses but you!" came the answer.

"Well, then, humble and unworthy as I am," Johnson shouted, "if no other better shall be found, I will indeed be your Moses, and lead you through the Red Sea of war and bondage, to a fairer future of liberty and peace." The applause was so tumultuous that Johnson must have felt that God himself was speaking from the burning bush. And he seemed genuinely puzzled when black Americans and their white allies called him inconsistent or even disingenuous in his later acts. After all, he had promised to lead them; he had not promised where.

Johnson's views were not unique; but they were extreme, and utterly inflexible. The key to this inflexibility may lie in his behavior at the moment that—had Lincoln not gone to Ford's Theater on Good Friday 1865—would have been the pinnacle of his career, a moment of triumph Johnson managed to convert into disgrace. On Inauguration Day 1865, Johnson went to the Capitol to meet with his outgoing predecessor, Hannibal Hamlin, before taking the vice-presidential oath before a crowd seated in the Senate Chamber. Johnson was unsteady on his feet; his health had been poor for a few weeks, and his condition had not been helped by a drinking bout the night before with his old friend John W. Forney, the secretary of the Senate. Just before Hamlin was to lead him into the Senate, Johnson impulsively asked whether there was liquor at hand. Hamlin, from the teetotal state of Maine, had none, but a messenger brought a bottle of brandy from the Senate restaurant. Johnson gulped two-thirds of a tumbler, then had a refill. As the two men were walking out the door, Johnson, seemingly in a panic, returned for yet another glass.

By the time he rose to give his inaugural address, the new vice president was drunk. He rambled through an account of his glorious career, and reminded the Cabinet members that they, like him, owed their eminence to the people. "I will say to you, Mr. Secretary Seward, and to you, Mr. Secretary Stanton, and to you, Mr. Secretary"—here he paused and in an audible whisper asked Forney, "Who is the Secretary of the Navy?" "Mr. Welles," Forney whispered—"and to you, Mr. Secretary Welles, I would say, you all derive your power from the people."

Cabinet members closed their eyes or hid their faces in embarrassment. "I was never so mortified in my life," Zachariah Chandler wrote. "Had I been able to find a hole I would have dropped through it out of sight." Johnson stopped only when Hamlin firmly tugged him on the arm.

Johnson had a drinking problem, and indeed, by current standards, the record seems to suggest that he was a full-blown alcoholic. His most recent biographer, Hans Trefousse, acquits him of the charge; but he does so by saying that on *some* days Johnson did not drink his usual two to four glasses of whiskey, and that Johnson "was inebriated in public only once." That occasion, however, was what any reasonable man would have expected to be the most important day of his life. No one but a compulsive drinker would have let his need for liquor overcome his prudence and self-interest.

Much that is shadowy about Lincoln's successor becomes clearer when viewed as the conduct of a man who was either drinking or fighting an overpowering urge to drink. His inner rage and resentment, rigidity, impulsiveness, self-pity, vindictiveness, and rampant egotism—his penchant for angry, even homicidal rhetoric and his habit of making public commitments without a moment's pause to consider where they would lead—suggest a man whose personality had been warped by alcohol.

Johnson's family life seemed, in contemporary terms, dysfunctional. That his son Robert was an open drunkard and a frequent patron of prostitutes, even when working in the White House, not even Johnson himself could deny. His wife, Eliza, was a recluse who lived in the smallest room of the White House's second floor and would never appear in public. Eliza suffered from consumption; but even so, there is something extreme in her withdrawal, suggesting the depressed and passive-aggressive behavior of an alcoholic's spouse.

It was a singular misfortune that this gravely flawed man had inherited the mantle of the modern presidency. Lincoln had forged the office by his prudence and his flexibility. He never spoke without thinking, he never committed himself before the right moment. He understood that the American earth was moving under his feet, and he let himself evolve to match. Johnson, by contrast, would never understand that history was not the lengthened shadow of his own experiences and beliefs.

That difficulty was made harsher precisely because the office he now held was so powerful. Americans now feared their president, and were anxious to placate him. And in their fear and flattery, Johnson misperceived love and vindication. In the first months after Lincoln's death, no one dared speak to him anything but soothing words and supplications. It was treatment that could turn the head and distort the judgment of any mortal—and in many ways, Andrew Johnson was more mortal than most leaders.

Historians continue to debate whether Andrew Johnson truly changed during the spring and summer of 1865, moving from his angry denunciation of Southern aristocrats into an alliance with them against the antislavery people of the North, or whether his Reconstruction policies were simply a continuation of his old-style Jacksonian unionism. Johnson did not perceive himself as changing, though to the outside world he seemed to veer 180 degrees. His "policy" was at all times, and always had been, focused on himself—his own leadership, his own enemies, his own allies. In many ways, the political world revolves around an American president. Johnson accepted himself as the center—and paid little attention to the revolutions around him.

Consider Johnson's conduct: The day after Lincoln's assassination, the new president made a first public speech in which he discussed at great length his own rise to power, the sacrifices he had made for the Union, and his intention to keep his principles intact in the months ahead. He seemed to view his elevation to the presidency as an inevitable result of his virtuous career, rather than the accidental result of a national tragedy. "My past public life, which has been long and laborious, has been founded, as I in good conscience believe, upon a great principle of right which lies at the basis of all things," he said, and added, "Toil and an honest advocacy of the great principles of free government have been my lot. The duties have been mine, the consequences God's." Conspicuously missing was any reference to Abraham Lincoln. After the speech, Senator John P. Hale of New Hampshire drily remarked that "Johnson seemed willing to share the glory of his achievements with his Creator, but utterly forgot that Mr. Lincoln had any share of the credit in the suppression of the Rebellion."

A week later, on April 21, Johnson met with a delegation of officials from Indiana and vowed bloody vengeance on the leaders of the Confederacy. "I know it is very easy to get up sympathy and sentiment where human blood is about to be shed, easy to acquire a reputation for leniency and kindness, but sometimes its effects and practical operations produce misery and woe to the mass of mankind," he said. "It is not promulg[at]ing anything that I have not heretofore said to say that traitors must be made odious, that treason must be made odious, that traitors must be punished and impoverished."

But while he espoused seemingly Radical intentions, historian Eric Foner notes, "the President embarked on a course of amazing leniency." In early May, he recognized the temporary wartime governments of Arkansas, Louisiana, Tennessee, and Virginia—created solely by Lincoln's presidential decree—as official and permanent members of the Union. On May 29, he recognized the provisional

North Carolina government headed by William W. Holden and instructed Holden to conduct an election under the state's restrictive, all-white voting rules. On the same day, he issued his amnesty proclamation, which restored full citizenship and all confiscated property to most participants in the rebellion. Later in the summer he ordered the Freedmen's Bureau to oust freed slaves from confiscated plantations, where the government had encouraged them to settle, and restore the land to its former owners.

Johnson made an exception to the restoration of civil rights: high officials of the Confederate government and all Southerners who owned property worth more than $20,000 would have to apply to Johnson personally for a pardon.

The drama of the pardon-seekers soon came to dominate Johnson's time and attention. Walt Whitman, true to form, was at its center, for his office handled all applications for pardon. "There is a great stream of Southerners comes in here day after day, to get *pardoned*—All the rich, and all high officers of the rebel army cannot do anything, cannot buy or sell, &c., until they have special pardons—(that is hitting them where they *live*) so they all send or come up here in squads, old & young, men & women."

One can only imagine the delicious vindication this proud, angry man came to feel as the cream of the old Slave Power crept humbly to the White House door to plead for their futures. All the slights and exclusions of Johnson's boyhood, the rage and resentment of his adult career, must have been assuaged by their humility, their flattery, and their supplication—or, more delicious still, by the decorous entreaties of the wives of officials and officers, such as Jefferson Davis, who were still in prison or too ill to travel to the capital. Every outsider dreams of the day when those who have mistreated him will cower and beg for his friendship. The Slave Power was at Andrew Johnson's mercy, and its members hastened to assure him that he was the wisest, fairest, most admirable leader in the Republic's history. While he held the sword above them, how could they say otherwise? But Johnson believed their flattery and considered these sycophants his only true and loyal friends.

Journalist Whitelaw Reid visited Washington during the summer of 1865. "All summer long the capital was filled with the late leaders in Rebel councils, or on Rebel battle-fields," he wrote. "They filled all avenues of approach to the White House. They kept the Southern President surrounded by an atmosphere of Southern geniality, Southern prejudices, Southern aspirations. Mr. Johnson declared that treason must be humbled—they convinced him that they were humble. That traitors must be punished—they showed him how they had suffered. That only loyal men should rule—they were all loyal now."

On his visit to the White House, Reid counted "two or three Rebel Generals, as many members of the Rebel Congress and at least a score of less noted leaders" as well as a former Confederate secretary of war. When the president's office door was opened, "the crowd rushed in as if scrambling for seats in a railroad car." Johnson was waiting with "a pile of pardons, a foot high, watched by a young Major in uniform."

In return for their pardons, Johnson's new friends offered him much more than friendship: "They cunningly showed him how he could secure the united support of the entire South and of the great Democratic party of the North, with which all his own early history was identified, for the next Presidency."

Stronger mortals than Andrew Johnson might have bent under that temptation. By comparison, the Republicans could offer him little. He and they had no history. Johnson must have known that these were men loyal to antislavery ideas he had never shared, to a Republican president he had barely known, and to a Northern Republican Party that would never embrace him. Beyond that, surely he knew that many of these men had seen and judged him on that terrible morning when he had stood in the Senate chamber and driveled like a drunken fool. In the faces of the supplicating Southerners he read no such derision or doubt.

His embrace of the conquered South must have been more palatable because it could be disguised as a dispute with the Radicals over the meaning of the Constitution. The real difference between

South and North lay in the future of Southern society. All agreed that slavery was dead, and most Southerners assured Johnson that they accepted its demise. All agreed that the South must repudiate secession and proclaim that the slave states had never truly left the Union. The Radicals and Johnson agreed that the Confederate debts, and the debts contracted by state governments during the war, must also be declared null and void.

What about the freed slaves? Even conservative Republicans believed that they must be granted their basic civil rights. In the nineteenth century, this term, from the common law, referred to the basic right to personhood under the law. "Civil" rights permitted an individual to marry, to follow a trade, to own land or property, to enter into contracts, to testify in court, and to sue and be sued. Free blacks in the antebellum South had not enjoyed any of these rights fully. The law restricted where they could live, what jobs they could perform, and what property they could own. No black witness, free or slave, could testify against a white man. To antislavery Northerners, full civil rights seemed like the minimum that would be acceptable.

Beyond those rights, however, lay what nineteenth-century Americans called political rights. Chief among them were the right to serve on juries and, most important of all, the right to vote. In 1787, even the most visionary Framers had understood the ballot as a privilege granted by society to those most suited to use it properly. A prudent republic granted the vote only to men (and a few women; in the eighteenth century, a few states, like New Jersey, allowed some women to vote, though by 1860 the ballot was again all-male) who had sufficient independence to make their votes true expressions of civic choice. Voters were free men, not indentured servants, apprentices, or slaves. They owned enough property to make them capable of resisting the corruptions of coercion and patronage.

The Founders saw little injustice in excluding most of society from the vote. They believed in representative government. Today that phrase denotes a system where elected representatives carry the authority of those who elect them; at the dawn of the Republic it meant something slightly different. Voting in elections was *itself* a "representative" act. The small minority of actual voters were the "representatives" of the people at large.

But that founding understanding, like so much else in early American thought, contained a contradiction. Two, in fact. To begin with, the rebellious colonists of 1776 had proclaimed that there could be "no taxation without representation." They did not send delegates to Parliament, they argued, and thus could not be bound by Parliament's decisions. To British thinkers, this argument was nonsense. The colonies *were* represented, because voters in England were "virtual representatives" of the colonists, precisely as women and the poor were "represented" by voters of property. The colonists rejected this argument, and that rejection began the subversion of the idea of the restricted franchise.

Beyond that, the patriots of 1776 had boldly proclaimed in the Declaration of Independence that "all men are created equal." Ever since, this ringing language had posed a theoretical problem for American political thinkers. If all men were equal in the eyes of God, why should some be less than equal before the law of man?

And in the 1850s, a few voices began applying Jefferson's language from the Declaration of Independence to black Americans as well. As a Senate candidate in 1858, Lincoln opposed black voting. Nonetheless, he asked persistently whether the South should be allowed to read the Declaration as saying "all men are created equal, *except Negroes*." Surely American equality meant more than that. To Lincoln, it at least meant that a black man had "the right to eat the bread, without leave of anybody else, which his own hand earns."

Even that meager equality was too much for the South, of course, and by 1850 or so Southern thinkers like John C. Calhoun and George Fitzhugh were adamant that the Declaration was meaningless. Any fool could see that men were *not* "created equal." The inequalities were part of God's plan. Andrew Jackson's old crony, Chief Justice Roger B. Taney, had written in *Dred Scott* that black people had not been Americans in 1776, and that under the Framers' Constitution they were not citizens now and never could become citizens, no matter what Congress might decide.

By 1865, though, black Americans had powerfully staked their claim for citizenship. By their thousands they had flocked to the Union colors, and once they were given the chance, they had fought bravely. Most knowledgeable Americans, North and South, agreed that, without these black soldiers, the North would not have won the war. Frederick Douglass, who took proudly upon himself the role of the voice of black America, had seen in 1863 what the success of black soldiers meant: "Once let the black man get upon his person the brass letters, U.S.; Let him get an eagle on his button, and a musket on his shoulder and bullets in his pocket, and there is no power on earth which can deny that he has earned the right to citizenship."

Citizenship meant, at a minimum, the basic civil rights that free blacks did not now enjoy. But to some Radical Republicans, it also meant the vote. Lincoln himself had begun to see this in the months before his death, and had rather timidly suggested to his military governor in Louisiana that "the very intelligent [black men], and those who have fought" should be entered in the voting rolls. Radicals had another reason for favoring black suffrage. Only with the votes of the freed blacks would a true two-party system be possible in the South, they argued. Without the political competition black voting would create, the Slave Power would re-create itself.

The Republican arguments—Radical or conservative—were lost on Andrew Johnson. He was no Republican; he was a Jacksonian Democrat who still held the pure faith as handed down a quarter-century earlier. Democracy to him meant rule by white men. "White men alone must manage the South," he remarked to an associate in 1865. A freed slave, he told George Luther Stearns, "will vote with the late master, whom he does not hate, rather than with the non-slaveholding white, whom he does hate." His personal secretary in the White House, Colonel William G. Moore, later remembered Johnson as showing a "morbid distress and feeling against the negroes." Moore recalled an occasion when the president espied a group of black laborers at work on the White House grounds. Angrily he ordered them sent away and replaced with whites.

In Andrew Johnson's Republic, there would be precious little black voting and no federal civil rights for blacks either. And here he was able to disguise his quarrel with the Radicals as a high-minded constitutional dispute. The Constitution gave authority over suffrage to the states, he argued. It would be a gross arrogation of power for any federal official to tell state governments whom to allow at the polls. More and more, as 1865 wore into 1866, Johnson came to see himself as the guardian of the true Constitution and of true democracy, the great defender of the people, fighting against new traitors— traitors to him, and thus, by easy extension, to the Union—not in the Southern cities but in the capital, indeed, in Congress itself.

That Johnson shifted in his views is clear from one fact. In June 1865, not long after his amnesty proclamation, Johnson turned to Carl Schurz for advice about the South. Anyone committed to a conservative course would have understood that Schurz would not give congenial counel.

Carl Schurz—"General Schurz," as he had been until a few weeks after the assassination—was as different from Andrew Johnson as chalk is from cheese. A legendary figure to German-Americans, he had been a major factor in the Republican victory in 1860. German-born immigrants that year held the margin of victory in a number of Midwestern states. Schurz had galvanized this powerful voting bloc with his speeches.

To those voters Schurz was, quite literally, a legend in his own time. In 1850, at the age of twenty-one, he had engineered a daring escape from Spandau Prison, the notorious sixteenth-century fortress near Berlin where Prussian authorities held their most dangerous political prisoners. Schurz had rescued a beloved professor, Gottfried Kinkel, a hero of the abortive German revolution of 1848. When the Prussian emperor, Friedrich Wilhelm IV, struck back against the liberal reformers, Schurz escaped to France. But Kinkel was sentenced to life in Spandau. Schurz surreptitiously reentered Prussia and bribed a guard to lower Kinkel from an attic window to the street sixty feet below. The professor and his star student slipped out of Prussia on a boat for England. Schurz went to London and tarried only long enough to woo and wed a wealthy German heiress, Margarethe Meyer, before embarking for the freedom of America in 1852.

In 1859, he won national fame with his speech, "True Americanism." The speech was a rebuke to Massachusetts voters who were flirting with the American, or "Know-Nothing," Party, which wanted to deny immigrants the vote. In the purity of its republicanism, in its nineteenth-century optimism, and in its implicit faith in America's special destiny, the speech stands today as a startlingly clear exposition of the beliefs of an entire generation of Republicans that inspired a constitutional revolution after the Civil War.

Standing in Faneuil Hall, where the patriots of 1776 had gathered, Schurz traced the history of European settlement of North America. Not just the English had come here, but also the French, the Dutch, the Norwegians, and the Germans. "All the social and national elements of the civilized world are represented in the new world" where "their peculiar characteristics are to be blended together by the all-assimilating power of freedom. This is the origin of the American nationality, which did not spring from one family, one tribe, one country, but incorporates the vigorous elements of all civilized nations on earth."

The disparate elements, Schurz said, represented not one people or one race, but the hopes and aspirations of all people everywhere. In "the colony of free humanity, whose mother-country is the world, they establish *the Republic of equal rights, where the title of manhood is the title to citizenship.*"

Schurz warned his audience that the Slave South showed how denial of equal rights led directly to tyranny. The whites of the South, he said, were no more free than their slaves. "Where is their liberty of the press? Where is their liberty of speech? Where is the man among them who dares to advocate openly principles not in strict accordance with the ruling system? They speak of a republican form of government—they speak of democracy, but the despotic spirit of slavery and mastership combined pervades their whole political life like a liquid poison," he said.

Massachusetts was in danger of taking the first steps down the road to oppression, he warned. "Ah, sir," he said, "is there a man in Massachusetts, except he be a servant of the slave-power, who cannot hear me advocate the equal rights of man, without feeling serious pangs of conscience" for the state's flirtation with nativism?

In 1860, Schurz barnstormed Wisconsin, Illinois, Indiana, Ohio, Pennsylvania, and New York; Lincoln, always eager to share credit, later said that Schurz's efforts had been decisive in his victory that year.

He received a commission from the president as a brigadier general. But his greatest war service probably came during the hard-fought campaign of 1864, when he rallied German voters behind Lincoln in widely publicized speeches in Philadelphia, New York, and Milwaukee.

After Lincoln's death, Schurz hastened to the White House to meet Andrew Johnson and offer his advice on treatment of the conquered land. Johnson, the nation would learn, was more of a talker and less of a listener than Lincoln had been. He showed Schurz a draft of a plan for reorganizing civilian government in North Carolina. The plan projected elections limited to white voters. Schurz suggested that the president delay. Johnson asked the former general to return to talk to him about the matter.

On May 29 Schurz learned that Johnson had issued the North Carolina proclamation without any change. He quickly wrote the president suggesting a different approach: "impartial suffrage" in the Southern states. South Carolina, for example, had a clause in its constitution limiting the vote to property holders. Why not require something like that, and allow those few blacks who held property to vote along with the whites? Schurz volunteered to go to the South and advise the president of conditions there. Johnson made no reply to this idea, but he invited Schurz to return to see him.

While on a long layover in Philadelphia waiting for the midnight train to Washington, Schurz dined at the home of a prosperous German-American doctor. The family had lost two sons in the fighting. Unsurprisingly, they had become enthusiastic believers in the "spiritual telegraph," and the family's fifteen-year-old daughter had begun to receive messages from the Other Side. After dinner the family urged Schurz to join in the thrilling pastime that was sweeping the country.

Schurz was somewhat skeptical when the séance began, but like many people who join this sort of paranormal play in fun, he was soon hooked. Impulsively Schurz asked to speak to Lincoln. When a message came through indicating that the fallen president was standing by, Schurz asked the question that was on his mind: Why had Johnson summoned him back to the capital?

"He wants you to make an important journey for him," "Lincoln" wrote, and added the admonition "Do not fail" to do what the new president asked. Writing years later, Schurz recalled that "Lincoln" also predicted that one day he would be a U.S. senator—not from Wisconsin or Pennsylvania, but from Missouri, where Schurz had seldom even visited.

We can forgive Schurz for believing the voice of Abraham when it told him what he wanted to hear. Spiritualism, to midcentury Americans, was scientific, not superstitious. As scholar David Reynolds notes, Walt Whitman came to think of himself as a kind of medium receiving poetry from the ether, and in 1855 he named the "Lawgivers of Poets": "the anatomist chemist astronomer geologist phrenologist spiritualist mathematician historian and lexicographer." In 1860, no less august an authority than Robert Dale Owen, son of the English socialist Robert Owen and himself by turns a champion of birth control, divorce, and abolition, produced a learned tome calling "the American Epidemic [of Spiritualism], more wonderful in its manifestations, far wider spread in its range, than any of the mental epidemics, marvelous in their phenomena as some of them have been, recorded by physicians and psychologists of continental Europe."

Not long after Owen wrote, the epidemic reached the White House, where President Lincoln and his wife, Mary Todd Lincoln, mourned the loss—a small one amid death's carnival, but as for parents everywhere, overwhelming in its private sorrow—of their beloved son Willie, who had died in February 1862 of what was probably typhoid fever. Mary Lincoln eagerly sought out mediums and conducted as many as eight séances in the White House itself. Owen read the president a paper on spiritualism. (Afterward, Lincoln was reported to have said, "Well, for those who like that sort of thing, I think it is just about the sort of thing they would like.")

Schurz arrived in Washington fresh from his spiritual conversation with Lincoln's voice, and hastened to the White House. He must have been uncomfortable—an abolitionist, a Radical, a German intellectual—waiting in the anteroom with the snuff-dipping, gray-clad chivalry of the defeated Slave Power. But Johnson saw him promptly. "His North Carolina proclamation was not to be understood as laying down a general rule for the reconstruction of all 'the States lately in rebellion,'" Schurz remembered the new president saying during their interview. "As to the Gulf States, he was very doubtful and even anxious. He wished to see those States restored to their constitutional relations with the General Government as quickly as possible, but he did not know whether it could be done with safety to the Union men and to the emancipated slaves." As Lincoln's ghost had foretold, Johnson asked Schurz to travel for him. Would Schurz take a trip through the Gulf states and write to Johnson about how he found conditions there?

Schurz said yes. He would go south and report what had become of the states that had been part of the old country, and that now lay at the feet of the new nation. As he departed, though, he must have cast his mind back to the scene at the White House, and to the obstinate Southern president he had met there. Perhaps he even wondered, as others around the country had begun to do, whether the new president, whose armies had crushed the Slave Power, was now thinking of giving back to his own region the victory Northern blood had won.

· 2 ·

DARK WISDOM

December 4, 1865, the opening day of the Thirty-ninth Congress, was a balmy clear day. The Capitol had a new cast-iron dome, finished in 1863 and topped with a statue of *Armed Freedom*. Within a few weeks, the scaffolding would be removed from the inside of the dome, marking the end of a decade of renovation. Despite the expense, Lincoln had insisted on finishing the work, as if replacing the dome could restore the Union; so workmen and artists had labored on throughout the war, while below them the Rotunda had been converted, first to a temporary barracks and then, after the disaster at Bull Run, into a makeshift military hospital. In 1863, while war continued, the statue of *Armed Freedom* had been placed atop the dome. To this day, *Armed Freedom* stands guard over the Republic in a Roman-style military helmet. The original design had pictured her in a Liberty cap of the kind made popular during the American and French Revolutions. But in 1856, in the waning days of the Pierce administration, the secretary of war had demanded a change. Liberty caps were associated with freedom for slaves; as long as Jefferson Davis was in the Cabinet, freedom would have nothing to do with emancipation.

Across First Street stood the Old Capitol, where Congress had met after the British burned the Capitol during the War of 1812; later it had been a boardinghouse, the temporary home, among others, of Southern patriarch John C. Calhoun. Lincoln had made Old Capitol a prison, where suspected war profiteers or Confederate spies were jailed, sometimes without formal charges, for months or years at a time.

The opening session was more crowded than any before in the nation's history. A brilliant parade of prominent citizens streamed into the building and jammed the galleries, the hallways, and even the floor of the chambers. A few must have turned to watch as the most important member of the House of Representatives—the leader who would become Andrew Johnson's most dangerous enemy—was carried onto the floor in a chair.

The symbolism, though unintentional, was profound. In 1787, when America's leaders gathered in Philadelphia, the oldest and most beloved of the delegates to the constitutional convention was carried to Independence Hall each morning in a chair. At eighty, Benjamin Franklin was then the living symbol of America and of its struggle for independence; his daily arrival in a chair carried by four strong men—prisoners from the city jail—seemed to onlookers to be a kind of benediction on the secret work of the convention.

The elder statesman of the Thirty-ninth Congress had also to be carried about in a chair. And like Franklin, Thaddeus Stevens worried that his countrymen would fumble away the gains of the struggle just past. But Stevens, who was seventy-three on December 4, 1865, comes down to us as a considerably more ambiguous figure than Franklin. Few American politicians—at least few who did not become president—inspired, and continue to inspire, such controversy as Stevens. Franklin's benign countenance seems to beam across the centuries with prosy good humor; Stevens, to most Americans who have heard of him, is a Saturnine figure, bitter, misshapen, and full of hate. If we picture Franklin, it is as a plain figure in a powdered wig, flying a kite with a key on the string to prove to the world that lightning was electricity. Thaddeus Stevens wore a wig, too, but only to hide his baldness. Franklin's hobby was science and the spread of enlightenment; Stevens passed many idle hours in the legal gambling hells that lined Pennsylvania Avenue, grimly wagering for small stakes at faro.

And when it comes to lighthearted anecdotes, the closest is a tale of how young Stevens and a few fellow students once fell upon a cow that wandered onto school grounds and hacked it to death. It is hardly the stuff of which kindly images are made. Eighty years after his death, his biographer, Fawn M. Brodie, noted that "the smell of brimstone, the suspicion of fanaticism, the aura of revolution, surround him still."

But Thaddeus Stevens was no devil—or at least, his devilishness was leavened with an admixture of something higher. Another biographer, Ralph Korngold, reached for a quote from Alexander Pope to characterize Stevens, calling him "[a] Being Darkly Wise and Rudely Great."

The words suit Stevens, who disturbs us not because he was an inhuman idealist, but because he was an all-too-human humanist. Unlike the godlike images we have graven of the eighteenth-century Founders—benign Franklin, noble Washington, mercurial Jefferson, far-seeing Madison—Stevens looks back at us with a face that is undeniably like our own, by turns passionate, self-doubting, merciful, and choleric.

The caricature of Thad Stevens created by D. W. Griffith in his film *Birth of a Nation*—of a malignant clubfoot inspired only by envy and contempt—is grotesquely off the mark. For there is much to respect in Stevens's character and career. He was persistent, creative, politically brave, intellectually honest, and above all motivated by a passion for equality. His legacy to his nation was, in its way, nearly as important as Franklin's. Like Franklin, he presided over a constitutional revolution, a new beginning for the Republic. Like Franklin, he himself contributed little to the specifics of the new design; but like Franklin, he was an animating spirit of the body that designed it, a presence without whom the result might not have occurred.

But while there is much to admire, there is not much about Stevens that inspires love. Part of the reason is physical. Even in the days before heart and liver disease robbed him of the power to walk, Stevens knew himself to be a figure out of nightmare. Born with a clubfoot (his elder brother had two club feet), Stevens disguised the deformity with a special boot, but for all his life he walked with a marked limp, and on occasion he purposely frightened children by brandishing his misshapen foot and snarling, "It won't bite!" As a young man he had been handsome of face and a famously skilled rider and athlete, but at the age of thirty-nine a "brain fever" (probably typhoid) left him completely bald. He covered his scalp ever after with an ill-fitting chestnut wig.

Politically, as well, Stevens has little of the noble aura history has bestowed on the Founding Fathers. As a lawyer and politician, he was at once crafty and self-destructive; as a debater and companion, he was at the same time vicious and principled. Above all, he was a practical, realistic professional politician, committed at every moment not only to writing a legacy for the future but to winning advantage for his party and his cause in the present.

Stevens's greatest contradiction was his admixture of genuine idealism and cynicism. In his view, most people were self-serving and cowardly; and yet throughout his life he fought to bring them greater knowledge and more freedom. The unrestrained viciousness of his wit, the rumors of bastardy and crime that dogged him through a largely honest life, even the very grotesquery of his appearance, were tools he seems to have consciously contrived and cultivated, as means of winning the larger political prizes for which he fought. Even though his causes eventually triumphed, he himself was immolated in the struggle: never once did he attain the high office he sought, either in the Cabinet or, most earnestly, in the Senate.

Stevens himself thought that one reason he never advanced politically was that popular rumor linked him romantically with his housekeeper, Lydia Smith. Lydia, who came to live in Stevens's house in 1848, was an attractive and refined widow twenty years his junior. But that was not where the scandal lay: Lydia Smith was black, or more properly a "mulatto." The daughter of a white father and a free black mother, she had never been a slave and had lived most of her life in Pennsylvania. She was clearly more than a servant; she mixed with his nephews and nieces on terms of equality, and Stevens insisted that they refer to her as "Mrs. Smith," an honorific almost never given to black servants in the North or the South. He himself respectfully called her "madam."

As so often in American life, it was thought more scandalous for a man to love one black woman than to enslave or oppress many, a peculiar delicacy that persists to this day. In her 1959 book, *Thaddeus Stevens, Scourge of the South*, Fawn Brodie drew the obvious conclusion. "The fact is," she concluded, "that there is a good deal more evidence [of the nature of their bond] than has been realized." (Stevens's most recent biographer, Hans Trefousse, rather primly admits no more than that "it is impossible either to prove or to disprove" Brodie's conclusion.) Yet Brodie related one telling episode that Trefousse omits: Jonathan Blanchard, a longtime friend and a clergyman, urged Stevens in 1868 to accept the sacrament of baptism; Stevens declined obliquely, stating that he had some vices, though not as many as some other political figures. The one historical figure he would compare himself to, he said, was Richard Johnson, a Kentucky slave owner who had become vice president under Martin Van Buren even though he openly lived with his slave housekeeper and had raised two children from the alliance.

In December 1865, Stevens had met his hour—the time of revolution, in essence, when, as historian Eric McKitrick notes, a "marginal politician" could move into the vacant centers of power and set national policy for generations to come. He had waited long enough for it. Educated at Dartmouth, he had moved to southeastern Pennsylvania and begun a modest practice of law, which took off when he defended a local farmer who killed a constable. Stevens argued that the man was insane; the jury rejected his plea, and his client was hanged. But his spirited defense of an unpopular client won him fame in the area, and by 1817 he was one of the best-known and most successful lawyers in Pennsylvania. He also argued a case in which a slave from Maryland claimed Pennsylvania residency—and thus freedom. Stevens won the case—for the slave owner, who regained his "property."

That was the last time, however, that Thaddeus Stevens appeared in court, or anywhere else, on behalf of the Slave Power. From then on, throughout his long and sometimes erratic career as a lawyer and a politician, Stevens's caustic voice was insistently raised in favor of the humanity of the slave and against the cruelty of the master.

Stevens's political career included some odd episodes. He was by turns a member of the Anti-Masonic Party (crusading against the danger of the Freemasonic "conspiracy"), a Whig, and a Know-Nothing. In 1838, he and his fellow Whigs in essence attempted to seize control of the state government by altering vote totals, an attempt that gave rise to what was called the "Buckshot War" and ended with Stevens ignominiously fleeing a lynch mob by jumping out an open window of the state capitol. But he also consistently gave his voice to crusades for betterment and brotherhood. His most successful fight in his native state was for a system of free public schools. Largely thanks to him, Pennsylvania in 1834 passed the first law outside New England to provide for free schooling for all children. Outraged at the "waste" of public funds, the voters subsequently swept into office a new legislature with a mandate to repeal the school bill. But when the new body met in 1835, Stevens's eloquent appeal single-handedly turned the tide. "Build not your monuments of brass or marble," he pleaded with his fellow lawmakers, "but . . . make them of everliving mind!" As if bewitched by his eloquence, the two houses then reversed a Senate repeal vote and actually voted to strengthen the new school system.

For much of the 1830s and 1840s, Stevens donated his services as a lawyer to the defense of escaped slaves seeking to avoid return to slavery. For Stevens, as for many Northern whites, the defining moment of the struggle against slavery came with the passage of the Fugitive Slave Act of 1850, a grotesque one-sided "compromise" brokered by Senator Henry Clay to reassure the militant South that its interests were safe inside the Union. The act set up a special federal bureaucracy with sweeping powers and one aim—to help slavemasters reenslave blacks in the North whom they claimed as their escaped slaves. The new federal commissioners were given the power to swear warrants for the capture of any black person in a free state whom a slave owner alleged to be an escapee. The warrants were executed by federal marshals—and the marshals were invested with the extraordinary power to require any citizen to join a slave posse on the spot or face imprisonment and fine. Once captured, the "escapee" was given a hearing, at which the master's testimony would be admitted, but the "slave's" would not. Afterward, the federal slave commissioner would receive a $10 fee for each slave he ordered returned, but only $5 for each free black he ordered freed.

In all, the act was a triumph for the slave states and for the Northern "dough-faced" politicians—chiefly members of Andrew Jackson's Democratic Party—who served their interests in exchange for support in Congress and national elections. But if it was a triumph, it was, like so many Southern victories, a Pyrrhic one. Black resistance broke out almost at once, near Stevens's home, in one of the most celebrated incidents of antislavery violence in American history—the Battle of Christiana, September 11, 1851.

Christiana, Pennsylvania, is in the southeast corner of the state, near the borders of Maryland and Delaware, then both slave states. The Quakers who lived there had long taken it as a religious duty to extend a welcome to free blacks and escaped slaves, and a small free black community had grown up there. One of that community's leading lights was an innkeeper named William Parker. On the night of September 11, a Maryland slave owner, Edward Gorsuch, appeared outside Parker's door with several relatives and three U.S. deputy marshals. Their aim was to reclaim two of Gorsuch's slaves who had slipped across the state line to freedom more than two years earlier. Waiting for them were more than twenty black men, armed with rifles, knives, axes, and other farm weaponry.

"I will have my property," vowed Gorsuch, "or go to hell." Hell soon followed. Sources are unclear about who fired first, but by the end of the exchange Gorsuch was shot dead and his corpse mutilated;

his son was seriously wounded, and four others—two black, two white—were less seriously hurt.

President Millard Fillmore, heavily indebted to slave-state interests, responded by calling out the U.S. Marines. Three of the black participants fled to Canada, but the federal government indicted thirty-six blacks and five whites for "wickedly and treasonously intending to levy war against the United States." The defendants turned to the state's best-known antislavery lawyer, Thaddeus Stevens.

The defendants, wearing red, white, and blue scarves, were tried in the second-floor courtroom of Independence Hall—one story above the hallowed chamber where the Constitution (including the fugitive slave clause) had been written seventy-five years earlier. Knowing that his antislavery reputation might inflame the federal judge hearing the case, Stevens engaged a defense team that included a prominent Democrat, John M. Read, to present the closing argument. But he himself conducted much of the examination of witnesses, and the trial record bears the mark of his famous sarcasm. "Sir—did you hear it?" he asked at one point. "That three harmless non-resisting Quakers and eight-and-thirty wretched, miserable, penniless negroes, armed with corn cutters, clubs, and a few muskets, and headed by a miller, in a felt hat, without arms and mounted on a sorrel nag, levied war against the United States!" The charge was such a grotesque overreaching that even the judge, a pro-slavery Democrat, felt obliged to instruct the jury considering the first case that the acts alleged did not "rise to the dignity of treason or levying war." When that jury acquitted the first defendant, the government dropped the indictments against the remaining prisoners.

After every pro-slavery outrage, a reaction occurred among ordinary Northerners, who began to see the Slave Power as a threat to their own freedom. But conversely, moments of resistance like Christiana brought their own backlash among free-state voters who wanted desperately to believe that the latest compromise had finally made the Union safe. So it is perhaps not surprising that in the fall of 1852, the notorious Thaddeus Stevens was defeated in his bid for a third term as Whig member of the U.S. House of Representatives. At sixty-one, Stevens seemed to have come to the end of an honorable, if somewhat idiosyncratic, career as a minor local politician.

Stevens, out of office and back in Lancaster, busied himself with his law practice and with rebuilding the iron foundry he had started in 1837 but that had nearly collapsed from mismanagement and debt. He also found time to attend meetings of the newly formed Republican Party, an awkward amalgamation of former Free-Soilers, Know-Nothings, Conscience Whigs, and "Barn-Burner" Democrats who came together around one overriding issue: to prevent the Slave Power from imposing its system of labor on the western territories held by the United States.

That issue had been "settled" by the Compromise of 1850, of course, when Congress solemnly vowed that the old Missouri Compromise line of 36° 30' would be extended to the Pacific: slave territory below it, free soil above. But one Congress cannot bind another. By 1854, at the urging of Illinois's Stephen A. Douglas, Congress unceremoniously junked the compromise to organize the new state of Kansas—well above the supposedly sacred Missouri line—under the principle of "popular sovereignty." What "popular sovereignty" meant was left artfully vague. At a minimum, it meant that when Kansas sought admission as a state, its people would be allowed to choose to adopt slavery in their state constitution, or to ban it.

Congress's vote for "popular sovereignty" was another self-defeating Southern victory. Northern voters became alarmed at the apparent arrogance of the Slave Power in casually breaking a solemn agreement it had made less than a decade before. The resultant political reaction brought Thaddeus Stevens back to Washington (that same year, 1858, the obscure Abraham Lincoln almost defeated Stephen A. Douglas, the "Little Giant" and Democratic president-in-waiting, for the Senate seat from Illinois). Returned to office as a Republican, Stevens this time quickly moved into a central role during the secession crisis and the beginnings of the Civil War. Once the South had seceded, he demanded that Lincoln turn the resulting conflict into a revolutionary struggle to emancipate the slaves and subdue, once for all, the haughty Slave Power.

No member of either house was more firmly committed to victory for the Union in the field and for the Party at the polls. But loyalty to a cause is not loyalty to a leader; Stevens and Lincoln were often allies but never friends. Their temperaments were simply too opposed— Stevens by temperament radical, by conviction antislavery and anti-Southern, and perhaps by the advance of age and illness hasty and almost desperate in his pursuit of change; Lincoln by temperament conservative and indecisive, by family background profoundly ambivalent about the South (from which his own forebears and his wife's had come), and patient beyond the ordinary measure of human nature. Lincoln used Stevens for his ends when he could; Stevens never hesitated to make the administration his target when, in his judgment, the president's temporizing seemed to threaten the Union cause.

For more than a year after Fort Sumter, Lincoln carefully dis-avowed emancipation as a war aim; for Stevens, freedom for the slave was from the first day the only rational aim of the civil conflict. Stevens was one of the moving forces that pushed through Congress the first emancipation measure—the Confiscation Act of 1861, which ordered Union commanders to "confiscate" escaped or captured slaves who had been used in the Confederate war effort and use them as paid workers in support of the Union. As word spread, "contrabands" flocked to the Union lines, until they formed a key part of the war effort. Congress widened the scope of confiscation, and in time, even the dilatory Lincoln saw that these runaways formed a legion devoted to the Union cause, leading to his decision in 1863 to allow the enlist-ment of black men as soldiers in the army, to his Emancipation Proclamation declaring all slaves inside Confederate lines "forever free," and to the Thirteenth Amendment to the Constitution, which in 1865 outlawed slavery forever. It is to this process that contempo-rary historians refer when they say that the slaves emancipated them-selves. So they did; but as America's black people marched to freedom during the war years, advancing in status from chattel to "contraband" to combat soldier to citizen, the spirit of Thaddeus Stevens limped by their sides.

Stevens, aware that a revolutionary moment in politics did not come more than once in a lifetime, openly schemed to replace Lincoln with a more radical nominee in 1864 if that would advance the cause. And when the Baltimore convention of the Republican Party (apologetically renamed the Union Party to make it more appealing to War Democrats) nominated Andrew Johnson as vice president, he exploded on the convention floor: "Can't you find a candidate for Vice-President in the United States, without going down to one of those damned rebel provinces to pick one up?"

The remark about "rebel provinces" was more than a momentary rhetorical flourish; it marked the radical cast of Stevens's mind, and a legal theory it produced in the early years of the war that Stevens stood by until his death. Civil war was a contingency neither the nation nor its Constitution had clearly thought about, and once the guns erupted at Fort Sumter in 1861, even the leading minds in Washington found themselves at a loss to describe what was happening to the United States. Could a state withdraw from the Union? The Confederates, echoing the late master theorist of "state sovereignty," John C. Calhoun, insisted that the Constitution had been a "compact" between state governments, one that could be dissolved whenever a state or its people saw fit. But James Madison, the Constitution's intellectual author, had regarded the new government as a national one, created by the only real "sovereign" in a free republic: the people.

If the Constitution, and the government it created, flowed directly from the people, then only the people—not the people of any individual state, but the people as a whole—could by their consent dissolve it. To the Lincoln administration, the war was never a "war between states," but a "rebellion," sparked, in Lincoln's words, by "combinations too powerful to be suppressed by the ordinary course of judicial proceedings, or by the powers vested in the Marshals by law."

But what had happened to the states? Conservatives argued that they remained as they were, under lawful but misguided state governments, and that peace could be restored if these states simply laid down their arms and returned to the Union by sending members back to Congress. "The Union as it was and the Constitution as it is" had been one of the slogans of the Democratic Party, which opposed Lincoln's policy of war.

But to Radical Republicans like Thaddeus Stevens, such a policy was unsatisfactory. To them, the catastrophe that had befallen the old Republic was not an accident of history, but a cool, calculated conspiracy of the Slave Power. Secession was illegal, and those who made war for secession were traitors. The states that had raised arms against the Union had ceased to exist and could claim no rights under the Constitution. The only law that applied to their territory was the law of war. As the Union armies marched across the South, Stevens and his Radical allies argued, they did not bring with them the old state laws and constitutions; they brought martial law, enforced by the conqueror upon conquered territory.

Steven's "conquered provinces" theory meant that the Union government had every legal right to alter—even to revolutionize—the governments and social systems of the conquered South. And that was precisely what Stevens proposed. His plan was to change forever the caste-ridden, undemocratic social system that had spawned the Slave Power. The great plantations of Confederate supporters would be confiscated and the land would be resold in small homesteads to the slaves who had worked it. A New England–style economy would result, in which each family would control its own destiny and work its own land. To make sure that the transformation took hold, the victorious North would encourage immigration by white veterans from free states into the old Confederacy, who would also have a chance to own confiscated land. The new class of freeholders would be buttressed by a system of free schools like the one Stevens had fathered in Pennsylvania. And the result would be a new South that would no longer march to a different beat than the rest of the nation. "I would send those soldiers [who fought for the Union] there with arms in their hands to occupy the heritage of traitors," Stevens had said in 1862, "and build up there a land of free men and of freedom, which, fifty years hence, would swarm with its hundreds of millions without a slave upon its soil."

That revolution would also break the back of the Southern-based Democratic Party. That aim was one that almost every Republican in the Thirty-ninth Congress shared, even those who did not endorse the Radicals' plans for social transformation. "The Democracy," as the party of Jackson proudly called itself—"the Locofocos," as Republicans scornfully referred to Democrats, after a name originally given to new-fangled friction matches politicians used to light their cigars—had been the executive committee of the Slave Power.

By 1865, the dislike between the parties had reached a pitch that we do not approach even in the partisan early years of this century. Republicans were well aware that slave interests had dominated the Democratic Party since at least the time of Jackson, three decades ear-lier. Slave-state Democrats vetoed any presidential candidate whose devotion to their interests was less than abject. With the collapse of their old rivals, the Whigs, in 1852, the Democrats ruled the states below the Mason-Dixon Line without any competition; and that was something Republicans particularly resented.

The simple fact, as Republicans had been pointing out for years, was that Republicans could not compete for Southern votes because the slave states did not permit freedom of speech, press, or assembly to any group that criticized or questioned the slave system. After the Nat Turner revolt in Virginia in 1832, the South had adopted a firm rule that any criticism of slavery must be prevented on the grounds of safety. Brick by brick, the slave-owning class of the South erected what historian Clement Eaton has called an "intellectual blockade" to prevent new ideas from the North—abolitionism, socialism, tem-perance, divorce, women's rights, spiritualism, or anything else that might rock the social boat—from polluting the Southern mind. Southern postmasters, with the encouragement of federal authorities, removed and destroyed any newspapers or books critical of slavery from the incoming mail in Southern cities. University teachers and clergymen who questioned the slave system soon found themselves unemployed and usually caught a steamer north. Abolitionists dared not speak or hold meetings in public. "Gentlemen" who questioned the propriety of slavery were "called out" and often killed; those of lower station were simply horsewhipped by Southern bravos.

Northern Republicans smarted under the Democrats' taunts that they were a mere "sectional party." If the Southern states were free, they said, Republicans would compete with the Democracy, and win, because they spoke for the interests of the laborer and small farmer. They bitterly resented the idea that one part of the country had been allowed to opt out of the American system of free elections and free debate. In 1859, Republican representative Henry Waldron of Michigan had portrayed the slave states in terms that seem familiar to anyone who remembers the rhetoric of the Cold War and the good-and-evil battle of democracy against twentieth-century totalitarianism:

> Today a system of espionage prevails which would disgrace the despotism and darkness of the middle ages. The newspaper which refuses to recount the blessings and sing the praises of slavery is committed to the flames. The press that refuses to vilify the memory of the fathers is taken by a ruthless mob and engulfed beneath the waters. The personal safety of the traveler depends not on his deeds, but upon his opinions. . . . Where slavery is there can be no free speech, no free thought, no free press, no regard for constitutions, no deference to courts.

To antebellum Republicans, the slave South had been something like Ronald Reagan's "empire of evil." Once the election of Lincoln broke slavery's hold on the national government, the South had tried to destroy the Union—and, as Republicans in 1865 saw it, many if not most of the Northern Democrats had been a fifth column inside the loyal North spreading defeatism and subversion.

Some Democrats had supported Lincoln. Lincoln's old antagonist, Stephen A. Douglas, had been one of the first; facing his own death and the ruin of all his hopes in 1861, he had reached out to his foe and wished him Godspeed in the battle ahead. Andrew Johnson, the only Southern senator to refuse to walk out of Congress after secession, was another; yet another was Indiana Democratic congressman Robert

Dale Owen, forever optimistic about projects for reform, secular and spiritual. But these "war Democrats" were a minority, as Stevens and the rest of the Republicans saw it. Most of the Democracy, it seemed to them, had been actively or passively disloyal—obstructing the war effort, defending slavery, and scheming to restore the Slave Power to its place at the center of the Constitution.

After the war began, Republicans like Stevens dropped "dough-face" as their insult—it was too polite. *Copperhead* was the new term, after the belly-crawling poisonous snake that lurked in Southern swamps. For some Democrats, the name was unfair, but many Democrats—far more than Americans today realize—had shown their Southern sympathies by trying to prevent Union victory. Copperheads and Southern sympathizers in the North talked openly of splitting up the stump of the Union into further fragments. Perhaps New York City, under its pro-Southern mayor Fernando Wood, should secede; perhaps the states of the Old Northwest—Ohio, Indiana, and others—would split off and make a separate peace with the Confederacy. Northern Democratic envoys traveled to Canada and Richmond to strategize with representatives of Jefferson Davis. In 1862 and 1863, Democrats organized their campaigns in state and federal elections around opposition to the Emancipation Proclamation, which many called unconstitutional and others seemed to promise to reverse. By 1863, Democrats had nearly won control of Congress and had taken over legislatures in key Northern states, including Lincoln's own Illinois.

By 1864, the Democrats smelled victory and the White House. To dislodge Lincoln, the Democrats had turned to General George B. McClellan, the "Little Napoleon" whose provoking slowness and timidity—to Republicans at least—had let Union victory slip away a dozen times since he had assumed command of the Army of the Potomac after First Bull Run. Over and over the handsome young general had hesitated, sometimes refusing direct orders from Lincoln to advance, until even the ever-patient Lincoln could bear it no more and exclaimed, "If McClellan is not using the Army, I should like to borrow it for a while." Meanwhile, McClellan had not been shy about allowing his many friends to know that in his view the president was unfit for his office—and further, that George McClellan was.

Relieved finally in 1862, McClellan at once began to campaign to replace Lincoln, and in 1864 he had become the nominee of the Democracy. That campaign brought a new word into the English language, created and popularized by Democratic operatives—what today might be called spin doctors—in an election hoax of mammoth proportions. The word was *miscegenation*, the interbreeding of blacks and whites, and its source was an anonymous pamphlet that pretended to emanate from the abolitionist wing of the Republican Party but that was actually the work of two hired hacks of the *New York World*, a violently antiwar, anti-Lincoln, and antiblack Democratic daily. The book called for immediate intermarriage of the two races, because "miscegenetic or mixed races are much superior, mentally, physically, and morally, to those pure or unmixed."

Democrats mailed the book to many prominent Republicans and abolitionists. Though most ignored it, a few credulous Radicals publicly hailed the idea—and the Democracy had an issue on which it appeared certain to win the White House. Democratic representative Samuel Sullivan Cox of Ohio galvanized his party when he raised the issue on the House floor. Cox, like many nineteenth-century politicians, had entered public office through journalism. In his first book, a volume about his European travels called *A Buckeye Abroad*, he had waxed so eloquent about the setting sun that ever after he was known as "Sunset" Cox. Now he applied the same eloquence to denouncing "the Abolition party." The book and its reception, he argued, proved that "that party is moving steadily forward to perfect social equality of black and white, and can only end in this detestable doctrine of Miscegenation!" Democrats then turned the election into a referendum on emancipation and civil rights. They ridiculed Lincoln as "Abraham Africanus I," who had proclaimed the new "Ten Commandments," which required that "Thou shalt have no other God but the negro," "Thou shalt swear that the negro shall be the equal of the white man," and "Thou shalt covet the slave-holder's man-servant and his maid-servant." So powerful was the response to the racist attacks, coupled with the weariness of the public with interminable and inconclusive fighting, that Lincoln himself despaired of his reelection by August 1864.

In the end, however, Lincoln prevailed, not because of a burst of racial enlightenment on the part of voters but because Admiral David Farragut won the Battle of Mobile Bay on August 5, General William T. Sherman captured Atlanta on September 2, and General Philip Sheridan routed the overconfident Confederate general Jubal Early at Cedar Creek on October 19. Like a horse sensing that its long ride has now turned in the direction of the barn, the Northern public rallied around a war effort that for the first time seemed to promise victory. Thanks to extraordinary efforts by the War Department to arrange mass furloughs, Union troops returned home for election day (marking the first time in American history that serving soldiers had voted in large numbers), and the soldiers voted for Lincoln and against McClellan, whom they now sadly regarded as a turncoat. Lincoln returned to the White House, Republicans won wide majorities of both houses of Congress, and within a few months the war was won.

But the victory was not as sweeping as it seemed. As he surveyed the House in December 1865, Thaddeus Stevens, like other Republican leaders, had good reason to wonder whether the loyal forces of the North would now promptly lose the peace—whether the Rebellion might not end, paradoxically, with the Rebels in charge of the unified nation, more powerful than before. Ironically, the completeness of the victory, the sudden and total collapse of the Confederacy and its government, seemed likely to leave the Slave Power politically triumphant.

As long as war had continued, the Union government was in a position to set the terms of the "reconstruction" of Southern states as they fell under Northern control. Lincoln had started the process in 1864, with his "ten percent" plan, which allowed Louisiana to form a new state government (and elect members of Congress) when 10 percent of its prewar voters had taken an oath of loyalty to the United States. Lincoln was seeking to split off Confederate states by offering them easy reentry into the nation they had left behind. And Lincoln, in his dilatory and often infuriating way, was always ready to consider new policies. When the war for the Union had failed, he had switched to a war against slavery. When compensated emancipation had failed, he had switched to immediate emancipation. When emancipation by presidential decree seemed constitutionally shaky, he had helped push through the Thirteenth Amendment. In time, Radicals suspected, Lincoln might realize that a more thoroughgoing reform of Southern society was needed.

But Lincoln was dead now, and the war was over. In the fallen president's place was Andrew Johnson, a Southerner and himself a former slave owner. He had authorized the former Southern states to organize new governments under the same state constitutions they had had before secession.

The newly restored states had responded to the invitation with alacrity. By December 1865, the Southern states had sent fifty-five claimants to the House of Representatives and twenty putative senators. They were a group that would provide little support for the Republican Party, or even the United States: they included at least nine former officers in the Confederate army, seven former members of the Confederate Congress, and three former members of Southern secession conventions. Alexander H. Stephens, senator-elect from Georgia, had until a few months before been vice president of the Confederate States of America.

If those "members" of Congress, or even most of them, took their seats, they would form a potential bloc with the Northern Democrats that could stymie any Republican initiative. And the situation would get worse because of the problem of the "slave seats."

Under Article I, Section 3 of the Constitution, seats in the House were handed out by "adding to the number of Free Persons . . . three fifths of all other Persons." The delicate phrasing fooled nobody. "Other Persons" were slaves. In the years since 1787, the "slave seats"—extra House seats (and presidential electors) given to slave states—had evolved into the heart of the Slave Power. As early as 1800, the extra electors had tipped the presidential balance against John Adams and handed the presidency to Thomas Jefferson's Democratic-

Republican Party, whose base was in the South. And since then, the disproportion had grown, as the invention of the cotton gin sparked an explosion in the number of slaves held in the lower South.

Between 1800 and 1850, the three-fifths clause endowed the slave states with somewhere between twenty and thirty "slave seats" in every Congress. So, if the Southern members marched back into Congress in 1865, they would again command disproportionate power. But worse was yet to come, because everyone in Washington knew that in a few days the secretary of state, William Seward, would announce that twenty-seven states had ratified the proposed Thirteenth Amendment, which abolished slavery. After it took effect, there would no longer be "Other Persons" in the South, because black Southerners—the overwhelming majority of America's black population—would legally be "free persons." Thus, when it came time to apportion members of Congress, and presidential electors, after the 1870 Census, the Southern states would receive representation for all the freed slaves rather than for three-fifths of them—which would give the region at least eighteen *more* House seats (and thus electoral votes). It was now clear to everybody that Johnson's "restored" state governments had no intention of allowing any freed blacks to vote, or even of changing their undemocratic prewar constitutions to guarantee minimal political rights for whites. The same gang of rich planters and conservative politicians was installing itself at every level of Southern politics, and they would choose the extra representatives and electors their states gained from emancipation. It was the Slave Power revived.

As early as the spring of 1865, Republican stalwarts like James G. Blaine, and War Democrats like Robert Dale Owen, had warned of the impending crisis. Fixing the problem would require another change to the Constitution; but even before the South reaped its windfall in 1870, the region's newly elected representatives and senators would be able to block any constitutional change once they took their seats. The Constitution required a two-thirds vote of both Houses to approve an amendment to the Constitution. Republicans had that many votes now; but if the Southerners were seated, they would not.

So the crisis was urgent; it must be addressed not later in the session but now, on opening day, while the eyes of the nation were turned toward Capitol Hill and the fashionable crowds packed the galleries and stood elbow to elbow on the back of the House floor. Thaddeus Stevens, who had been chased from one legislative chamber by Democratic ruffians, was determined to win this final battle.

This time around, Stevens and the Republicans held the high ground. In this case, the strategic redoubt was the usually obscure office of the Clerk of the House. It was a battleground where the Republicans had fought two years earlier against a plot of conservatives and Democrats to destroy the Lincoln administration. In the heady days after the election of 1862, Democrats believed that they could derail the Lincoln government. Popular revulsion at the Emancipation Proclamation had decimated the Republican margin in the House. If just a few votes could be shifted in the House, the Democrats could elect the new Speaker and send a powerful message (sure to be heard below the Mason-Dixon Line) that the Northern public no longer supported Lincoln and his war.

The chief plotter was crusty old Emerson Etheridge, a former Whig from Tennessee who had opposed secession and had been rewarded in 1861 with election to the office of Clerk of the House of Representatives. Etheridge was disgusted by the Emancipation Proclamation, which he branded "treachery to the Union men of the South." Now he began scheming to make "Sunset" Cox the new Speaker and hand the rebels a victory that might undo Gettysburg and Vicksburg. Etheridge told Democratic leaders that he might find irregularities in the credentials of just a few Republican members-elect—just enough, that is, to give control of the House to the anti-emancipation forces.

Republicans reacted with alarm. "I can think of nothing but a Bull Run so disastrous to our cause as that they might hear in Richmond and abroad that our own House of Representatives was in a state of Revolution," one wrote. Despite his flair for intrigue, Etheridge was no match for Lincoln, a consummate practical politician whose political resolve never wavered. During the months before the first meeting of Congress in December 1863, the president worked behind the scenes to make sure that loyal Republicans arrived in the capital with their credentials in order.

On opening day, Etheridge called a truncated roll, leaving out sixteen members-elect and including three conservative members from occupied Louisiana. Thad Stevens immediately stepped into the breach, asking for inclusion of the omitted loyal names, but Etheridge explained that he had concluded that their credentials were not in order. Another Republican moved that the omitted names be read, and the opposition moved to "lay the motion on the table," which would have killed chances for seating the Republican members. When the voting roll was called, five Democrats and six conservative Unionists voted with the Republicans. Etheridge's scheme failed.

But it would not have succeeded no matter what the vote. Lincoln, Stevens, and the Republican leadership were prepared to use "any means necessary" to foil the plot, one Republican member wrote at the time. In fact, the president had military forces standing by in the Capitol itself. "We have planned a small campaign which has a fight as one of its remote contingencies," Representative James A. Garfield wrote home at the time. And Lincoln made clear that violence would be preferable to defeat: "If Mr. Etheridge undertakes revolutionary proceedings," he grimly told Schuyler Colfax of Indiana on the eve of opening day, "let him be carried out on a chip, and let our men organize the House."

Once the Republicans were unquestionably in control, they fired Etheridge as clerk. His replacement was now the Republican caucus's not-so-secret weapon. Edward S. McPherson was someone Thaddeus Stevens could trust. In fact, Edward McPherson might serve as an allegorical figure in the Stevens story. In a story of intrigue and striving, one in which dark legends hover around Stevens's head, McPherson could symbolize the redemptive power of generosity. Thad Stevens, childless and seemingly forbidding, had always found a spot in his heart for the young lawyers he trained in his law office, and now one of these protégés would ride to his rescue, and that of the nation.

Stevens's office was always full of young men "reading" the law. An aspiring lawyer worked as a combination clerk and pupil in a lawyer's office until he felt ready to try the bar exam. For Stevens, these young men—many not yet out of their teens—were as close as nature would allow him to children of his own, and in later life he followed their exploits with pride, fussed over them, and lectured them sternly when they disappointed him. One of these foster sons, whom Stevens took in when he was just eighteen and fresh out of Gettysburg College, was Edward J. McPherson.

McPherson had quickly left Stevens's office for the other job that prepared a young man in nineteenth-century America for a job in public office—journalism. By the age of twenty-one, McPherson was editor of the *Harrisburg American*, and he kept his fingers well inked for the next decade, until in 1858 he was elected to Congress as a Republican from a district neighboring Stevens's.

McPherson was determinedly antislavery, and he backed the Union war effort and the Emancipation Proclamation. That steadfastness cost him his seat in 1862. So in December 1863, he was drafted as House Clerk. On December 4, 1865, McPherson's political astuteness saved the Republican majority. The alliance of Democrats and conservatives knew it would be politically unpalatable for an entire phalanx of former Confederates and Southern conservatives to arrive in Washington on opening day and clamor for their seats. It would be far easier for the new members to take their seats one by one as the session went on, until they formed a Southern bloc that, in alliance with the Northern Democrats, could paralyze the Radicals' efforts to shape Reconstruction.

The plan was to begin with one member from a Southern state: Horace Maynard of Tennessee, whom the Republicans might be ashamed to exclude. For one thing, Maynard was a Unionist of unquestioned loyalty. For another, he had actually served in Congress from Tennessee during the war, when Lincoln had chosen to recognize a military government there that conducted elections among the loyal minority. It might be embarrassing for the Republicans to exclude this one man from his seat, a man whose Unionism was unquestioned and whom they had cheerfully seated during the war, when they needed his vote.

But if the Thirty-ninth Congress seated Maynard, they would have set a precedent. How would the Republican majority find a legal basis to bar the door to other members from "reconstructed" states? There would be no dramatic scene of ex-Rebels strolling coolly into the Capitol on opening day, but over the next weeks or months, one by one, the Southern members would arrive, until before long they and the Northern Democrats would have, if not control, then at least the power to block any but the most lenient terms of reconstruction. All they needed to do was delay and stall, until in 1870 the redrawn congressional apportionment would mean that once again the Slave Power would be the dominant force in national affairs.

The weekend before the opening of Congress had been a time of feverish activity in Washington. Lawmakers and lobbyists had gathered privately in hotel rooms and saloons to plot strategy. The most important meeting was the Republican House caucus, held in the House chamber on Saturday night, December 2, to consider what would be done when the House opened the next Monday. In no uncertain terms, Stevens warned his colleagues that they must stand together on Monday or lose everything they had built. He laid out the plan: as Etheridge had tried to use the Clerk's office to break up the Union, now McPherson would use it to preserve the victory.

The battle would be fought in the dry language of parliamentary procedure, in which enemies were always "gentlemen" or "distinguished friends"; but for all the politesse, it was war just as much as Cold Harbor or Shiloh.

When the members met at noon on December 4, the House of Representatives of the Thirty-ninth Congress did not yet legally exist. Unlike the Senate, which is a "continuing body," each House of Representatives is a new creature. All of its members are elected at each election, and so its officers must be chosen anew every two years. Under the House rules, McPherson was empowered to convene the new House because he had been clerk of the last one. He would preside over the House only until it could elect a new Speaker, who would then take over the chair. Convening the members is what is usually called a "ministerial" duty, involving little discretion. But these were not ordinary times, and even the smallest act could take on overwhelming significance. The moment came when McPherson's call of the roll reached the letter *M;* Horace Maynard should have been next; but instead, McPherson called the name of William E. Niblack, a Democrat from Indiana.

At once Maynard was on his feet demanding recognition. "Mr. Clerk," he began. "I beg to say that in calling the roll of members—"

McPherson cut him off. "The Chair will be compelled to object to any interruption of the call of the roll," he said.

"Does the Clerk decline to hear me?" Maynard asked.

"I decline to have any interruption of the call of the roll," said McPherson.

Maynard fared no better when McPherson was done calling the members' names. As soon as the list was complete, Justin Morrill rose to move that the House proceed to elect its own officers. Rising again, Maynard managed to get out only a few words: "Before that motion is put—"

Stevens now cut him off. "I call the gentleman to order," he said. And McPherson then said, "The Clerk rules, as a matter of order, that he cannot recognize any gentleman whose name is not upon his roll."

At this point, the Democratic Party's champion, such as he was, entered the battle. James Brooks was the Democratic candidate for Speaker. He had entered politics by the time-honored route of newspaper editorship, and in fact was still editor in chief of the *New York Daily Express*. In the Democratic landslide of 1863 he had won election to the House. In 1864, with Union sentiment on the rise even in New York City, Brooks had had a harder time holding on to his seat. In fact, as he spoke, the election that had returned him to office was under challenge, perhaps giving him a special sympathy with Horace Maynard and the other Southern representatives whose credentials had just been brushed aside.

Now he bitterly protested the move to elect a new Speaker without settling the issue of Maynard's seat. "I trust that we shall not proceed to any revolutionary step like that without at least hearing from the honorable gentleman from Tennessee," he said.

McPherson replied, "If it be the desire of the House to have my reasons, I will give them; but I have not felt justified or called upon to give any reasons; I have acted in accordance with my views of duty, and I am willing to let the record stand."

Stevens quickly moved to prevent discussion of McPherson's motives. "It is not necessary," he said. "We know all." And in fact everyone in the room knew what McPherson was doing and why, because his plan had been agreed upon the previous Saturday night. But Brooks attempted to make the moment as embarrassing as he could for the Republicans. "This is not parliamentary propriety, if it is even decency," he said. "Are gentlemen afraid to face debate?"

Thaddeus Stevens was never afraid to debate anyone, but he would not be drawn by Brooks. He protested that Brooks was out of order. The issue before the House was election of a Speaker. McPherson ruled Brooks's motion out of order. Stevens then moved "the previous question," asking that the motion to elect a Speaker be put to an immediate vote. Once again, Maynard rose to try to plead his case in person, but Stevens responded, "I cannot yield to any gentleman who does not belong to this body."

The House then held the vote; Colfax, to no one's surprise, defeated Brooks by 139 to 36. Colfax ascended the Speaker's rostrum and delivered a brief speech on the work before the House. In his vision, that work mostly concerned imposing democratic ways on the former rebel states. The new Congress's duties "are as obvious as the sun's pathway in the heavens," he said. "Its first and highest obligation is to guaranty to every State a republican form of government. The rebellion having overthrown constitutional State governments in many States, it is yours to mature and enact legislation which, with the concurrence of the Executive, shall establish them anew on such a basis of enduring justice as well as guaranty all necessary safeguards to the people, and afford what our Magna Charta, the Declaration of Independence, proclaims is the chief object of government—protection to all men in their inalienable rights."

Next, Representative Elihu Washburne of Illinois rose to read to the House a telegram forwarded to him by William Seward, the secretary of state. It was from L. E. Parsons, the provisional governor of Alabama, and it said simply, "The amendment is adopted by an overwhelming vote." Even more thunderous applause from the floor and the gallery greeted this announcement. "The amendment" was the Thirteenth Amendment abolishing slavery. It was the first amendment to the Constitution to be made since 1803, and Alabama's accession meant that it had now been approved by twenty-seven state legislatures, making it officially a part of the Constitution. Slavery—at least the old Southern institution in which people were treated as property and counted as three-fifths of a human being for political purposes—was dead beyond the power of political change to revive it. Now the heirs to victory were left to grapple with the uncertainty left by its demise.

TURNS IN THE SOUTH

Among those who thronged onto the House floor at the opening of Congress was Carl Schurz, remembered by journalist Whitelaw Reid on that day for his "fiery whiskers, and an asserting nose with the blooded race-horse thinness of nostril." Schurz was no longer Andrew Johnson's emissary to the conquered lands; instead, he was the Washington correspondent for Horace Greeley's *New York Tribune*. Newspaper correspondents were allowed on the floor of the House and Senate, but rarely did they enter into the debates. Schurz, however, was no ordinary correspondent, and within days of the opening of Congress he had become the subject of heated speeches. Led by Charles Sumner, Senate Republicans had a question: *Where was the Schurz report?*

Schurz had reported back to Johnson in November 1865. But once Johnson got the report, it had disappeared. Schurz had not told Johnson what he wanted to hear, and the president had responded by pigeonholing the report and sending other emissaries southward who could be expected to tell him more congenial news.

It is difficult for Americans in the twenty-first century to appreciate just how mysterious the former Confederacy seemed to Northerners in the months after Appomattox. In 1866, *Harper's Weekly* announced a new series of woodcuts of Southern life with the remark, "To us the late Slave States seem almost like a newly-discovered country." It was not simply that four years of war had made communication between the two halves of the nation difficult—though that was true—or that both North and South had changed during the searing years of war in ways that people in the other region could hardly imagine. The brute historical fact was that North and South had always been separate societies, culturally different and mutually incomprehensible. Now, for the first time, the two halves were to become part of one whole, and Northerners found themselves wondering what their new countrymen were like, and how they planned to behave in the new nation created by the war.

Throughout the second half of 1865, the states of the old Confederacy were aswarm with Northern visitors carrying notepads. All had similar questions: How severe was the destruction visited on the former Rebel states? How did Southern people live? What money did they spend, what clothing did they wear, how did they travel, what did they eat? What were their feelings toward the North, and toward the Union? What were their plans for the four million Southerners of African descent, most of whom had until the surrender been held as slaves, persons without rights? And, perhaps most important for the anxious officials in Washington, what were their plans when they regained their place in the United States? Would they accept that the war had changed the nation, and the Constitution, forever? Or would they seek to return to the place of mastery they had occupied before Fort Sumter?

The last question seems strange to us today. The South of late 1865 was a land devastated by war. The North had for decades been richer and more populous than the South. And yet for half a century before the outbreak of war, Northerners had hated, resented, and feared the South, and, more than that, had seen the Southern states and their political leaders as the real rulers of the United States.

For some, the Slave Power was a sinister conspiracy that pulled every string and manufactured every seeming coincidence in American life. John Smith Dye, a devoted conspiracy seeker, wrote three books during the 1850s and 1860s explaining that the Slave Power had murdered Zachary Taylor when he proved unresponsive to its wishes and had poisoned the sugar at a Washington political gathering in 1857, nearly killing President James Buchanan and terrorizing him into slavish obedience to the Slave Power agenda. (Most accounts, then and now, suggest that the barrels of oysters served to the gathered politicos were the real cause of the outbreak of dysentery that affected the president.)

But it wasn't just conspiracy theorists who saw the South as the uncrowned monarch of nineteenth-century America during the years before Fort Sumter. As historian Leonard Richards notes:

> The notion that a slaveholding oligarchy ran the country—and ran it for their own advantage—had wide support in the years before and after the Civil War. It was the basic theme that Abraham Lincoln and his fellow Republicans used in the 1850s to gain political power. Before that, it was deemed a self-evident truth by scores of prominent northerners. John Quincy Adams, former president of the United States, was a true believer. So were Charles Sumner, senator from Massachusetts; Salmon P. Chase, senator from Ohio; Josiah Quincy, president of Harvard; Horace Greeley, editor of the *New York Tribune;* and Henry Wilson, future vice president of the United States. Oddly enough, many southerners also regarded the Slave Power thesis as a self-evident truth. Among the more prominent were Alexander Stephens, future vice president of the Confederacy, and the South Carolina hotspur James Henry Hammond.

Many Northerners had fought to end the Slave Power rather than to end slavery itself. Now, like frightened villagers in a fairy tale, they were asking themselves if the giant was really dead. Northern journalists, military officers, missionaries, and teachers were the eyes and ears of the Northern public as they asked whether the Slave Power had learned its lesson.

Sumner wanted the Schurz report because he knew the answer Carl Schurz had come to. Schurz's reports had appeared in the *Boston Daily Advertiser* every few days for most of the time he spent on tour in the South. He had bombarded his Northern friends—including Sumner—with letters detailing what he saw. But Sumner and his allies in Congress were outraged that Andrew Johnson had received the report and stuck it in a drawer. Johnson seemed to want to pretend it had never been written. He had reckoned without Charles Sumner, however, and that was always a mistake. For if there was one human being in the North who symbolized opposition to the Slave Power, it was Charles Sumner.

In his landmark biography of Sumner, historian David Herbert Donald calls him "one of the most potent and enduring forces in the American government" during his long career. He was almost the only American white leader of the nineteenth century willing to embrace the idea that black and white Americans should be equal in all things, whether education, politics, or social relations. In 1849, he was the first American lawyer to argue that segregating school-children by race violated the Constitution. In *Roberts v. City of Boston*, Sumner attacked American racism as an attempt to create a caste system—hereditary, hierarchical, and lifelong—like that of India; it was an analysis that would be echoed by Gunnar Myrdal in his path-breaking 1944 work, *An American Dilemma*, which formed one key basis of the Supreme Court's rationale in *Brown v. Board of Education*. Sumner's argument did not convince the Massachusetts court, but in 1855, the Massachusetts legislature forbade racial segregation in schools.

Wealthy, intellectual, and pretentious, Sumner was no man of the people. A colleague, George Boutwell, once observed that in his pre-war career Sumner had managed to pass only one bill—a measure allowing Mongolians to become naturalized citizens. But he was relentless in his insistence that American slavery, whether in Southern states or in western territories, was a violation of the principles of the Declaration of Independence, of the Constitution, and of the laws of God. He scorned the courtesies associated with political debate and laid the guilt of slavery at the feet of Southern society, of Southern legislators, and of Northern "doughfaces." His insistence on calling his colleagues to account transformed Sumner from a marginal politician into a living symbol of antislavery zeal.

On May 29 and 30, 1856, in the heat of the controversy over slavery in Kansas, Sumner delivered an address in the Senate called "The Crime Against Kansas." Sumner denounced the attempt of Missouri "border ruffians" to force a pro-slavery constitution on the new territory. He pilloried Southern senators for their complicity with an inhumane system. Turning to South Carolina senator Andrew P. Butler, he compared the aristocratic lawmaker to Don Quixote, who insisted that the pig-tender Dulcinea was his fair maiden. Butler, Sumner said, "has chosen a mistress to whom he has made his vows, and who, though ugly to others, is always lovely to him; though polluted in the sight of the world, is chaste in his sight . . . the harlot, Slavery."

Sumner had directly challenged the Southern code of honor, a code that had been enforced for decades with dueling pistols and sabers. On May 22, Butler's cousin, South Carolina representative Preston Brooks, quietly entered the Senate chamber, where Sumner sat at a desk making notes on the session that had just ended. Without giving Sumner a chance to rise, Brooks began to beat him with a gold-handled gutta-percha cane. In a few seconds, Brooks delivered at least thirty blows across Sumner's head and shoulders. Bloodied and stunned, the muscular Sumner was trapped by the desk. At last he wrenched the desk from the floor and staggered into the aisle, where he fell, semiconscious and covered in blood.

The assault on Sumner was a turning point in the struggle over slavery. To many Northerners, even those with little interest in the issue, it became a psychological milestone, like the Kennedy assassination for a later generation. The full arrogance of the Slave Power was on display; not only was Brooks willing to invade the sacred precincts of the senate and to assault a defenseless opponent without allowing him to defend himself, but Brooks's Southern colleagues, both in Congress and across the region, lionized the man—dubbed

"Bully Brooks" by the Northern press—who had apparently tried to murder freedom's champion. Sumner's injuries were severe; he was not able to resume his seat in the Senate until 1859. During those turbulent years, Sumner's empty seat became a standing reproach to the South, so much so that the Massachusetts legislature reelected him to another term, not knowing when or if he would be fit to serve. And when Sumner finally resumed his place, he had become something more than an ordinary senator. He was a symbol, revered in the North, hated in the South.

During the Lincoln years, Sumner had been a thorn in the administration's side, pushing always for the president to go faster and farther toward the goal of emancipation and equality. Yet Lincoln and Sumner had become close friends. Sumner's elegant manners and fluent French charmed Mary Todd Lincoln, and Sumner had held Robert Lincoln in his arms as the young man stood sobbing at his father's deathbed.

Sumner had eagerly volunteered to be a member of Johnson's official family. But by the opening of Congress, he had deduced that Johnson, whatever he had said during the war, had now committed himself to propitiating the old Slave Power. The final straw had come just two days before the Senate assembled, when Sumner called on Johnson at the White House and implored him to impose more stringent conditions on the South. The president angrily repelled his pleas, and when Sumner arose to take his leave, he discovered that Johnson had also—perhaps inadvertently—spat tobacco juice into the fastidious Sumner's pristine silk hat.

So, on December 12, when Sumner introduced a resolution that called for publication of the Schurz report, he was doing so to embarrass the president. Schurz had submitted his report to Johnson in late 1865. Before that, the two men had held a chilly meeting at the White House, where Johnson urged Schurz not to bother writing one. But when he saw that Schurz was determined, Johnson decided, even before he saw the document, to counter it. In late November, he sent General Grant south to test the temper of the former Rebels. The head of the occupying army found few Southern whites who were anything but obsequious. As expected, Johnson received from Grant a brief report stating that "the mass of thinking men of the South accept the present state of affairs in good faith." They had given up their belief in "State's rights" and secession, Grant said, and stood ready to accept any Reconstruction measures "not humiliating to them as citizens." There was a crisis of law and order, Grant admitted, one that would require small federal garrisons in the South for the near future. But the trouble did not come from the leaders of the old South, but from the "ignorant" whites and from the "late slave," who might help himself to his former master's property. Grant recommended that the substantial numbers of black troops in the South be withdrawn right away. Their presence "demoralizes labor" because the black soldiers furnished subversive "advice" to the freed slaves and their camps offered freedmen a refuge from work on the plantations. All in all, the report supported Johnson's policies nicely, and for Johnson it made up in congeniality what it might lack in detail.

With his resolution, Sumner put Johnson to the choice of refusing a reasonable request for a presidential document—thus defying Congress—or of making public a document that directly contradicted the administration's claims. Six days later, on December 18, Johnson responded by sending the reports by Grant and Schurz. He made only passing mention of the Schurz document, but said that "the attention of the Senate is invited" to Grant's report. Senator Edgar Cowan of Pennsylvania, a conservative Republican, promptly moved that Grant's report be read into the record. There was no objection to reading such a brief document—about two thousand words—from a revered figure like Grant. But when the reading was finished, Sumner rose and demanded that Schurz's report—nearly thirty thousand words, with almost as many appended in supporting documents—also be read aloud and printed in the *Congressional Globe*. Groans greeted this suggestion, and several voices cried, "It is very long."

Senator John Sherman, a moderate Republican, proposed a compromise. Why not print the report as a Senate document, sparing the chamber the ordeal of a reading? Grumbling like a rabbit flung into the brier patch, Sumner acquiesced and the Schurz report went to the printers. From there, as Sumner had intended all along, it became a best-selling government publication. More than 100,000 copies were requested within a few weeks, and Northern public opinion got the message Sumner had hoped to send: like Cadmus in the ancient Greek myth, the president's lenient policy was sowing the burned earth of the South with serpent's teeth. From these seeds, the Slave Power was springing up anew.

Schurz was not the only traveler to the South who reached that conclusion in 1865. Four important American journalists had undertaken tours of the South in the months after the surrender, and all reported that the Slave South, though vanquished, was unbowed and that its people intended to dominate the Union.

The travel book was a staple of nineteenth-century publishing—a vicarious chance for readers to journey to distant and exotic lands. And the South was as exotic to Northern readers as Ireland or Bohemia. One of the bestsellers of the 1850s had been *A Journey to the Slave States* by Frederick Law Olmsted, the journalist and landscape architect who is today best remembered as the designer of Central Park. In 1865, Olmsted was associate editor of a new magazine, *The Nation*. Olmsted and the magazine's editor, E. L. Godkin, commissioned a twenty-seven-year-old Harvard graduate named John Richard Dennett to repeat Olmsted's travels and report to the magazine's readers under the weekly heading of "The South as It Is."

Horace Greeley, the premier antislavery newspaperman of the North, commissioned Whitelaw Reid to travel south at about the same time. Dennett had to jostle over Southern railroads; Reid traveled in style down the coast in a military packet carrying Salmon P. Chase, chief justice of the Supreme Court, a veteran antislavery politician, former secretary of the Treasury, and perennial presidential hopeful (he had actively schemed to displace Lincoln on the ticket in 1864). Sidney Andrews reported on his own Southern travels for the *Chicago Tribune* (a Republican newspaper that jousted with Greeley's *New York Tribune* for the title of leading antislavery paper) and the even more deeply antislavery newspaper, the *Boston Daily Advertiser.*

Most prominent of the literary travelers was John Townsend Trowbridge, at thirty-eight already a well-known antislavery novelist and poet. The subscription publisher L. Stebbins now sent him south to prepare a travel volume for the spring list of 1866.

Taken together with Schurz's report, the dispatches filed by these reporters tell us a good deal about life in the South during 1865 and early 1866—the period in which the Thirty-ninth Congress was reshaping the Constitution. But inevitably they tell us as much if not more about what *Northerners* were thinking—and fearing—about their traditional foes. Their real curiosity was about the white planters, politicians, and merchants who had made up the Slave Power. And even though each reporter brought different experiences to bear on what he saw, and traveled different itineraries across the defeated South, their observations were remarkably consistent.

The white South, though defeated in battle, did not realize how much the war had changed America, they reported. On one level, Southerners owned themselves beaten. Andrews reported one octogenarian delegate to the South Carolina convention who said, "If the youngest of you lives to my age even, you will not see another musket shouldered in the South against the Union." Everywhere they traveled, the reporters met former Confederate officials and soldiers who freely confessed their defeat and their weariness of war. But there was another field of battle—politics, Congress, and the Constitution—and in that struggle the South expected nothing less than victory.

The Southern spirit of confidence was more striking because it came from a region so thoroughly devastated by war. Most of the correspondents felt obliged to visit Charleston, the cradle of secession. Schurz, arriving there on the *Arago*, remarked on the "desolate and melancholy" look of the waterfront, the grass growing between the paving stones of once-busy streets, and the crowds of turkey buzzards massed on the roofs of the warehouses and fashionable homes. Andrews visited the tomb of John C. Calhoun, patron of the South, and found dogs and ragged children roaming above it, surrounded by "a wealth of offal and garbage and beef-bones." Whitelaw Reid rather maliciously recalled the reports of frenzied celebration in Charleston's streets when secession was voted in December 1860. Now, he reported, the streets were thronged with armed soldiers—most of them black and all clad in Union blue—and "the restaurants are closed and the shutters are up; the occupants of the club rooms are dead, or in prison, or in exile; there is still carousing in taverns, but it is only by the flushed and spendthrift Yankee officers who are willing to pay seventy-five cents for a cobbler (wine punch)."

But it was not just Charleston that was devastated. Richmond, the Confederate capital and the South's largest city, had been burned by retreating Confederate troops. Walking from the city's waterfront toward the capital, Dennett found its downtown changed into a kind of moonscape: "For a quarter of a mile one passes nothing but toppling walls, forlorn-looking chimneys, heaps of bricks, with here and there a ruined safe lying in the midst, warped and red from the effects of intense heat." A few miles south, in Petersburg, Trowbridge reported that the months of siege and bombardment had left it a city of "tenant-less and uninhabitable houses, with broken walls, roofless, or with roofs smashed and torn by missiles."

And yet, these once-proud cities were fortunate. Farther south and east, William Tecumseh Sherman, the dark angel of modern warfare, had passed like Death on a pale horse, and Hell had ridden with him. "They destroyed everything which the infernal Yankee ingenuity could devise means to destroy," one Southerner told Andrews, "hands, hearts, fire, gunpowder, and behind everything the spirit of hell, were the agencies which they used." Sherman would later report that his troops had destroyed property to the then-unimaginable value of $100 million. Of that sum, only about one-fifth was actually taken for army use. The rest, Sherman said, was "simple waste and destruction."

The Northern reporters saw the footprints left by the Angel of Death. South Carolina's capital, Columbia, had once been esteemed the most beautiful city in the South; now, Andrews reported, "it is in the heart of destruction . . . a wilderness of ruins. Its heart is but a mass of blackened chimneys and crumbling walls." On the road to

Atlanta, Reid marked the "track of the destroyer" by the trail of "solitary chimneys and the debris of burnt buildings."

Particularly hard hit by the ravaging Union forces was the South's already inadequate system of roads and railways. Columbia had once been a railroad hub, Andrews noted; now, no viable railroad approached the city within thirty miles. Former Rebel soldiers expressed admiration for Sherman's thoroughness in bending and twisting the rails so they could never be relaid. "We could do something in that line, we thought," one told him, "but we were ashamed of ourselves when we saw how your men could do it."

Military devastation of transport was not the only problem. For four years, the Confederate governments had devoted little or no expense to maintenance and repair of rails, roadways, and rolling stock. By 1865, it was common for passengers to be hauled in old box cars, seated on rude wooden benches or on the floor. Dennett reported a recent derailment on the line between Richmond and Danville in which passengers, injured when the train fell from a crudely repaired bridge, lay groaning all night on the embankment while thieves robbed them by the light of the burning cars. Travel by wagon and stage was not much safer; besides the danger from returning troops turned highway robbers, the roads themselves were so poorly maintained that passengers sometimes had to fling themselves back and forth in a group in order to keep a sunken wheel from overturning the rig.

The problem of travel was only one part of the general economic breakdown of a society that had been on a war footing, encircled by a naval blockade, for four years, Reid explained:

> Everything has been mended, and generally in the rudest style. Window-glass has given way to thin boards, . . . Furniture is marred and broken, none has been replaced for four years. Dishes are cemented in various styles and half the pitchers have tin handles. A complete set of crockery is never seen. . . . A set of forks with whole tines is a curiosity, hats, bonnets, and ladies' and children's shoes, are nearly all homemade. Hair-brushes and

tooth-brushes have all worn out; combs are broken, and are not yet replaced; pins, needles, thread, and a thousand such articles, which seem indispensable to housekeeping, are very scarce. Even in weaving on the looms, corn-cobs have been substituted for spindles. Few have pocket-knives. In fact, everything that has heretofore been an article of sale at the South is wanting now. At the tables of those who were once esteemed luxurious providers, you will find neither tea, coffee, sugar, nor spices of any kind. Even candles, in some cases, have been replaced by a cup of grease, in which a piece of cloth is plunged for a wick.

Northerners had not esteemed Southern cuisine even in flush times; now that most meals consisted of pork, lard, and cornmeal, the region's diet seemed positively subhuman. By the time he reached Corinth, Mississippi, though, Trowbridge's culinary standards had sunk; he reported with satisfaction a particularly sumptuous repast of "fried pork, fricasseed gray squirrel (cold), boiled 'back of hog' (warmed up), a pitcher of milk, cold biscuit, cold corn bread, and 'sweet bread' (a name given to a plain sort of cake)."

But most desperate of all was the Southern need of money—any form of it—that could be spent for things they could not sew or shoot themselves. Confederate notes were valueless. In their place were only scant reserves of silver and gold—most citizens had lent their hard money to the Confederate government in exchange for now-worthless paper—and something Southerners had never seen before: national money, issued and backed by the federal Treasury. Merchants who would accept these bills at all insisted on a steep discount from prices set in silver or gold. From bitter experience with the Confederate government, most Southerners assumed the notes would be repudiated by the Union. "Won't be worth a copper in two years," one merchant assured Dennett.

But the "Lincoln green" was welcome everywhere for now. For Whitelaw Reid, traveling with Chief Justice Chase was something like traveling with a twenty-first-century rock star. In his eagerness to boost his presidential prospects, Chase had used his position as secretary of the Treasury to put his own face on the new federal $1 bill, and black and white Southerners in the street recognized him almost at once. When the group reached Key West—unimaginably remote and accessible only by water—one prominent free black man looked from Chase's face to the face of a bill in wonderment. "'Now I knows you,' he broke out at last, 'you's Old Greenback hisself. You mout come heah fifty yea from now and I'd know you just de same. . . .'"

Yet amid the poverty and destruction, there were signs of immediate growth. In the spring of 1865, Reid found Mobile "a city of ruins." Returning six months later, he rubbed his eyes in amazement at the sight of frantic rebuilding, as former Rebel soldiers thronged the bars to do business with Northern speculators. Atlanta, burned by Sherman, presented an even more electric prospect when Andrews got there— "narrow and irregular and numerous streets are alive from morning till night with drays and carts and hand-barrows and wagons . . . with a never-ending throng of pushing and crowding and scrambling and eager and excited and enterprising men, all bent on building and trading and swift fortune-making."

But what Southern phoenix would rise from the ashes? To the visitors in 1865, the portents were ominous. There were, to be sure, "Unionists" everywhere abroad in Dixie in 1865, but even for those who had not adopted scalawag garb only after Appomattox, "Unionism" was insubstantial stuff, made up mostly of class antagonism toward the planters and hatred of the freed slaves. "These men loved not the Union more," Reid reported, "but Jeff. Davis less." Andrews reported from North Carolina that "much of the 'Unionism' of the State is mere personal bitterness toward Jeff Davis, or Governor [Zebulon] Vance, or some less noted secession leader." Such Unionism, he concluded, was "a cheat, a will-o'-the-wisp, and any man who trusts it will meet with overthrow."

On most of the issues that concerned the Northern public in 1865, the Unionists and the old Rebels were pretty much in agreement. Most white political figures in the South agreed that the Southern states were entitled to immediate reentry into the Union. The Constitution as they had known it guaranteed the sovereignty of every state, and made it in all but a few spheres superior to the Union. The battles of the past four years had changed the military facts, Southern whites argued; they had not changed the Constitution or the power of the individual state. Visiting the Georgia state convention, Andrews reported, "The State rights heresy was as dominant in this Convention, almost, as in [the secession convention] of 1861." Among the educated classes, there was "not merely a broad assertion of the rights of the States, but an open enunciation of the supremacy of the State over the general government."

Most Southerners were willing to admit that slavery was abolished, though they were often careful to add words like "by the military power of the United States" to indicate some legal doubt about the issue. The Thirteenth Amendment (which most Americans in 1865 called simply "the Amendment," because it was the only one in their lifetimes) was not yet ratified. Many Southern whites told Carl Schurz that they would be willing to "accept" it; but they wanted it rewritten to omit the section granting Congress the power to enforce its provisions. That provision, they argued, would compromise their state's prerogatives.

Those prerogatives were absolute, they said, and Congress could do nothing to abridge them. When Southern members reached Congress, one Georgian told Sidney Andrews, "We're not going there to ask favors, by G-D, but to demand our rights!" Another was more pacific, but no less firm, in his words to Whitelaw Reid: "We tried to leave the Union. You have defeated us in our effort. What can there be, then, for us to do but to return our Senators and Representatives to the Congress from which we tried to withdraw forever? We acknowledge the defeat, and are ready to send back our Congressmen. That is what you have been fighting for; what more can the General Government have to do with the matter?" As for civil liberties, the privilege of voting, and the rights of the freed slaves, Southerners of all stripes agreed: these were internal matters, given over entirely to state government, about which a meddling Congress could have nothing whatsoever to say.

As far as many white Southerners were concerned, it was not just a matter of resuming their representation in Congress. The South, with its political unity and its lucrative cotton crop, had always dominated American politics, and expected to do so again. "We'll unite with the opposition up North, and between us we'll make a majority," one former federal officeholder told Whitelaw Reid. "*Then* we'll show you who's going to govern this country."

In fact, as far as many Southerners were concerned, the process of restoring regional rule had already begun. Andrew Johnson was a Southerner, and in the months since Appomattox he had abandoned the angry rhetoric about treason and set to work restoring the South to eminence. White Southerners hailed his efforts and expressed hearty support. Wade Hampton, a former secessionist firebrand and Confederate general, told the people of South Carolina that "it is our duty to support the President of the United States so long as he manifests a disposition to restore all our rights as a sovereign State." In Georgia, politically savvy Southern men explained to Andrews that Johnson clearly had chosen the South as his base for a presidential run in 1868 and that "the South and the Democratic party could elect him then." Another Georgian explained that "We must strike hands with the Democratic party of the North, and manage them as we always have.... [T]hey were ready enough to give us control if we gave them the offices; and I reckon they've not changed very much yet."

Whitelaw Reid found that politically involved Mississippians expected Johnson to sweep away Republican opposition in Congress, by fair means or foul. "There's no use in you Yankees talking," one said. "Johnson can force through Congress anything he wants." Others suggested that Republican opposition might anger the president and lead him to a coup d'état. "Hasn't he the army?" one group asked archly, while another was less subtle. "Johnson isn't going to put up with your radicals any longer. He is going to prorogue [dissolve] Congress at once, to get rid of its meddlesome interference with his policy!"

Dennett found much the same spirit in Vicksburg. "Johnson's doing very well now. He don't believe much in the niggers, neither, and when we're admitted into congress we're all right. The men that tyrannize over us now won't be in a majority then," one Southern pundit explained. "All the men, North and South, that are conservatives, must unite together. There are some men at the North that behaved very well all through the war, and we must unite with them."

Once they returned to authority, Southerners said, they would make a few changes in the postwar economic setup. Ever since the rise of Andrew Jackson in 1828, low debt had been a watchword in American politics. But when Lincoln in 1861 found himself with an empty treasury and half the Union in revolt, he and Secretary Chase had persuaded Congress to throw caution to the wind. By 1865, the national debt totaled $2.6 billion—nearly thirty times what it had been in 1861—and required regular interest payments of $137 million a year. Federal taxation to pay off the Union debt was, Schurz reported with some understatement, "very unpopular in the South." One South Carolinian told Sidney Andrews that "the President would not require the south to pay any part of the national debt. 'What, ruin us, and then make us help pay the cost of our own whipping? I reckon not!'" Indeed, the only question to many Southerners was whether the South should be exempted from taxation—or the entire national debt should simply be repudiated, like the Confederate debt after Appomattox. A tavern keeper in Southside Virginia assured John Richard Dennett that the Union bonds "were going to be repudiated in less than twelve months." In Georgia, a state convention delegate pointed out to Whitelaw Reid that it wasn't fair for Union bonds to be paid off while Confederate securities were worthless. "If that Confederate debt isn't honestly due no debt in the world ever was," he said. "If we've got to repudiate that, we may as well help the Democrats repudiate the debt on the other side too. What's fair for one is fair for the other."

And the whole issue of Southern debts incurred to pay for the war would get another look once the South was back. The Northern travelers found few Southerners who were willing to argue for repayment of the $700 million debt run up by the Confederate States of America. But the Confederate state governments also owed about $54 million. Much of that had been borrowed from well-to-do whites in each state, and many of the leaders of the new state governments thought they ought to repay that money. True, it had been borrowed to fund a war against the Union; but few whites in the South thought the attempt at secession had been wrong or illegal, and the fact that the Union army had defeated Lee's troops didn't change that. Andrew Johnson had suggested to the new governments that they repudiate that debt, and had found them remarkably reluctant to do so. Sidney Andrews found overwhelming majorities of the conventions in both South Carolina and Georgia in favor of requiring repayment of the state debts. When it became clear that even this lenient president would not accept them back into the Union without repudiation, the conventions rather reluctantly assented—for the moment. One Georgia delegate pointed out that the issue could always be revisited: "Let us repudiate only under the lash and the application of military power, and then, as soon as we are in independent sovereignty, restored to our equal rights and privileges in the Union, let us immediately call another Convention and resume the debt."

Beyond the state debt, though, Southerners had another financial issue they expected the federal government to deal with. Lincoln's Emancipation Proclamation had freed the slaves. Now the South was ready to present its bill for this confiscation of valuable property. "There are abundant indications in newspaper articles, public speeches, and electioneering documents of candidates, which render it eminently probable that on the claim of compensation for their emancipated slaves the Southern States, as soon as readmitted to representation in Congress, will be almost a unit," Schurz told Johnson. "I 'low the gov'ment won't take away all our niggers for nothin'," one North Carolinian explained to Andrews. "The Cons'tution makes niggers prop'ty, and gov'ment is bound to pay for them."

Southerners were quite confident that their congressional votes, coupled with those of Northern Democrats, would get them a good deal economically. Domestically, too, the restored Union these Southern political thinkers envisioned would be much like the antebellum republic—complete with Southern control over words written and spoken in the South. As Reid noted, "Persons writing from here in the spring of 1861, said there was no feature of the feeling among the leaders more marked than their scarcely disguised hostility to the freedom of the press." He found that feeling still general: "The newspapers found it difficult to realize that free speech and free press were at last established. The Montgomery Mail thought these correspondents from the North ought to be kept in their own section—they did nothing but misrepresent and slander." Schurz in his report reminded Johnson:

> One of the greatest drawbacks under which the southern people are laboring is, that for fifty years they have been in no sympathetic communion with the progressive ideas of the times. While professing to be in favor of free trade, they adopted and forced a system of prohibition, as far as those ideas were concerned, which was in conflict with their cherished institution of slavery; and, as almost all the progressive ideas of our days were in conflict with slavery, the prohibition was sweeping. . . . This spirit, which for so long a time has kept the southern people back while the world besides was moving, is even at this moment still standing as a serious obstacle in the way of progress.

Before the war, informal violence by individuals and secret "vigilance committees" had driven dissenting whites into silence or exile. Now those committees were reappearing. One Alabama Unionist showed Dennett a note he had received:

> Sir: We, the undersigned citizens of Mobile, Ala., give you one week from date to leave the place, and if found within the limits of the city or State after the time specified as above, you and your traitorous offspring will be wiped into eternity as sure as there is a God above you.
>   By order of
>   SPECIAL COMMITTEE.

In New Orleans, Dennett was told of a secret society that had made plans to drive all "Yankees" out of the city as soon as federal troops withdrew. And a planter in a rural Louisiana parish was subjected to another secret missive for the crime of leasing land to black farmers: "We have decided to burn more than your gin-house, and will kill you if you don't break up your infamous nigger camps." Dennett warned that any Northerner emigrating South "would be compelled to restrict his accustomed freedom of speech and action and defer to the social and political theories and opinions of his neighbors." Sidney Andrews found that out personally, when rumors spread around Albany, Georgia, that this Yankee visitor had taken the side of a black man in a fistfight with a white. Andrews was tracked by a lynch mob, and had to slink out of town.

Having been united so long on slavery, white Southerners were now, the correspondents reported, united in their fear and hatred of the freed slaves. It was, Sidney Andrews found, almost all they talked about: "Everybody talks about the negro, at all hours of the day, and under all circumstances. . . . Let conversation begin where it will, it ends with Sambo." With Emancipation, one Union officer told Schurz, the whites had concluded that "the blacks at large belong to the whites at large." Andrews noted that whether or not Southern whites had "accepted" emancipation, almost none of them accepted that blacks were human beings, much less fellow citizens. " 'The negro is an animal whose character the North seems utterly unable to comprehend,' " one South Carolina convention delegate told him. That, he concluded, was the voice of Southern opinion: "[T]he negro is an animal; a higher sort of animal, to be sure, than the dog or the horse, but, after all, an animal."

What that meant, to many Southerners, was that a legal system would have to be devised quickly to keep the freed slaves in their proper place—on the plantations, laboring for their old masters. These "black codes," which were passed by many restored Southern legislatures in the fall of 1865, in essence made black Southerners wards of the state, granting officials authority to bind them out under contract to planters in need of hands. Blacks who had no regular employment for a white master were subject to whipping and imprisonment. Black families were to be broken up again, as in slavery times, as well—a number of the "black codes" empowered local judges to seize the children of black parents and "apprentice" them to white masters. Preference, in some of the codes, was to go to the children's former "owners."

Such harsh measures—slavery in all but name—shocked Northern readers. But to many Southerners, the "black codes" were just a way station toward reestablishment of the old "peculiar institution" in all its glory. One man in Lynchburg told Dennett that the blacks "seem to think they be" free—but that "we can tell better when the next Congress meets and after the Supreme Court has decided." The reliance on the Supreme Court was not as quixotic as it seemed. Southerners had dominated the Court since its establishment, and the vast majority of justices had been slave owners and pro-slavery men. The hope that they could win back in Congress or in court what they had lost in war was not completely absurd.

Schurz reported to Johnson that he had found throughout the old Confederacy "a desire to preserve slavery in its original form as much and as long as possible . . . or to introduce into the new system that element of physical compulsion which would make the negro work." This "new system," he wrote, would not be "slavery in its old form," but instead a system "intermediate between slavery as it formerly existed in the south, and free labor as it exists in the north, but more nearly related to the former than to the latter."

Many of the South's best brains were at work on how the new system could be smoothly installed. Andrews reprinted a speech by one Confederate veteran in Georgia, which explained that the new constitutional amendment allowed involuntary servitude as "punishment for crime." Thus, all that was needed was a law that would "enable the judicial authorities . . . to sell into bondage again those negroes who should be found guilty of certain crimes." Another Georgia veteran cheerfully told Andrews of "private talk" of making "the penal code take [the Negro] back into the condition of slavery. It'll be called 'involuntary servitude for the punishment of crime,' but it won't differ much from slavery." In Selma, Alabama, Trowbridge found, city authorities were already putting such a system in place; he saw a chain gang of black men working on the streets; they had been convicted of " 'using abusive language towards a white man,'" or of selling produce at the public market before the opening bell. "That's the beauty of freedom!" onlookers told him as they pointed to the "criminals" at work. *"That's what free niggers come to!"*

The whites of the South, all the reporters agreed, were uniformly convinced that only one thing could keep the region safe and solvent—the whip. Hardly had Carl Schurz stepped aboard the *Arago* leaving Washington than he met a Southern planter returning in order to restore his old lands. Schurz asked whether he expected to make contracts with his former slaves.

> This remark stirred him. He became animated. . . . Contracts with those niggers? It would never work. Yes, he had heard of that emancipation business. He knew that was the intention. But—and here he approached me with an air of confidentiality as if to coax my secret, true opinion out of me—now really did I think that this was a settled thing? Now, he could tell me that niggers would not work unless compelled to. . . . Why, was not President Johnson a Southern man, and did he not know equally well that the nigger would not work without compulsion?

This encounter set the pattern thereafter. "In at least nineteen cases of twenty," Schurz reported to Johnson, Southerners told him flatly, " 'You cannot make the negro work without physical compulsion.' I heard this hundreds of times, heard it wherever I went, heard it in nearly the same words from so many different persons, that at last I came to the conclusion that this is the prevailing sentiment among the southern people." Reid found the same thing: "Nothing could overcome this rooted idea, that the negro was worthless, except under the lash," he wrote. Many of the "black codes" prescribed the whipping post for blacks who committed offenses that led only to fines for whites. And even some Union officers stationed in the South—under orders to protect the freed slaves—assumed that regular whipping would be part of the system, and sometimes volunteered to administer the lash themselves on behalf of "aggrieved" whites.

Whites tended to regard a whipping, or a beating, or even worse treatment as the prerogative of any white who was displeased by any black person, regardless of their previous relationship. One white told Sidney Andrews, "I would shoot one just as soon as I would a dog." Andrews reported that he had seen a black man gunned down in Columbia, South Carolina, at high noon in the doorway of a store, with no more notice taken than if the freed slave had been a domestic animal.

White Southerners saw no reason why "freedom" for black people should carry any additional rights, such as the right to testify in court against whites. "Nothing would make me cut a nigger's throat from ear to ear so quick," a shoemaker told John Richard Dennett, "as having him set up his impudent face to tell that a thing wasn't so when I said it was so. The idea of letting one o' them be sworn to give his evidence!"

Votes for the freed slaves were simply beyond imagination. "We don't believe that because the nigger is free he ought to be saucy," one South Carolinian—a proud self-proclaimed Unionist—told Whitelaw Reid, "and we don't mean to have any such nonsense as letting him vote. He's helpless, and ignorant, and dependent, and the old masters will still control him."

Anyway, the vote was none of the Union's business. Nothing in the Constitution gave Congress any right to meddle in the Southern states' voting practices—and the general Southern sense was that too many white people were voting already, and that blacks were out of the question. Sidney Andrews found South Carolina leaders opposed even to white voting. "It will not do to put power in the hands of the common people," they told him. Others remarked sadly, "It was a great mistake when we passed our free-suffrage law."

The issue of black voting, however, seemed less important to Southern whites in 1865 than we might think. That's because many whites expected the freed slaves to disappear within a generation or two. Before the war, many antislavery Northerners had concluded that the only answer to the slavery question was colonization of freed slaves—either in Liberia, or in Haiti, or in the American Southwest. Lincoln himself had pursued these strange-seeming colonization schemes even after issuing the Emancipation Proclamation in 1863. Now Southerners clutched at the idea that the federal government might simply deport the former slaves. In Virginia, a congressional candidate proclaimed, "I shall favor and encourage the emigration and colonization of the Negro population as a measure calculated, under present circumstances, to promote the interest of both races." On a train between Knoxville, Tennessee, and Atlanta, Whitelaw Reid met a former Confederate major, who explained that "the only effective and satisfactory policy which could be adopted was that which General Jackson had pursued towards the Indians—they must be colonized."

The reference to Andrew Jackson was a reminder of the forced removal from the Southeast of the so-called Five Civilized Tribes—the Cherokee, Chickasaw, Choctaw, Muskogee Confederation (Creek), and Seminole. Jackson had sponsored the Indian Removal Act, which required these educated, agricultural tribes to leave their land and migrate west to Indian Territory (present-day Oklahoma) along what came to be known as the Trail of Tears. The fate of the Indians showed white Americans what happened to racial "inferiors" when confronted with white civilization. "I pity the poor niggers, after what you've done for them," said one Southerner whom John Townsend Trowbridge met literally outside Andrew Johnson's office door. "In a little while they'll be exterminated, just like the Indians." Others affected less pity for the doomed race. "I candidly confess that I look forward to the extermination of the freedmen," a Pedee River planter told John Richard Dennett. Trowbridge reported passengers on a Southern train who spotted through the windows a ragged camp of freedmen huddled against the cold around a fire. "That's freedom! That's what the Yankees have done for 'em!" the white passengers began to cry with a grim satisfaction. "They'll all be dead before spring." What made the scene remarkable, he said, was that the same train was crowded with well-dressed blacks traveling in groups to Memphis to buy Christmas presents. These passengers, who showed no sign of imminent demise, were in a different car, however, and the white passengers affected not to see them.

All in all, the prospects for the Union seemed to these Northern observers to be grim. The prospect, Andrews reported, was for "a sullen and relentless antagonism to the idea of national sovereignty,— from which will breed passionate devotion to local interests, unending persecution of the freedmen, never-ceasing clamor in behalf of State rights, and continual effort to break away from the solemn obligations of the national debt." Schurz warned that there was a possibility that the South would build up "another 'peculiar institution' whose spirit is in conflict with the fundamental principles of our political system." Trowbridge warned that Southern leadership was determined "to govern not only their own states but to regain their forfeited leadership in the affairs of the nation; to effect the repudiation of the national debt or to get the Confederate debt and the Rebel state debts assumed by the whole country; to secure payment for their slaves, and for all injuries and losses occasioned by the war."

The picture of the reemerging Slave Power was remarkably consistent among all the accounts. Of course, all were written by Northern partisans, who could be expected to sympathize with the Republican Party. But in case anyone was in doubt about the message, the *Richmond Examiner* ran a short report on the political situation in January 1866. No one could accuse the *Examiner* of Northern bias; it had been a consistent voice for secession and violence since before Fort Sumter. (Once, when Robert E. Lee suggested offering black men freedom if they would fight for the Confederacy, the *Examiner* had attacked even Lee as a disloyal Southerner.) Now the paper announced for all to read, "Universal assent appears to be given to the proposition that if the States lately rebellious be restored to rights of representation according to the federal basis, or to the basis of numbers enlarged by the enumeration of all the blacks in the next census, the political power of the country will pass into the hands of the South, aided, as it will be, by Northern alliances. The South claims that this will be the fact, and the North does not dispute it."

THE MIGHTY HEART
OF THE WORLD

In 1787 the drafters of the new federal constitution worked in secret, with windows closed even in the July heat to prevent the public from learning that they were remodeling America's government. In 1865, the Thirty-ninth Congress met amid a blaze of publicity. With the guns silent, legions of newspaper reporters found themselves drawn to Washington and the unfolding conflict over the shape of the restored Union.

Americans in the mid-nineteenth century devoured political news. In a culture that had no mass entertainment and no professional sports, politicians were among the most recognizable public figures. Newspapers across the country devoted many columns to summaries or transcriptions of their speeches, which ordinary people read and debated among themselves in homes that had no radio or television. In such an environment, the daily *Congressional Globe* (the Congress's official record of its debates) was the equivalent not only of today's C-SPAN but even to some extent of ESPN. Just as members of Congress today tailor their speeches for the audiences watching on TV, members of the

Thirty-ninth Congress often delivered long addresses aimed as much at public opinion as at persuading their colleagues.

But constitution-making in public is hard. Much of the maneuvering that went into the Fourteenth Amendment in fact took place outside the public eye, in the proceedings of the joint committee of Fifteen on Reconstruction. Like the Philadelphia delegates, the members of the joint committee kept no official record of their debates. What little we know of the committee's doings is pieced together from the committee's bare-bones journal and from unofficial sources—letters, diaries, newspaper reports. The journal itself vanished after the Thirty-ninth Congress adjourned; it surfaced again only two decades later, when former congressman Roscoe Conkling, arguing a case for a powerful railroad in front of the Supreme Court, pulled a battered copy from his pocket and assured the justices that the committee had always intended the "due process" clause to apply to corporations as well as to natural persons. Though the text contains little support for that idea, the Court, perhaps cowed by Conkling's lordly manner, wrote that idea into law, where it remains today.

The first major struggle was over the very makeup of the committee. Charles Sumner wanted the chair. He had long dreamed of remaking the South, turning it into a model New England–style society of small independent farmers and schoolhouses. On the very first day of the session, he had offered a set of bills to do exactly that. His bills would have required Southern states to do away with all laws making any distinction among citizens "founded on race, former condition, or color." Former Confederate officials—the leaders of the Slave Power—would be disfranchised and excluded from politics. Not only former officials but veterans of the Confederate military would be denied the ballot. The Southern states would be required to repudiate all Confederate debt and renounce forever secession and slavery. Most important, the South would lose its "slave seats" forever—representation in Congress would henceforth be based on the number of legal voters rather than on population. States that refused to make these changes would be kept under direct rule from Washington indefinitely.

It was a comprehensive program for the future of the South, and no instrument in Washington could have been better suited for carrying it into enactment than a joint congressional committee. In a joint committee, the two houses send members to one body with one chairman. The result can be a uniquely powerful platform from which to influence the executive branch and to broadcast Congress's view of national affairs to the people.

Sumner's program faced insuperable problems, however. To begin with, it was by no means clear that Congress had the power to make these changes in Southern internal institutions. Sumner, like many antislavery politicians in the years before and during the war, claimed that the power to alter these state arrangements lay in the Constitution's so-called Guaranty Clause—the provision in Article IV requiring the national government to "guarantee to every State in this Union a Republican Form of Government." This provision had been rarely invoked in the years before the war. But antislavery thinkers had begun in the 1830s to argue that the Southern system—in which a small elite of rich whites exercised political control, while blacks were held in lifelong chattel slavery—could not be considered "republican." If it wasn't, then Congress would have power under the Guaranty Clause to step in and redo the state's political system.

Sumner and other antislavery leaders argued that Congress need not seat any Southern member of Congress until the majority was satisfied that the new Southern state governments were truly "republican"— what we would call "democratic." That might mean requiring new civil rights guarantees, demanding rewritten state constitutions, and even interfering with state voter qualifications.

It was an elegant argument. But the reconstruction bills Sumner based on it went nowhere. In fact, there was actual laughter from the gallery when he first introduced them. The problem these bills encountered was not constitutional; it was political, and it was the same problem Sumner himself encountered when he tried to secure the chairmanship of the Joint Committee on Reconstruction. It was not the program, it was the proposer.

Charles Sumner, to put it mildly, was not a party man. At heart he was not a politician but a revolutionary intellectual. He lived in a world of abstract principles, and he saw compromise as betrayal. Serious congressional Republicans in late 1865 saw that the problem was not pure principles but adroit governance. For that, Sumner was not their man.

The congressional leadership faced a number of problems, and the more prominent Sumner became, the worse each of these problems would be. The president—with wide popularity in the country and the unprecedented power of the office Lincoln had forged—was not one of their own. They had a majority in Congress, but many congressional Republicans were nervous about picking a fight with the White House. Unless the leadership moved very carefully, it risked an outright rupture with Johnson, who might rally enough Republicans and Democrats to cut Congress out of Reconstruction altogether. Even Radical leaders like Thad Stevens wanted to avoid a break with Johnson until the time was right. The joint committee was no place for a revolutionary, or for a man given to gallant but futile gestures. The leadership needed finesse, intelligence, and party loyalty.

The chair of the Senate Republican caucus, Henry B. Anthony of Rhode Island, turned to someone who had the qualities Sumner lacked. His choice—William Pitt Fessenden of Maine—must have galled Sumner. Acerbic, aloof, and intellectual, Pitt Fessenden would have seemed perfectly at home among the delegates to Philadelphia in 1787. The godson, personal and political, of Daniel Webster, he was a curious combination of antislavery zeal, Whig nationalism, and what Thaddeus Stevens called "that vile ingredient, called conservatism." Languid in manner, conspicuously handsome, and beautifully dressed on all public occasions, he was a respected figure in the Senate, and a feared opponent in debate. During the antebellum years, he had always stood up to Southern bullies, and had even fought Stephen Douglas to a rhetorical standstill on more than one occasion. During the Kansas-Nebraska crisis in 1854, when Andrew Butler of South Carolina threatened yet again that an unfavorable vote would mean

Southern secession, Fessenden electrified Northern public opinion with his blunt reply: "[D]o not delay it on my account."

Fessenden embodied respectability, but he had been born in 1806 under scandalous circumstances: his father, a young lawyer, had sought to marry a local belle; she gave birth to young Fessenden but refused his father's hand in marriage. Samuel Fessenden—later known as "General Fessenden" for his role in the Maine militia—raised and personally educated his son, to whom he remained close until his death (the two men died only months apart); Fessenden never saw his mother again—and indeed refused her written pleas later for a meeting. General Fessenden named his son William Pitt in honor of the conservative British prime minister. The young Pitt Fessenden was throughout his life far less radical on every question than was his father and mentor.

As a child, Fessenden was delicate, bookish, and aloof. He shunned athletic pursuits to spend solitary hours with his books; as an adult, however, he embodied the Down Easter's love of cool weather, gardening, and trout fishing. For most of the last fifteen years of his life, Fessenden also suffered from health problems that often left him unable to attend Senate sessions. The nature of the malady is not clear, but it seems likely that he had contracted malaria from the mosquitoes that thrived in Washington. On more than one occasion, during a particularly fierce debate, Fessenden would give way to fatigue and stretch out in a window seat in the back of the Senate chamber for a quick nap. His wife, Emily, had died in 1857, leaving Fessenden with a sense that he had little to live for; after her death, almost all his letters include a few sentences expressing his sense that death was approaching and would be welcome.

Fessenden was educated at Bowdoin during the Maine college's golden era. He counted among his schoolmates one future president, Franklin Pierce, and two future authors, Nathaniel Hawthorne and Henry Wadsworth Longfellow. The greatest tragedy of Pitt's early life was the unexpected death of his fiancée, Emily Longfellow, the poet's sister.

His father began his career as a strong Federalist, but in the 1840s the general became a Garrisonian abolitionist, favoring immediate abolition of slavery and if necessary the breakup of the Union. The younger Fessenden was no abolitionist; his opposition to slavery was inspired by the disproportionate influence the Slave Power exercised in Washington. He was resolutely nationalistic and antislavery, first as a Whig and then, after his first election to the Senate in 1852, as a Republican. When the war came, he had served as chair of the Senate Finance Committee. It was a demanding role; Union victory depended on a steady flow of funds. Fessenden had worked closely with Treasury secretary Chase on the new income tax and on the issue of long-term government bonds. In 1864, when Lincoln finally grew tired of Chase's constant threats to resign, he had turned to Fessenden as Chase's replacement. Fessenden accepted reluctantly; entering the Cabinet would mean forgoing his chief joy, his summers among his roses in Portland. He had resigned as soon as possible to reenter the Senate.

During Fessenden's first term in the Senate he and Sumner had been friends and allies. After Bully Brooks's assault drove Sumner out of the Senate, Fessenden moved into Sumner's rooms while his colleague wandered Europe in search of a cure. But Fessenden wrote to friends that the Charles Sumner who returned to the Senate in 1859 was not the same man who had been carried out three years before; the assault and his prolonged convalescence seemed to have driven Sumner away from the land of living people and into a system of abstract principles. Fessenden, true to his Federalist roots, believed first and foremost in the necessity of governing the nation. Moral issues played a secondary role to practical legislative politics. And while Sumner's first loyalty was to principle as he conceived it, Fessenden was a strong party man. "I would vote for a dog," he once said, "if he were the candidate of my party." That the two men were rivals for leadership of New England's congressional delegation made relations worse. By 1864, he had referred privately to Sumner as a "dirty dog."

Fessenden's party was firmly in charge of the committee, and the leadership of the two houses made sure he had a number of strong antislavery Republicans to rely on. Jacob Howard of Michigan and James Grimes of Iowa were two of the antislavery senators named to the committee; from the House came a delegation headed by Thad Stevens himself and including a number of members with solid records of opposition to the Slave Power: Elihu Washburne of Illinois had been a member of the Joint Committee on the Conduct of the War, and he had belabored Lincoln ceaselessly to turn the war into an antislavery revolution. George S. Boutwell of Massachusetts was a former Democrat who had broken with his party over Kansas and had also pushed for vigorous prosecution of the war.

Steven's final House ally was Roscoe Conkling of New York, a kindred spirit in his devotion to the Republican Party, but utterly devoid of Stevens's idealism about reform. (Indeed, later in life, Conkling said scornfully that "[w]hen Dr. Johnson defined patriotism as the last refuge of a scoundrel, he was unconscious of the then undeveloped capabilities and uses of the word reform.") Conkling, like Stevens, was an accomplished political infighter; unlike Stevens, though, he was physically magnificent, tall, broad, and muscular, and he used his size and physical power to intimidate political foes. Once, during the tense days before secession, Southern members of the House had made a rush at Stevens, as if to silence his mocking tongue; they turned back when Conkling calmly interposed himself between the mob and his leader.

More conservative, but also a more formidable intellect, was Representative John A. Bingham of Ohio, whom Whitelaw Reid called "the best-natured and crossest-looking man in the House." Stevens would be the tactical leader of the House delegation; but he was not an intellectual. Bingham, who was in his way as formidable a constitutional lawyer as Fessenden, would fill that role. Bingham had served in the House until the Republican debacle of 1862, when opposition to the Emancipation Proclamation cost him his seat. During his antebellum career in Congress, Bingham had been withering in his denunciations of the Slave Power. Beyond that, he had attacked the Southern states for their repressive political systems, which denied basic democratic rights—free speech, assembly, and press, for example—to their people.

Bingham had insisted for years that no state could have a "republican form of government" that did not allow free discussion of political issues; beyond that, he had long insisted that the Constitution should be changed to apply the Bill of Rights to states as well as to the federal government. "The equality of the right to live; the right to know; to argue and to utter, according to conscience; to work and enjoy the product of their toil, is the rock on which [the] Constitution rests," he had argued in 1857, "its sure foundation and defense." Bingham admitted that the Constitution of 1787 did not give Congress power to regulate the states' voting systems. But he did argue passionately that the Bill of Rights, and the Fifth Amendment's requirement of "due process of law" generally, limited the states' power to set up political oligarchies or racial caste systems. And beyond that, he rejected the idea that states had any power to determine who was a citizen—either of the state or of the nation. The Constitution did that, he claimed, and rightly interpreted it made everyone—black and white, male and female—a citizen, and an equal. "One people," he had long proclaimed in presciently nationalistic tones, "one Constitution, and one country!"

Those words were more than political sloganeering for Bingham. From his childhood on, Bingham had been raised in the austere tradition of dissenting Presbyterianism. This small minority within the faith insisted that the mission of God's people on earth was not simply the salvation of their own souls, or even that of others. They were to realize on earth the ideal commonwealth they saw in the New Testament—a republic of complete legal and social equality. Bingham's vision of "one country" was far more radical than that of many of his colleagues; on the joint committee, he would steadily push to embody it in the Constitution, and would succeed better than many historians fully recognize.

In January 1865, John Bingham was fifty-two years old. A decade earlier, a journalist had described him as "a sandy-haired middle aged man, rather tall, vigorously built, with a broad and commanding forehead; . . . the expression of the face conveys the idea of a strong will inclined to extreme convictions, an intellect practical in the guerilla support of every opinion, and a temperament which is inclined to antagonize on every possible occasion with all or any, who do not think in precisely the same channel." Friends and foes alike admired his oratory; his Ohio colleague, Republican Albert Gallatin Riddle, wrote that "it was like a steady, strong, onsweeping wind, roaring through and over a great old forest, a powerful, steady, pealing blast."

Bingham was the principal force behind the adoption of Section One of the Fourteenth Amendment, which contains most of the provisions that affect us today. But history has not paid this stubborn, principled, intellectual Framer his due. Perhaps it is because he fits uneasily at best into the scheme of "Radicals" versus "Conservatives" that historians use to understand the early years of Reconstruction. Perhaps it is because he was a small-town boy from the heartland—he made his political base in the tiny frontier town of Cadiz, Ohio. Unlike Stevens, a Dartmouth man, and Fessenden, of venerable Bowdoin, Bingham traced his intellectual roots to modest Franklin College, in New Athens, Ohio, which has long since disappeared. Franklin, founded in 1825, was a fountainhead of hardshell Presbyterianism, as expressed in the Associate Presbyterian and Associate Reform Presbyterian movements. Both at home and at Franklin, Bingham absorbed an old-style Protestantism that equated republicanism with God's will, and the United States with His kingdom on earth.

John Bingham represents the full flowering of Protestant America's republican and utopian phase. On the floor of the House in 1858, Bingham explained that the movement against slavery was simply part of the fruition of God's plan for perfection of mankind: "It is the high heaven of the nineteenth century. The whole heavens are filled with the light of a new and better day. Kings hold their power with a tremulous and unsteady hand. The bastilles and dungeons of tyrants, those graves of human liberty, are giving up their dead," he said. "[T]he mighty heart of the world stands still, awaiting the resurrection of the nations, and that final triumph of the right, foretold in prophecy and invoked in song."

Throughout his career, Bingham combined pure antislavery fervor with reverence for the Constitution; he regarded the Slave Power, or "the slavocracy," as he called it, as a conspiracy to destroy the Founders' Republic. In 1860, he had stood on the floor of the House and arraigned the Slave Power for its crimes against the nation:

> [T]he repeal of laws for the protection of freedom and free labor in the Territories; the conquest of foreign territory for slavery; the admission into the Union of a foreign slave state; the rejection by this sectional party of the homestead bill; the restriction of the right of petition; the restoration of fugitive slaves at national expense; the attempt to reward slave pirates for kidnapping Africans; the attempt to acquire Cuba, with her six hundred thousand slaves; the attempt to fasten upon an unwilling people a slave constitution [in Kansas]; the attempt to enact a sedition law, thereby restricting the freedom of the press and the freedom of speech, in direct violation of the Constitution . . . ; and the attempt, by extra-judicial interference to take away from the people and their Representatives the power to legislate for freedom and free labor in the Territories.

At Franklin College, he had been a classmate of the Reverend Titus Brasfield, a former slave who became one of the first black men admitted to an American college. The two men remained lifelong friends and correspondents. But the crimes of "the slave interest" went far beyond its inhumanity to the slaves themselves, in Bingham's view. Southern demands for censorship of the mails and suppression of antislavery publications threatened to destroy freedom everywhere in the nation, convert the United States from a Christian republic into a despotism, and pervert the Constitution—"a sublime and beautiful scripture—into a horrid charter of wrong."

To Bingham, the "sublime and beautiful scripture" was something far more vigorous than the limited compact state-sovereignty theorists promoted during the Civil War. To begin with, it complied with what he saw as the basic requirement of a republic: that all those within its borders be equal. The Constitution was "a new evangel to the nations, embodying the democracy of the New Testament, the absolute equality of all men before the law, in respect of those rights of human nature which are the gift of God," and "a great written charter of liberty, which is no respecter of persons, which declares that the poor and the rich, the citizen and the stranger within your gates, are alike sacred before the sublime majesty of its laws."

There was no pretense of bipartisanship on the joint committee. The Republican Party dominated Congress; at opening day, it held 145 of 191 seats in the House and 39 of 50 in the Senate. This already lopsided advantage translated into an even more overwhelming preponderance on the committee, which had just three Democrats among its fifteen members. But again, the Senate Republican leadership reached into American history to give even the hapless opposition the luster of the early Republic by choosing the nation's foremost constitutional lawyer, Senator Reverdy Johnson of Maryland, as one of three Democratic members.

If Fessenden, in his reserved elegance, seemed a living link to the Federalism of the Founders, Reverdy Johnson was a proud descendant of Jefferson and Jackson. A supporter both of the Union and of "states' rights," he had always mildly regretted slavery and strongly defended the rights of slaveholders. At seventy, Johnson was the oldest member of the Senate. Though he had been identified with Southern rights and slavery for much of his career, he managed to transcend partisan and sectional tensions by his unfailing good humor.

He had not always been quite so equable: as a young lawyer, he had challenged a rival to a duel. The other party had Johnson jailed until he agreed to a reconciliation; the two men then became lifelong friends. A few years later, Johnson had volunteered to help a friend prepare for another duel. While demonstrating proper pistol technique, Johnson deflected a bullet off a hickory tree. It ricocheted into his left eye, leaving him half-blind. Eventually, his right eye failed as well; by the opening of the Thirty-ninth Congress, Johnson retained only minimal sight. Perhaps as a result, he was notorious for his illegible penmanship. On one occasion, a political rival accused Johnson of hypocrisy on a political issue. The rival claimed to have a letter in his possession proving the charge. One of Johnson's allies suggested that Johnson demand the critic produce the original. "No one on earth can read it but yourself," the friend explained, "and you can read it to suit yourself."

Though Maryland was a slave state, Johnson had resolutely opposed secession in 1861. He supported the Union war effort and was personally close to Lincoln—but he had defended Mrs. Mary Surratt, accused of complicity in the assassination, without charging a fee. He had voted for the Thirteenth Amendment outlawing slavery, but he remained a states' rights man; on one occasion he had even denied that, as a senator, he was a federal official or part of the federal government at all. Senators were *state* officials, he claimed. The states were "creators of the government." For this reason, senators should represent their states even if it meant voting against the national interest: "We should look at the matter from the point of view of the country," he admitted, "but we should not let our patriotism run wild."

Johnson's two party allies on the committee were Henry Grider of Kentucky, as old as Johnson but by no means as distinguished, and Andrew Rogers of New Jersey, young and flamboyantly pro-Southern. Remarkably enough, the members seemed to get along with one another despite the yawning political gulf dividing them. Johnson, as leader of the opposition, said later that he had never found any bias in the committee's procedures.

The committee first met on January 6, in the Senate's Pacific Railroad committee room. It began by adopting a strict rule that its proceedings would be secret, a rule that most committee members observed until their deaths. The only document reporting its deliberations is a brief journal, recording the dates and times of meetings, brief summaries of subcommittee reports, formal proposals offered for adoption by members, and votes on specific measures. At the first meeting, Stevens proposed that three of its members "wait on the President and request him to defer all further executive action in regard to reconstruction until this Committee shall have taken action on that subject."

The committee picked Fessenden, Elihu Washburne, and Reverdy

Johnson to visit the White House—one conservative, one Radical, and one Democrat. The group went to the White House the following Monday, and the committee reassembled on Tuesday, January 9, to hear their report. Fessenden, the journal says, recounted a friendly meeting with Johnson, in which the delegation told him that "the Committee desired to avoid all possible collision or misconstruction between the Executive and Congress." Johnson was noncommittal, but did allow that "it was not his intention to do more [about Reconstruction] than had been done for the present."

The committee then fell to work. By late January, it would begin taking testimony from witnesses in the South—officers in the Union army, freed slaves, and local whites, including some of the major leaders of the Confederacy and its army. The objective was officially to determine whether the white citizens in the South were loyal and disposed to accept Emancipation and equal rights for blacks. After the evidence was gathered, the committee was to make a recommendation about when and how each state should be readmitted. But at its very first session, the committee also began to debate the other important business before it: making sure that the South did not reenter the Union under the old constitutional system, which had allowed it to run the show for more than half a century.

Stevens had already made clear his own program for the South. In a speech to the House on December 18, he unveiled the "Dead States" theory, which envisioned a lengthy period of territorial government for the former slave states. Stevens's speech represents the best single summary of Radical thought about Reconstruction and constitutional renovation. Neither Stevens nor his radical faction was ever in a position to dictate the outcome of the committee's deliberations. But the more cautious members, like Fessenden and Bingham, knew they must operate with Stevens watching them closely. Thus, the December 18 speech exercised a gravitational influence on the committee and on the Thirty-ninth Congress.

The Southern states, Stevens reasoned, had committed a kind of political suicide when they illegally attempted to break the Union.

They could no longer claim the powers of states within the federal government. "Dead States," he said in a slap at the Democratic slogan, "cannot restore their own existence 'as it was.'" That restoration could only be done by the national government acting as a unit. That meant that Johnson could not order the "restoration" of these states without the approval of Congress. "Congress—the Senate and House of Representatives; with the concurrence of the President—is the only power that can act in the matter. . . . A law of Congress must be passed before any new State can be admitted, or any dead ones revived."

Until Congress agreed, then, the Southern states had no claim to enter Congress. They should be governed under Article IV, Section 3, which gave to Congress the power to "make all needful Rules and Regulations respecting the Territory or other Property belonging to the United States." In particular, Congress should create elected territorial governments—with rules of suffrage set by Congress itself, and presumably including at least some blacks as voters. The experience of sharing the polls with former slaves would eventually convince Southern whites that impartial suffrage was not the disaster they imagined.

While the South waited for readmission to the Union, Stevens said, Congress must amend the Constitution "to make it what its framers intended; and so as to secure perpetual ascendancy to the party of the Union; and so as to render our republican government firm and stable." Here Stevens, in his blunt way, proclaimed a purpose that other Republicans sometimes preferred to obscure. In his analysis, there were two parties in the nation. One—the Republican, now called the Union, Party—was loyal to the nation and its Constitution. The other was "the party of treason," the Democratic–Slave Power axis that had run the country for much of its history. To Stevens, that was not an indictment of the voters, but of the Constitution. The Framers' document had allowed the South to set up a racial caste system and a political oligarchy that stifled internal debate. Now that caste system must be broken up, and the constitutional flaws that gave the South its power must be repaired.

The first change, Stevens said, must be a change in the way repre sentatives and presidential electors were assigned. If a Southern state denied the vote to black citizens, then its all-white electorate should not be entitled to representatives for those citizens. If the basis of rep- resentation were changed, the readmitted states might still exclude blacks from the suffrage. But if they did so, they would yield the "slave seats." If, on the other hand, the South decided to allow black voting, the result would be a breakup of the one-party South and the oppressive system that protected the Slave Power oligarchs from internal criticism and political competition. Under such a system, "there would always be Union white men enough in the South, aided by the blacks, to divide the representation and thus continue the Republican ascendancy."

While the Constitution was being reformed, Stevens said, the document should also be amended to require all state laws to be uniform—thus making "black codes" unconstitutional—and to pro- hibit the Southern states from paying off their Confederate debts.

Finally, Congress should begin a homestead program for the South like the one it had adopted in the West in 1862. The federal govern- ment was now holding a vast amount of cropland in the South, some confiscated from Southern planters who had supported the Confederacy. Instead of meekly returning it to the lords of slavery, the federal government should break it into small holdings and sell it cheaply to freed slaves who would farm it. At a stroke, this would break the economic basis of the Slave Power and create a new class of independent freeholders.

All American citizens should be part of the body politic, Stevens said. Here he obliquely drew on James Madison's famous argument that a large country must of necessity be more democratic than a small one, because the many different groups and factions within it would block one another from assuming despotic power. The extent of a republic, Stevens implied, might be measured in the breadth of its electorate as well as in the square mileage it covered. Black suf- frage, "joined with just white men, would greatly modify, if it did not entirely prevent, the injustice of majorities."

All that stood in the way of such an outcome, he suggested, was the idea that the United States Constitution created a "white man's government." He was flinging down a challenge to Andrew Johnson, but he was careful to phrase the challenge in the language of loyalty. He did not remark that Johnson had been quoted using just those words; as the White House had never directly confirmed the quote, he pretended that they had never been uttered, attributing the heresy to "Copperhead" figures. The idea that American democracy was racial was as heretical and dangerous as the theory of *Dred Scott* that no black person could ever be a part of the American political system. "This doctrine of a white man's government," he said, "is as atrocious as the infamous sentiment that damned the late Chief Justice [Roger B. Taney, author of *Dred Scott*] to everlasting fame; and, I fear, to everlasting fire."

Stevens's program was but one alternative the joint committee would consider behind closed doors. Looking back at the long struggle for what became the Fourteenth Amendment, it is striking how quickly the committee—and much Northern sentiment—moved to embrace what would become two of its most important features: reduced representation for the South and national power to enforce civil rights. Almost every Republican in Congress had by now noticed the looming paradox that Emancipation would shortly make the former slavemasters more politically powerful than ever. Clearly the South must be blocked from claiming representation for the freed slaves while denying them the vote. That much was easy. The question was how to achieve it.

The most straightforward way would be simply to change the Constitution to bar racial discrimination in voting. One hundred and forty years later, it's hard to understand why antislavery veterans didn't want to do that. But the majority of Republicans—and even some abolitionists, like William Lloyd Garrison—weren't ready to take that step. Many were still mired in the old view of the vote as a political privilege granted to a few citizens rather than as a right belonging to all. To contemporary Americans, a citizen without a vote is a second-class citizen. But by 1865, Americans were still affected by the Framers' old view of representation as something that a small body of voters did for the larger body of citizens. Freed slaves, these thinkers argued, were not "ready" for the vote. Largely illiterate and uneducated, they would be unable to make an intelligent choice at the polls. A number of antislavery politicians feared that the former slaves would remain in psychic thrall to their old masters and would vote as the white aristocracy directed them to.

Beyond that lay an uncomfortable fact: even in the North, most states did not allow black men to vote. Early records suggest that free blacks did vote in most of the Northern states during the Revolutionary Era, and some even served as delegates to the state conventions that ratified the Constitution of 1787. But in the nineteenth century, Jacksonian politicians had increasingly viewed the ballot as the property of white men only; thus, even as the right of whites to vote grew broader after about 1828, it was taken away from free blacks and Indians. By 1865, only a few New England states guaranteed black suffrage—and even in New England, the idea was not universally accepted. (In fact, in November 1865, Connecticut had held a referendum on whether to allow the vote to the state's few black men—and soundly rejected it.)

A constitutional amendment requiring suffrage would face an uphill struggle in the North, so radicals turned to another idea. Only the Southern states had a black population of any size in 1865. Why not leave the question of voting up to each state, as it always had been—but penalize states that disfranchised their black populations? Disfranchised blacks would not be counted in assigning seats in the House. That would confront the South with a difficult choice: they could cling to their old undemocratic political systems, and thereby forfeit the extra votes that had made the Slave Power so formidable; or they could open the polls to blacks, in which case they would no longer be able to maintain a one-party system.

But there was yet another problem. If representation was not to be based on sheer population, what could it then be based on? The most logical possibility seemed to be legal voters. Stevens had proposed this in Congress; even Andrew Johnson had suggested this as a potential basis. But, on January 8, the same day the committee's delegates went to the White House, Representative James G. Blaine had made a speech pointing out that this plan would have unforeseen consequences. In some Northern states, as few as one-fifth of the population were actual voters; in others, particularly those of the West and Midwest, the percentage rose as high as 58 percent. A rule basing congressional numbers on voting population would thus produce wildly inequitable results in the North, with the New England states losing votes to the western states.

The reasons for this discrepancy were twofold. First, more New Englanders were female than were male. The war had produced some of this disparity—thousands of men from New England had died in battle. But that problem simply made worse one that had been growing for half a century. To young men in cold and rocky New England towns, the West offered a grand vista of opportunity—cheap land, silver and gold mines, the American dream of a new life. For decades men had left the Northeast for the Midwest and West, leaving behind sisters and sweethearts. In antebellum America women were not voters, and so, if legal voting population became the basis, the Eastern population of women would not provide a basis for representation.

Beyond this was the issue of immigration. Europeans continued to stream into the United States—more than 200,000 in 1865 alone. Most of them settled in the East. They would not count if legal voting was the basis of representation—at least in the East. But some Western states, eager to boost their populations in order to qualify for statehood, were offering new foreign immigrants the immediate right to vote.

The committee agreed upon an ungainly solution. They proposed to reduce the basis of representation only for those states that restricted the ballot by race. States would continue to have authority to set educational or wealth requirements. The issue of sex would be irrelevant, and so would immigration. By January 20, the committee agreed on a proposed constitutional amendment to send to the House. It read:

Representatives and direct taxes shall be apportioned among the several States which may be included within this Union, according to their respective numbers, counting the whole number of persons in each State, excluding Indians not taxed; provided that whenever the elective franchise shall be denied or abridged in any State on account of race or color, all persons of such race or color shall be excluded from the basis of representation.

It looks something like the language eventually adopted in the final amendment; but it was subtly different, and stronger. The difference can be appreciated by understanding that many politicians, Northern and Southern, were suggesting some kind of compromise on black suffrage. Perhaps, for example, voting rolls could be open to all whites—and to all black men who could pass a literacy test, or who held a certain amount of property. Even though some black men would be allowed to vote, there would still be different standards for black and white voters. Under the committee's version, any state with such a rule would still lose representation for all black people—even for those allowed to vote. If passed and enforced, it would nudge the Southern states powerfully toward impartial rules for voting.

The representation amendment was the joint committee's first product. It did not pass. But it bears a strong resemblance to what became Section 2 of the eventual Fourteenth Amendment, and so the debate over this first attempt at a constitutional fix is relevant to understanding the real amendment that eventually resulted. But beyond that, the debate shows us that the members of Congress in 1866 were men who literally felt the ground shifting under their feet.

The war had changed the Constitution. State rights, or "state sovereignty," as Southern thinkers had called it, was now in disrepute. (Even the old Southern Jacksonian, Andrew Johnson, dismissed "state sovereignty" as a Rebel myth. "'The sovereignty of the States,'" he wrote in his first state of the Union address, "is the language of the Confederacy, and not the language of the Constitution.") The leaders of secession had loudly brayed that citizens owed allegiance to their state governments, not to the Union. States had a "right" to secede, they had argued; now many of those same leaders were back in Washington, arguing that their states had a "right" to return to Congress, stronger than before; and that they had a "right" to impose any limits on their own people that they chose, without federal interference. The argument rang hollow to Northerners who had sacrificed to keep the Union together—and, eventually, to bring freedom to Southern slaves. Northerners now paid income taxes to the federal government, spent "federal cash," and served in the Union army. The minimal confederation of prewar state's rights theory did not fit the living reality they saw around them.

And America had changed. Four million new freed people of African descent fit uneasily into the prewar scheme. The Supreme Court in 1857 had proclaimed that African Americans, free or slave, constituted no part of the national community and could never be made American citizens, even by act of Congress. Yet now, by constitutional amendment, these Americans were free, and must be accounted for. Beyond that, the war had made everyone, North and South, aware that the United States was (before the war, most writers would have said, "the United States *were*," but by 1865 the Republic had begun to be written of as a single thing, a nation) what we today would call a multicultural society. Whatever changes Congress proposed in the Constitution would not only affect Southern blacks. They might also have profound implications for the political status of the European immigrants, many not yet citizens, who thronged the farms and cities of the North, and for the nearly fifty thousand Chinese at work on railroads and in mining camps across the American West. Beyond that, the war had profoundly stirred America's women, inspiring them with a vision of human equality and propelling them into economic and social roles that had been closed to them before the men marched off to fight.

Finally, ideas about freedom and equality had changed. The "lords of the lash" had been refuted by the egalitarian armies of the North, made up of laborers—the men Southerners had scorned as "mud-sills of society"—and former slaves. They had humbled aristocrats like

Jefferson Davis and Robert E. Lee. The equality genie was out of the
bottle.

On January 20, Thaddeus Stevens rose in the House to report the
first results of the joint committee process. He told the House that he
wanted the proposed amendment approved "before the sun goes
down." Voices from the chamber echoed, "We are ready!" At that
point, Stevens had reason to believe that this first adjustment to the
Constitution would be a relatively smooth one. The committee's
work was backed by members of all the Republican factions; the
measure seemed moderate, and while it would disappoint the more
advanced Radicals who favored votes for freed slaves, it seemed
likely to gather enough support to make that fact irrelevant. Beyond
that, Stevens was a master of party discipline and expected his members to stand with him against the feeble Democrats.

The opposition in the House, in fact, must have warmed Stevens's
heart. Most of the rhetoric deployed against the proposal was pure pro-
Southern, Copperhead rhetoric, all but unchanged since the days when
Southerners had ruled Congress with the help of their "dough-faced"
allies. Andrew Rogers of New Jersey, as a member of the minority on
the joint committee, began the assault on the amendment, and every
word he uttered strengthened the Republicans' resolve.

Under the tyrant Lincoln, Rogers said, "the war power, imbedded
in usurpation, trampled [the Constitution] under foot." Now the
usurpers wanted to deform the Constitution to place black people
over America's whites. "[B]ecause there are in certain States negroes,
men of an inferior race, men who by the laws of God are stamped with
an inferiority so indelible that nothing can wipe it out, it is proposed
that such States shall only enjoy their full right to representation here
on the condition that they will allow these negroes the unqualified
right of suffrage on a perfect equality with the white citizen." Rogers
seemed to regard Emancipation as the greatest of Lincoln's crimes. It
had robbed the slave owners of their property and now sought "to
inflict a disgrace upon the Anglo-Saxon race of the South by coercing
them to bestow upon these slaves political rights after they have

been taken away from their masters without compensation. I think it time we should begin to legislate for white people."

Roscoe Conkling, acting as Stevens's lieutenant, answered Rogers. To begin with, he said, the Framers had never foreseen or planned for the current situation. They had believed that slavery was dying and that slaves would gradually be set free. "Did the framers of the Constitution ever dream of this? Never, very clearly. . . . They never peered into the bloody epoch when four million fetters would be at once melted off in the fires of war. . . . No one foresaw such an event, and so no provision was made for it."

Left untouched, the Framers' Constitution would give the former slave states twenty-eight additional votes in Congress: "Twenty-eight votes to be cast here and in the Electoral College for those held not fit to sit as jurors, not fit to testify in court, not fit to be plaintiff in a suit, not fit to approach the ballot box. . . . This is privilege, class, aristocracy, in its most hateful form. It is not democracy or republicanism or free government at all."

Free government would be assured, instead, by providing representation only for those who actually could vote, Conkling argued. And that principle would force states to live by the principles most Americans thought essential: "'Fair play,' 'A fair day's wages for a fair day's work,' 'Live and let live'—these mottoes, if blazoned over the institutions of a State, will insure it against being cursed for any length of time with inhabitants so worthless that they are fit only for beasts of burden."

It was a powerful defense, delivered with Conkling's characteristic self-assurance. But there was a flaw in the argument. As proposed, the amendment did not blazon "fair play" into the Constitution. It punished only one form of disfranchisement, that of race. Many other potential voters could be disfranchised, mostly in the North. On January 23, the good-humored James Brooks of New York—whose candidacy for Speaker had reduced the members, including himself, to amiable laughter at the opening of Congress—rose to spring this trap. What about "coolies," he asked Stevens—the Chinese workers in the West? Stevens admitted that states would lose representation for Chinese inhabitants if they limited the vote to whites. What about Indians? Brooks asked. That was different, Stevens answered. Tribal Indians were not taxed and had never figured in the basis of representation.

Ah, then, said Brooks, what about white women?

Here was an issue that would bedevil and almost confound the framers of the Fourteenth Amendment. In no state of the Union were women allowed to vote. Yet they were counted in the census and formed the basis of representation. Why didn't the argument apply to them?

James Brooks turned grandly to the galleries—thronged with women who had been forewarned that this issue would come up—and proclaimed, "I raise my voice here in behalf of fifteen million of our countrywomen, the fairest, brightest portion of creation, and I ask why they are not permitted to be represented under this resolution. . . . Why, in organizing a system of liberality and justice, not recognize in the case of free women as well as free negroes the right of representation?"

At this point, Brooks produced a letter from Elizabeth Cady Stanton and a petition written by Susan B. Anthony. The two pioneer feminists had been stalwarts of the antislavery movement. Now the feminists asked Congress for "an amendment of the Constitution that shall prohibit the several States from disfranchising any of their citizens on the ground of sex."

Stevens lumbered to his feet to ask whether Brooks himself was in favor of extending the vote to women. The wily New Yorker evaded the question. He said only, "I am in favor of my own color in preference to any other color, and I prefer the white women of my country to the negro." This brief speech set off a storm of applause from women in the gallery.

The Democrats had planted the feminist flag, but now they returned to their more accustomed arguments. Blacks were inferior, not fit to vote or even to remain in the United States, and the Republicans were seeking to give them power over more-deserving whites. John Winthrop Chanler of New York told the House on

January 23 that the real agenda of the amendment was to shut white immigrants out of the South and turn it over to blacks. "This country is the refuge of and is maintained for the white race," he said.

The Democrats were addressing the Northern public, and the potential white voters of the South, with an eye to harvesting antiblack votes in the next election. Many Republicans were worried about the long-term politics of being identified with black interests; but the white-supremacy rhetoric had little real effect on the vote now before the House. If the party stuck together, they could easily pass the committee's recommendation.

On January 29, however, the amendment faced a more serious challenge from within the Republican caucus. The speaker who rose in opposition was Henry J. Raymond. Raymond, a newcomer to the House, was a formidable political power. He was chair of the Republican National Committee and had served as one of the leaders of Lincoln's reelection campaign. Beyond that, Raymond was editor and owner of the *New York Times,* one of the most powerful Republican papers in the country. With his enthusiasm, his eloquence, and his determination, Raymond cast a giant shadow in the world of politics and journalism, but physically he remained always the boy wonder he had been when he burst into politics at the age of twenty as a firebrand orator backing the Whig ticket of William Henry Harrison and John Tyler. (After one of his speeches in that campaign, a Democratic foe wondered aloud "what that little Raymond, with a face no bigger than a snuff-box, meant by coming round there to make political speeches.") Raymond was very much of the conservative wing of the party, and early in the session he had decided that the party's only hope lay in embracing Andrew Johnson as its leader. Now he rose to defend the president's restoration policy and to declare open war on Thaddeus Stevens and the joint committee: "a committee which sits with closed doors, which deliberates in secret, which shuts itself out from the knowledge and observations of Congress, and which does not even deign to give us the information it was appointed to collect, and on which we are to base our action—but which sends its rescripts into this House and demands their ratification, without reasons and without facts, before the going down of the sun!"

Raymond instead proposed his own conservative program. Congress should simply accept Johnson's restored governments and admit their representatives—excluding, on a case-by-case basis, leaders of the Rebellion; it should legislate to give the freed slaves their basic civil rights "in courts of law and elsewhere"; and it should only then consider political rights for blacks, "freely and without coercion."

On January 30, the House voted to send the proposed amendment back to the joint committee. The next day, the joint committee voted to amend the measure slightly by removing the words "and direct taxes." When the bill returned to the House that afternoon, Stevens's party whips had the votes to force its adoption by 120 to 46.

Now the action passed to the Senate, where the opposition was to be of an altogether different order. For one thing, Reverdy Johnson was not a Copperhead like Rogers or a clown like Brooks. His objections would carry more weight. For another, the Republicans in the Senate were not a united group like those in the House. There was no Thaddeus Stevens to crack the party whip above their heads. Unity in the caucus could not be achieved by force, but only by persuasion.

But one member was not open to persuasion. Charles Sumner had resolved to kill the amendment. When debate opened on February 5, everyone in the chamber knew that the days ahead would see a battle of giants. Sumner, the living symbol of opposition to the Slave Power, would range himself against his former friend Fessenden, the party's leading constitutional lawyer. And Sumner was no more generous to his fellow Republicans than he had been to Andrew Butler and Preston Brooks.

Sumner's two-day opening speech is a masterpiece of florid nineteenth-century rhetoric, drawing on the Bible, the philosophy of Immanuel Kant, and the thought of constitutional Framers like Madison and Hamilton to argue that the amendment, by recognizing the power of states to disfranchise racial minorities, violated the sacred

American rule against "taxation without representation." Beyond that, it would betray the black Americans who had rallied to the Union cause during its darkest days.

Sumner's speech represents, in its purest form, the heritage of one thread of antebellum antislavery thought. During the 1830s, abolitionist thinkers had disagreed over the meaning of the Constitution of 1787. One wing, led by William Lloyd Garrison and Wendell Phillips, had taken the position that the Constitution was a "pro-slavery compact" designed to protect the interests of the Slave Power above any concept of popular self-rule or human rights. Garrison had burned a copy of the Constitution at a public meeting in 1854 and had branded it "a covenant with Death and an agreement with Hell."

But another wing of the movement had questioned the accuracy— and the tactical wisdom—of this history. Abolitionists like Frederick Douglass preferred to view the Constitution as actually antislavery. The Framers, they argued, had provided clues that slavery was unconstitutional. The most important clue was the guaranty clause, with its promise that each state's government would be "republican" in form. Republicanism required equality of all men, as promised in the Declaration of Independence. From the day the new government began in 1787, Sumner now declared, the federal government had possessed full power under this clause to restrict or even outlaw slavery. And if the clause was not enough, he said, the Thirteenth Amendment gave Congress authority to hobble the Slave Power. All that was needed was a federal statute proclaiming the equality of all Americans.

Sumner offered such a statute as a substitute for the representation amendment. His proposed statute read, "There shall be no Oligarchy, Aristocracy, Caste, or Monopoly invested with peculiar privileges and powers, and there shall be no denial of rights, civil or political, on account of color or race anywhere within the limits of the United States or the jurisdiction thereof; but all persons therein shall be equal before the law, whether in the court-room or at the ballot-box. And this statute, made in pursuance of the Constitution, shall be the supreme law of the land, anything in the Constitution or laws of any State to the contrary notwithstanding."

Since the founding, Sumner said, "slavery thus far has been the very pivot, round which the Republic has revolved, while all its policy at home and abroad has radiated from this terrible center. Hereafter the Equal Rights of All will take the place of Slavery, and the Republic will revolve on this glorious pivot, whose infinite, far-reaching radiations will be the happiness of the Human Family."

It was time, Sumner said, to break with the very idea of "state's rights," which had brought on the Civil War. "The Rebellion began in two assumptions, both proceeding from South Carolina: first, the sovereignty of the States, with the pretended right of secession; and, secondly, the superiority of the white race, with the pretended right of Caste, Oligarchy, and Monopoly, on account of color."

Sumner's rhetoric rings sweetly in modern ears. Certainly it sounds more principled than the committee's proposal, which accepted that the Southern state governments, left to themselves, would bar freed slaves from the polls.

So seductive is his rhetoric—and so inspiring the image of Charles Sumner, the saving victim of Brooks's cane, as the lone defender of racial equality—that a reader may not realize that the major force behind his stand was not so much principle as Massachusetts politics. In fact, the committee's proposal was almost identical to a bill Sumner himself had introduced on the opening day of the Thirty-ninth Congress, Senate Resolution Number One. That measure would have amended the Constitution to provide that representation would be based on "the number of male citizens of the age of twenty-one years having in each State the qualifications requisite for electors [voters]."

That amendment did not mention the state government's power to exclude voters on the basis of race, but it assumed it as surely as the committee's proposal did. And if Sumner had thought a constitutional amendment necessary in December, it raised questions about his insistence that one was not needed in February.

In fact, Sumner's original proposal had brought him serious political trouble back in Boston. Apportioning representation by "male citizens," most people in Massachusetts believed, would cost Massachusetts seats in Congress. John Andrew was the outgoing governor of the state; he had his eye on Sumner's seat in the Senate at the election of 1866. In his farewell address as governor in January 1866, Andrew had mounted a frontal assault on Sumner's amendment. Andrew criticized Sumner in much the same language that Sumner now deployed against the committee, accusing him of "political cupidity." Sumner had been outflanked at home on the left; as biographer David Herbert Donald explains, he now felt compelled to abandon his own earlier proposal and assault the joint committee.

When he rose on February 7 to answer Sumner's assault, Fessenden did not adopt Sumner's language of principle and purity. He rejected Sumner's argument that the vote was already guaranteed to all men by the Guaranty Clause and the Thirteenth Amendment. Neither history nor political theory, he said, regarded the vote as an inescapable part of basic civil rights. "In a republican government it may be that it may receive the name of a right, although most people call it a privilege; but a voter is an officer, not in the same degree, perhaps, but as much so in substance as the man who enters the jury box, as any one who holds an office," he said.

He also pointed out to Sumner that his taxation-without-representation argument "would just as well apply to women as to men; but I noticed that the honorable Senator dodged that part of the proposition very carefully. . . . I should like to have him tell me why every female that is taxed ought not to vote," a challenge Sumner, the champion of equality and principle, did not accept.

For himself, Fessenden said, he would favor an amendment outlawing all distinctions of race or color. But he was not an individual, he said. He was a senator, and the chair of a Senate committee that wanted to do something now. The main objection to an equalizing amendment of that sort is that it probably couldn't be adopted. "The argument that addressed itself to the Committee was, what can we accomplish? What can pass?" A constitutional amendment would require two-thirds of the legislatures to approve; states would be unlikely to vote to void their own voting systems. The committee proposal, he argued, was the best thing that could pass.

Fessenden echoed the cool, rational rhetoric of the eighteenth-century Framers when he argued that his amendment would quickly induce all the states to extend the ballot as far as they safely could. "Men love political power; they do not part with it easily; they love to increase it," he said. "Having a little, they are ready to grasp more. If this is the case, have we not done something if this amendment is passed, to say to men, 'Your political power shall be in exact proportion to your action in the right direction?'"

By contrast, Fessenden compared Sumner's seemingly more radical substitute to "a very small dipper with a very long handle. . . . Does this clause provide the machinery by which it is to be carried into execution? Does it provide courts to protect rights? Does it provide a military force? Does it provide anything? . . . It is a mere legislative declaration, and a legislative declaration of a fact that exists, as the Senator says, and as I am willing to concede for the sake of argument, in the Constitution itself."

Sumner rose to his full magnificent height and said grandly, "That is all I intended."

Fessenden pounced: if Sumner merely meant to pass "a word upon the statute-book, what good has he done to him who was once a slave in securing him his rights? Sir, I am afraid that there are too many of these things—protections of human rights consisting of words alone!"

The next day, February 8, Reverdy Johnson rose to give the Democratic critique of the committee's amendment. His speech demonstrates why Sumner's performance had driven Fessenden to the end of his patience. Johnson spent most of his speech attacking Sumner's equal-rights statute, rather than the proposed amendment. It's hard not to conclude that he was deliberately confusing the two. This gave him, and his party, the political benefit of attacking the Republicans on two contradictory fronts; the committee proposal did not go far enough, he suggested, and Sumner's proposal went too far. Former slaves had no right to vote if the majority deemed them unfit to do so. And if only voters were free, he said, "The whole female sex not only are not, but never have been, free women. . . . Is any inherent and natural right violated by such an exclusion? Certainly not."

There was no need for constitutional nostrums, Johnson insisted. All that was needed was an immediate restoration of the Southern states, which might, though he did not mention it, restore Johnson's Democratic Party to its traditional place of power. He pointed to the conciliatory conduct of the Union generals as an example of how to treat the Southern states. "How do Grant and Sherman and Meade and Sheridan and Thomas meet their former comrades, lately their enemies, now that the war is over?"

Fessenden, dry as an old Maine farmer, rose and said, "They do not put them in command of the Army."

On February 15, Sumner produced a petition signed by Frederick Douglass opposing the committee's amendment. Douglass read the proposal the way Sumner professed to: as an open invitation to the Southern governments to exclude Southern blacks from the vote. Douglass had fought against slavery and white supremacy since his escape from bondage in 1838. During the war, he had been a major weapon in the Union arsenal, traveling the North to recruit black soldiers into the new regiments of "colored volunteers." More than that, his own family had flocked to the colors: one son, Lewis, had been sergeant major of the 54th Massachusetts, and a second, Charles, had served in that storied unit as a private. Now Douglass and a group of black Northern leaders had sent an indignant protest against anything less than full equality for the emancipated slaves. Their petition said that they "most respectfully but earnestly pray this honorable body to favor no amendment to the Constitution of the United States which will grant or allow any one or all of the States of this Union to disfranchise any class of citizens on the ground of race or color for any consideration whatever."

By now, the committee's proposal was caught in a fatal whipsaw. The more Radical senators, following Sumner's lead, scorned it because it did not guarantee immediate equality. "The negro is a man!" Daniel Clark of New Hampshire had said on February 14. "And however degraded, inferior, abject, or humble, it is our duty to elevate and improve him, and give him the means of elevation or improvement." Democrats, preparing for the next election, meanwhile denounced it as a measure to give power to an inferior race. "I am not in favor of giving the colored man a vote, because I think we should remain a political community of white people," Thomas Hendricks of Indiana said. Beyond that, Northern Democrats began to echo the Southerners quoted by Schurz, Dennett, and the other travelers to the South. The Congress should not bother to protect the freed slaves, they argued, because black people were fated to die off quickly, just as the Indians had done. "We know that when there comes that strife of races between the white men of the United States, the mixture of the best blood of Europe on this continent, and the black man, what will be the fate of the black man," Hendricks added.

Sumner stood to deliver his closing blast on March 6. With magnificent scorn, he compared the committee's work to the droppings of the Harpies in Greek mythology, to a mouse stillborn from a mountain, and to the legendary black diamond of the Middle East. "Adopt it," he said, "and you will cover the country with dishonor. Adopt it, and you will fix a stigma upon the very name of Republic. As to the imagination, there are mountains of light, so are there mountains of darkness; and this is one of them. It is the very Koh-i-Noor of blackness."

The ever-mournful Fessenden, acting out of duty rather than hope, rose on March 9 to make one final defense of the committee's measure. Dapper as always, weary of debate and of life itself, Pitt Fessenden seemed to shake his head at the folly and ingratitude of his colleagues. "I have no expectation that this proposed amendment of the Constitution will be adopted," he said. "I know, to use a common expression, that noses have been counted." But he felt duty-bound to offer a defense of himself and of the committee's measure. It was not a party measure, he said; not a measure to benefit New England; not, as Sumner had claimed, a measure to license the slave states to discriminate and reward them with power over the freed slaves. It was a halfway measure, true—but Fessenden suggested that halfway measures were the true route to Constitutional reform.

The committee's proposal would convince the leaders of the South to move toward black voting as soon as possible. Leading the people by their own self-interest, he suggested, was better than forcing suffrage on them by decree. An immediate suffrage amendment "will create ill-feeling, generate discord, and produce, perhaps, undying animosities," he said, adding with characteristic irony that "this, however, is my own private opinion, and perhaps it is of little value."

He concluded by noting that Sumner was making common cause with the Copperheads, crypto-Confederates, and racists on the Democratic side. "Just imagine," he said, "all the gentlemen opposed to this resolution met in caucus together and looking round at each other, would there not be a smile on all their faces to see what company they had fallen into?"

Then the vote was taken, nearly six weeks after the committee had recommended the amendment. The vote was 25 to 22. Sumner had carried seven Republicans into opposition with him, more than enough to deprive the amendment of the two-thirds vote needed to pass. The committee's first recommendation was dead.

This split in the Republican ranks seemed to bode ill for the committee, but the congressional Republicans would soon come together again in self-defense. For while the Senate had been high-mindedly debating the nature of representation, Andrew Johnson had declared war on the majority in Congress.

THIS GOOD RIGHT HAND

Andrew Johnson had begun the New Year with a grand reception at the White House. It was a rather soggy affair, held on a gray, drizzly day. "The day was murky and roads intolerable," Gideon Welles, the secretary of the navy, remarked in his diary. "The persons who got up the programme were evidently wholly unfit for the business.... Consequently there was neither order nor system." Top officials, jammed cheek by jowl with ordinary citizens, waited in long lines to shake the president's hand. At one point the ushers threw open the door to the Blue Room, allowing guests to enter and find the president and his official party neatly facing away from them. Still, Welles loyally insisted, "The affair passed off very well." With the help of his daughter, Martha Patterson, Johnson had begun to rescue the White House from its prewar shabbiness. Mrs. Patterson presided as hostess in an austere silk dress trimmed with black lace. Eliza Johnson remained out of sight.

January 1866 marks the high point of Johnson's fortunes. As of that New Year's party, the brave tailor could still see himself as a historic figure, destined to reunite a shattered nation and preside over a realignment of its parties. He had a few sworn enemies in Congress, to be sure—Thaddeus Stevens was implacable. But Stevens and his allies were the exception. From the very beginning of the Thirty-ninth Congress, much of the Republican leadership tiptoed around Andrew Johnson like skittish soldiers skirting a field of mines. They hoped to influence him as they had influenced Lincoln so often in the past; to forge a compromise policy that would preserve the facade of Republican unity, permitting the "perpetual ascendancy" of the party of Union in a new, purified republic. If Johnson had possessed some shred of Lincoln's skill and flexibility, the history of Reconstruction might have been very different. "If there was a time when Johnson could have come to an agreement with the moderates of the Republican party, it was the period following the return of Congress in January 1866," writes Hans Trefousse, his biographer.

But Johnson was no Lincoln. He saw those who questioned him as more than just wrong; they were enemies, traitors as repellent as the Rebels he had defied in 1862. He saw no difference between the pacific Fessenden and the feisty Stevens. And in Welles, he had as alter ego another former Democrat to whom the president's critics—the leaders of the party that had put Johnson in the White House—were also at best deluded and at worst traitors. Johnson, in his drunken vice-presidential inaugural speech, had been publicly unable to remember Welles's name; but since his accession to office, Welles had become Johnson's closest ally in the Cabinet. A grizzled graybeard whom Lincoln had called "Father Neptune," Welles was, at sixty-three, an elder statesman among Johnson's advisers. He was a former Democrat who in 1854 had joined the Republican Party. Welles, like Johnson, remained in his heart a state's-rights Democrat. Indeed, before the war, his great objection to the Slave Power was that its control of the federal government threatened the rights of Northern states.

As described in Welles's detailed diary, the Johnson White House seems to have begun 1866 with what today would be called a full-blown "bunker mentality." "The President is satisfied that his policy is correct, and is, I think, very firm in his convictions and intentions to maintain it," Welles wrote in his diary on January 30. The next day,

Senator Henry Wilson of Massachusetts took Welles aside at a Washington reception and almost begged him for help avoiding a split. Welles calmly replied that only complete surrender by the congressional Republicans would bring peace. Johnson "could not abandon his conviction to gratify mere factious schemers." Over and over, Welles and Johnson mulled over their contempt for the Radicals and dismissed moderates who sought peace. On January 2, Johnson exploded in rage at "this little fellow Colfax," who had had the effrontery to make a speech after his election as Speaker, claiming attention that Johnson felt should be his alone. "I do not hear that the colored people called or were invited to visit Sumner or Wilson," Johnson said waspishly, "but they came here [to the White House on New Year's Day] and were civilly treated." In February Johnson "alluded with some feeling to the extraordinary intrigue which he understood was going on in Congress, having nothing short of a subversion or change in the structure of the government in view. The unmistakable design of Thad Stevens and his associates was to take the government into their own hands, the President said, and to get rid of him by declaring Tennessee out of the Union. A sort of French Directory was to be established by these spirits in Congress, the Constitution was to be remodeled by them, etc." Both Welles and Johnson seemed to regard conciliation as either a sign of weakness or a trap. "[T]he President cannot yield and sacrifice his honest convictions by way of compromise," Welles wrote on February 16, implicitly dismissing the idea that those in Congress might also hold honest convictions.

"By late January, if not before, Johnson himself had concluded that a showdown with the radicals was necessary to the success of his policy and ambitions," writes one historian of his presidency. "Johnson decided to challenge the Radicals on what he deemed—correctly—to be their most vulnerable ground: Negro suffrage."

Black voting was not popular with the white public, North or South. In 1860, New York voters had refused to revoke their state's property qualification for black voters; in the fall of 1865, voters in the solid Republican states of Connecticut, Minnesota, and Wisconsin had rejected measures to open the polls to black men.

Looking back at these referenda from the standpoint of the twenty-first century, it is easy to assume that white opposition to black voting demonstrated pure and simple racial hypocrisy by ordinary Northerners. Today, the term *civil rights* suggests legal guarantees against discrimination, whether in employment, public accommodations, or voting rights. But to nineteenth-century Americans, *civil rights* meant something very different from "political rights" like voting. Every American—at least in the North—had the basic civil rights to marry, buy and sell property, enter into contracts, and otherwise participate in society. Only a minority—men only, and often men who had some minimum amount of property—exercised the political rights of voting and jury service. These rights were intended for those who were "fit" to exercise them, by virtue of education and wealth.

Many Northerners who opposed black voting also fervently believed that freed slaves were fully entitled to civil rights. In fact, for more than a decade before Fort Sumter, the Northern states had been systematically eradicating state laws that discriminated against blacks in *civil* rights. As historian Paul Finkelman has shown, the legal position of blacks in the free North was complex. The idea of equal *civil* rights, he has written, moved back and forth like a pendulum.

> The period between 1780 and 1817 saw advances in the protection of blacks. With the advent of the Colonization Society in 1817, the position of blacks in the North began to decline. By the early 1830's, black rights were under severe attack in the North. This was the nadir for antebellum northern blacks, and by the end of the decade the pendulum began to swing back towards protecting free blacks. With some exceptions, the legal rights of blacks continued to expand in the North until the Civil War.

But a majority seemed to feel that blacks were not ready to exercise political power, North or South. So if the Republican Party made voting the centerpiece of its program of Reconstruction, Johnson would have an opportunity to portray himself as a moderate, and the congressional Republicans as extremists seeking radical change in the American form of government.

There was only one problem: Congress wouldn't cooperate. At the opening of Congress, radicals brought forward a proposal to open the vote in the District of Columbia to blacks. The district's white residents made it abundantly clear that they didn't want blacks voting: in December, the Washington and Georgetown city councils tried to preempt black suffrage by holding a referendum. The black-voting proposal failed in Washington 6,591 to 35, and in Georgetown by 465 to 0. Nonetheless, the House on January 18 passed a bill striking the word *white* from the D.C. voting bill, and the Senate opened debate on a similar measure. But Senate leaders recommitted the measure to committee, where it languished. And instead of the black vote, civil rights for blacks—a considerably more popular proposition—emerged as the point of dispute between Johnson and Congress.

To a leader who has decided on open warfare, moderates and compromisers are at best distractions, and at worst outright enemies. And so it proved in January and February 1866; the Republican moderates, striving desperately to stay in Johnson's good graces, spoiled his opening shot. None was more assiduous in striving for compromise than Senator Lyman Trumbull of Illinois, who was at the White House almost every other day to assure himself that he was acting with the president. Johnson and Welles hid their contempt for Trumbull and prepared for the battle ahead.

In his diary, Welles had dismissed Trumbull as "freaky and opinionated." But in fact, the Illinois senator was far closer to the center of Republican thought than either Welles or Johnson. And however much Johnson might insist that the Constitution had not changed since the days of Jackson, Trumbull knew it had. He, as much as anyone living, had changed it.

In 1866, Trumbull was fifty-two years old. He was tall for his time—just over five feet ten inches—slender but sturdily built. He had a slight stoop, which may have stemmed from a spinal injury he suffered as a young man, or from his severe myopia, for which he wore gold-rimmed glasses. The pince-nez and his high collars gave him the look of a pedagogue; and in fact he had begun his career as a schoolmaster at Greeneville Academy in Greeneville, Georgia. Trumbull was Connecticut-born, but like many young men in the early part of the century he saw opportunity to the west and south. He studied law in Georgia and was admitted to the bar there, but soon moved to Belleville, Illinois. His views on slavery were not recorded during his Georgia days, though later in life he showed a flinty awareness of the determination and ruthlessness of the slave interest; but if he had thought he was avoiding the issue by moving to Belleville, he was wrong. Belleville was just across the state line from the slave metropolis of St. Louis, and even in the 1830s many Southern-born residents of the area continued to hold black "indentured servants" in a relationship they rather impudently called "voluntary servitude." Many of the area residents were slaveholders or relatives of slaveholders. One such was the vivacious Mary Todd, who wrote to a friend in 1841 that she was planning to "lay my claim" to Trumbull, "as he is talented and agreeable & sometimes *countenances me.*"

As it turned out, Mary Todd married another rising lawyer, Abraham Lincoln. Her close friend, Julia Jayne, was a bridesmaid at that wedding. Soon after, Trumbull married Julia, and Mary Todd Lincoln was her bridal attendant.

The young lawyer quickly became involved in advising local blacks who sought the freedom guaranteed to them by the Illinois state constitution—and, before that, by the Northwest Ordinance of 1787. Trumbull charged no fee for this work, and in 1845 he persuaded the Illinois Supreme Court that the ordinance had freed all slaves held in the territory, thus freeing their descendants as well.

Trumbull was well equipped for the intellectual cut-and-thrust of appellate law. He lacked the emotional warmth that makes for great advocacy before a jury. His mind was logical and remorseless. Appellate judges liked his style and respected the depth of his knowledge of the law and the Constitution. (Political opponents quickly came to respect and even fear this as well; once, in 1856, Trumbull asserted in Senate debate that Congress possessed the same power over a territory as a state legislature had over a state. Clearly, that would mean that Congress *could* abolish slavery in the territories. At once the formidable Lewis Cass, seventy-four years old, a former Democratic presidential candidate and a future secretary of state, rose to give Trumbull the lie direct. Where had the Court ever so held? Cass demanded. With no show of discomfiture, Trumbull directed a Senate attendant to bring him a specific volume of the Supreme Court reporter; when he got it, he turned directly to the page and read aloud Chief Justice Marshall's words. The old man was humiliated; the spectators howled.)

In 1855 Mary Todd Lincoln and Julia Jayne Trumbull had sat companionably together in the gallery when the Illinois legislature met to choose a new senator. Lincoln was the favorite—he had forty-five votes on the first ballot. Trumbull, an antislavery Democrat, was a dark horse candidate, with only five votes. But Lincoln's support did not grow, and by the ninth ballot he received only fifteen votes to Trumbull's thirty-five. At that point, Lincoln threw his support to Trumbull, who won on the next ballot by one vote. Mary Todd Lincoln never forgave Julia Jayne Trumbull.

Lincoln, though, was not one to hold a grudge, and he found Trumbull a useful instrument for his policies. As the war went on, Trumbull was vociferous in his insistence that the law of war permitted the Union to confiscate the slaves of rebel masters. He wrote and piloted through the Congress two confiscation bills designed to allow emancipation, but he was disappointed that Lincoln did not use them more successfully. He battled Lincoln, too, on the administration's policy of arresting dissidents without charge or legal authorization. Trumbull favored jail for traitors and Copperheads, but he insisted that, under the Constitution, Congress must authorize any emergency detention. The president alone did not have the power to suspend habeas corpus. The war power existed under the Constitution, Trumbull argued; it did not supersede it. "I am for suppressing this monstrous rebellion according to law, and in no other way," he said in 1861. Trumbull was equally insistent on constitutional procedures when it came to freeing the slaves. Charles Sumner and other Radicals argued that Congress could enact emancipation by statute.

Trumbull rebuked them: "[I]t is not because a measure would be convenient that Congress has authority to adopt it." A constitutional amendment was needed.

Many years after the war, Trumbull addressed the students of Union Law College in Chicago about the Thirteenth Amendment, which outlawed slavery. He stood before the assembly, solemnly raised his right hand, and said, "Gentlemen, this good right hand wrote this amendment to the constitution." It was an exaggeration, but only a slight one. Trumbull was chair of the Senate Judiciary Committee; in February 1864, the committee had proposed a constitutional amendment to make the Emancipation Proclamation irrevocable. "Neither slavery nor involuntary servitude, except as a punishment for crime whereof the party shall have been duly convicted, shall exist within the United States, or any place subject to their jurisdiction," said the draft. This was moderate language—Sumner, only a few days before, had proposed his own amendment, based on the Declaration of the Rights of Man and Citizen promulgated by the French Revolutionaries in 1789. Sumner's amendment would have proclaimed all Americans "equal before the law." Trumbull's committee draft was based instead on the language of the Northwest Ordinance of 1787. That choice was designed to make the amendment appear less radical, linking it to the Founding Fathers rather than to the French regicides.

In fact, Trumbull was not and never had been a Radical Republican. He opposed voting rights for blacks and sometimes expressed a wish that all the free blacks could be resettled somewhere in the West, like the Mormons, "where they would not be dominated and where they could develop their powers." But his biographer Mark Krug calls him a conservative radical—like Gouverneur Morris at Philadelphia. To begin with, the amendment proclaimed a new right—the right not to be enslaved—and it was the first right in American constitutional history to be protected not only against the government but *against fellow citizens*. And if that was not radical enough, Trumbull's draft included a second section, the "enabling clause," which provided that "Congress shall have power to enforce this article by appropriate legislation." This promised a change in the place of states in the federal system. But at the time of the amendment's adoption, neither Trumbull nor any other member of the committee had been eager to spell out exactly what the two sections together meant. Artful ambiguity is always a part of constitution-making, and the sponsors of the amendment left the promise of the new text deliberately vague.

By January 1866, however, the amendment was part of the Constitution. Now Trumbull was prepared to spell out his idea of the new shape of the nation and the Constitution. Using the amendment as a basis of power, Trumbull introduced two bills to serve as a moderate program of Reconstruction—the renewal of the Freedmen's Bureau and the Civil Rights Act of 1866. These two bills were designed to bring a free, multiracial society to the South. But they were also designed to appease Northern opinion—which was possible—and to avoid a break with Johnson—which was not.

The Freedmen's Bureau bill was first. The bill Trumbull produced was extraordinary—as extraordinary as the agency itself. The Bureau of Freedmen, Refugees and Abandoned Lands was America's first attempt at a comprehensive social-welfare agency, designed to provide for the masses of newly freed slaves and Unionist refugees displaced across the South. In retrospect, the bureau reeks of anachronism, like a jet plane streaking across the nineteenth-century sky. What is remarkable is not that the bureau failed, but rather that it was ever tried.

The Freedmen's Bureau sprang from the imagination of the abolitionist movement, which began agitating long before the Emancipation Proclamation for an agency that would supervise and protect former slaves, who were then being warehoused in "contraband camps." Like most nineteenth-century American experiments that came before their time, the bureau was in part the brainchild of Robert Dale Owen, the doyen of American reformers. In his prewar career, Owen had championed birth control, divorce, communitarian living, and spiritualism. Starting in 1862, as head of the War Department's American Freedmen's Inquiry Commission, Owen toured the camps and plantations where former slaves had gathered. The commission's report proposed a temporary agency to ease the slaves' transition to

independence. It would supervise relief and education; it would settle freed slaves on lands confiscated from rebel planters; and it would
provide a justice system where former slaves would have an equal
voice with their former masters. "The essential thing is that we
secure to them the means of making their own way," Owen wrote in
his final report; "that we give them, to use the familiar phrase, 'a fair
chance.'"

In its first year, the bureau was given a taxing mission and an
inspiring leader—General Oliver O. Howard, the "Christian general"
whose idealism and piety were famous in the Union ranks. Howard
had lost his right arm at Fair Oaks in 1862. Even his critics agreed he
was brave—after his amputation, he was back in action at Second
Bull Run barely a month later. Henry Ward Beecher wrote that
Howard was "of all men, the one who would command the entire
confidence of [the] Christian public." Later he would serve as president of the first federally funded university for black students, which
to this day takes its name, Howard University, from the brave pious
little white man who tried so hard to do justice to the freed slaves
after the war.

But Congress gave the bureau no budget at all. As the war ground
to a close, Howard began to borrow military officers, sending them
into the occupied South as "agents" for the bureau. Often one agent
was responsible for an entire county or district, and was given virtually
no policy direction from bureau headquarters. In midsummer of 1865,
Howard ordered agents to settle freed slaves on forty-acre plots of
land broken off from confiscated plantations; one of Andrew Johnson's
first actions had been to cancel this tentative step toward land reform
and order the plantations restored to pardoned Rebels.

Congress saw the bureau as temporary; in the March 1865 bill, it
was given a one-year life span. Now, with the Southern states passing
"black codes" to put the former slaves into a subordinate position,
antislavery leaders saw a need for an extension of its life. Trumbull's
bill made the bureau a permanent government agency and permitted
it to hire at least one agent for every county in the South at a salary of
$1,500 a year. It authorized the bureau to build schools for the freed

slaves and to acquire land for them to farm; it permitted the bureau to distribute public lands held in the lower South for homesteads; and it would have given permanent title to the freed slaves farming the so-called Sherman lands, farm acreage in Georgia that had been allotted to them by General Sherman during his march to the sea.

The bill also erected a system of military courts in any part of the nation "wherein the ordinary course of judicial decisions has been interrupted by the rebellion" and local "law, ordinance, police, or other regulation, custom or prejudice" denied to black people "any of the civil rights or immunities belonging to white persons." Included among these "civil rights" were "the right to make and enforce contracts, to sue, be parties, and give evidence, to inherit, purchase, lease, sell, hold and convey real property, and to have full and equal benefit of all laws and proceedings for the security of person and estate." Beyond that, any person—North or South, private person or official—who subjected any freed slave to "the deprivation of any civil right secured to white persons," or who subjected any black person to a different punishment for crime than that given to whites, was liable to a year in prison, a $1,000 fine, or both.

The bureau bill, then, gave to the freed slave everything that a mid-nineteenth-century American would regard as a "civil right." And it did it under the authority of the Thirteenth Amendment. For Trumbull, and for many of those who had written and passed the Thirteenth Amendment, the constitutional ban on slavery empowered Congress to make sure that the freed slaves were not just emancipated but made equal, fully functioning members of society. It provided the tools to revolutionize Southern society.

Johnson must have gnashed his teeth in frustration; even a moderate senator like William Stewart of Nevada approved the bill when Senate debate opened on January 18. "It goes to the utmost extent that I think we are entitled to go under the Constitutional Amendment," Stewart said. But to the Democratic opposition, the whole idea of a government bureaucracy providing direct help to freed slaves—or, for that matter, to anyone—was a monstrosity, a blasphemy against Andrew Jackson's vision of the Constitution. Thomas Hendricks, a loyal Indiana Democrat who had opposed all antislavery measures since before the Kansas-Nebraska Act, argued that permitting the federal government even to buy land for freed slaves would mark the end of constitutional government in the United States. "Upon what principle can you authorize the Government of the United States to buy lands for the poor people in any State of the Union?" he demanded. "What has occurred, then, in this war that has changed the relation of the people to the General Government to so great an extent that Congress may become the purchasers of homes for them?"

In reply, Trumbull explained his theory of constitutional change. The former slaves were entitled to full federal protection against any organized effort to treat them as less than free people. Trumbull explained, "With the destruction of slavery necessarily follows the destruction of the incidents to slavery." Trumbull pointed to the "Black Codes" as examples of slavery's incidents. "I have no doubt that under this provision of the Constitution we may destroy all these discriminations in civil rights against the black man; and if we cannot, our constitutional amendment amounts to nothing. It was for that purpose that the second clause of that amendment was adopted, which says that Congress shall have authority, by appropriate legislation, to carry into effect the article prohibiting slavery. Who is to decide what that appropriate legislation is to be? The Congress of the United States; and it is for Congress to adopt such appropriate legislation as it may think proper, so that it be a means to accomplish the end."

The bill's supporters insisted that their program was the same as Andrew Johnson's. On January 23, Fessenden himself ridiculed the idea of a breach with the White House. Talk of a split was "all idle, ridiculous rumors, without the slightest foundation except the wish of those who invent them and give them currency."

At the same time, Fessenden answered Democratic constitutional arguments with a declaration that the war had endowed the federal government with power needed not only to win military victory but to preserve the peace by providing guarantees of freedom in the old slave states. To Democrats, his theory was full-throated radicalism;

but in his words we can actually hear echoes of Chief Justice John Marshall. "Whether you call it the war power or some other power," Fessenden said, "the power must necessarily exist, from the nature of the case, somewhere, and if anywhere, in us [Congress], to provide for what was one of the results of the contests in which we have been engaged." Southern resistance confronted the nation with a crisis akin to civil war. "We must meet it, and we must meet it under some power. There is no positive prohibition. It is a thing to be done." Democratic speakers denounced the idea of "implied powers" under the Thirteenth Amendment, but on January 25 the measure passed, 37 to 10.

The House debate centered around the same questions. Democrats attacked the bureau as a giveaway to lazy and undeserving blacks and invoked the old doctrine of state's rights. Republicans defended it as a measure to defend American citizens—many of whom had served bravely in the war—against unrepentant Rebels who sought to reduce them to serfdom. As for state's rights, they argued, *that* doctrine had died at Cemetery Ridge. Ignatius Donnelly, the midwestern freethinker who would enliven postwar American culture as a Utopian novelist and founder of the Populist movement, told the House that the war had renewed and expanded the Constitution. "This is a new birth of the nation. The Constitution will hereafter be read by the light of the rebellion; by the light of the emancipation; by the light of that tremendous uprising of the intellect of the world going on everywhere around us," he said.

James A. Garfield of Ohio, a future president, outlined his own view of the proper relation of the states to the union: "What is the meaning of the word State as applied to Ohio or Alabama? . . . They are only the geographical subdivisions of a State; and though endowed by the people of the United States with the rights of local self-government, yet in all their external relations, their sovereignty is completely destroyed, being merged in the supreme Federal Government," he said. "We call them States because the original Thirteen had been so designated before the Constitution was formed; but that Constitution destroyed all the sovereignty which those States were ever supposed to possess in reference to external affairs."

The individual states, Garfield explained, were like planets; the Union—the sovereign creation of the American people—was the sun. Legally, the states were to the Union as counties are to a state: subdivisions set up for the convenience of the people. "This *is* a nation," he said. "The rebel States are not sovereign States."

Reassured by its leadership that Johnson supported the bill, the House passed it, 136 to 33. The leaders were wrong; but they were not lying. They believed they were advocating a moderate policy that Johnson supported, and that they were acting with Johnson's approval. Johnson was careful not to disabuse them of this notion. In effect, in modern terms, the president set them up, though in retrospect they could have discerned the warning signs. On Sunday, January 28, Fessenden had visited Johnson at the White House. He went away convinced that Johnson had promised not to break with the emerging policy of Congress. But no sooner had Fessenden departed than Johnson called in Senator James Dixon of Connecticut, one of his key allies on the Hill, and gave him a very different interview. Dixon was one of the three Republican senators who had signaled that he would follow Johnson's line on all points. He dutifully relayed Johnson's views to the press, which quoted only a "distinguished senator." In the interview, Johnson opposed the entire project of remodeling the Constitution. The most he could support, he said, was an amendment basing representation on "qualified voters." Johnson also attacked proposals for black voting in D.C. and said that Congress should not meddle in matters of "the political equality of the races." Fessenden was doubly embarrassed: he believed Johnson had lied to him and then manipulated matters to make it seem as if the "well-known senator" was Fessenden himself. Thaddeus Stevens wasted no time denouncing the interview, proclaiming it open defiance of Congress. "Centuries ago," Stevens said dramatically, "had it been made to Parliament by a British king, it would have cost him his head."

A few days later, Johnson had a cold interview with a delegation of Northern blacks, led by Frederick Douglass. He pronounced himself opposed to the vote for freed slaves and accused Southern blacks of being potential allies with their former masters against the poor white class Johnson claimed to represent.

But the Republican leadership had convinced itself that Johnson would sign the bureau bill. The Joint Committee on Reconstruction, in fact, was preparing to meet Johnson's gesture with a peace offering of its own. On February 19, the committee heard the first draft of a resolution recommending the immediate restoration of Tennessee, Johnson's home state, to representation in Congress. But that afternoon, word swept the capital that the president had vetoed the Freedmen's Bureau bill—and had done so, moreover, on terms that in effect proclaimed himself the sole arbiter of Reconstruction.

The Bureau Bill, Johnson said in his veto message, was "not warranted by the Constitution." It was expensive, it would tend to centralize authority in Washington, and its military commission and land-reform provisions violated the Bill of Rights. In addition, it would "keep the mind of the freedman in a state of uncertain expectation and restlessness," making him look to Washington for protection instead of to his former masters.

Johnson then turned to an argument that suggested that he would not approve any Reconstruction bill, no matter how moderate or careful. Congress, he argued, was simply not a legitimate legislative authority as long as the Southern states were not represented. "The principle is firmly fixed in the minds of the American people, that there should be no taxation without representation," he wrote. "At present all the people of eleven States are excluded—those who were most faithful during the war not less than others."

Johnson proclaimed himself the sole legitimate authority in the wake of the war. "Each member of Congress is chosen from a single district or State," he said. "The President is chosen by the people of all the States. As eleven States are not at this time represented in either branch of Congress, it would seem to be his duty, on all proper occasions, to present their just claims to Congress." This was a remarkable claim. To begin with, most of the states not represented in Congress had also not been represented in the presidential voting in 1864; the National Union ticket had no greater claim to represent the whole nation than did either house of Congress. Nonetheless, Johnson gravely informed Congress that he would be in sole control of Reconstruction from now on. "I feel not only entitled, but bound to assume that, with the federal courts restored, and those of the several States in the full exercise of their functions, the rights and interests of all classes of the people will, with the aid of the military in cases of resistance to the laws, be essentially protected against unconstitutional infringement or violation," he said. "Should this expectation unhappily fail, which I do not anticipate, then the Executive is already fully armed with the powers conferred by the act of March 1865, establishing the Freedmen's Bureau, and hereafter, as heretofore, he can employ the land and naval forces of the country to suppress insurrection or to overcome obstructions to the laws." Congress's role, the message suggested, was essentially that of a bystander; the power of the government rested solely in him.

John W. Forney, the secretary of the Senate, read the message aloud to the Senate floor on the afternoon of February 19. After he had finished, the Senate galleries erupted in "loud applause and hisses," as black and white spectators nearly came to blows. The sergeant at arms cleared the west side of the gallery while senators wrangled over whether to proceed at once to a vote to override the veto. The original measure had passed by well over a two-thirds vote; supporters of the bill were ready to rebuke Johnson right away. But some senators hadn't heard the whole message and wanted a chance to think overnight (and consult political allies); in the chaotic conditions of the afternoon, the leadership permitted a postponement until 1 P.M. the next day.

When debate had opened, Trumbull rose to defend his bill. "Is it not most extraordinary that the President of the United States returns a bill which has passed Congress, with his objections to it, alleging it to be unconstitutional, and makes no allusion whatever in his whole message to that provision of the Constitution which, in the opinion of its supporters clearly gives the authority to pass it." That was, of course, the Thirteenth Amendment, and Trumbull spoke in his authorial voice when he said that "so far from the bill being unconstitutional, I should feel that I had failed in my constitutional duty if I did not propose some measure that would protect these people in their freedom. And yet this clause of the Constitution seems to have escaped entirely the observation of the President."

Trumbull turned to Johnson's attack on Congress for passing laws without Southern members present. The Rebel states had not been represented because—as even Johnson admitted—they had closed themselves off from the Union by secession. But the provisional governments of the South, staffed by former Confederates and determined to return blacks to serfdom, were no more legitimate than the old rebel regimes had been. Congress was fully empowered to legislate for all parts of the nation—States, territories, or occupied former Rebel areas—until they were restored by congressional vote.

Edgar Cowan of Pennsylvania popped to his feet and asked "by what rule the rebel is to be treated after he submits—by what law?"

Trumbull responded, "He is to be hung, if he is a big rebel." At this, the galleries exploded once more, and the chair threatened to clear them again.

As for Johnson's claim to represent all the people, Trumbull said, "If it would not be disrespectful, I should like to inquire how many votes the President got in those eleven States. Sir, he is no more the representative of those eleven states than I am."

He concluded more in sorrow than in anger, "I thought, in advocating it [the bill] I was acting in harmony with the views of the President. I regret exceedingly the antagonism which his message presents to the expressed views of Congress. . . . Now, sir, with these remarks, made without any unkind feeling toward the Executive, with whom I should be glad to agree, but in justification of my own position, I submit the bill, so far as I am concerned, to the decision of the Senate."

Spectators watched the ensuing roll call with interest, but there was not much suspense. Since the beginning of the Republic seventy-five years earlier, no presidential veto on a substantive bill had ever been overridden. And when the votes were cast, five conservative Republicans now switched in order to support the president. The bureau bill had failed by 30 to 18. Again, the galleries exploded.

Johnson had won a significant victory. But there are certain personalities—men and women used to living on the edge—for whom danger lies not in adversity but in triumph. Johnson was exalted by the success of the veto, exalted almost to madness. On February 22, Washington's birthday, he made sure that everyone within earshot understood that for him this was not a difference of opinion with members of the party that had put him in office, but a life-and-death struggle against traitors and would-be assassins.

The occasion was a "serenade," a now-lost nineteenth-century political custom whereby crowds of supporters would march to the home of their leaders and call them to the window for an impromptu address. February 22 had been "a day of soft air, and a clear sky, and a warm sun." The march came from a midday meeting in Grover's Theater, now the National Theater, at Thirteenth and E Streets NW, only a few blocks from the White House. A boisterous crowd had assembled, with boys darting around hawking peanuts and apples. It seems likely that those attending the "Endorsing the President" meeting refreshed themselves alcoholically as well during a long afternoon of florid oratory about the greatness of Johnson and the perfidy of his congressional critics. One antislavery newspaper, the *Boston Daily Advertiser*, had a correspondent in the crowd. He noted the presence of many prominent "peace Democrats," including Andrew Rogers of New Jersey, James Brooks of New York, and Senator Willard Saulsbury of Delaware. These were men who had only barely disguised their hope for Southern victory during the war. Now they joined hands with administration figures like Frank and Montgomery Blair and Judge David Patterson, Johnson's son-in-law. "If there were few heretofore known as promoters of the cause of the Union, there were many known of all men as promoters, a year and a half ago, of peace at any price," the *Advertiser*'s man reported. "If there was a noticeable absence of men who have worn the army blue, there was also a noticeable presence of men who wore rebel gray." On the other hand, as one attendee assured the correspondent, "There wasn't a nigger present."

As darkness fell on the capital, the crowd, inspired by the speeches and liquor, descended on the White House, carrying torches and shouting for Johnson as the man of the hour. Like the parade that brought forth the "Moses" speech, the scene was one Andrew Johnson relished: flaring torches, an adoring crowd, himself high above them in a position of power. And once again, as he gazed from the portico of the White House, some demon seemed to seize his tongue. In the days to come, many of his enemies, and even a few of his friends, wondered aloud, in fact, whether it had not been demon rum. Count Adam Gurowski, a Polish exile who had the sharpest tongue in town, spread the word that Johnson had drunk too much bad whiskey to make a good speech. But the president's manner apparently betrayed none of the confusion and hesitancy that had disfigured his vice-presidential speech. Instead, what he told the crowd seems more like the words of what alcoholism counselors call a "dry drunk"—a man who has neither conquered his inner demons nor temporarily stilled them with alcohol.

It was a vintage Johnson speech. As Eric McKitrick notes, in a speech of six thousand words, he referred to himself no fewer than 210 times. He linked himself and his policies with George Washington, Andrew Jackson, and "the Founder of our holy religion." "Who has suffered more than I have?" he asked plaintively. "I shall not recount the wrongs and the sufferings inflicted on me." But like Jesus himself, Johnson was now for "clemency and kindness, and a trust and a confidence" in all the people of the South except for the Confederate leaders.

But his Christlike policy was opposed by a set of traitors, as disloyal as Jefferson Davis, who were using the joint committee to "bring about a consolidation of the Republic" and destroy constitutional government. Just as he opposed Davis and the other traitors, he would oppose those in Washington who were "still opposed to the Union."

From somewhere in the audience, a voice called for Johnson to name the villains. A prudent politician would have held his tongue—but then, a prudent politician would have hesitated to compare himself with Jesus. "Suppose I should name to you those whom I look upon as being opposed to the fundamental principles of the Government, and as now laboring to destroy them. I say Thaddeus Stevens, of Pennsylvania; I say Charles Sumner, of Massachusetts; I say Wendell Phillips, of Massachusetts."

Later Welles wrote, "I was sorry he had permitted himself to be drawn into answering impertinent questions." Indeed, a president seeking secure legislative victories usually should avoid calling members of Congress traitors; it gives his enemies a stick to beat him with, and embarrasses his congressional allies, who are often friends with the "traitors" and even if not must work with them day after day.

But Johnson was not content with declaring war on Stevens and Sumner. There was something so delicious in that comparison between himself and Jesus that he could not resist spinning it off for almost an hour longer. The object of his enemies was not only to depose him but to seek his life. "Are those who want to destroy our institutions and change the character of the Government not satisfied with the blood that has been shed? Are they not satisfied with one martyr?"

If need be, then, he, Andrew Johnson, would wear the martyr's crown: "[I]f my blood is to be shed because I vindicate the Union and the preservation of this Government in its original purity and character, let it be so; but when it is done, let an altar of the Union be erected, and then, if necessary, lay me upon it, and the blood that now warms and animates my frame shall be poured out in a last libation as a tribute to the Union; and let the opponents of this Government remember that when it is poured out the blood of the martyr will be the seed of the church."

All in all, the speech was a revealing glimpse into the mind of Andrew Johnson, and Count Gurowski was not the only observer who, over the next morning's papers, suggested that the speaker must have once again been drunk. A few days later, however, Thaddeus Stevens rose gleefully to the president's "defense." The reports of the speech were a slander by the newspapers. Johnson, whom Stevens professed to admire, would never have made such a speech. It had been invented out of whole cloth. Why? Well, Stevens said, the president's enemies were like lawyers seeking to hale Johnson before a court on the common-law writ *de lunatico inquirendo*—a charge that the named person had lost his mind. A lawyer in such a case "would cautiously lead the alleged lunatic to speak upon the subject of the hallucination, and if he could be induced to gabble nonsense, the intrinsic evidence of the case would make out the allegation of insanity. So, Mr. Speaker, if these slanderers can make the people believe that the President ever uttered that speech, then they have made out their case."

As so often when Thad Stevens grabbed hold of an enemy, he reduced his listeners to laughter. But there was little real mirth in it for either side. Johnson was now on record asserting that his own party was honeycombed with traitors; prominent members of his party were freely suggesting that he was out of his mind. Meanwhile, the great question of the postwar political order was unsettled, and more was still to come.

BIRTH OF A NATION

On February 7, in the midst of the debate over the Freedmen's Bureau, Frederick Douglass and a delegation of prominent black Americans came to the White House to meet with Andrew Johnson. Douglass was a global figure: the former slave who had escaped bondage to become a famous writer, lecturer, and editor—and a superweapon in the intellectual struggle against the Slave Power.

Frederick Douglass in 1865 was forty-seven years old, in his intellectual prime, a dazzling orator whose brilliance, eloquence, and physical magnetism set audiences afire (and female hearts aflutter) on two continents. He was born in 1818 on the eastern shore of Maryland as Frederick Bailey; the surname, it is thought, was an Anglicization of Belali, a common African surname. Fred Bailey was probably the son of a white father, whose identity he never knew. Like so many slave children, he was motherless as well as fatherless. Though he met his mother a few times, he was raised by his grandmother and then, at the age of six, taken into the plantation household of Edward Lloyd, a rich Maryland planter.

From his earliest youth, Fred Bailey was proud and fiercely

ambitious. With the collusion of the white family he lived with, he (illegally) taught himself to read and practiced the rich, allusive oratorical style common in the nineteenth century. He was nearly hanged for an attempted escape in 1836; two years later, carrying forged "free papers," he boarded a train from Baltimore to New York and left slavery behind forever. He reached New York and sent for his wife, a free black woman named Anna Murray. The two were formally married in New York and then hastened on to New Bedford, Massachusetts, where they joined one of the oldest communities of free blacks in America. Once there, he changed his name to Frederick Douglass. Within a very few years, "Frederick Douglass" would be one of the most famous names in America.

In 1841, he attended a convention of the Massachusetts Anti-Slavery Society on nearby Nantucket Island; at that gathering, the twenty-three-year-old Douglass rose and delivered an impromptu account of his life as a slave and his escape from bondage. His words were not set down, but they impressed the mostly white audience into silence. Then William Lloyd Garrison, the abolition firebrand, rose to his feet and asked the crowd, "Have we been listening to a thing, a chattel personal, or a man?" "A man! a man!" roared the crowd.

A star had been born. Garrison arranged for Douglass to become a traveling lecturer for the society. Douglass mesmerized audiences with his eloquence and perfect diction. Equally impressive was his own physical magnificence. A contemporary observer wrote that he was "more than six feet in height, and his majestic form, as he rose to speak, straight as an arrow, muscular, yet lithe and graceful, his flashing eye, and more than all, his voice, that rivaled Webster's in its richness, and in the depth and sonorousness of its cadences, made up such an ideal of an orator as the listeners never forgot." Douglass throughout his life (during travels that frequently took him away from Anna and the children for months or years at a time) formed close alliances with beautiful white women, at least two of which were clearly full-blown love affairs.

So impressive was Douglass at the lectern that soon pro-slavery propagandists spread the rumor that he had never been a slave at all. To answer those charges, Douglass in 1845 published one of the classic works of American literature, *The Narrative of the Life of Frederick Douglass, Written by Himself*. With introductory notes by Garrison and his abolitionist colleague Wendell Phillips, the book became a best seller almost overnight and made Douglass famous throughout the civilized world. During his life, he would twice more write book-length accounts of himself—*My Bondage and My Freedom* in 1855 and *Life and Times of Frederick Douglass* in 1881. This multivolume autobiography illustrates that the great achievement of Douglass's life was the creation of "Frederick Douglass"—a former slave who gave no quarter to American racism, and who insisted that he was—intellectually, morally, politically, and sexually—the equal of any white man. In the end, "Frederick Douglass" was the gift to history of the black man born Frederick Bailey, a flag planted for complete human equality at a time when even the most advanced whites tended to regard black Americans as somewhat childlike. So powerful is Douglass's presence in American history—and so subversive of the comforting myths the nation has told itself about its long, painful encounter with matters of race—that Douglass as an individual, proud, touchy, ambitious, has been all but swallowed up in Douglass the symbol.

By 1865, Douglass was not only a famous writer and speaker but the editor of one of the most influential antislavery newspapers, at first called *The North Star* but later *Frederick Douglass' Paper* and *Douglass' Monthly*. He had broken with his mentor, Garrison, who scorned practical politics. He had become a staunch ally of the abolition movement's female wing and counted among his closest friends the feminist pioneers Elizabeth Cady Stanton and Susan B. Anthony. He had briefly conspired with John Brown, who asked Douglass to join his doomed rebellion at Harper's Ferry in 1859. Once the war began, he had implored Lincoln to make ending slavery the Union's chief war aim; once Lincoln issued the Emancipation Proclamation, Douglass had become a tireless Union propagandist. He had traveled the country to recruit black men for the Union army, proclaiming that military service was the ticket to citizenship. Two of Douglass's sons served in the fabled 54th Massachusetts Infantry, the first Northern black regiment.

For his services to the Union cause, Douglass had several times met with Lincoln, to advise him on efforts to recruit black troops and to spread the word of emancipation among the still-enslaved blacks within the Confederate lines. "Mr. Lincoln was not only a great President, but a GREAT MAN," he wrote later. "In his company I was never in any way reminded of my humble origin, or of my unpopular color."

Douglass could not say the same of Andrew Johnson. Douglass later remembered meeting Johnson on the day of his inauguration as vice president. "Mr. Lincoln touched Mr. Johnson and pointed me out to him," Douglass wrote. "The first expression which came to his face, and which I think was the true index of his heart, was one of bitter contempt and aversion. Seeing that I observed him, he tried to assume a more friendly appearance, but it was too late." Scholars dispute whether this incident could in fact have occurred on Inauguration Day; but there is little doubt that Douglass correctly read the inclination of Johnson's heart. As a poor white from East Tennessee, Johnson had little use for any black American; the very *existence* of Frederick Douglass must have galled the man who fancied himself the "Moses" of black America. Frederick Douglass did not seek white redeemers for himself or for his nation; he regarded equality for himself—and for every black American—not as an aspiration for the future or a potential gift from whites, but as a right.

It was to ask for that right that Douglass and the delegation came to the White House in February 1866. They were at that moment the cream of black America, or at least of *male* black America. (The antislavery movement had created many strong female leaders, but none was included in the delegation that waited upon the president.) The group had been picked by the National Convention of Colored Men, a group that had first met in Syracuse, New York, to agitate for equal rights. Meeting again in Washington, the group designated

Douglass and ten others to speak for them in an audience with Johnson. The head of the delegation was George T. Downing, one of the richest and most important African Americans in the country. Downing, born free in New York, lived among the rich whites of Newport, Rhode Island, and owned restaurants there and in Providence, and even a whites-only resort in Newport. During the war, he had come to Washington to operate the restaurant in the House of Representatives; by war's end, he had amassed large real estate holdings in the Northeast. But he had always been an advocate for equality; beginning with service on the Underground Railroad in his twenties, he had consistently supported efforts to end segregation of black schoolchildren and to win the vote for Northern blacks on equal terms with whites. Also included in the delegation were John M. Brown, a bishop of the African Methodist Episcopal Church; John Jones, a wealthy Chicago tailor and opponent of Illinois's antiblack statutes; William Whipper of Pennsylvania, another veteran of the Underground Railroad; and Douglass's son Lewis Douglass, who had fought with the 54th Massachusetts.

The meeting was cold and correct. All the members stood in Johnson's presence. The president remained upright as well and did not invite them to sit. Douglass, as the most eminent of the delegation, briefly saluted Johnson. "[Y]ou have the power to save or destroy us, to bless or blast us," he told the president. "The fact that we are the subjects of Government, and subject to taxation, subject to volunteer in the service of the country, subject to being drafted, subject to bear the burdens of the States, makes it not improper that we should ask to share in the privileges of this condition."

Johnson had prepared carefully for this moment, and he responded with a classic example of his pugnacious style. As always, the main subject of his remarks was himself and the many virtues he brought to the office. "If I know myself, and the feelings of my own heart," he said, "they have been for the colored man. I have owned slaves and bought slaves, but I never sold one." In fact, Johnson, for all the world like a Southern planter, complained, "I have been their slave instead of their being mine."

When Andrew Johnson reviewed the victorious Union armies in May 1865, he was the most powerful president the United States had ever known. (*The National Archives*)

BELOW LEFT: Johnson asked Carl Schurz, a former Union general and German-American political leader, to visit the Deep South; but Schurz's report displeased Johnson and encouraged Radical Republicans. (*Collection of the Library of Congress*)

BELOW RIGHT: Thaddeus Stevens, the most powerful member of the House of Representatives, was implacably opposed to Johnson's plan to "reconstruct" the South with all-white governments. (*Collection of the Library of Congress*)

Southern congressman Preston Brooks nearly killed Massachusetts senator Charles Sumner on the Senate floor in 1856, galvanizing antislavery opinion. (*Collection of the Library of Congress*)

By 1866, Sumner had become the living symbol of opposition to the Slave Power. (*The National Archives*)

Charles Sumner, here with the poet Henry Wadsworth Longfellow, was a classic revolutionary intellectual—more interested in abstract ideas than in particular people. (*Collection of the Library of Congress*)

Senator William Pitt Fessenden, by temperament conservative, tried to compromise with the White House but to no avail. (*The National Archives*)

Senator Lyman Trumbull, an old friend and rival of Lincoln's, was amazed when Johnson vetoed his Civil Rights and Freedmen's Bureau bills. (*Collection of the Library of Congress*)

Representative John Bingham of Ohio, principal author of Section One of the Fourteenth Amendment, despised "the devilish Slavocracy." (*The National Archives*)

LEFT: Northern public opinion gradually swung against Johnson, who, one historian notes, treated Southern slavecowners with "amazing leniency." (*Collection of the Library of Congress*)

BELOW: Johnson's vetoes delighted Southern whites, but ended up costing him any control over Reconstruction policy. (*Collection of the Library of Congress*)

Frederick Douglass bitterly protested language in the Fourteenth Amendment that seemed to recognize a state's power to deny the franchise to black Americans. (*Collection of the Library of Congress*)

Susan B. Anthony and Elizabeth Cady Stanton, the two founding mothers of the women's suffrage movement, felt betrayed by the amendment's use of the word *male*. (*Collection of the Library of Congress*)

Robert Dale Owen, America's chief voice for utopian reform, wrote the "omnibus" draft that, much watered down, became the Fourteenth Amendment. (*Collection of the Library of Congress*)

HARPER'S WEEKLY.
A JOURNAL OF CIVILIZATION.

VOL. X.—No. 491.]   NEW YORK, SATURDAY, MAY 26, 1866.   [SINGLE COPIES TEN CENTS. $4.00 PER YEAR IN ADVANCE.

Entered according to Act of Congress, in the Year 1866, by Harper & Brothers, in the Clerk's Office of the District Court for the Southern District of New York.

THE MEMPHIS RIOTS.

There was in Memphis, on the first two days of May, an excitement unequaled since the close of the war. The origin of the disturbance between the whites and negroes of that city was highly discreditable to the colored soldiers, and the riotous proceedings which followed were a disgrace to civilization. For the riot the lower class of white citizens were as responsible as were the soldiers of the Third United States Colored Infantry for the original difficulty. This regiment, whose reputation has been a bad one, had been mustered out, since which they had frequented whisky-shops in the southern part of the city, and had been guilty of excesses and disorderly conduct. On the evening of May 1 some drunken members of the regiment were on South Street, talking noisily, when in an insolent manner they were ordered by two policemen to cease their noise and disperse. Words ensued, followed by blows, throwing of missiles, and firing of revolvers.

To understand what followed it must be remembered that the police force of Memphis is composed mostly of Irishmen, whose violent prejudice against negroes was so shamefully displayed in the New York riots of 1863. The *Times* correspondent thus described the riot:

Word was sent to police head-quarters, and the whole force at once proceeded to the scene of the fray, being joined on the way thither by armed and excited citizens. Meanwhile the firing had brought other negroes to the spot, some armed with clubs and some with revolvers, so that by the time the police force came up the two parties were nearly equal in number. The negroes held the original

SCENES IN MEMPHIS, TENNESSEE, DURING THE RIOT—BURNING A FREEDMEN'S SCHOOL-HOUSE.

[Sketched by A. R. W.]

SCENES IN MEMPHIS, TENNESSEE, DURING THE RIOT—SHOOTING DOWN NEGROES ON THE MORNING OF MAY 2, 1866.—[Sketched by A. R. W.]

position, and, upon the approach of the police, showing no determination to abandon it, were fired upon by the police and citizens who accompanied them. This fire was returned, and for a while both parties united themselves in discharging their revolvers as rapidly as possible. Meanwhile word was sent to General Stoneman, who promptly dispatched to the scene of action a company of Regulars (white), when the negroes were quickly dispersed and driven in every direction.

During the evening the wildest and most exaggerated reports soon spread throughout the city. Every commandant of the intelligence of the fight told a different story, and the highest excitement prevailed. Each rumor gained a worse aspect upon the safer than the preceding one, and only served to develop the pent-up prejudice against the negro. Soon after dark this excitement and prejudice found vent. Large numbers of armed citizens repaired to the scene of the fight and commenced firing upon every negro who made himself visible. One negro upon South Street, a quiet, inoffensive laborer, was shot down almost in front of his own cabin, and after life was extinct his body was fired into, cut and beat in a most horrible manner. In all parts of the city, wherever they could be seen, negroes were fired upon by persons as well as citizens. They were shot while driving hacks, and quietly walking in the streets about their business. The police seemed to make it their special business to shoot every negro they could see, no matter where he was or what he was doing. The result was that by 9 o'clock the colored population were in-doors trembling with wild alarm. How many negroes were killed during the night it is impossible to ascertain, as firing was continually heard during the earlier hours in all parts of the city. It is estimated that from 15 to 20 were killed. So far as I have been able to learn, not a white man was fired upon by a negro during the whole night.

After the fight of Tuesday evening the negro soldiers and most of the colored population residing in the vicinity of the fight fled to the fort for security. They were perfectly quiet—in fact, were terrified, frightened for their own safety. At an early hour yesterday morning every thing

---

Final debate on the amendment opened a few days after a bloody antiblack riot in Memphis. (*Collection of the Library of Congress*)

After Johnson was repudiated in the 1866 elections, the Republican members of the House impeached him. (*The National Archives*)

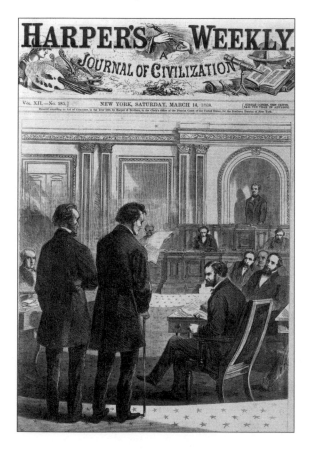

Thaddeus Stevens and John Bingham, two of the House impeachment "managers," argued for removal; their committee colleague Fessenden refused to vote against Johnson, who was acquitted by one vote. (*Collection of the Library of Congress*)

Johnson made it clear that black voting was one of those "theoretical, hollow, unpractical" ideas that a practical man like himself need not consider. "[S]uppose by some magic touch you could say to every one [of the freed slaves], 'you shall vote tomorrow,' how much would that ameliorate their condition at this time?" He walked "very near" Douglass as he spoke, but would not allow him to respond to his rhetorical question. The problem, Johnson said, was that the "slave power," a minority of Southern whites, had oppressed the poor whites as much as, or more than, the black slaves.

Johnson turned to Douglass now. "Have you ever lived upon a plantation?"

"I have, your excellency," Douglass answered.

"When you would look over and see a man who had a large family, struggling hard upon a poor piece of land, you thought a great deal less of him than you did of your own master's negro, didn't you?" Johnson asked confidently.

"Not I!" Douglass replied.

"Well," Johnson said, "I know such was the case with a large number of you in those sections." The poor white man hated blacks, Johnson said, because "the colored man and his master combined kept him in slavery, by depriving him of a fair participation in the labor and productions of the rich land of the country."

Black Americans should be content with freedom, Johnson suggested. "[W]hen you come back to the objects of the war," he said, "you find that the abolition of slavery was not one of the objects." The war had been fought for the Union, and emancipation was only "an incident to the suppression of a great rebellion." So the black man should recognize that "there is a great deal done for him on this point" that he did not really earn or deserve. In fact, the worst injuries had been suffered by poor Southern whites, who had been "forced into the rebellion" but had "come out of it with nothing gained, but a great deal lost."

For this reason, Johnson said, it would be a gross injustice to the whites to force black suffrage on them. Consent was the basis of American government, after all, and the Southern people (by which

Johnson meant Southern whites) had not consented to the inclusion of blacks in their political system. "It is a fundamental tenet in my creed that the will of the people must be obeyed," he said. "Is there anything wrong or unfair in that?"

Douglass sought to soften his reply with a smile. But he said, "A great deal that is wrong, Mr. President, with all respect."

Douglass, at Downing's invitation, attempted to respond to Johnson's arguments. But the president was in no mood for back talk. "I merely wanted to indicate my views in reply to your address," he said, "and not to enter into any general controversy." He went on, having taken back the floor, to suggest that it was the duty of black leaders to convince the freed slaves that "the colored people can live and advance in civilization to better advantage elsewhere than crowded right down there in the South."

Johnson suggested that there was an inevitable conflict between blacks and whites. "[H]ence I suggest emigration," he said. "If [the freed slave] cannot get employment in the South, he has it in his power to go where he can get it."

Johnson made it clear that the delegates were dismissed, without a chance to respond. "The President sends us to the people," Douglass said to his colleagues.

"Yes, sir," Johnson answered. "I have great faith in the people. I believe they will do what is right."

After the delegates had left, Johnson's private secretary told a friend that the president snarled, "Those d——d sons of b——s thought they had me in a trap. I know that d——d Douglass; he's just like any nigger, & he would sooner cut a white man's throat than not."

The next day, the *Washington Chronicle* published a reply, written by Douglass for the delegation. The policy Johnson had announced at the meeting, he wrote, was "entirely unsound and prejudicial to the highest interests of our race as well as our country at large." The hostility Johnson perceived between poor whites and freed slaves "has its root and sap in the relation of slavery, and was incited on both sides by the cunning of slave masters." Slaves had feared poor whites, to be sure—they were the "slave-catchers, slave-drivers, and overseers" of the plantation South. But with emancipation, "the cause of his hatred removed, the effect must be removed also."

Even if the opposition between whites and blacks in the South was insuperable, Douglass added, the conclusion that blacks should not vote was illogical. "Peace between races is not to be secured by degrading one race and withholding it from another; but by maintaining a state of equal justice between all classes."

Finally, Douglass told the president, "it is impossible to suppose" that black Americans would emigrate to some other country. "[T]here can never come a time when [blacks] can be removed from this country without a terrible shock to its prosperity and peace." And it would be a lasting blot on the honor of white Americans if they were to decide that "negroes could be tolerated among them in a state of the most degrading slavery and oppression, and must be cast away, driven into exile, for no other cause than having been freed from their chains."

Had it been a diplomatic negotiation, the meeting with Johnson would have been called "a frank exchange of ideas"—code for a bitter disagreement between the ruler of a powerful nation and the leaders of a weaker one that had been cruelly wronged by its stronger neighbor. And in fact this tense and tragic encounter was very much like a summit meeting between the leaders of two nations groping toward peace or war. Black America in 1866 was like a country and a people emerging from colonial rule into an uncertain independence.

Freedom had come slowly to the new nation. Lincoln had first hinted at emancipation in the fall of 1862. He had followed through with the Emancipation Proclamation on the first day of 1863. The freedom it promised slaves within rebel lines came slowly as the blue armies moved through the South; freedom for slaves in Texas was not formally proclaimed until "Juneteenth," June 19, 1865—more than two months after Appomattox. Slaves within the Union, moreover, were not permanently freed until December 1865, when the Thirteenth Amendment was ratified. Now, three months later, neither blacks nor whites could agree on just what the promised freedom would consist of.

Black America in 1865 had a population of nearly five million,

500,000 in the North and more than four million in the black heartland of the plantation South. The population was overwhelmingly concentrated in the Deep South—in South Carolina, Georgia, Alabama, and Louisiana, in fact, blacks formed a majority of the population. Viewed as a nation, black America had formidable problems. Only one in ten of its adults could read and write. Years of slavery had left its people virtually penniless. Black labor had built the plantations and cities of the South; cotton and tobacco grown by black slaves had enriched mercantile families of the Northeast; but those who had done the work had received no payment. Its people were landless, too, and their indigenous leaders were just emerging. Douglass's delegation was made up of freeborn Northern blacks and escaped slaves; like many other colonized peoples, black Americans at first could rely only on leadership from exile.

But black America had potential assets as well. Its people were galvanized by freedom; it had a potentially sustainable land base in the fertile farming regions of the lowland South; and it even had, in 1865, a powerful military arm. In the aftermath of Appomattox, however, black Americans were divided about how to employ these assets. Some of their leaders, like Frederick Douglass, believed that votes for black men would ensure the future of both nations; others believed that land ownership alone promised a successful future. Some believed that blacks should stay in the South and live side by side with their former masters; others, echoing Andrew Johnson, believed that the South would never allow dignity and freedom to the former slaves, who would do better to seek their fortunes in the West.

Frederick Douglass had no doubts. What black Americans needed was the vote—nothing more, nothing less. "I am for the immediate, unconditional, and universal enfranchisment of the black man, in every state of the Union," he proclaimed even before the guns had fallen silent. Black men were entitled to vote, and could not consent to their own disfranchisement, even when suggested by their white allies. "No class of men can, without insulting their own nature, be content with any deprivation of their rights."

Besides that, the slave power was still committed to dominance within the reunited nation. "Now, where will you find the strength to counterbalance this spirit [of rebellion], if you do not find it in the Negroes of the South?" If black men possessed the vote, it would form "a wall of fire for [every loyal citizen's] protection."

Blacks might be ignorant at present, Douglass admitted; so were many whites. The vote would educate them. Besides, if blacks could not vote, they would in effect be slaves to white Southerners in general. "[I]f we restore the Southern states without" the vote, Douglass warned a few weeks after the disastrous interview with Johnson, "[W]e shall establish an ownership of the blacks by the communities among which they live."

For this reason, Douglass scorned the kind of compromise that was embodied in the joint committee's representation amendment. Within days of its introduction in the Senate, he had presented Charles Sumner with a petition denouncing the amendment's implicit recognition of states' rights to disfranchise blacks. In that protest, Douglass noted that in the Constitution "as it now stands, there is not a sentence or a syllable conveying any shadow of right or authority by which any State may make color or race a disqualification for the exercise of the right of suffrage." The signers "will regard as a real calamity the introduction of any words, expressly or by implication, giving any State or States such power."

Other leaders of black America in 1865 thought that economic self-sufficiency, not the vote, was the most important thing the new nation needed. Among the most colorful of these was Sojourner Truth, the legendary former slave, abolitionist, and feminist. Truth had been born Isabella van Wagenen, a slave not in the Deep South but on Long Island; freed when New York abolished slavery in 1817, she had transformed herself into a living symbol of the black quest for freedom and of the female quest for equality. Six feet tall, angular, and strong, she was a visual shock to white people, a black woman who did not fit any known stereotype. The impression she made was strengthened by the symbolic name she assumed in 1843. In the years before the Civil War, she had become a celebrity—as famous, in her way, as Douglass—and a frequent speaker before antislavery and women's rights assemblies.

To Truth, the immediate needs of black America were practical. The vote she did not care for; after all, neither Douglass nor any other male leader had any notion that women like her should get the franchise. For Truth, black folks needed work—and good jobs might be much more easily found in the North than in the old slave states. Truth helped black refugees leave Washington, D.C., for new lives in towns like Battle Creek, Michigan, and Rochester, New York. Meanwhile, she kept up a never-ending fight for recognition of black Americans' right to equal treatment on streetcars and other places of public accommodation; to the end of her life she suffered pain in her shoulder from a struggle aboard a Washington streetcar—officially desegregated—when a white conductor tried to throw her off in 1865.

Other leaders of black America thought that the key to the future lay neither in the vote nor in emigration, but in acquiring land in the South, where blacks had labored without pay for generations. Tunis Campbell, a freeborn black man from New Jersey, was almost as well known nationally as Frederick Douglass for his abolition speeches. In 1863, he journeyed south to the coast of Georgia to begin his plan of helping blacks acquire a thriving agricultural land base. His design called for a separate, economically self-sufficient community, with its own legislature and free common schools; by the next spring, the model republic was up and running.

The profound tragedy of Reconstruction, of course, is that black America got none of these things. Despite a promising start, white society eventually refused to permit the emergence of the black nation as an equal component part of the complex tapestry of American nationality. The constitutional change wrought by the Thirty-ninth Congress did set in motion a renewal of American freedom for all its people, but in the end the nation did little specifically designed to make sure that blacks were able to use the freedom they had won for themselves during the Civil War.

Many white Americans—today as in 1865—cling to Andrew Johnson's comforting notion that white Americans had altruistically freed the slaves. But the reality is far more complex. From its outset, Lincoln had insisted that the Civil War was *not* an "abolition war." "If I could restore the Union by freeing the slaves, I would do so; if I could restore the Union by leaving slavery alone, I would do so," he said in 1862. "If I could restore the Union by freeing some slaves and letting others alone, I would do so."

But black Southerners had other ideas. War between the whites was their opportunity, and they had seized it, making their way to Union lines in search of freedom and citizenship. At first, Union commanders politely returned escaped slaves to their masters. Northern public opinion was scandalized by this callousness, and farsighted Union officials perceived that a secure slave population would give the Confederacy a tremendous advantage in wartime. In 1861 Union general Benjamin F. Butler had come up with the notion of calling escaped slaves "contraband of war," as if the refugees were ammunition or weapons liable to seizure under the laws of battle. Congress had adopted this idea in the two confiscation acts, which freed any slaves used by their masters to support the Rebellion. In time, this formed a major drain on Rebel resources; by war's end, one Southern slave in eight had made his or her way to Union lines, draining the Confederacy of desperately needed labor.

The growing numbers of black refugees had put pressure on Lincoln to recognize them as human beings, to guarantee to them by law the de facto freedom they had won for themselves. More than that, as the conflict spread and deepened, changing from a picturesque clash of Napoleonic armies into a grim industrial abattoir, the "contrabands" represented a well of manpower that the Union could not afford to ignore. "You say you will not fight to free the negroes," Lincoln wrote to a white correspondent in 1864. "Some of them seem willing to fight for you."

In fact, as white Americans began to resist marching to the killing fields of the South, black Americans were begging the Union to give them a chance to fight. The Emancipation Proclamation of January 1, 1863, as most Americans know, did not actually free a single slave. It applied only to slaves held behind Confederate lines—slaves, that is, whom federal authority could not affect at all. The proclamation did succeed in making emancipation the Union war aim, and it promised escaping slaves that "the Executive Government of the United States, including the military and naval authorities thereof, will recognize and maintain the freedom of said persons." It also announced that "such persons of suitable condition will be received into the armed service of the United States." Reluctantly, Lincoln had agreed that the slaves themselves should fight for their own freedom.

Black Americans flocked to the colors. "Six months after the Emancipation Proclamation," historian Leon F. Litwack writes, "more than thirty black regiments had been organized, camps had been established to receive and train them, recruiting was taking place almost everywhere, and several units had already participated in combat action." Eventually 186,000 blacks would enter the army, and by war's end one active-duty soldier in four was black. Most of the new Union troops came from the South and the border states. But the most fabled black regiment of the war, immortalized today in a famous sculpture by Augustus Saint-Gaudens and in an award-winning film, was the 54th Massachusetts Infantry, mustered into service on Boston Common in May 1863.

"Glory enough for one day," said William C. Nell, a black abolitionist who watched the new soldiers of the 54th as they passed in parade before the Massachusetts State House. "Aye, indeed for a lifetime." Two months later, on July 18, 1863—barely two weeks after Pickett's Charge failed at Gettysburg—the 54th led a Union assault on Fort Wagner, a heavily fortified Confederate bunker at the mouth of Charleston Harbor. The mission was all but hopeless: the attackers were forced to advance through a narrow defile between the ocean and a salt marsh, where the massed Confederate artillery could hardly miss them. Though they reached the wall and fought desperately for an hour, the 54th was eventually pushed back, with the loss of half its soldiers, including Colonel Robert Gould Shaw, the young Boston

Brahmin who had volunteered to command black troops. But the courage of the 54th—which had volunteered for the mission—impressed Northern opinion deeply and came to symbolize the black sacrifice for the Union.

There were other place-names in the list of black battles. At Port Hudson and Milliken's Bend in Louisiana, at Cabin Creek and Honey Springs in Indian Territory (present-day Oklahoma), and at Jenkins Ferry in Arkansas, black troops fought bravely, and sometimes put Confederate detachments to flight. But another name that resounded in the story of black soldiers was Fort Pillow, Tennessee. On April 12, 1864, Confederate general Nathan Bedford Forrest—later a founder of the Ku Klux Klan—conducted a massacre of black Union soldiers who had already surrendered and laid down their arms. His report gloated that the Mississippi River beside the fort "was dyed with the blood of the slaughtered for 200 yards," and he concluded by suggesting "that these facts will demonstrate to the Northern people that negro soldiers cannot cope with Southerners." Many Northern whites disagreed, including a number of veterans who had resisted serving alongside blacks. As one cavalry officer said after the Battle of Cabin Creek, "I never believed in niggers before, but, by Jesus, they are hell in fighting."

At the war's end, the black veterans promised to provide leadership—and protection—to the freed slaves of the South, a kind of military arm of the new black nation. Black troops formed the core of the Union occupation force after Lee's surrender. But white Southerners regarded them with fear and horror. One of the most important aims of the Black Codes was to deny to black men the "right to bear arms," either as individuals or as members of the state militias, which the provisional governments sought to re-create as all-white forces.

Freedom of movement: that was the first liberty the former slaves sought to exercise in 1865 and 1866. "To look at the congested railroad depots, the makeshift camps along the tracks, the hastily constructed freedmen villages, and the stragglers crowding the country roads, bundles under their arms or slung over their shoulders, many of them hungry, sick, and barely clad, the impression conveyed was that of an entire people on the move," Litwack writes. White Americans were often befuddled by the mass migration of blacks from one part of the South to another. Many of them had tended to think of black slaves as attached to the land, like livestock, and had expected they would stay attached after emancipation. But the rush to the roads made perfect sense to the freed slaves. Some wanted to travel just to prove they could, or to escape from their former masters; but many were looking for their loved ones, for wives, husbands, sons, daughters, brothers, and sisters who had been sold or shipped away from home. Frederick Douglass himself had such a reunion: in February 1867, his brother Perry Downs appeared at his door in Rochester, New York. "The meeting with my brother after nearly forty years of separation is an event altogether too affecting to describe," he wrote.

Far too often, the quest was in vain. Many families were never reunited. And even when the search did succeed, the damage wrought on family life by slavery was not easily repaired. Often a husband or wife sold south, or left behind, had taken another spouse on the assumption that the old one was gone forever. Children separated from their parents at an early age often found it hard to accept them when they reappeared. And there were legal problems. Marriage was the fundamental civil right, as the common law defined that term. White masters had denied to blacks the legal right to start a family; now a free man might have two competing wives, or vice versa. Black people hurried to be formally wed, often in mass ceremonies. Sometimes the Freedmen's Bureau organized these events and required couples to take part. One Freedmen's Bureau official wrote, "Whenever a Negro appears before me with two or three wives who have equal claim upon him, I marry him to the woman who has the greatest number of helpless children who otherwise would become a charge on the Bureau." The children, too, proved an obstacle to freed slaves attempting to put together a free household. White slave masters often insisted on keeping children born to their slaves, even after emancipation, and some Southern Black Codes required black children to be "apprenticed" to whites.

The question of labor loomed over every other issue in the new nation. The postemancipation South faced a momentous choice. The plantation South, with its crops of cotton, tobacco, and rice, was in essence a colony controlled by British merchants (and to a lesser extent by Northern industrialists) who bought the crops. These crops could only be grown on huge landholdings with intensive labor—either by slaves or by "free" workers in a condition of semislavery. That need for huge numbers of hands willing to work under brutal conditions had fastened the slave system on the South in the seventeenth century. Most white Southerners—and many white Northerners—couldn't imagine the South without its plantations, or the North without Southern crops.

To these whites, the solution to the South's problems seemed quite simple. The freed slaves should accept contracts from the owners of the plantations and perform for wages the same work they had performed as slaves. When freed slaves objected, whites—even some agents of the bureau—interpreted their desire for a new life as simple laziness. "Whence comes the assertion that the 'nigger won't work'?" one former slave said. "It comes from this fact: ... the freedman refuses to be driven out into the field two hours before day, and work until 9 or 10 o'clock in the night, as was the case in the days of slavery."

There was a road not taken, for black Southerners, for the region as a whole, and for the nation. Some Northern leaders, white and black, believed the way to unify the nation was to dismantle the Slave Power at its base—to substitute for the plantation system a New England–style economy of small farms, market towns and villages, public schools and churches. To this day, Americans are conditioned to laugh at the old slogan of "forty acres and a mule." Yet it was a serious proposal for the kind of land reform that has followed other revolutionary upheavals. If small parcels of land could be distributed to freed slaves and poor whites, the social consequences might have been far-reaching. Historian Eric Foner writes that "land distribution would have had profound consequences for Southern society, weakening the land-based economic and political power of the old ruling class, offering blacks a measure of choice as to whether, when, and under what circumstances to enter the labor market, and affecting the former slaves' conception of themselves."

Nor was land distribution an imaginary or impractical policy. In fact, it had begun out of necessity during the war and in some parts of the South was well advanced even before Appomattox. The most famous example was the Port Royal Experiment in the Sea Islands of South Carolina. These remote and lush islands fell to the North in November 1861. Panicked, the white masters of the plantations fled at the approach of Union ships, leaving their slaves behind. Left with vacant land and hungry civilians, federal authorities put the former slaves—who were not yet even clearly legally free—to work on the old plantation lands. Over the next two years, the experiment prospered modestly. The freed slaves worked in gangs raising Sea Island cotton and were given small plots of their own to cultivate for food.

Another large-scale experiment was begun by General William Tecumseh Sherman during his famous March to the Sea in 1864–1865. In a gamble that changed the face of warfare, Sherman left Atlanta late that year and burned his way toward Savannah on the Atlantic Coast. He defied Napoleon's adage that "an army travels on its stomach" by cutting his own supply line and sending his men to live off the plantation lands they passed through. The advance was so rapid that some of Sherman's own horses and mules starved because there was no time for them to graze. Not only could Sherman's Army of the West advance more quickly without its logistical "tail," the foraging of its "bummers" for food and equipment meant that it left behind almost nothing that the Confederates could use for their own war effort.

But as Sherman's armies passed, they were followed by throngs of former slaves, unwilling to wait on their old plantations for starvation or reenslavement. Feeding these refugees was impossible; returning them to slavery was unacceptable. After a meeting with a group of black leaders from Savannah, Sherman on January 16, 1865, issued Special Field Order No. 15. The order set aside all the Georgia Sea Islands, and the rich coastal plantation country between Charleston,

South Carolina, and Jacksonville, Florida, for settlement by freed slaves. Each family allotment would be forty acres; the new occupants would hold "possessory title" until Congress decided the final ownership of the conquered lands. A few weeks later, apparently inspired by Sherman's makeshift land reform, Congress passed the first Freedmen's Bureau bill. In language that appeared without fanfare in the conference version of that bill, Congress ordered the bureau to distribute to "every male citizen [of the South], whether refugee or freedman" an allocation of forty acres. The new occupants would be guaranteed the right to rent the land for three years, and then to buy from the government "such title as it could convey."

The words were artfully ambiguous. No one knew exactly what title the government held to the confiscated and abandoned plantations of the South. Lincoln and many other more conservative Republicans shuddered at the prospect of outright confiscation. Even if the landowners had actively supported the Rebellion, the Constitution itself suggested that government had no power to seize their property permanently; in Article III, Section 3, the document said that "no Attainder of Treason shall work corruption of blood, or forfeiture except during the life of the person attainted." The provision was aimed at the practice, so tempting to impecunious English kings, of declaring one's rich subjects traitors and seizing their lands.

But to the freed slaves, the prospect of forty acres seemed like a promise from the United States. It was one that could easily have been fulfilled. Even if every eligible family had received a forty-acre plot from confiscated plantations, the new allotments would have used only 10 percent of the eligible Southern land. In addition, nearly a third of the South was still property of the federal government. Much of this was swampy, hilly, or arid, but there was still some good land to be distributed, the way the federal lands in the West had been granted to white settlers. A temporary title to these lands might have enabled black families to establish themselves and generate enough wealth to rent or buy other farms when the confiscation lapsed. To Thaddeus Stevens and a few other congressional Radicals, possession of land seemed a far better guarantee of freedom than did the ballot. Without land, the freed slaves would be dependent on the former masters, Stevens said, who would restrict the suffrage to "their former menials, their house servants, those that they can control."

Eventually, Congress pulled back from the idea of land reform as a Reconstruction policy. A change in the South's agricultural system would have meant less cotton flowing to Manchester and Massachusetts. For every social revolutionary like Stevens or Sumner, the party had a dozen hardheaded businessmen prepared to defend the interests of Northern industry. And, of course, Andrew Johnson was dead set against any confiscation. During the months before Congress convened in late 1865, he had restored land to pardoned Rebels at such a rapid clip that by April 1866, General Howard reported to Congress that virtually all confiscated plantation land had been restored to its former owners.

In October 1865, Howard journeyed to Edisto Island, a few miles south of Charleston, to tell the hardworking people of the Port Royal experiment that the president had turned his back on them. The freed slaves gathered under the live oaks and Spanish moss in a churchyard. Howard, in full uniform, explained Johnson's orders. "[A]s the meaning struck them," wrote one white witness, "that they must give up their little homestead gardens, and work again for others, there was a general murmur of dissatisfaction." Howard begged the people to stay, and asked them to allow him to work out a compromise with the planters. Reluctantly they agreed. "In the noise and confusion no progress was had," Howard wrote later, "till a sweet-voiced negro woman began the hymn 'Nobody knows the trouble I feel—Nobody knows but Jesus,' which, joined in by all, had a quieting effect on the audience." Howard did not mention it, but some witnesses recall that even he, a veteran warrior, broke into tears as the song went up.

The Port Royal experiment was over, abandoned not in failure but in success. Further to the south, the Freedmen's Bureau evicted Tunis Campbell's model black republic on the Georgia Sea Islands. Bureau officials returned the land to the white planters and spread false rumors that Campbell had been caught in corrupt dealings. All over the South, the dream of black land ownership and self-sufficiency was ending.

Blocked from land ownership and facing a future of peonage on the plantations, many of the people of black America began to think that life would be better in the cities and towns of the South. As Leon Litwack writes:

> Between 1860 and 1870, census statistics confirmed what the white South had already strongly suspected—a striking increase in the black urban population. In Mississippi, for example, the black population of Vicksburg, to which so many slaves had fled during the war, tripled while that of Natchez more than doubled; the four largest cities in Alabama—Mobile, Montgomery, Selma, and Huntsville—showed an increase of more than 57 percent in black residents; three of Virginia's principal cities—Richmond, Norfolk, and Lynchburg—now had nearly as many blacks as whites, and Petersburg found itself with a black majority; in Charleston, too, blacks moved into a majority position, while the black population of Memphis increased with a rapidity that made it a likely candidate for a race riot.

White Southerners found this a frightening development. In the Black Codes, they sought to bar blacks from cities and towns or restrict the occupations they could follow. Black Americans, however, used the comparative freedom and gregariousness of the cities to launch institutions that remain important today—distinctly black churches, fraternal organizations, newspapers, banks, insurance companies, and schools. Not least important were the mass meetings, freedmen's conventions, and Union Leagues that sprang up across the South almost as soon as the fact of emancipation sank in. Even as whites were, at Johnson's invitation, writing new state constitutions that shut them out, freed slaves were gathering to ask respectfully to be allowed in. At these meetings, former plantation slaves, Northern freeborn blacks, mixed-race people from the cities, and proud Union veterans met to debate the future and establish the foundations of a black political elite.

Some sought immediate suffrage; others thought land more important. But virtually all agreed that the freed slaves must have fair and equal treatment before the law and protection by those charged with enforcing it. "When blacks drew up their postwar demands," Leon Litwack writes, "equal justice almost invariably superseded all others. Even those who argued the primacy of the suffrage or economic grievances conceded that without equal protection under the law, neither the property they accumulated, the wages they were promised, nor the vote they might someday cast would be safe." Under the slave laws, and the new Black Codes, black witnesses could not testify against whites; penalties that were levied by fining whites could subject a black offender to the lash or the chain gang. Blacks were required to carry passes on the roads at night and to yield the sidewalk to any white person. Blacks were forbidden to own weapons or to gather in groups. And they might be whipped, or even killed, by almost any white person dissatisfied with their deportment.

Bands of vigilantes and "regulators" sprang up even before Lee's surrender; as Johnson began to remove the Union forces during 1865 and 1866, these irregular groups grew bolder. In December 1865, a small group of whites in Pulaski, Tennessee, formed a white social club called the Ku Klux Klan. Within months, the Klan (and other secret lodges such as the Knights of the White Camellia) had spread across the South. "Our main and fundamental objective is the MAINTENANCE OF THE SUPREMACY OF THE WHITE RACE in this Republic," new members of the group were told. Robert E. Lee genially declined to be the head of the "Invisible Empire"; Nathan Bedford Forrest, who had proudly dyed the Mississippi with black blood at Fort Pillow, eagerly accepted.

From the very beginning of Reconstruction, individual whites and vigilante groups unleashed a reign of terror against black veterans, Northern schoolteachers, and anyone, white or black, who showed a disposition to accept the humanity of former slaves. Southern sheriffs and courts either ignored the carnage or joined in.

For black America, the war had begun, not ended, at Appomattox. Though the new nation began this period with a vision of power, land, autonomy, and freedom, by 1866 many were just praying to survive. And in Washington, it was becoming clear that the leaders of Congress were not disposed to give them either the vote or land. At most they could hope for a guarantee of equal justice; or, if Andrew Johnson had his way, not even that.

· 7 ·

THE JEWELED WORD

Even now, moderate Republicans were not ready to give up. Surely a way could be found to save Johnson and the party—or at least to make it clear to the voters that the party had been willing to go the extra mile to placate the president. In the wake of the veto of the Freedmen's Bureau bill, hopeful Republicans clutched at the president's suggestion that he favored protection of civil rights. Two theories quickly emerged about how best to do that, and both gave rise to legislation that forms an important part of the story of the Fourteenth Amendment. The diligent Lyman Trumbull wished to push ahead with another bill, the Civil Rights Act, based on the Thirteenth Amendment. But John Bingham and a few others insisted that the Constitution needed another amendment to make sure that Congress had power to force the states to live by the rules of republicanism and to write those rules into the Constitution so that they could not subsequently be repealed. Both approaches came before Congress in the period after Johnson's first veto; both eventually became part of the law. Trumbull's Civil Rights Act was approved by Congress over the president's objection and remains a part of the United States Code today. Bingham's constitutional amendment came forward, was debated, and disappeared—only to reappear in different form as the first section of the Fourteenth Amendment. Scholars over the years have tended to view them as the same, arguing that Section 1 of the Amendment was merely intended to ratify the Civil Rights Act. The reality is quite different. The two provisions had different authors and were inspired by different constitutional theories. Trumbull offered a bill that was modest and conservative in its aspirations; Bingham offered an amendment that was almost breathtaking in its breadth and ambition. Together, they offer a vivid map of the new constitutional geography the second founders designed.

Neither measure was presented as a direct challenge to Johnson. Indeed, the Republicans eagerly propitiated the president. Fessenden rose in Congress the day after Johnson's February 22 outburst to shower the president with deferential praise. "I am not aware that there has been any effort anywhere to get up a political wrangle or engage in a political wrangle with the President," he said. "No man has ever heard me speak of him except in terms of respect, in my place here and elsewhere." But the praise had a sting in its tail; Fessenden was rising to move that the Senate agree to a House concurrent resolution committing both houses not to admit any Southern member "until Congress shall have declared such States entitled to representation." Under the resolution, proposed by the joint committee, neither house would act alone.

Congress needed to act together, Fessenden said, because Johnson ("and I mean to speak of the President with respect, because I entertain for him respect") had suggested in his veto message that "Congress has no right to pass any bill affecting the interests of the late confederate states while they are not represented in Congress." That language questioned the legitimacy of anything the Thirty-ninth Congress might do, Fessenden said. "I decline to give my assent to any such proposition."

The Senate promptly passed the bill; the houses of Congress had closed ranks against a direct challenge to their power. Fessenden began to consider his practical options. His private view of Johnson was not as respectful as his public one. On February 25, he wrote to his beloved Cousin Lizzy that "[t]he long agony is over. [Johnson] has broken the faith. . . . I see nothing ahead but a long indecisive struggle for three years, and, in the mean time great domestic convulsions and an entire cessation of the work of reform—perhaps a return to power of the Country's worst enemies—Northern Copperheads."

The Republicans needed a firm two-thirds majority to override a presidential veto. And under Article V, Congress could propose an amendment by two-thirds vote, which would then become valid if ratified by three-quarters of the states; the president had no veto of a proposed amendment. So Republican members began an anguished process of nose-counting in the two houses. By party label alone, they were unassailable. In the House, Republicans numbered 145 to a mere 46 Democrats, while the Senate had 39 Republicans to only 11 Democrats. But the Freedmen's Bureau veto override vote showed that not all the Senate Republicans could be counted on. Fessenden began to look around for some way to improve their numerical position.

As for Trumbull and other moderates, Johnson could still have salvaged a deal with them without yielding his claim to be a guardian of the old Constitution. In his veto message, Johnson had said, "I share with Congress the strongest desire to secure to the freedmen the full enjoyment of their freedom and property, and their entire independence and equality in making contracts for their labor." He objected to bureau courts, but he also said that "the freedman should be protected, but he should be protected by the civil authorities, especially by the exercise of all the constitutional powers of the courts of the United States and of the States." As it happened, Trumbull had another bill pending to empower the courts to do exactly that. Perhaps Johnson would sign that, and peace could be restored.

The story of the Civil Rights Bill forms an important part of the background of the Fourteenth Amendment. But while the bill was still pending, John Bingham also brought forward his proposed constitutional amendment. Even without Trumbull's bill, Bingham believed, American citizens were not at the mercy of states for their civil and natural rights; they were guaranteed basic rights by Article IV,

Section 2 of the federal Constitution, which provides that "[t]he Citizens of each State shall be entitled to all Privileges and Immunities of Citizens in the several States." Most constitutional thinkers had read this provision to require only that a state treat visitors from other states no worse than it treated its own citizens; they had given it the nickname "the Comity Clause," meaning that it ensured only equal treatment. But Bingham, like other antislavery constitutional thinkers, read it as much more. To Bingham, it meant that "citizens of each State, all the citizens of each State, being citizens of the United States, shall be entitled to 'all privileges and immunities of citizens in the several States.'"

What were those "privileges and immunities"? Bingham had a ready answer; they were the rights guaranteed by the federal Bill of Rights, which applied as much against the states as they did against the federal government. "Whenever the Constitution guarantees to its citizens a right, either natural or conventional, such guarantee is in itself a limitation upon the States." Foremost among these was the Due Process Clause of the Fifth Amendment, which provides that no "person" may be deprived of "life, liberty or property, without due process of law." The basic rights of speech, assembly, petition, the guarantee of due process, the protections against arbitrary arrest and unfair trial—these were the rights of every American, which states could not legally abridge.

Bingham dismissed the idea that states had the "right" to use their power in ways forbidden by the Constitution. The Constitution was supreme, he had explained in 1861: "States have no inherent rights; they have only derivative or delegated rights."

And just as state governments owed their existence to the Constitution, Bingham argued, all Americans—black or white—were citizens of the United States, and that citizenship automatically made them citizens of any state where they chose to live, whether the state government liked it or not. In 1859, when the Oregon Territory sought statehood under a constitution that barred "free negroes or mulattoes" from even *entering* the state, Bingham lashed out at the impertinence of a prospective state discriminating against any American. "I maintain that the persons thus excluded from the state by this section of the Oregon constitution, are citizens by birth of the several states, and as such are entitled to all the privileges and immunities of citizens of the United states, amongst which are the rights of life and liberty and property, and their due protection in the enjoyment thereof by law."

One other constant appears in Bingham's thought—his opposition to the "slavocracy," the "slave interest," the Slave Power that, as he and many others believed, was conspiring against the Constitution and the freedom of Northern states. Having lashed the slavocracy throughout the antebellum years, he saw no reason to reexamine his view now, particularly because he had helped punish what he regarded as evidence of its worst crime—the murder of Abraham Lincoln.

In 1862, amid a general reaction against the war and the Emancipation Proclamation, Bingham had lost his seat in Congress. Lincoln named him judge advocate general of the army's Department of the Susquehannah. He protested to Lincoln that he knew no military law; the president gravely replied, "[Y]ou will learn as soon as anybody I know of." In the weeks after Lincoln's murder, Bingham's old friend, Secretary of War Edwin Stanton, appointed him judge advocate of the special military commission that would try the ill-assorted group accused of plotting the assassination along with John Wilkes Booth.

Lincoln's is the only presidential assassination in American history that was clearly the result of a conspiracy. One of Booth's confederates came to the home of Secretary of State William H. Seward and stabbed him repeatedly; another had been assigned to murder General Grant, who thwarted the plot by leaving town; a third, by subsequent accounts, stalked Andrew Johnson at the Kirkwood House hotel, but lost his nerve and fled without attempting to kill him; another was detailed to kill Secretary of War Stanton. Had all five succeeded, the United States government would have been paralyzed and decapitated. Booth had been in contact with the Confederate Secret Service before the assassination (though the subject under discussion was supposedly only kidnapping, not killing, the president). And news reports at the time said that Confederate president Jefferson Davis, when told about the assassination, had said only, "If it were to be done it were better it were well done." Bingham had only a short time to immerse himself in the evidence—Lincoln was shot on April 14, 1865; Booth was killed twelve days later; and the trial of the surviving conspirators opened before a military commission on May 9. But the evidence convinced Bingham that the assassination had been a Confederate intelligence operation. "My own conviction," he told the military court, "is that Jefferson Davis is as clearly guilty of this conspiracy as is John Wilkes Booth."

"My intellect detected a merciless conspiracy of Jefferson Davis, Jacob Thompson (a Confederate agent in Canada) and associates to murder President Lincoln, Vice-President Johnson, Secretary Seward and General Grant in order to destroy the glorious Union and to perpetuate the devilish slavocracy," Bingham told an Ohio friend not long after the trial. Because the assassination was an act of war, Bingham told the court, President Johnson had every right under the War Power to require trial in front of a military commission rather than a civilian federal court. Bingham's final speech to the court defended both its military jurisdiction and the evidence of a conspiracy, and was important in gaining the guilty verdict against all eight defendants. Four were sentenced to hang, including Mrs. Mary Surratt, who kept a boardinghouse that Booth had used as a message center. (The commissioners sent President Johnson a recommendation for clemency to Mrs. Surratt, which Bingham signed, but the president either ignored the document or did not see it, and Mrs. Surratt was hanged with the rest.)

To the end of his life, Bingham would from time to time issue dark hints that he knew more about the Lincoln plot than he could tell because the true dimensions of the conspiracy would wreak havoc on the nation. His doctor reported years later that, on his deathbed, Bingham had said, "The truth must remain sealed."

Bingham was thus a formidable opponent to anyone who would seek to revive or protect the Slave Power. He believed that the Constitution took precedence over any "right" of the states; that all Americans, regardless of color, were American citizens and entitled to protection by federal law; and that the proper role for states within the Union was as models of republican self-rule, free discussion, and enlightenment. Bingham did, however, admit one flaw in the original Constitution. Though its Supremacy Clause bound the states to observe the Bill of Rights, the document did not give Congress power to enforce that obligation.

The problem was not that the guarantees did not *apply*, but the Framers had neglected to put in language giving Congress the *power* to enforce the amendments. Bingham had long thought that an amendment giving Congress that power would be a fatal blow to the slavocracy. Now, in the aftermath of Johnson's veto, he was ready to strike it.

He had come to Washington in December with his proposed amendment in mind, and he first introduced it on December 6; it was referred to the Judiciary Committee. When Speaker Schuyler Colfax appointed him to the joint committee, he proposed it to the committee less than a week after its first meeting. The committee's journal shows that Bingham brought it up over and over again during January; on February 10, as the Freedmen's Bureau debate neared its end, the committee voted to send it to the full Congress.

Debate, however, did not open until February 26, after Johnson's outburst against the joint committee. As edited by the committee, the proposed amendment read: "The Congress shall have power to make all laws which shall be necessary and proper to secure to the citizens of each State all privileges and immunities of citizens in the several states, and to all persons in the several states equal protection in the rights of life, liberty, and property." The ensuing debate offers a brief but fascinating glimpse into the meaning of the words Bingham used—words that he noted were "the very words of the Constitution of the United States as it came to us from the illustrious framers." Later historians have puzzled over the meaning that Bingham gave to the terms *privileges and immunities*, *equal protection*, and *due process*. During the long years of conservative backlash against the Civil War and the very idea of equal rights, many pro-Southern historians sim-

ply insisted that Bingham was an addlepate who did not even understand the words he used. Thus, they reasoned, when he said "bill of
rights" he did not mean *the* Bill of Rights but some *other* bill of rights,
made up of snips and snaps of the original Constitution. But the pure
contemporary record does not seem very complex—Bingham was
talking, as he said on February 28, about "a proposition to arm the
Congress of the United States, by the consent of the people of the
United States, with the power to enforce the bill of rights as it stands
in the Constitution today."

Those rights most particularly included free speech. Before the
war, Representative Hiram Price noted, "if a citizen of a free State
visiting a slave State expressed his opinion in reference to slavery he
was treated without much ceremony to a coat of tar and feathers."
Congressional legislation to protect free speech would prevent the
slave system from reasserting itself.

The opponents of the amendment had two interrelated arguments. The amendment would abridge "state's rights," they argued—
and in case anyone missed the point, it would particularly abridge a
state's right to keep black Americans from voting and even marrying
white women. The irrepressible Andrew Rogers rose to reply to
Bingham on the opening day of debate, and his attack brought such
lusty cheers from the galleries that Elihu Washburne of Illinois finally
asked the Speaker to call him to order: "He is addressing the galleries
and not the speaker." Rogers had excoriated the amendment as "but
another attempt to consolidate the power of the States in the Federal
Government. It is another step to an imperial despotism." And what
would happen if despotism triumphed? "This amendment would
make all citizens eligible [to be elected president], negroes as well
as whites," he warned, and would "run the pure white blood of the
Anglo-Saxon people of the country into the black blood of the negro
or the copper blood of the Indian."

But it was not only Copperhead Democrats who opposed Bingham's
dream, and it was not only opponents of the amendment who showed
a little anxiety about the prospect of too much racial or sexual equality.

William Higby of California rose to support the amendment because it would "give vitality and life to portions of the Constitution that probably were intended from the beginning to have life and vitality, but which have received such a construction that they have been entirely ignored." Democrat William Niblack of Indiana asked whether the amendment would "have any effect on the condition of the Chinamen in California." Higby was quick to say no. "The Chinese are nothing but a pagan race," he explained. "You cannot make good citizens of them." Since they weren't allowed to become citizens, the amendment would not give them protection—and anyway, "they do not propagate in our country."

But what really sank the amendment was a suggestion that it did not go far enough. Giles Hotchkiss of New York, a Republican, warned that the amendment, by focusing exclusively on Congress, left the meaning of constitutional rights "to the caprice of Congress." Hotchkiss drew laughter from the galleries when he said, "I think the gentleman from Ohio is not sufficiently radical in his views upon this subject. I think he is a conservative." Hotchkiss warned, "Should the power of this Government, as the gentleman from Ohio fears, pass into the hands of the rebels, I do not want rebel laws to govern and be uniform throughout this Union."

Surrounded by old-style Copperheads and state's rights men on the right, and those even more radical than he on the left, Bingham was stymied for the moment. On February 28, the House voted 110 to 37 to postpone further consideration of his amendment until April 2. Bingham's amendment disappeared forever; but its ghost would reappear in the language of the Fourteenth Amendment, which would guarantee equal protection and due process—and, in its final section, give to Congress the power Bingham had sought for it.

But the Bingham amendment debate was, at the time, merely a sideshow to the main event in Congress in February and March—the ongoing debate on Trumbull's civil rights bill. The bill's provisions, and the arguments advanced for it, show us what some of the framers of the Fourteenth Amendment meant by civil rights. But the debate on the civil rights bill was actually a debate about the meaning of the

Thirteenth Amendment. The sponsors of the bill believed that Congress already had the power to outlaw discrimination in civil rights. No one during the Bingham amendment debate suggested that his amendment needed to be passed to justify the civil rights bill. The Fourteenth Amendment, passed later, was designed to push Congress's power over the states even further.

Trumbull had pushed the civil rights bill through the Senate on February 2. The bill required that every "inhabitant" of the United States—regardless of race or previous condition of slavery—must be afforded "the same right to make and enforce contracts, to sue, be parties and give evidence, to inherit, purchase, lease, sell, hold and convey real and personal property, and to full and equal benefit of all laws and proceedings for the security of person and property," and also not be subject to any discrimination in legal "punishments, pains, and penalties," despite any state law to the contrary. State officials who discriminated in awarding these rights would be guilty of a federal crime, punishable by up to a year in prison. Lawsuits and criminal proceedings in state courts against federal officials who protected blacks (an increasingly favored tactic of the new Johnson government) would be removed to federal court. Federal courts could appoint commissioners to arrest offenders—and federal law enforcement officials could demand help from any citizen, as a posse comitatus, or from the military, to ensure that local officials did not resist arrest. Finally, in case of massive defiance, the president could use the "land and naval forces of the United States . . . to prevent the violation and enforce the due execution of this act."

The posse comitatus provisions were copied verbatim from the Fugitive Slave Act of 1850, hated by all who opposed slavery. The Supreme Court had upheld the posse comitatus rule for fugitive slaves. Trumbull must have felt that he stood on solid constitutional ground in using a similar provision to further the enforcement clause of the Thirteenth Amendment. As written, the bill went far toward providing enforcement for a federal rule of civil (though not political) equality. But almost immediately, Trumbull himself pushed it further, moving an amendment to clear up the question of citizenship;

now the bill began: "all persons of African descent born in the United States are hereby declared to be citizens of the United States."

Trumbull once again explained that the bill was designed to ensure that the Thirteenth Amendment's aims were fulfilled. "It is difficult, perhaps, to define accurately what slavery is and what liberty is," he said. But "any statute which is not equal to all, and which deprives any citizen of civil rights which are secured to other citizens, is an unjust encroachment on his liberty; and is, in fact, a badge of servitude which, by the Constitution, is prohibited."

The opposition made several arguments. The citizenship provision was unconstitutional, they contended, and would grant citizenship, not only to freed slaves, but to Indians living off their reservations, to Chinese born in the United States, and even to gypsies. Trumbull agreed that it would, opening a chorus of cries that the bill would cede California to China and make America a mongrel nation. But the greatest animus was reserved for freed slaves, the chief beneficiaries of the bill. Willard Saulsbury of Delaware, who had earlier rejoiced that his state was the last to abolish slavery, sarcastically complained that he had heard all he wanted to hear about the problems of black people. "I think the time for shedding tears over the poor slave has well nigh passed in this country," he said. Under this bill, Delaware would be required to allow blacks to testify in court, to buy and sell real estate—and even to own guns and ammunition! "Sir," he admonished Trumbull, "stop, stop: the mangled, bleeding body of the Constitution of your country lies in your path; you are treading upon its bleeding body when you pass these laws."

But Saulsbury was moderate compared to Garrett Davis of Kentucky, who could be as verbose in defense of his conservative values as Sumner ever was in his Radical fervor. Davis had nearly been expelled from the Senate for the sarcasm with which he opposed the Thirteenth Amendment. One of his serious objections to the Thirteenth Amendment had been the possibility that it might make blacks into citizens; now his nightmare was unfolding. As Davis droned on about the danger that black citizenship would lead to black voting and black supremacy, one of the Senate's best debaters,

Daniel Clark of New Hampshire, attempted to pin him down: "Is a woman a citizen under our Constitution?" he asked. "Not to vote," Davis replied.

"I did not ask about voting," Clark answered. "I want to know if she is a citizen."

Davis refused to answer, saying only that a black man was not a citizen "because he is no part of the governing power."

"The Senator only begs the question," said Clark, clearly aware of the galleries. "It only comes back to this, that a nigger is a nigger."

Lot Morrill of Maine offered a more substantive rebuttal: "The Senator from Kentucky tells us that the proposition is revolutionary, and he thinks that is an objection. I freely concede that it is revolutionary. I admit that this species of legislation is absolutely revolutionary. But are we not in the midst of revolution? Is the Senator from Kentucky utterly oblivious to the grand results of four years of war? Are we not in the midst of a civil and political revolution which has changed the fundamental principles of our Government in some respects?"

Apparently a majority of his colleagues agreed because the bill passed the Senate on February 2, by a vote of 33 to 5. But then it disappeared into the committee process, and did not reach the House floor until March 1, after the veto of the Freedmen's Bureau bill and Johnson's Washington's Birthday outburst. Even then, Trumbull and other proponents of the bill clung to the hope that, if it could be got through the House, Johnson would sign it. In hindsight, that belief looks naive, but they had read his Freedmen's Bureau veto message and believed that this bill was more conservative than that one. To begin with, the bill had no applicability to voting for former slaves. Beyond that, this bill did not set up a new bureaucracy or a parallel enforcement system, as the Freedmen's Bureau bill had. "It is a court bill," Trumbull had said to the Senate, perhaps hoping the White House was listening as well. "It is to be executed through the courts, and in no other way."

Beyond that, Trumbull had taken pains to keep Johnson apprised of the progress of the bill. They met twice during this period, and

Trumbull gave the president a summary of the bill in his own hand-writing. Johnson apparently gave little hint that he opposed it. Signing it would be a conciliatory move toward the conservative wing of the party and would furnish Johnson with a platform from which he could oppose black voting without being accused of hostility toward the freed slaves.

But Trumbull, Fessenden, and the others had not fully reckoned with the absolute cast of Johnson's mind. "The Administration must be supported or opposed," Welles noted in his diary around this time. "Congress must be with the Administration or against it." Neither Johnson nor his confidant was disposed toward any compromise, no matter how small.

One reason for the leadership's desire to avoid a split was the fear that they could not overcome another veto. Not many minds would be changed, but a seat might come open. Democratic senator John P. Stockton had been elected by the New Jersey Legislature in 1865 under somewhat irregular circumstances. A group of Republicans from New Jersey protested that the senator-elect had not gotten a majority of the vote in both houses of the state legislature. Instead, the two houses had met in joint session and had voted by a one-vote margin to suspend the requirement of double majorities. Stockton then won the seat on a party-line vote.

The judiciary committee, chaired by Lyman Trumbull himself, had concluded on January 30 that the New Jersey election wasn't illegal. Stockton was serving in the Senate, but by March 1, when House debate began on the civil rights bill, the full body had not yet voted to accept his credentials. A few covetous members of the majority noted that Stockton's seat—one they needed for a veto-proof majority—was just sitting there for the taking.

On March 1, though, the action wasn't in the Senate, but on the other side of the Capitol, where Representative James F. Wilson of Iowa brought the civil rights bill to the House floor. Wilson, a careful lawyer and fervent prohibitionist from staunchly Republican Iowa, gave the House a careful lawyer's brief that stressed the limited, non-political nature of the "privileges" protected by the bill: "Do they mean that in all things civil, social, political, all citizens, without dis-tinction of race or color, shall be equal?" he asked. "By no means can they be so construed. Do they mean that all citizens shall vote in the several States? No, for suffrage is a political right which has been left under the control of the several States, subject to the action of Congress only when it becomes necessary to enforce the guarantee of a republican form of government. Nor do they mean that all citizens shall sit on the juries, or that their children shall attend the same schools."

As for the "immunities," these meant only "equality in the exemp-tions of the law" regardless of race, he explained. "It is not the object of this bill to establish new rights, but to protect and enforce those which already belong to every citizen."

As for authority, Congress had probably always had it, but cer-tainly did now in the wake of the Thirteenth Amendment. "I assert that we possess the power to do those things which Governments are organized to do," he said, "that we may protect a citizen of the United States against a violation of his rights by the law of a single State; that by our laws and our courts we may intervene to maintain the proud character of American citizenship."

The debate that followed was fundamentally different from the one in the Senate. The real quarrel, it quickly became clear, was within the Republican Party. On one side were those who followed Trumbull and Wilson's theory that the Thirteenth Amendment gave Congress power to protect a limited set of nonpolitical "civil rights." On the other were John Bingham and a few others, whose argument was at once more radical and more conservative. Congress did not yet have the power to protect civil rights, they insisted; a constitutional amendment was needed. And once that amendment was passed, Congress would be able to protect a much broader set of rights, whether they were called civil or political; Congress would, in fact, be able to transform the Southern states into genuine republics, real parts of the larger nation.

Bingham pointed out that the amended version of the bill pro-tected only citizens, not all persons in each state. "If this is to be the language of the bill, by enacting it are we not committing the terrible enormity of distinguishing here in the laws in respect to life, liberty, and property between the citizen and stranger within your gates?" he asked. "Sir, that is forbidden by the Constitution of your country."

On Tuesday, March 13, there was a desultory debate—one sardonic Democrat offered an amendment to retitle the bill, "A Bill to Abrogate the Rights and Break Down the Judicial System of the States"—but the bill was quickly passed, 111 to 38. The Senate, the same day, voted to accept the House amendments. Now the only obstacle was Johnson.

The pro-administration *New York Herald* predicted he would sign. The *Herald* approved of the bill as a "practical, just, and beneficial measure," noting that the effect of the bill would be limited: "It does not touch the question of negro suffrage, and it does not provide for the encouragement of laziness among the Southern blacks and white refugees by inviting them to laugh and grow fat upon the public treasury." Both *The Nation* and *Harper's Weekly* took much the same tack.

Inside the White House, however, Johnson was finding the bill a bitter pill to swallow. Compromise was weakness to him, and the intrusion of federal power into the internal life of a state—particularly on behalf of the undeserving freed slaves—went against his antebellum principles. His alter ego, Gideon Welles, told him that signing would destroy the Constitution and blight Johnson's own political future. "The Alien and Sedition Laws were not so objectionable," Welles argued melodramatically.

Johnson's stand was profoundly wrongheaded and politically inept, but it is possible to feel some sympathy for the brave tailor, surrounded suddenly by voices cautioning him that his own entire future was at stake. He liked to compare himself to Christ; on this occasion, he may have felt a bit like Jesus in the wilderness, taken up to a high place by Satan and offered all the kingdoms of the world. The Republicans would take him to their bosom, many of them suggested, if he compromised on the civil rights bill. The majority of his Cabinet urged him to sign. John Sherman was still hoping for compromise, and

Senator Stewart and Representative Rutherford B. Hayes both left meetings with Johnson convinced he had promised to sign.

Or perhaps Satan was a Democrat. Certainly Democrats, North and South, were issuing their own temptations to the accidental president. From New York, Pennsylvania, and Illinois came offers of Democratic support if he jettisoned the Republicans. One correspondent from Texas had attended the state constitutional convention there and assured Johnson that his only opposition came from "what was called Union men." The good news was "there is not a secessionist in the state of Texas who is opposed to you or your policy."

As March wore on, Johnson showed the strain. Oliver Morton, the governor of Indiana, had supported Johnson during the difficult weeks after Lincoln's death. Now he made a special trip to Washington to urge him to sign. Johnson's reaction was almost alarming: "Johnson was laboring under great emotion. Large beads of perspiration stood on his forehead. He was stubborn and seemed to think he was strong enough to build up a new party." On another occasion, the president was closeted with his private secretary, Colonel W. G. Moore. Johnson paced the floor in agitation, then turned and said, "Sir, I am right. I know I am right, and I am damned if I do not adhere to it."

By the last week of March, rumors of an impending veto were general around Washington. And so the wretched John Stockton of New Jersey found himself on the wrong side of history.

The scion of a prominent family—one New Jersey historian likened the Stocktons to the Adamses—Stockton was only thirty-nine. He had supported the war effort, but—in keeping with the New Jersey Democratic Party's firm view—had insisted throughout that the old Calhoun "state sovereignty" theory of the Constitution was the correct one. So while "supporting" the war, he had opposed most of Lincoln's measures to win it—including most particularly the Emancipation Proclamation. Nonetheless, he had a first-rate intellect and was well regarded on both sides of the aisle. But (as Americans relearned in 2000) when only one vote stands between politicians and power, they will get it by any means they can.

The problem the Senate faced was that the Constitution provided only that senators should be "chosen by the legislature." The Constitution also gave Congress the power to "make or alter" the rules for electing senators, but Congress had never done so, leaving each state legislature to make its own rules for election. New Jersey had usually required that the two houses meet together and that the winning candidate had to get a majority of all the members. But in December 1865, the joint session had voted to drop the majority requirement, permitting a candidate to win with only a plurality. One group in the session (now supported by New Jersey Republicans), however, argued that only the two houses, voting separately, could change the rules for the joint session; the other (supported by Stockton and the Democrats) argued that the joint session had the authority to enact its own rules. The question was vital: Stockton had received 40 votes in the joint session, while a group of opponents together got 41. Trumbull's judiciary committee had recommended that Stockton be seated. But now that recommendation came unstuck, and (as so often in politics) what began as simple farce suddenly ascended into high drama.

On March 22, New Hampshire's Clark cataloged the reasons why Stockton's election was not legal: under the constitution and under New Jersey law, a majority was necessary to take any action unless a specific rule provided otherwise. The legislature had not provided such a rule; therefore Stockton had not been elected.

If he did not know it before, Stockton must have known he was in trouble when Pitt Fessenden rose to speak against him. Fessenden was regarded as a constitutional authority on both sides of the aisle, and he proceeded to make the kind of metaphysical argument constitutional lawyers adore and ordinary citizens find opaque: because the Constitution instructed "the legislature" to elect a senator, the *state* legislature when electing senators was actually a *federal* body, and its powers could only be changed by either a state *law* or by a congressional statute. The convention that enacted the new rule was not making a state *law*—that could only be done by the two houses acting individually. So no rule of a state *convention* could alter the majority requirement prescribed by parliamentary procedure.

It was one of those moments—common in politics then as they are today—in which the contending parties talk about everything except the real issue. Not a soul in the chamber doubted that the issue being decided was the one Fessenden put to his son in a letter a few days later: "It is all important now that we should have two-thirds in each branch."

The matter came to a vote on Friday, March 23, at the same moment that, across the Mall, Andrew Johnson was reading his Cabinet the draft of a veto message. On a preliminary vote, the anti-Stockton forces had only 19 votes, while Trumbull had attracted enough Republicans to give Stockton 21 votes. The Republicans quickly found Senator Henry Wilson and got him to the floor, as the roll call began on the question, Should Stockton take his seat? With Wilson voting, the pro-Stockton vote was 21; the nos were only 20.

At this moment, Lot Morrill of Maine, who had not answered the roll call, rose to his feet. "Call my name," Morrill said.

"Mr. Morrill," said the secretary.

"I vote nay." The vote was now tied, meaning the measure would fail and Stockton would lose his seat.

Now Stockton rose in protest. Morrill had agreed with New Jersey's other senator, William Wright, to "make a pair" on this vote, he said. Wright was seventy-two years old and in ill health. Before departing, he had agreed with Morrill that neither would vote. Wright's "aye" would cancel Morrill's "no," and the result would not be affected.

Now Stockton played his last card. "Mr. President," he said, "I ask that *my* name be called."

If what Morrill had done seemed somewhat beyond the rules, to many senators what Stockton was now doing was worse. *Nemo judex in sua causa*—"no one shall be judge in his own case"—was a Latin maxim that every common lawyer knew. When a senator's legitimate claim to his seat was before the body, the member himself was expected not to vote.

Stockton had won by one vote—for the moment. But his action rankled. In the interim, Johnson's veto message confirmed that the Republicans would need that extra vote. On Monday, March 26,

182 · DEMOCRACY REBORN

Charles Sumner rose and moved "that the Journal be amended by striking out the vote of Mr. Stockton." Two days of ferocious wrangling ensued, in which, once again, no one mentioned the necessity of overriding a presidential veto. By the afternoon of March 27, the weary Senate voted to unseat the hapless Stockton, 23 to 20. The extra vote was secure.

That margin of safety came not a moment too soon. Johnson's veto message arrived officially on the floor immediately after the unseating of Stockton. Johnson's stated reasons for rejecting the bill were many, but the most salient was his rejection of the idea that black people—or any nonwhite Americans—were really citizens of the United States. "This provision comprehends the Chinese of the Pacific States, Indians subject to taxation, the people called Gipsies, as well as the entire race designated as blacks, people of color, negroes, mulattoes, and persons of African blood," he complained. "Is it sound policy to make our entire colored population and all other excepted classes citizens of the United States?" Why shouldn't they go through "a certain probation" and be required to prove themselves worthy of citizenship? Moving blacks to the head of the line "proposes a discrimination against large numbers of intelligent, worthy, and patriotic foreigners."

In addition, Johnson complained that the limited list of civil rights guaranteed in the bill attempted to create "a perfect equality of the white and colored races," brushing aside state polices that treated the races differently. If Congress could abrogate these laws, might it not next choose to strike down laws barring interracial marriage? Or to require states to allow blacks to vote, to sit on juries, or to hold office? These questions were state matters, over which the federal government should have no control. The bill would hale state officials into federal court for no crime other than enforcing discriminatory state laws.

Congress, Johnson said, had no power to do any of these things, regardless of the Thirteenth Amendment. "Slavery has been abolished," he said, which meant that the amendment had no more scope to operate. The bill was antiwhite. "The distinction of race and color is, by the bill, made to operate in favor of the colored and against the white race." And finally, it would lead to "an absorption and assumption of power by the general government which, if acquiesced in, must sap and destroy our federative system of limited powers, and break down the barriers which preserve the rights of the states."

His partisans hailed his firmness. James Gordon Bennett's *New York Herald* had previously praised the bill and predicted he would sign it. But now it proclaimed that "the great contest for the constitution has now commenced in earnest. . . . Mr. Johnson has taken his stand upon the great principles which underlie and are the foundation of the republic. There is no middle ground between him and the revolutionists in Congress."

The two houses were ready to take up the president's veto by the first week in April. William Wright of New Jersey, whose illness had probably cost Stockton his seat, managed to make his way back to Washington to vote to uphold the veto. Johnson's ally, James Dixon of Connecticut, was also badly ill, but made clear that he would come to the chamber if his vote was needed. On April 6, after two days of debate, the Senate overrode the veto by a vote of 33 to 15. Of the Republicans present, only James H. Lane of Kansas voted with the president; for Lane, it would turn out to be a fatal vote. Three days later, the House overrode as well. The vote was 141 to 22.

In the seventy-seven years since the ratification of the Constitution, no Congress had ever before overridden a presidential veto on an important measure. A line had been crossed; perhaps sensing it, the House gallery broke into applause, the members themselves joining in, that lasted a long time. Johnson, who had seemed so well positioned three months before, had now lost control of events and would never get it back.

Fessenden, Stevens, Bingham, and the rest were in charge now. No one—not even they—knew what they would do next.

THE UGLIEST AMERICAN

Walt Whitman stayed busy during the winter and spring of 1866. He had his clerk's job at the attorney general's office, and, like civil servants everywhere, yearned for promotion. The job was dull, though there were diverting moments, like the time that Mary Ann Lamar Cobb, wife of former senator (and later Confederate general) Howell Cobb, came in to seek pardons for friends—"some profitable job for her," Whitman suspected. He found Mrs. Cobb amusing— "what most people would call a very pretty little woman," he wrote to his mother with a certain air of detachment. He was preparing yet another edition of that never-finished epic, *Leaves of Grass;* he had also published a new volume, *Drum-Taps*, containing his wartime poems, and he followed the reviews avidly. As always, there were visits to wounded veterans; there were sporting events and the opera, and he was excited about having new shirts made (if a bit shamefaced about the expense).

Though he was barely forty-seven, Whitman was now "the good grey poet." He was beginning to experience dizziness and weakness, which foreshadowed the strokes he would suffer during the 1870s; he was past, or just passing, his poetic prime; but he had not lost his nose for the cultural moment. In the midst of everything else, he found time to spend some afternoons in the House and Senate galleries, where grim-faced men in frock coats fought over America's future. "The contest between Congress and the President is quite exciting," he wrote to one of the innumerable soldiers he had met during his years as unpaid nurse. "Sometimes I feel as if one side had the best of it and then the other."

The contest was exciting, but it was also turning deadly. A certain indecision had set in after the failure of the representation amendment and the success of Trumbull's Civil Rights Bill. By early April, the joint committee had not met for more than a month and a sense of drift was alarming Republicans and their allies. At the end of March, *The Nation* had called on Congress to come forth with its alternative Reconstruction policy. Congress "has now . . . sat for nearly four months" without producing "any well-defined plan." Unless the Congress got to work immediately, the magazine warned, the voters might use the fall elections to "let the President and his friends have their own way." Three weeks later, it said, "The time has arrived at which [Congress] must visibly begin to shape a policy," even if its efforts faced a certain veto, in order to provide a political alternative to Johnson.

Late in March, a private citizen named Robert Dale Owen "became, to borrow the Quaker term, greatly exercised in regard to this matter." He traveled to Washington, sat down to breakfast with his old friend Thaddeus Stevens, and told him in no uncertain terms exactly what should be done. It should have surprised no one that when the cause of reform was in trouble, rescue appeared unbidden in the person of Robert Dale Owen. Nor was it remarkable that even a salty old campaigner like Stevens should listen carefully when Owen spoke. The document Owen presented at that breakfast is the mother document of what became, a few weeks later, the Fourteenth Amendment.

Though he was a former member of the House, Owen in 1866 held no public office; but that didn't matter to him and never had.

Nineteenth-century America was the Utopia of Utopians, where idealists of every stripe followed a million corduroy roads, certain that the New Jerusalem must lie at the end of one of them. And in that yeasty, optimistic Oz, Robert Dale Owen had been for nearly half a century the wonderful wizard himself. Whether the cause was socialism, communal living, free thought, divorce, feminism, women's rights, birth control, public education, abolition of hanging and debtors' prison, labor reform, temperance, spiritualism, plank roads—even, belatedly, the abolition of slavery—Owen was for some time during the antebellum years one of the movements' strongest voices.

His was invariably a powerful voice; one of the most prolific and skilled polemical journalists of his time, he broke lances with all foes in the pages of his many publications—*The New Harmony Gazette, The Free Enquirer, The New York Daily Sentinel*—in an array of magazine articles, speeches, and pamphlets, and in the astonishing variety of books he wrote on a dizzying array of subjects—*Moral Physiology; or a Brief and Plain Treatise on the Population Question* (birth control—the first American volume on the subject); *Pocahontas: A Historical Drama in Five Acts; Hints on Public Architecture; A Brief Practical Treatise on the Construction and Management of Plank Roads; Biography of Joseph Lane, "Not Inappropriately Styled by His Brother Officers and Soldiers, the Marion of the War"; Footfalls on the Boundary of Another World* (spiritualism); and finally, in 1864, *The Wrong of Slavery, the Right of Emancipation, and the Future of the African Race in the United States.*

Yes, he was truly the voice of change, of optimism, of Utopia— but, though he had adorned many a stage at athenaeum and lecture hall, no reformer would have wanted Robert Dale Owen as the *face* of reform. Owen's own doting wife, Mary Jane Robinson Owen, to whom he remained uxoriously faithful for nearly forty years, once told her sister that Owen was the ugliest man in the world. His face centered around an oversized nose and thick lips. All his features— the sandy hair, the blue eyes as well—seemed oddly mismatched atop his short body. A photo of him today bears an unfortunate resemblance to a bad police artist's sketch of an unknown suspect: illassorted, unfinished, and improbable. Luckily for Owen, though,

Mary Jane first saw him on the lecture platform, where his eloquence, not his face, set audiences afire; and when she told her sister about his ill looks, she quickly added that if she couldn't marry this homely little Scot, she would marry no one at all. The two had reformed marriage before entering it (on the morning of the ceremony, Owen signed a formal document denouncing the "unjust rights" of husbands over wives, stating, "I consider myself, and earnestly desire to be considered by others, as utterly divested" of them). They were improbably happy ever after.

A capsule summary of Owen's career makes him sound like a Dickensian figure, a kind of Mrs. Jellyby in trousers flitting from cause to cause in a feckless rapture of ignorant goodwill. Biographers notoriously fall in love with their subjects. But even Owen's sole biographer, the historian Richard William Leopold, was chaste in his claims for Owen's significance as an original thinker. "Possessed of a mind more facile than consistent, more receptive than original," Leopold wrote in 1940, "Owen frequently changed his opinions, even on such fundamental issues as capitalism, religion, educational methods, and the rights of the Negro." But history can be changed by the facile as easily as the profound. And Owen combined the vision of a Utopian with the hard-nosed political skills of a heartland ward heeler. He became a power in Indiana politics, and his legacy endures today in that state's fabled university system. Beyond that, no matter what the subject, Owen's real ideology remained the same, and was always close to the heart of America's own view of itself and of the world. He believed in progress; he believed that reason and science had brought nineteenth-century humanity to a place where its own efforts could realize paradise here on earth, without needless suffering or divine intervention. Most of all, Owen believed in the future of mankind shimmering just over the horizon, as knowledge, medicine, and science brought light and new hope to mankind. "I may seem an enthusiast," he said rather mildly in his birth control tract, *Moral Physiology,* "and so let me seem then—when I express my conviction, that there is not a greater physical disparity between the dullest, shaggiest race of dwarf horses, and the fiery-spirited and silken-haired Arabian, than between man degenerate as he is, and man perfected as he might be." And with each setback—each panacea that failed, each Utopia that melted in the Midwestern rain—he reminded his comrades that success was inevitable: "Men may be sacrificed," he wrote in 1832, but "the human race will still survive, will still improve; each coming day richer in knowledge than its predecessor, and every succeeding generation wiser and happier than the last."

The worst insult Owen's enemies could think of was to compare him to the "infidel" Tom Paine, the pamphleteer of the American Revolution ("These are the times that try men's souls. . . ."), who questioned revelation and clerical authority in his 1794 book, *The Age of Reason*. Owen wore the comparison proudly. Like Paine, Owen was an immigrant to the United States from Britain; arriving in the New World for the first time in 1848, the twenty-three-year-old Owen was so taken with the impudent vigor of the New York waterfront that he went straight from the wharf to a notary's office to sign the required declaration of intent to become a U.S. citizen. It was a marriage as favorable in its way as his later union with Mary Jane.

If John Bingham represents a link to the lost revolutionary world of Christian republicanism, Robert Dale Owen was a direct connection to another facet of the Founders' world—the bluff good sense of the Scottish Enlightenment, the optimistic rationality of the eighteenth-century Deists. In political terms, Owen was the heir of Hume and the other liberal skeptics; in religion, he kept alive what historian Daniel J. Boorstin called "the lost world of Thomas Jefferson." And he also represented that strand of Jeffersonianism that had settled in the Democratic Party during the age of Jackson and had not been tempted by the new gods of Republicanism. That intellectual lineage was direct: Owen's closest friend in the new country, and his tutor in American politics, was Nicholas P. Trist, the Virginia diplomat who had grown up literally at Jefferson's knee, a boarder at Monticello, and who completed his education by marrying the great man's granddaughter.

The connection to Scotland was even clearer: Owen was born in

Glasgow in 1801, the son of Robert Owen, hardheaded Scottish manufacturing tycoon and woolly-minded global socialist messiah. The elder Owen was as ambitious in reform as he had been in business, and was given to dashing off articles with titles like "A Few of the Innumerable Reasons for an Immediate Entire Change of the Existing System of Society in the United States, in Europe, and Over the World." He was listened to respectfully not only in Parliament but in the U.S. Capitol, where he addressed a capacity audience in the House of Representatives chamber in 1825.

As a true reformer should, Robert Owen made sure that his children received unconventional educations in the spirit of Rousseau's *Emile*. Robert was sent to Switzerland to study at Hofwyl, where educational reformer Emanuel von Fellenberg broke with the rote memorization of standard Continental education and set his students to work at practical projects, manual labor, and rhythmic physical movements. Then Robert Owen gave Robert Dale—as he did with his other three sons—$50,000, and sent him forth to do well by doing good.

That quest took Robert Dale to America, where his father had purchased a defunct religious commune, Harmony, built on the banks of the Wabash in what was then the frontier state of Indiana. The new plan was to build a model community based on socialism and democracy rather than on religion. Anyone would be welcome at New Harmony—and the turnout was enthusiastic and motley, entomologists, geologists, and painters blending with farmers, mechanics, and fortune-hunting drifters. The resulting town almost immediately began splitting into subtowns and rebel colonies with names like Macluria and Feiba-Peveli, which would secede and reenter New Harmony, then recombine and subdivide until the community sputtered into complete incoherence in 1827, and dissidents called the sheriff to arrest the elder Owen—not only the town's benefactor but nominally its owner—for unpaid debts.

But one part of the Indiana experiment was a rousing and lasting success. In 1826, Robert Dale Owen temporarily assumed the editorship of the *New Harmony Gazette*, then little more than a newsletter for the quarreling settlement. The resulting love affair with journalism lasted the rest of his life. He made the *Gazette* a nationally known voice for newfangled reforms—and a potent power base for himself in old-style Indiana politics.

As editor, Owen could no longer propagandize for Owenite socialism (it didn't work even with his father's money behind it). But other causes soon appeared. In his first months at the helm, Leopard notes, the *Gazette* tackled accepted fashions in "English grammar, medicine, and female costume" and openly espoused free thought and divorce.

All that was just throat-clearing for the aria of radicalism Owen would sing over the next decade or so. Just as the original New Harmony dream was dissolving, Robert Dale Owen met Frances Wright. Fanny Wright, as she was suggestively known, was then the most intoxicating and frightening feminist in America, one so radical and unorthodox that the American women's movement could not explicitly acknowledge its debt to her until 1889, when Elizabeth Cady Stanton and Susan B. Anthony daringly used her portrait as the frontispiece of volume 1 of their monumental *History of Woman Suffrage*.

The problem was not just that Wright was antislavery, or critical of private property, or a freethinker on theological matters. These heresies were bad but not quite bad enough to mark her as "The Great Red Harlot of Infidelity."

No, the truth was worse. Fanny Wright was—well—sexy.

The trouble was not merely in her personal charms, though these were real. Fanny (like Owen) was a wealthy Scot, a towering five feet ten inches tall. She was connected by birth to Scottish commonsense philosophy and by affinity to the Founding generation. Born in 1795 in Dundee, she had been orphaned at three and had inherited a huge fortune at the age of eight. She met and favorably impressed both James Madison and Thomas Jefferson, who devoted a full seven pages in his commonplace books to quotations from her precocious travel memoir, *Views of Society and Manners in America*. As a young woman of twenty-six, she seems to have besotted the aging Marquis de Lafayette, then sixty-five. Biographers debate whether she and

Lafayette were lovers. What is certain is that the friendship carried a strong erotic charge for both parties, and French society and the marquis's family were scandalized by the intimacy. Tiring of the gossip, Wright in 1824 demanded that her "paternal friend" put an end to it by either marrying her or adopting her (and her sister Camilla). The old lion would do neither. The rumors about Lafayette—scandalous, aristocratic, and revolutionary at once—followed Fanny for the rest of her life.

Beyond the scandalous past, there was her insistence on appearing as a speaker in front of mixed-sex audiences, unheard of in the manly age of Andrew Jackson. There was her advocacy of birth control, though the idea of divorcing sex from reproduction seemed to most Americans of the time, male or female, a dangerous opening to debauchery and vice. And finally there was her insistence that sex— licit sex, sex between man and woman rather than between customer and prostitute—ought to bring pleasure, and to both partners. Only "false opinion and vicious institutions" had "perverted the best source of human happiness—the intercourse of the sexes—into the deepest sources of human misery," she wrote in 1828. Society sacrificed the health of well-bred women by requiring "the unnatural repression of feelings and desires inherent in their very organization and necessary alike to their moral and physical well-being."

This was bold stuff indeed. It was an age in which passion was seen as degrading and literally dangerous to the health of both sexes. What most feminists wanted was admission to the spheres of reason and power.

Robert Dale Owen and Fanny Wright met while both were still single; they were apparently never lovers (indeed, the homely Owen got a letter from Mary Wollstonecraft Shelley urging him to be kind to "our Fanny," on the grounds that it would do him good to show "constant attention to a woman, with whom you are not in love, yet for whom you have affection and kindness"). Owen was facing the end of New Harmony as a utopia (though the village itself remained, and would be his political power base for years to come). Wright was at the end of a project as subversive and exciting as any of her other causes: a communal living experiment designed to show the South how to free and deport its slave population in one process, without financial loss or social upheaval.

The Nashoba experiment began near Memphis in 1825, with eight slaves Wright had purchased. They were to work side by side with whites for five years, generating income that would pay off the cost of their purchase; then they would be freed and resettled in Haiti. Alas, by the time Wright met Robert Dale Owen in 1827, the community was in ruins. The white idealists were all but broken by the physical labor demanded by Southern agriculture. And disturbing rumors had surfaced that some of the community's members believed in equality in all things, including free love between the sexes and the races.

Fanny Wright had formed an instant bond with Robert Dale, who was five years younger. She persuaded him to escort her to Europe to recover her strength; and when they returned to the United States in 1828, they began one of the most dizzyingly creative partnerships in the history of American radicalism. She bought a half interest in the *Gazette*, and the two collaborators began a three-year assault on organized religion that galvanized the free-thought community and made them both infamous.

That year Wright took the first of her scandalous lecture tours, while Owen published articles in the *Gazette* that attacked Sabbath observance, denied the authority of scripture, and opposed Bible reading and religious influence in education. By the next year, the two took their movement to New York and established *The Free Enquirer*, a skeptical weekly so scandalous that the Commonwealth of Massachusetts was able to convict a Boston editor of blasphemy for merely reprinting the *Enquirer*'s copy. On the off chance that there was some major group he had not scandalized, Owen also chose at this point to publish *Moral Physiology*, the first American book to discuss methods of birth control. (Owen favored "complete withdrawal, on the part of the man, immediately previous to emission," which he thought to be *"in all cases, effectual."* It would have the added benefit, he reported, of making American men and women more relaxed and comfortable with each other and with sex, not unlike "the cultivated classes" of France and Italy.)

As partners in heresy, Wright and Owen achieved so much that it is startling to realize that their active partnership lasted only about three years. Wright returned to Europe in 1830, and the next year she married a Parisian, a physician whose name seems to have been Guillaume (or William) Sylvan Casimir Phiquepal D'Arusmont.

Wright's marriage marks the turning point of Owen's career. They would never again share the kind of incandescent partnership that had briefly lit up the American sky, and by 1836 a permanent breach between them had opened, caused apparently by understandable friction between D'Arusmont and Owen. It was at this point that Owen and Mary Jane fell in love at first thought. They were married on April 12, 1832. For the next three decades, the labor reformer and sexual radical would be a New Harmony civic booster and hardworking local Democratic politician. Within three years he was a member of the Indiana state legislature, and in 1843 he became a Democratic member of the U.S. House of Representatives.

As a politician, Owen was a complex figure. He had a skill and flair for the rough-and-tumble of party caucuses and stump debates. He never forsook the idea of reform—public education and women's rights remained important parts of his legislative agenda. He also supported westward expansion, plumped lustily for war with Mexico, and opposed efforts to prohibit slavery in the territory seized during that conflict. All these were orthodox Jacksonianism, of course; but an honest observer cannot overlook the fact that Owen's constituents were, in the main, antiblack and pro-slavery, and Owen's stands were highly politic (as was his support, a few years later, for a clause of the new state constitution that banned free persons of African descent from settling in the state). And they kept him in good standing with the national Democracy as well—enough that President James K. Polk in 1853 rewarded him for his service with the coveted post of American chargé d'affaires to the Kingdom of the Two Sicilies, which required him to live in baronial splendor in Naples and entertain the nobility in the American mission, the opulent Palazzo Valli.

It was in Naples that Owen became interested in spiritualism. He investigated the phenomenon carefully, attending more than a hundred séances in an attempt to detect fraud. By 1859, he had become convinced that the phenomena were real. What seems like credulity to us was actually much more plausible in the 1850s. Electricity was a revolutionary technology, though no one fully understood it. If electrical impulses could travel thousands of miles over small wires, who could say for sure that the brain itself was not simply another electrical phenomenon, one that might survive death itself? Spiritualism was not a throwback to superstition; it was a modernist theory that sought to supplant religion and the mystical idea of a soul. Historian R. Laurence Moore puts the phenomenon in context by noting that "[t]he professional medium appeared in America at about the moment Thoreau heard a locomotive whistle penetrate the woods around Walden Pond." On January 1, 1860, Owen published the most exhaustive study of the new American creed, *Footfalls on the Boundary of Another World*.

The new book might have marked a third phase of Owen's career, as a traveling evangelist for the new rational religion of the spirit world. It might even have been the final chapter, but history had other ideas. Owen was now fifty-nine years old, with not one but several careers behind him. But in a sense, his real career was about to begin.

As a politician, Owen had closed his eyes to the humanity of the slave and sought to propitiate the Slave Power with concessions and flattery. During the "secession winter" of 1861, Owen publicly begged for "compromise" between the sections—meaning new guarantees to the South. But "compromise" failed, and in April 1861 the Confederate artillery opened fire on Fort Sumter in Charleston Harbor, bringing on civil war. In the crisis of the Union, most Midwestern Democrats retreated into sullen semiopposition. These anti-Republican Northerners became, in time, the Peace Democrats and Copperheads who were always ready to declare the Union war effort a failure and plump for policies that would in effect concede independence to the South.

Not Robert Dale Owen. Owen rallied to the flag in the wake of Fort Sumter and never wavered in his support for the war, for Lincoln, and for emancipation of the slaves. He became one of the strongest of the minority War Democrat wing of his party, and with the energy of a much younger man he threw himself into promoting the war effort and exploring winning political strategies for war and reconstruction. His real service to his new country began when the balloons went up over Charleston Harbor that April day.

Owen plunged into the practical aspects of war when, at the request of Governor Oliver Morton, he took on the task of outfitting the Indiana militia units being raised in response to Lincoln's call for troops. At the war's outset, he proclaimed that the Union, not slavery, had to be the sole aim of the war. But as he grappled with manpower and logistical problems, Owen quickly concluded that the Rebels could not be beaten as long as they could count on a docile slave population to keep the Southern economy running. By the summer of 1862, he was campaigning for an immediate decree of emancipation.

Having entered the abolitionist camp, Owen did not hang back. He became a Radical, a confidant of men like Sumner and Thaddeus Stevens. At Sumner's urging, Secretary of War Edwin Stanton in early 1863 named Owen one of three members of the American Freedmen's Inquiry Commission, which was intended to plan the transition of the South from a slave society to a free-labor, republican social order.

The Inquiry Commission, like the Freedmen's Bureau to which it gave rise, reeks of anachronism. It was as close as the wartime North came to the kind of far-seeing social engineering of the World War II allies, who, long before the surrender, carefully planned the resurrection of Japan and Germany. Owen and his fellow commissioners sent exhaustive questionnaires to everyone they could think of who had experience with Southern slaves and free blacks (Frederick Douglass got one, and carefully filled it out in his own hand). The commissioners also visited the front, speaking with freed slaves themselves in the contraband camps, the black Union regiments, and the free-labor plantations of the Sea Islands. Their final report, written mostly by

Owen and issued on May 15, 1864, stated that the freed slaves were ready to take their place as equal participants in the economy of free labor. All that would be needed was legislation to give them equal civil and political rights; once those were granted, the freed slaves would quickly become self-supporting members of the American nation.

Democratic members of the Senate sought to suppress the report, but Republicans voted to release it and Owen published a revised version under his own name.

The resulting document is Owen at his best—exhaustive, thorough, radical, and optimistic. Wherever it is practiced, he wrote, slavery injects "a certain element of barbarism" into the society that tolerates it. For this reason, America could not become a "true union" until slavery had ended. And emancipation would be an act of mercy, not only to the slave, but to the slaveholder. Until the latter was divested of his human chattel, "there will be between him and us a lack of the conditions necessary to a true union; there will be no loyal, concurrent sentiment of citizenship."

Once freed, Owen predicted, the slaves would settle in the South, learn agriculture and useful arts, and become in all respects contributing members of society. His vision of their role most definitely included the vote. Many whites believed that the years of slavery and ignorance made Southern blacks unfit to exercise this political right, but from his contact with freed slaves, Owen reached the precise opposite conclusion: "The habit of the slave is, while assenting to whatever his master says, secretly to hold his own opinion, and to act upon it whenever opportunity offers. His sagacity is developed. I do not think the freedman will be found a ready tool for the political demagogue."

Only two things were needed, then, to create a society into which the freed slaves would fit happily, to the advantage of all. A freedmen's bureau should be created to provide temporary aid to the freed slaves. And the Constitution must be amended. To Americans, he wrote, the Constitution "stands in the place occupied, under the monarchical system, by the sovereign in person." To ensure that slavery was dead and that republicanism would live, a brief amendment would do the trick: "Slavery shall not be permitted, and no discrimination shall be made, as to the civil or political rights of persons, because of color."

Owen's report for the commission has been called the "Blueprint for Radical Reconstruction." It was probably the clearest single vision laid out anywhere in the wartime North of how the two regions could come back together as one nation after a century of estrangement and four years of civil war. It unquestionably spurred Congress to create the Freedmen's Bureau, and there was reason to believe that Lincoln, with his infinite capacity for taking advice, was listening to Owen as well as to others as he hesitantly mapped a postwar strategy. (There were rumors that he considered naming Owen the first head of the Freedmen's Bureau, but in the end the appointment went to Oliver Howard, who was a soldier.)

Owen was equally eager to be of service to Andrew Johnson, who was a comrade from his days in Congress and a fellow son of the Jacksonian tradition. As early as June 1865 he was publicly warning Johnson of the political trap that awaited the Union if the Southern states were restored without permitting black suffrage. Owen was one of the first voices to publicly note the paradox caused by the three-fifths clause. In his letter to Johnson (later published in the *New York Tribune*), Owen told Johnson that, if freed slaves were denied the ballot, each Southern white voter would exercise three times the political power of a Northern voter. The Constitution gave Southern whites every incentive to exclude blacks from political rights because so doing would make them the political masters of the new nation. They would, by his calculations, gain an additional ten House seats from the end of slavery; and "if color be deemed cause of exclusion [from the vote], then *all the political power which is withheld from the emancipated slave is gained by the Southern white.*" This would give them "a preponderance of political power, such as no class of men, in a democratic Republic, ever enjoyed since the world began." Southern whites, already corrupted by "a system the most cruel and demoralizing the world ever saw," should not be given "privileges of an oligarchical character." The federal government must step in to prevent this, using its authority to guarantee a "republican form of government." If it did not do so, "an oligarchy, on an extended scale, will grow up in one large section of the country, working grave injustice toward the voters of another section." Johnson's reply is not recorded. By November 1865, Owen had progressed to recommending a constitutional amendment to make voter qualification a federal matter, with no discrimination of color.

Owen watched closely as the Thirty-ninth Congress and the joint committee struggled with the twin problems of a recalcitrant South and an obstinate president. With characteristic modesty, he set off in mid-March for Washington to propose his own solution.

Owen by this time was formally a Republican. He proceeded to the brick house on B Street, near the Capitol, where Thaddeus Stevens lived during congressional sessions. Owen and Stevens had never served in the House at the same time. But Owen had come to know Stevens during his years as a war Democrat. "He was rough in expression, had strong prejudices, and was sometimes harsh in his judgments," Owen wrote later, "but he was genuine to the core, upright and patriotic beyond the reach of sinister motive, inflexible and enthusiastic of purpose in the right; above all he was a stanch friend of the poor and the oppressed." The two men met early on an April morning, in the little house surrounded by flowers tended by Lydia Smith. Owen read Stevens an omnibus amendment he had drafted, intended to settle the outstanding questions of Reconstruction for the time being.

Owen's draft amendment had five sections. The first barred any state (and the federal government) from discriminating in "the civil rights of persons, because of race, color, or previous condition of servitude." The second section granted black Americans the vote—but not for ten years. After July 4, 1876, no state could restrict the "right of suffrage, because of race, color, or previous condition of servitude." The Southern states could maintain an all-white electorate for the next decade if they chose; but if they did, the third section removed all the freed slaves from the basis of representation, thus preventing the white South from achieving dominance in the Congress. Section 4 barred both states and the federal government from paying any debts incurred by the Rebel states and any compensation "for loss of involuntary service or labor." Section 5, echoing the Thirteenth Amendment, gave Congress enforcement power "by appropriate legislation."

Owen finished reading the draft aloud. "Read that to me again," Stevens said. Owen complied, then asked whether his powerful friend had time to listen to his explanation. "I have nothing half so important to do as to attend to this," Stevens replied. "Take your own time."

Owen laid out his argument. His work on the Freedmen's Inquiry Commission had convinced him that the freed slave was not ready for the vote, even though that had "occurred through no fault of his." But the slaves would be ready soon. "We must think and act for [the former slave] as he is, and not as, but for life-long servitude, he would have been," Owen said.

Stevens objected that this provision delayed "full justice" for the freed slaves; but Owen countered that what they needed—and wanted most—was education, and that it would be irresponsible to "call him away from the school-room to take a seat which he is unfitted to fill in a legislative chamber." If black Southerners did not get the vote, Stevens objected, power would pass to "impenitent traitors," a result he considered at least as bad. Owen, the idealist, gave a carefully realistic answer: in the next few years, the political forces running the South would probably "make a mess of it and lose character." If so, "I'd rather it should be the planters."

Stevens sat silent for a minute, looking over Owen's manuscript. "I'll be frank with you, Owen," he said. "We've had nothing before us that comes anywhere near being as good as this, or as complete. It would be likely to pass, too; that's the best of it." Stevens concluded, "I'll lay that amendment of yours before our committee tomorrow, if you say so. And I'll do my best to put it through."

Owen then explained that his proposed amendment was designed as a kind of treaty of peace between North and South. When a Southern state had ratified the amendment, and had purified its legal code, its white voters would be entitled to send the representatives of their choice to Congress. The only disqualification would be for former Confederate military officers, members of the Thirty-sixth Congress, and Cabinet members who had later broken their oaths by joining the Confederacy. "That will never do!" Stevens exploded. "Far too lenient. It would be dangerous to let these fellows off on such easy terms."

Once again the "idealistic" Owen schooled the "cynical" Stevens in his version of political reality. If the Southern states withheld the vote before 1876, they would lose the House seats based on the black population. This would reduce the South (by Owens's calculation) to a mere forty-two House members. "'Surely,' said I, 'you can manage that number, even if they should happen to be ultra secessionists.'"

Owen next went to Fessenden, the committee's other chair, whose response was characteristically restrained. "Cold, dispassionate, cautious, he heard me patiently, but with scarcely a remark." Fessenden studied the proposal for two days, then told Owen that the draft was "the best that had yet been presented to their committee." Elihu Washburne, Roscoe Conkling, Jacob Howard, and G. S. Boutwell all indicated their support. Bingham also was favorable, but said "the first section ought to specify, in detail, the civil rights which we proposed to assure."

In fact, the only discouraging words came from Charles Sumner, who was not a member of the committee but who—as the members had learned when he torpedoed the representation amendment— had the influence to make passage of any Reconstruction measure difficult or impossible. As Owen remembered his meeting with Sumner, the Massachusetts senator (who had been quick to adopt a political stratagem to protect his left flank when Governor Andrew was mulling a challenge earlier that year) now presented himself as such a rigid man of principle that he seemed to have ascended to a kind of heaven of constitutional purity. "I cannot vote for this amendment," he told Owen. "It contains a tacit recognition that the ex-slaveholders have a right to withhold suffrage from the freedmen for ten years longer." He brushed aside Owen's practical arguments about the political state of the country in an election year. "It is a question of abstract principle," Owen records his saying, "not of expediency."

Owen asked whether Sumner thought immediate suffrage could pass in the current Congress, or the next. "Probably not, this session," Sumner replied. "And it may be several years before it does. If so, let the responsibility rest on those who reject it."

Owen pointed out that Sumner's approach would leave the freed slaves without "the protection even of a prospective right."

"I shall be sorry if that prove so," Sumner said. "I think no one feels the wrongs of the negro more strongly than I do. But not even to mitigate his sufferings for the time can I consent to palter with the right, or to violate a great principle. I must do my whole duty, without looking to consequences." Owen left the interview admiring Sumner's stubbornness, but not his common sense.

After the meetings, Stevens submitted the draft to the committee on April 21. All the members were there that day, except Senator Howard, Representative Conkling, and, perhaps fatefully, Fessenden. Never robust in health, the chairman had fallen victim to the varioloid, a mild form of smallpox that tended to hit people who had been vaccinated with the relatively hit-or-miss vaccination techniques available in the nineteenth century. Though varioloid was rarely life-threatening, it could produce a lingering illness marked by a rash, a few raised pustules on the skin, swollen glands, diarrhea, and general lassitude. (Lincoln had come down with varioloid in 1863, on his way back from delivering the Gettysburg Address.)

So in place of Fessenden, old Reverdy Johnson, the good-natured conservative Democrat, was the chair as the committee considered the Owen draft. The members adopted it, section by section, on a more or less straight party-line vote. Bingham offered a new section as Section 1: "No state shall make or enforce any law which shall abridge the privileges or immunities of citizens of the United States; nor shall any state deprive any person of life, liberty or property without due process of law, nor deny to any person within its jurisdiction the equal protection of the laws." But the language of the resolution to accompany the draft—specifying whether ratification of the proposed amendment would mean readmission of a state to Congress—still needed to be worked out, and the committee adjourned until April 23.

Over the next week, the committee met three times, and the Owen plan underwent a drastic remodeling. While the meetings were closed, all of Washington seemed to know what went on in the Pacific Railroad room of the Capitol as soon as the committee adjourned each day. Johnson knew the committee's plans at every step, and the *Cincinnati Commercial* reported a few days later that the committee itself was wondering which of its members was responsible for the "leakiness" of the proceedings. With each set of votes and leaks, the public pressure grew on the committee to alter Owen's original plan to make it more acceptable to Northern voters in an election year. Probably for this reason, the committee voted on April 25 to drop Bingham's civil rights section and to adopt the Owen plan basically intact, including the guarantee of votes to black men after 1876. That vote laid out a complete proposed amendment and the members voted to send it to Congress.

But there was the varioloid to contend with. Fessenden had not been able to attend meetings since March 5, and on April 25 the committee voted to wait until the chair could attend and approve what had been done. Members of Congress began meeting in small caucuses, and the verdict seemed to be that votes for freed slaves would not be a good basis to fight the November elections. By April 28, when Fessenden had recovered enough to attend a session, the mood had perceptibly shifted. The committee met in secret, and what emerged was far different from the Owen proposal.

The next morning, Owen read the new text amendment in the newspapers. "It had evidently been hurriedly thrown together," he recalled, "and it contained no reference whatever to negro suffrage, present or prospective." He hurried to Stevens's house. "'So that was all labor lost?' said I."

"Yes," Stevens answered, "but not by my vote. Don't imagine that I sanction the shilly-shally bungling thing that I shall have to report to the House tomorrow." Then Stevens told Owen that the plan that had been approved on the twenty-third had unraveled while the committee waited on Fessenden's recovery. "Our action on your amendment had, it seems, got noised abroad," Stevens said. Caucuses from New York, Illinois, and Indiana had organized against the black voting provision, and "our committee hadn't backbone enough to maintain its ground." The two men regarded each silently for a minute, and then Stevens exclaimed, "Damn the varioloid! It changed the whole policy of the country!"

The story that Owen's utopia was lost because of the committee's delay has persisted to this day. The reality—and Stevens's role in it—was more complex. In fact, the journal shows that it was Stevens himself who the day before had moved that the black voting provision be stricken from the proposed amendment. The old Radical had attempted to stick by prospective suffrage; but Stevens was, before anything else, a practical politician with the ability to count noses. The results of the caucuses made clear that there would not be two-thirds majorities in both houses for a measure that mentioned black suffrage, and failure to pass an amendment would be far more dangerous to the party than merely passing a "shilly-shally bungling thing." It was literally true that Owen's prospective suffrage plan had not been "lost by my vote"; the committee vote was 12 to 2. But the impression Owen walked away with was somewhat inaccurate nonetheless, and Stevens was content to leave him ignorant of the full story.

As a result of the vote to remove Owen's black voting plan, the committee made another decision that was to prove fateful in the long term. Without the guarantee of the vote, the freed slaves would indeed be defenseless against their former masters. Immediately after the vote to strip the voting provision, the committee reconsidered Bingham's civil rights amendment. By a vote of 10 to 3, the committee put Bingham's vision back in. Without the vote, blacks would need civil rights to protect themselves against a new form of slavery. But beyond that, by incorporating Bingham's vision, the committee kept alive the vision of a new republicanism in the states, enforceable by the federal government, as an antidote to the reemergence of the Slave Power.

Section 1 guaranteed civil rights; Section 2 prescribed loss of representation for any state that denied the vote "to any portion of its male citizens . . . except for participation in rebellion or other crime"; Section 3 banned anyone who had "voluntarily adhered to the late insurrection" from casting a vote before July 4, 1870; Section 4 forbade states and the federal government to "assume or pay any debt . . . incurred . . . in aid of insurrection" or to compensate former slaveholders; and the final section mirrored the enforcement provision of the Thirteenth Amendment, granting Congress power "by appropriate legislation," to enforce the amendment's provisions. All told, the new amendment was an ungainly construct, a mix of the idealism of an Owen or a Bingham with the calculation of a Fessenden or a Stevens; it promised radical change in the Constitution created by the Framers but clothed the coming changes in oracular language. Nevertheless, it seemed likely to pass. And in April 1866, any amendment that could pass, however ungainly, promised potential salvation to the Republican Party—and the cause of emancipation—in its death duel with Andrew Johnson and the ghost of the Slave Power.

The proposed amendment was a rough beast, but it was one whose hour had come round at last.

· 9 ·

THE PROSPECT OF
A GOOD LONG LIFE

In 1866, New York's Union Square was the center of a neighborhood of brownstone and brick mansions. On the square's west side stood the Romanesque Church of the Pilgrims, a Presbyterian church built in 1847 to the design of James Renwick, who would later design St. Patrick's Cathedral. On May 10, 1866, the church was home to something the nation had not seen since the attack on Fort Sumter—a national woman's rights convention. Though no one present fully understood it, that meeting would begin a turning point in the American women's movement.

The church was crowded to well over its capacity of thirteen hundred, and the crowd represented the royalty of American feminism. On the dais were Elizabeth Cady Stanton, Lucretia Mott, Susan B. Anthony, and Francis Ellen Watkins Harper, the freeborn black abolitionist, feminist, poet, and novelist. Only one man was granted the honor of the platform—Theodore Tilton, the abolitionist editor of *The Independent*. (Tilton had not yet achieved additional notoriety because of the scandalous affair between his wife, Elizabeth Richards, and his mentor, the Reverend Henry Ward Beecher, who was seated in the front row.)

Newspaper writers found the appearance of women's-rights advocates an endless source of fun. The *New York Herald*'s correspondent said that the audience was largely made up of ladies "from the interior of New England, where the mental and physical culture of females is attended to more closely than the art of adornment in dress."

The convention had originally been called to celebrate the victory over slavery and to look forward to a bright future of equality. Since the abolition movement had begun, women had been its heart and soul—the shock troops that had brought antislavery from the fringes of political discourse in the 1840s to the very center of national politics in 1866. Until the spring of that year, antislavery and feminism were not allied; they were the *very same movement*, springing from a common core of passion and looking forward to a common future of racial and sexual equality.

With victory, that unity would be shattered forever.

The American women's movement, as a separate intellectual and political current, had in effect been born at the World's Anti-Slavery Convention in London in June 1840. American antislavery groups had selected both male and female delegates to the gathering, which was held in Freemasons Hall in Drury Lane. But British abolitionists were scandalized by the idea of men and women sitting promiscuously together on the convention floor. This was worse than immoral—it was un-British. Wendell Phillips, one of the two most prominent American abolitionists, led the opposition to the exclusion of women, but when the matter came to a vote, British propriety prevailed. The female delegates were shunted off to a side gallery, separated from the floor by a rope, where they could hear without being seen.

The furor over female delegates brought to the fore an upstart American man, William Lloyd Garrison, whose version of the antislavery creed would not countenance any compromise with gradualism or colonization. Garrison arrived five days late for the meeting, in a delegation that included Charles Lenox Remond, a prominent black abolitionist. Garrison and his associates genially announced that a convention that excluded women excluded *them* as well. They watched the meeting from prominent seats in the gallery, where English radicals ostentatiously paid them court. The group "presented a picture that no one ever forgot," writes Garrison's biographer, Henry Mayer. One female delegate wrote, "They are a glorious crew. Garrison is one of God's nobility. I don't think I ever saw such an angelic, holy-looking face."

Garrison's emergence was a fateful turn for the antislavery movement. But perhaps even more consequential in the long run was an alliance forged by two of the women whom the delegates had excluded. "As Lucretia Mott and Elizabeth Cady Stanton wended their way arm in arm down Great Queen Street that night, reviewing the exciting scenes of the day, they agreed to hold a woman's rights convention on their return to America, as the men to whom they had just listened had manifested their great need of some education on that question," three founding mothers of the women's movement wrote years later. "The movement for woman's suffrage, both in England and in America, may be dated from this World's Anti-Slavery Convention."

That first woman's rights convention, dreamed of on Drury Lane, took place eight years later, in Seneca Falls, New York. Ironically, it was not organized by the well-known Quaker activist, Lucretia Mott, but by Stanton, the young pupil. Elizabeth Cady was born in 1815 near Albany, New York. In 1840, she had married Henry B. Stanton, a determined, though moderate, abolitionist. (The trip to the London antislavery convention was in fact the young couple's honeymoon.) Elizabeth's true radicalization began in 1847, when she and Henry left a happy home in Boston and moved to a relatively isolated house in Seneca Falls. There she took on the life of a housewife and (eventually) the mother of seven children. In Massachusetts, she had been at the center of a circle of reformers, artists, philosophers, and poets, but "[i]n Seneca Falls my life was comparatively solitary," she recalled years later, "and the change from Boston was somewhat depressing." Henry was away traveling much of the time, and

Elizabeth had to "keep a house and grounds in good order, purchase every article for daily use, keep the wardrobes of half a dozen human beings in proper trim, take the children to dentists, shoemakers, and different schools, or find teachers at home." Forever after those years in Seneca Falls, Elizabeth Cady Stanton's feminist thought would be grounded in awareness of the concrete drudgery that made up the lives of even the most privileged American women.

On a visit to mutual friends in nearby Waterloo, New York, Stanton was reunited with Mott, and confided to her and other women the desperate unhappiness of her daily life. The group decided that the long-dreamed-of "convention" was the answer. The group took out an advertisement in a local paper, and then drafted a "Declaration of Principles" based on the Declaration of Independence. "We hold these truths to be self-evident," they wrote, "that all men *and women* are created equal. . . ."

Even in a time and place where radicalism flourished, the demand for full equality—at the polls, at home, and even in church—was strong stuff. Henry Stanton, for one, vowed to have nothing to do with such nonsense and left town before the convention's opening day, July 19, 1848. On the appointed day, more than 250 women appeared. Even though Henry was absent, so many men also showed up that the organizers quickly decided to let them stay, and to draft Lucretia's husband, James Mott, "tall and dignified, in Quaker costume," as the chair. Also in attendance was the young Frederick Douglass, recently established not far away in Rochester. Douglass, who had grown up surrounded by strong and compassionate women, would be a firm advocate of women's equality for the rest of his life; and when some in the audience protested that the demand for the vote was too radical, Douglass supported Stanton. The suffrage resolution passed narrowly, the only one of the reform proposals not adopted unanimously.

The meeting at Seneca Falls, historic though it was, had attracted women only from the areas nearby. Another meeting was held in Rochester just two weeks afterward; then, eighteen months later, another in Salem, Ohio. In 1850, the first national convention convened in Worcester, Massachusetts; national groups convened almost every year thereafter until the Civil War broke out, along with countless local and regional meetings.

The Seneca Falls meeting had one other effect that changed the world. About 120 miles away, in the village of Canajoharie, New York, a young schoolmistress named Susan B. Anthony read "The Woman's Declaration of Independence" passed at Seneca Falls. The presumption of these women at first amused her. Anthony was twenty-eight years old, and already a supporter of abolition and temperance, the daughter of Quakers. Indeed both her parents and her sister, she learned afterward, had been at the second meeting, in Rochester. Not long after that, Susan Anthony realized that women's rights— even women's suffrage—were not a laughing matter. They became, in fact, the great quest of the rest of her life.

Anthony and Stanton met for the first time in 1851, and from then on they are invariably discussed as a unit. Their story is not the entire story of American feminism before and after the Civil War. The generation of women who came after Fanny Wright's—educated, ambitious, optimistic, strong—is a bright galaxy. To name some almost at random, there was Clara Barton, who almost single-handedly created a volunteer nursing organization during the war that saved thousands of lives; Antoinette Louisa Brown, the first female ordained minister in American history; Amelia Bloomer, who gave her name to a costume designed to liberate women from the tyranny of stays and petticoats; Anna Dickinson, whose mesmerizing antislavery oratory swung statewide elections before she herself turned twenty-one; and Frances Ellen Watkins Harper, the pioneering black abolitionist and author who toured the Southern states at risk of her life during Reconstruction to bring the gospel of equality to audiences of former slaves.

And these women were aided by remarkable men, who grasped instinctively that the cause of slaves and that of women were both parts of the long fight for human equality. Pioneer abolitionists like

William Lloyd Garrison, Parker Pillsbury, Frederick Douglass, and Charles Lenox Remond also belong in the constellation of a brilliant generation of feminists.

But the complex double-star system that was Stanton and Anthony has come to symbolize the nineteenth-century women's struggle much the way Martin Luther King Jr. symbolizes the civil rights movement of the next century. In part that is because the two of them were active for so long. "You and I have the prospect of a good long life," Stanton wrote to Anthony in 1857. She was forty-two and Anthony five years younger. "We shall not be in our prime before fifty, and after that we shall be good for twenty years at least." In fact, the two went on in partnership into the next century; Stanton died at eighty-seven, Anthony at eighty-six.

In part it is because they symbolized the span of possibilities available to white, middle-class women in the America of the time: Stanton, the hardworking housewife and mother, struggling to take part in public affairs while meeting the needs of husband and family; Anthony, the perennial spinster, constantly on the road, seemingly scornful of even the possibilities of personal life. (Indeed, the two visually form a kind of memorable Mutt-and-Jeff pair: Stanton was plump, sunny, and maternal, while Anthony was sharp-faced and somber, though in person she was far from grim.) In part it is because the two women were not just intellectual peers but allies in all the details of their lives. Often when Stanton was tormented by a writing deadline, Anthony would hie herself to Seneca Falls to handle housecleaning and child care. Stanton, pinned down by her duties at home, was the movement's philosopher; Anthony, always on the move, was its organizer. "[I]t has been said that I forged the thunderbolts," Stanton wrote, "and she fired them."

But more than all this, the story of Susan B. Anthony and Elizabeth Cady Stanton fascinates because it is a story of selfless female love and devotion, like the tale of Ruth and Naomi in the Bible. In their letters there is something of Naomi's calm avowal: "Whither thou goest, I will go; and where thou lodgest, I will lodge: thy people shall be my people, and thy God my God." The letters are also playful, affectionate, funny, and inspiring in their selflessness and seriousness of purpose. Biographers speculate about the extent of their sexual feeling for each other, but more important, in the end, is a friendship that was a triumphant illustration of the feminist dictum that for women "our real life is our common life"; a cooperative activism that contrasts with the solitary drama of ego and ambition that is most male nineteenth-century politics. "Our speeches may be considered the united product of our two brains," Stanton wrote. Together they formed a mighty force that—though it did not win the vote in their own lifetimes—transformed the world around them.

Women in 1850 had many needs; indeed, for many, the vote was far down the list. So far from voting, women, particularly married women, were barely persons under the law. "In fine, it appears that the husband's control over the person of his wife is so complete that he may claim her society altogether," wrote one legal scholar in 1845, "that he may reclaim her if she goes away or is detained by others; that he may use gentle constraint upon her liberty to prevent her going away, or to prevent improper conduct; that he may maintain suits for injuries to her person; that he may defend her with force; that she cannot sue alone; and that she cannot execute a deed or valid conveyance without the concurrence of her husband. In most respects she loses the power of personal independence, and altogether that of separate action in legal matters."

When divorce was even available, fathers, not mothers, almost always got custody of their children. Women were often subject not only to "gentle constraint" but to physical violence by their husbands (or fathers, if unmarried) with the connivance, though not the sanction, of the law. Women could not own property—indeed, if a husband *wanted* to deed land to his wife, he could do so only by creating a trust and giving legal title to the trustee. Women could not sue their husbands—or anybody else, for any reason. To some female reformers, a few basic civil rights seemed more urgently needed than the vote.

Beyond the law, life for women was physically arduous. Wives and daughters were responsible for all the household chores. Women could not attend most colleges or enter most professions. A few could serve (while unmarried) as ill-paid schoolteachers. Others might hire themselves out to other families as domestic servants. During the first half of the nineteenth century, though, a new economic role opened up for Northern women—work in the New England cotton mills.

Ironically, the rise of cotton transformed the lives of America's women, black and white. Black women were pushed into the fields alongside men to pick the crop; white women were in demand to spin the cotton into yarn and weave it into textiles. As early as 1831, nearly forty thousand Northern women were at work in the mills; by the eve of the Civil War, a quarter of those working in factories were female. Mill work offered a shred of independence to these women. It also sparked economic conflict and strikes by the female employees; for them, wages and working conditions were more urgent issues than voting.

Many American women indignantly denied that the antebellum social order oppressed women. According to the prevailing theory, men were made for the rough-and-tumble of the marketplace, where their decisions must be given primacy; women were supreme in a "separate sphere," protected from competition and conflict, the world of home and children. The vote would weaken, not strengthen, women in this work. "In civil and political affairs, American women take no interest or concern, except so far as they sympathize with their family and personal friends," explained Catherine Beecher, sister of Henry Ward Beecher and prominent exponent of "domestic science" as woman's proper place. "In matters pertaining to the education of their children, in the selection and support of a clergyman, in all benevolent enterprises, and in all questions relating to morals or manners, they have a superior influence." Submissive though this sounds, Beecher and her fellow "scientists" were actually seeking to carve out some kind of role for women that did not depend on their men; for these theorists of the "separate sphere," the idea of women as political beings threatened these tenuous aims.

For most men, the idea of women at the polls was simply ridiculous. Even many female reformers cautioned that asking for votes would open the movement to ridicule; and so it did. When Susan B. Anthony first petitioned the New York Legislature for modest reforms that would allow women to keep their own wages and gain custody of their children in a divorce, the legislative committee solemnly responded that if the two sexes were not equal, "the gentlemen are the sufferers." Their only recommendation was addressed to the married couples who had signed Anthony's petition. These couples should "apply for a law authorizing them to change dresses, that the husband may wear petticoats and his wife the breeches."

Nonetheless, Stanton and Anthony instinctively understood that there would be something fatal in conceding validity to any inequality, no matter on what issue, between men and women. Feminism was part and parcel of antislavery, and the central insight of both movements was the urgent necessity of full equality for all people, male or female, black or white. Just as Frederick Douglass always insisted that real justice required full political rights for blacks, Anthony and Stanton sought the same recognition for women. That commitment to human equality bound the two movements together during the antebellum years; it made Douglass, for example, as firm a supporter of women's rights as Stanton and Anthony were of freedom for the slave.

The antebellum women's movement did make some progress in reforming divorce laws and securing the passage of Married Women's Property Acts, which allowed women to retain their land and belongings even when they married. Women also sparked the greatest successes of the antislavery movement. It was women who flooded the state legislatures and Congress with antislavery petitions, sparking the great debate of the 1830s over the House's "gag rule" that forbade members to discuss any petitions against slavery. Harriet Beecher Stowe's antislavery novel, *Uncle Tom's Cabin*, revolutionized public debate over slavery after its publication in 1851. Ten years later, when Lincoln met the author, he is said to have remarked, "So you're the little woman who wrote the book that made this great war!"

During the Civil War, the female legions of antislavery flocked to the cause of the Union. Clara Barton and Dorothea Dix organized thousands to volunteer for nursing duties. A few women, not content with that, disguised themselves as men and fought at the front. A small army of young women went into government service as clerks and secretaries, replacing the men who had marched off to war.

Nor was all the service behind the scenes. Anna Dickinson, the beautiful and precocious angel of antislavery, used her fiery oratory to sway off-year elections for the Republican cause. In 1863, at the Church of the Puritans, Stanton and Anthony founded the Women's National Loyal League, which promptly resolved that "[t]here never can be a true peace in this Republic until the civil and political rights of all citizens of African descent and all women are practically established." Over the next year, the Loyal League collected a stunning 400,000 signatures on petitions demanding an amendment to the Constitution to end slavery—more signatures than had ever been presented to Congress on behalf of any cause. When presented to the Senate by Charles Sumner, the massive bundle of petitions was so heavy that two strong black men had to carry it. That petition first focused public opinion on the need for what became, in time, the Thirteenth Amendment.

Feminist leaders made a conscious decision to stop agitation over "women's issues" for the duration of the war. Some accounts have it that Lincoln personally asked for this change of strategy and promised to support women's suffrage after the Union was saved. That encounter has the smell of legend—Lincoln was a cautious and conservative man, and temperamentally averse to making promises. Stanton does not record such a meeting in any of her published works. In fact, the decision to emphasize Union over women's rights caused the first serious quarrel between the two friends. Anthony wanted to press on for equal rights and suffrage; Stanton, like other feminists, wanted to focus on victory and emancipation.

Anthony was stung by the quarrel. "I am sick at heart," she wrote to Lucretia Mott in 1861, "but I cannot carry the world against the wish and will of our best friends." Stanton later publicly apologized for her faintheartedness. "When they asked us to be silent on our question during the War, and labor for the emancipation of the slave, we did so, and gave five years to his emancipation and enfranchisement," she wrote in 1897. "To this proposition my friend, Susan B. Anthony, never consented, but was compelled to yield because no one stood with her. I was convinced, at the time, that it was the true policy. I am now equally sure that it was a blunder, and, ever since, I have taken my beloved Susan's judgment against the world."

War rarely bodes well for women, either on the battlefield or at home. Even before the guns fell silent, there were grim omens: in 1862, without women to lobby for their cause, the New York Legislature quietly reversed some of the legal reforms women had won only two years before, reducing a mother's share of guardianship over her children and stripping widows of their statutory interest in marital property. "This cowardly act," Stanton and Anthony wrote bitterly in 1889, "is the strongest possible proof of woman's need of the ballot in her own hand for protection."

After Appomattox, Robert Dale Owen—a passionate feminist since his New Harmony days—was the first to alert Anthony and Stanton of the plan to allot state representation according to the rules governing "male" voters. Owen related what he claimed were behind-the-scenes discussions in the joint committee. When one member suggested using "persons" instead of "males," Owen said, another replied, "That will never do . . . it would enfranchise all the Southern wenches." Another supposedly chimed in that "Suffrage for black men will be all the strain the Republican party can stand."

Even as the joint committee was preparing the first representation amendment, Anthony and Stanton began a petition drive to prevent the implicit recognition of the ballot as a man's prerogative. "[U]nder the Federal Constitution, as it now exists, there is not one word that limits the right of suffrage to any privileged class," Stanton wrote in the *National Anti-Slavery Standard* in January 1866. "This attempt to turn the wheels of civilization backward . . . should rouse every woman to a prompt exercise of the only right she has in the Government, the right of petition." When the petitions were gathered, though, their old ally, Sumner, brought them to the Senate only under protest; in the House, the women could find only the clownish Democrat James Brooks to present them. That first amendment failed, not because old antislavery allies had rallied around women, but because Charles Sumner fought for the vote for black men. (Sumner later said he had written "over nineteen pages of foolscap" to devise constitutional language that could pass without using the word "male"—"but it could not be done.")

Now, however, it was May, and the fatal language was back in the draft Fourteenth Amendment proposed by the joint committee. The issue caused consternation and division among the crowd at the Church of the Puritans. The call for the convention had proposed the slogan of "Equal Rights to All," and warned that "while our representatives at Washington are discussing the right of suffrage for the black man . . . they deny that 'necessity of citizenship' to woman, by proposing to introduce the word 'male' into the Federal Constitution." Stanton convened the meeting and said, "Now in the reconstruction is the opportunity, perhaps for the century, to base our government on the broad principle of equal rights to all." Henry Ward Beecher, one of the nation's most eminent clergymen, for the first time addressed a women's convention and proclaimed that "*[i]t is more important that woman should vote than that the black man should vote.*" At the meeting's conclusion, the members resolved that the proposed language of the Fourteenth Amendment was "a desecration of the last will and testament of the Fathers, a violation of the spirit of republicanism, and cruel injustice to the women of the nation." They unanimously voted to create a new body called the American Equal Rights Association, dedicated to the proposition that "the negro and woman now hold the same civil and political *status*, alike needing only the ballot."

The movement had come to a turning point, a moment when innocence was forever lost. Beecher's question symbolized the

Pandora's box that had been opened. Who "needed" the vote *more*—black men or women? No more were women and African Americans to be partners in the work of liberation. Instead, they would fight each other for the spoils of victory, and that battle would leave scars for a generation.

Wendell Phillips, the aristocratic abolitionist who had been a close ally of Anthony, spoke up at the meeting and reproved Stanton and Anthony. Echoing the mocking language of the New York Legislature, he proclaimed that women already held power and did not need the ballot. The issue of women's suffrage was not important enough to obstruct the effort to protect the freed slaves. "I do not feel by any means that keen agony of interest in this question that I did in the slavery question," Phillips wrote in the *National Anti-Slavery Standard* shortly afterward. "[H]ere is woman, educated, influential, walking down the highway of society, wielding all her power."

Stanton and Anthony were outraged. For them, women needed the vote as much as men of any color. And the word *male* in the Constitution would offer antisuffragists an argument that votes for women were unconstitutional as well as unimportant. Anthony presciently remarked that the new language would delay female voting for a hundred years.

And besides, there were those insidious questions that, once asked, could not be unasked—who "needed" the vote more, who "deserved" it more, who would make "better" use of it? As early as December 1865, Stanton had pretty clearly decided. "[N]ow, as the celestial gate to civil rights is slowly moving on its hinges, it becomes a serious question whether we had better stand aside and see 'Sambo' walk into the kingdom first," she wrote in a letter to the *Anti-Slavery Standard*. What about the black *women* of the South? "In fact, it is better to be the slave of an educated white man, than of a degraded, ignorant black one." So enthusiastic was her criticism of the Southern black man that a few years later, her old friend and comrade Frederick Douglass publicly rebuked her at a meeting of the Equal Rights Association:

There is no name greater than that of Elizabeth Cady Stanton in the matter of woman's rights and equal rights, but my sentiments are tinged a little against *The Revolution* [the newspaper she had started in 1867]. There was in the address to which I allude the employment of certain names, such as "Sambo" . . . I must say that I do not see how any one can pretend that there is the same urgency in giving the ballot to woman as to the negro. With us, the matter is a question of life and death, at least, in fifteen States of the Union. When women, because they are women, are hunted down through the cities of New York and New Orleans; when they are dragged from their houses and hung on lamp-posts; when their children are torn from their arms, and their brains dashed out upon the pavement; when they are objects of insult and outrage at every turn; when they are in danger of having their homes burnt down over their heads; when their children are not allowed to enter schools; then they will have an urgency to obtain the ballot equal to our own.

Douglass and many others—black and white, male and female— saw the moment differently than did Stanton and Anthony. To them, the postwar opportunity was fleeting and the impulse of reform fragile. The demand for the ballot had always been controversial, even within the women's movement itself. Democrats and allies of Andrew Johnson were eager for a female-vote proposal, calculating that it would carry the proposed amendment to defeat in Congress and ridicule in the country. To men like Douglass, Stanton and Anthony were being not only naive but selfish.

Not only Douglass, but pioneer abolitionists like Wendell Phillips and Charles Sumner implored Stanton and Anthony to put the woman-suffrage question aside until black men had won the ballot. A month after the convention at the Church of the Puritans, Phillips told a Boston equal-rights meeting that "suffrage was a great question of the hour, [but he] thought, nevertheless, that in view of the peculiar circumstances of the Negro's position, his claim to this right might fairly be considered to have precedence." Sumner, who had found women's energy so valuable in the quest for the Thirteenth Amendment, disavowed their activism now, telling Congress that it was not "judicious for them at this moment to bring forward their claims so as to compromise in any way the great question of equal rights for an enfranchised race now before Congress."

Stanton, Anthony, and their allies felt betrayed and alienated from their old allies. "[W]omen educated to self-sacrifice and self-abnegation readily accepted the idea that it was divine and beautiful to hold their claims for rights and privileges in abeyance to all orders and classes of men," they wrote later in the *History of Woman Suffrage*. They began to look for new allies—including some whom they would have scorned during their antislavery days. One prominent conservative Democrat underwrote their new suffragist newspaper, *The Revolution*. And the next year, Anthony accepted election as a delegate to the Democratic National Convention. When their former allies criticized this strange alliance, Anthony and Stanton responded that "the hypocrisy of Democrats serves us a better purpose in the present emergency than does the treachery of Republicans."

During the antebellum years, the ideology of abolition and feminism was identical. Human equality was the axiom; all *people*, white and black, male and female, were "endowed by their creator with certain unalienable rights." But now, in the wake of what they saw as male betrayal, Anthony, Stanton, and their allies began to argue that women needed the ballot—and deserved it—not because they were human, but because they were female. Not only would voting be a means of self-protection; it would elevate the political process by bringing the influence of women—purer, nobler, and more peaceable—into public life.

The change is probably best symbolized by a split that occurred in 1869. By January of that year, Stanton was calling for a separate amendment to guarantee women's voting rights. When the Equal Rights Association met in New York that May, the group broke in two over the issue. Stanton and Anthony at once announced a new organization, the National Woman Suffrage Association. Membership would be all-female. (To complete the split, the "mainstream" suffragists, male and female, formed a competing group, the American Woman Suffrage Association.) That year, the Equal Rights Association met and resolved that "[t]he extension of suffrage to woman is essential to the public safety and to the establishment and permanence of free institutions" because "as woman, in private life, in the partnership of marriage, is now the conservator of private morals, so woman in public life, in the partnership of a republican State, based upon Universal suffrage, will become the conservator of public morals." American feminism had come full circle; it was the antebellum idea of "separate spheres" again. Thus was born the movement for *woman* suffrage, rather than for suffrage for all; and at the same moment the separatist impulse in American feminism came to the fore.

Stanton and Anthony worked on together into the new century; but neither lived to cast a legal vote. (Poignantly, one and only one woman who had been in the church at Seneca Falls in 1848 lived to celebrate the Nineteenth Amendment; as Charlotte Woodward, she had signed the Declaration of Principles; seventy-two years later, as Charlotte Woodward Pierce, she cast a vote in the 1920 presidential election.)

Frederick Douglass and other black feminists continued to support votes for women. But a certain suspicious coolness developed between advocates of black rights and the feminists of the suffrage movement. Its effects lasted well into the 1960s, when a new wave of feminists criticized the male leaders of the civil rights movement. And even today, advocates of women's rights are split over whether women are *equal to* men or *different from*—and in some ways better than—men. Women have come to share in the rights guaranteed by the Fourteenth Amendment. (In 1995, for example, the U.S. Supreme Court held that the Equal Protection Clause means that the state of Virginia could not close its prestigious military college, Virginia Military Institute, to qualified female applicants.) But the struggle to write women into the new freedoms created during Reconstruction illustrates one of history's cruel paradoxes. Most advances in one area of democracy and equality have been accompanied by retreats on other fronts. The framing of the Constitution in 1787, and the Bill of Rights two years later, are milestones in the history of democracy and freedom. But they came at a cost: to make the Constitution palatable to the South, the Framers provided guarantees for slavery that spawned the Slave Power and a bloody civil war. Now, as a new generation of framers struggled to cure the Constitution's defects, their efforts retarded the progress of the nation's women. As black Americans gained formal guarantees of citizenship, women were forced to accept a gender distinction in the reformed Constitution.

Stanton had predicted that the loss would set women back a century. She was slightly pessimistic—but only slightly. In the wake of the second founding, justice for women was delayed for nearly sixty years.

NOT AMONG ANGELS

The joint committee had now made the key decisions that would lead to the amendment's adoption. There would be one "omnibus" amendment, whose sections addressed the different facets of the Slave Power. Suffrage for black men would be put on hold. And Bingham's theory of republicanism and equality would be embodied in the first section.

Viewed from the twenty-first century, the emergence of the proposed Fourteenth Amendment seems like the major news story of the spring of 1866. But in fact the joint committee's proposal, printed in the newspapers on April 29, did not electrify the nation. The proposed amendment was swiftly overshadowed by the news from Memphis, Tennessee, where white Southerners began a coordinated attack on their black neighbors that swiftly escalated into a full-scale pogrom. The Memphis riots marked the beginning of a new and ominous chapter in black-white relations in the post-Confederate South.

The day after the draft's release, April 30, was also the last day of service for hundreds of black Union soldiers who had been stationed in Memphis. The soldiers surrendered their rifles and uniforms and dispersed through the town to celebrate; according to some reports, fighting immediately broke out between the former soldiers and the all-white Memphis police. The next day, a chance collision between two cabs set off a full-scale confrontation between black soldiers and white police, which escalated into an organized assault on the city's black population.

The elements of the explosion were far from random. Memphis, like many Southern cities, had seen an explosion in its black population since the outbreak of war. The city had about three thousand black residents in 1860; by mid-1865, there were as many as twenty thousand. This was not the only change wrought by the war and occupation. Tennessee's provisional government had zealously excluded secessionists and former Confederates from official posts. But pro-Union did not mean pro-black, in Tennessee or elsewhere in the South. "If there is anything a loyal Tennessean hates more than a rebel," Tennessee's governor, W. G. "Parson" Brownlow, explained at about this time, "it is a nigger." The result was a city government and a police force dominated by recent white emigrants to the city, mostly Irish and Irish American. It was the police who led the anti-black violence in Memphis.

Police officers in uniform commanded groups of whites who burned black schools and homes. Individual officers shot peaceful black residents on the street and in their houses. John C. Creighton, the city recorder, mounted the stump shortly after the first face-off between police and former soldiers. He urged the white crowd to "go ahead and kill the last dam[n]ed one of the nigger race." Even the state's attorney general, William Wallace, raced into town, urged white residents to "organize and arm yourselves," and handed out weapons to the crowd.

White officials who did not join in the butchery were at best ineffective. Memphis mayor John Park, according to the Freedmen's Bureau report, was "in a state of intoxication during a part or most of the time and was therefore unable to perform the high and responsible functions of his office." The local sheriff stayed off the street, but sent messages to General George Stoneman, military commander of the district, begging him to send Union troops to restore order. Stoneman waited nearly three days before declaring martial law. By that time, historian James Gilbert Ryan wrote, "46 blacks and 2 whites lay dead. Seventy-five other persons had received bullet wounds. Moreover, during the forty-hour span of anarchy, predatory gangs had raped at least 5 Negro women, robbed over 100 victims and dealt severe beatings to 10 others. Property destroyed included the houses of 91 families (89 belonging to blacks, 1 owned by a white man and 1 of an interracial couple), 4 churches, and 12 schools. A contemporary estimate placed the damage at over $100,000."

The damage was not confined to Tennessee. The white rioters in Memphis had also given the lie to Andrew Johnson's claim that the laws of the free market would guarantee the safety of the freed slaves. "When the Freedmen's Bureau Bill and the civil rights bill were first talked of," *The Nation* noted on May 15, "one of the strongest arguments used against them by their opponents was that they were unnecessary, that 'the laws of political economy' would eventually secure protection for the negroes from their white neighbors themselves without any interference on the part of the federal government." The Memphis riots made clear, the editors argued, that the court remedies provided by those statutes were needed to protect black Southerners; even more, they suggested that blacks needed the vote immediately. "[T]he riot at Memphis reveals another gap which no legislative enactment can stop that does not in some way make the officers of the law responsible to those for whose protection they are appointed."

Other Northern observers drew a different moral, however. Henry Raymond's *New York Times* placed the blame for the riots squarely on the shoulders of "those 'philanthropists' among us who are attempting to keep up strife and ill-feeling in the South," whom it called "the very worst foes of the unhappy negroes."

Andrew Johnson showed no sign of reconsidering his view that the freed slaves needed no protection and Southern society no reform. He had convened the Cabinet on May 1 and forced a vote of every member on the proposed amendment. He led off with an impassioned denunciation of the draft and of the committee, and perhaps not surprisingly, no one spoke out for it—not even Secretary of War Edwin Stanton, whom Republican Radicals counted as one of their own. Within hours all the major newspapers carried an inside account of the meeting—furnished by Johnson himself. It was designed to embarrass Stanton and his congressional allies; and it was also, as Eric McKitrick notes, "a declaration of war on the men who had drafted and supported the committee's amendment."

When debate on the draft amendment opened in the House on May 5, Johnson and his obstinacy formed the background for the debate. The speeches showed a kind of double consciousness. On the one hand, the Republican members knew that they were reforming the fundamental law of the nation. As Vermont's Frederick Trowbridge had said in February, they were leaving "footprints . . . upon the rocks of the mountains." At the same time, everyone knew that the proposed amendment was also designed to serve as a political platform for the coming election—as a declaration that Republicans could rally around in a desperate electoral struggle that might determine not only who ran government for the next two years but who ran the Republic for the next generation—and in fact what kind of republic it would be. The House members debating the measure spent far more time discussing the second section, which governed representation, and the third, which would control who could vote, than they did talking about the first section, which embodied Bingham's view of the Bill of Rights and the proper role of state government.

Eben Ingersoll, an Illinois Republican, rose on the first day of debate to warn the nation that the stakes were the same as those of the war: "Carry out the policy of Andrew Johnson, and you will restore the old order of things, if the Government is not entirely destroyed: you will have the same old slave power, the enemy of liberty and justice, ruling this nation again, which ruled it for so many years."

Stevens, in his long speech on May 7, spoke not of the immediate political prospect but of the principles involved. The amendment was the beginning of a process of rebuilding the nation around the principles of the Declaration of Independence, he said. "In rebuilding it is necessary to clear away the rotten and defective portions of the old foundations, and to sink deep and found the repaired edifice upon the firm foundation of eternal justice." Admittedly, the proposed amendment was a compromise: "It falls far short of my wishes, but it fulfills my hopes. I believe it is all that can be obtained in the present state of public opinion."

Then he explained the amendment by section. Section 1 "allows Congress to correct the unjust legislation of the States, so far that the law which operates upon one man shall operate *equally* upon all. Whatever law punishes a white man for a crime shall punish the black man precisely in the same way and to the same degree. Whatever law protects the white man shall afford 'equal' protection to the black man." The amendment was necessary despite the Civil Rights Act, not because the act was unconstitutional but because "a law is repealable by a majority. And I need hardly say that the first time that the South and their copperhead allies obtain the command of Congress it will be repealed."

But to Stevens, the practical politician, the second section was "the most important in the article," because it would "either compel the states to grant universal suffrage or so . . . shear them of their power as to keep them forever in a hopeless minority in the national Government." As for the disfranchisement provisions of Section 3, "My only objection to it is that it is too lenient." The debt guarantees needed no defense— "none dare object to it who is not himself a rebel."

John Bingham defended his Section 1 as a necessity for the completion of the work of the Framers. "There was a want hitherto, and there remains a want now, in the Constitution of our country, which the proposed amendment will supply. What is that? It is the power in the people, the whole people of the United States, by express authority of the Constitution to do that by congressional enactment which hitherto they have not had the power to do, and have never even attempted to do; that is, to protect by national law the privileges and immunities of all the citizens of the Republic and the inborn rights of every person within its jurisdiction whenever the same shall be abridged or denied by the unconstitutional acts of any State." And Bingham added that "this amendment takes from no State any right that ever pertained to it. No state ever had the right, under the forms of law or otherwise, to deny to any freeman the equal protection of the laws or to abridge the privileges and immunities of any citizen of the Republic, although many of them have assumed and exercised the power, and that without remedy."

Bingham recalled the theory of state sovereignty, as practiced by South Carolina, which during the Nullification Crisis of 1832 had enacted a statute requiring its citizens to swear allegiance to the state and the state alone, to the exclusion of the Union. "That great want of the citizen and stranger, protection by national law from unconstitutional State enactments, is supplied by the first section of this amendment," he said.

The Democratic opposition also proceeded on two tracks. They dismissed the amendment as a useless contraption designed only for temporary partisan advantage; at the same time, they warned that the measure would transform the nation into a centralized despotism.

Andrew Rogers of New Jersey gave the fullest explanation of the opposition when he warned that the first section would take away the government's traditional power to choose groups among its citizens who were worthy of "privileges and immunities," and would instead confer these treasured prerogatives as rights on the unworthy. "The right to vote is a privilege," he said. "The right to marry is a privilege. The right to contract is a privilege. The right to be a juror is a privilege. The right to be a judge or President of the United States is a privilege. I hold if [Section 1] ever becomes a part of the fundamental law of the land it will prevent any State from refusing to allow anything to anybody embraced under this term of privileges and immunities," he said. "That, sir, will be an introduction to the time when despotism and tyranny will march forth undisturbed and unbroken, in silence and in darkness, in this land which was once the land of freedom. . . ."

The "despotism" Rogers warned of was not even a land where blacks held political power over whites, but one where blacks held *any* share of political power. The creation of a multiracial republic would mean the end of civilization. "I want it distinctly understood that the American people believe that this government was made for white men and white women," he said. "God save the people of the South from the degradation by which they would be obliged to go to the polls and vote side by side with the negro!"

Bitter as the language was, however, the House debate was short and orderly. Stevens had command of his troops, and though the opposition could orate in outrage it could do little to stop the Republican juggernaut. By Thursday, May 10, the House was ready for the vote. At the close of debate, Stevens told his troops that their votes were needed by their country. "Gentlemen say I speak of party," he said. "Whenever party is necessary to sustain the Union I say rally to your party and save the Union." And he pointed to the events in Memphis to refute Democrats who had preached "Christian forgiveness" and "charity" to the white South. "Let not these friends of secession sing to me their siren song of peace and good will until they can stop my ears to the screams and groans of the dying victims at Memphis."

Stevens quickly moved "the previous question," hoping to ensure that the bill would be voted on as it was. He knew that Henry Raymond and a few others were trying to find language that would weaken the disfranchisement clause, and he hoped to forestall any compromise at least until the bill reached the Senate. After a brief parliamentary skirmish, his motion for an immediate vote passed 84 to 79. Many Republicans voted no; but they were canceled out by Democrats who voted aye, hoping the draft amendment would be so harsh as to be unpopular in the nation. Once the draft was put to an up-or-down vote, party unity kicked in; the draft amendment passed 128 to 37, with nineteen members not voting. The galleries and the floor both burst into an ovation, and the Speaker struggled to maintain order. One Democrat protested against interruptions by "the nigger-heads in the galleries." As the mixed-race crowd hissed and booed him, Stevens wryly asked the chair, "Is it in order for members on the floor to disturb those in the galleries?" Amid general laughter, the Speaker admonished the Democrats not to "insult the spectators."

The proposed amendment did not come before the Senate for two weeks after it passed the House. House Republicans who opposed the disfranchisement section had been robbed of the chance of voting against it; they began to lobby Senate colleagues to change it. Meetings around the country began to consider the draft amendment, and letters to senators poured in from their home states.

The Senate was also embroiled in other struggles with Johnson, including an argument about patronage, a subject that tends to engage politicians' minds very closely. And lurking behind the patronage issue were even more ominous questions. Some Washington observers had begun to predict that, after the elections in the fall, Johnson would call a session of his own supporters, North and South, "recognize" it as the "real" Congress, and use military force to disband the Republican members who insisted on opposing him.

William Pitt Fessenden, meanwhile, was working himself into a state of near nervous collapse. Still not fully recovered from the varioloid, he plunged into the task of writing the joint committee's report. The report, by tradition, should have been submitted along with the proposed constitutional amendment. But Fessenden's illness had delayed him, and now he sat down to write "in weary hours, when I could find time, in which I should have rested." The report was not presented until June 6, while debate on the amendment was well under way in the Senate; but it was aimed at an audience beyond the Capitol walls and became an important part of the political campaign of 1866, which centered around the proposed Fourteenth Amendment as a plan for Reconstruction.

The majority report's 15,000 words laid out the Republican case for congressional Reconstruction. Johnson, the report argued, had based his lenient policy on "incomplete and unsatisfactory" knowledge of the condition of the defeated South. Southerners had taken advantage of the president's leniency to elect "notorious and unpardoned rebels" as prospective members of Congress, and the committee's interviews with Southerners and federal officials produced "no evidence whatever" among white Southerners "of repentance for their crime," or any real regret, "except that they had no longer the power to continue the desperate struggle."

The committee had also examined the situation of the freed slaves, who "had remained true and loyal, and had, in large numbers, fought on the side of the Union." These black citizens would be in danger under the rule of the unrepentant rebels. "It was evident to your committee that adequate security could only be found in appropriate constitutional provisions." Those provisions should first and foremost address the "increase of representation necessarily resulting from the abolition of slavery," but they should also recognize the basic rights of all citizens, black and white, and entrust them to the care of the federal government. This was not merely charity to the freed slaves, but self-defense for the Union. Without it, a new Slave Power might arise to renew the Rebellion: "Slavery, by building up a ruling and dominant class, had produced a spirit of oligarchy adverse to republican institutions, which finally inaugurated civil war. The tendency of continuing the domination of such a class, by leaving it in the exclusive possession of political power, would be to encourage the same spirit, and lead to a similar result."

The obvious solution to this problem, of course, would have been universal suffrage. But "it was doubtful, in the opinion of your committee, whether the States would consent to surrender" their previous monopoly of power over the franchise. Thus, "your committee came to the conclusion that political power should be possessed in all the States exactly in proportion as the right of suffrage should be granted, without distinction of color and race."

"So far as the disposition of the people of the insurrectionary States," it said (meaning, without saying it, the *white* people), "the prospects are far from encouraging." The Southern whites generally clung to "a generally prevailing opinion which defends the legal right of secession, and upholds the doctrine that the first allegiance of the people is due to the States, and not to the United States." They also remained "totally averse to the toleration of any class of people friendly to the Union, be they white or black" and nursed "an expectation that compensation will be made for slaves emancipated and property destroyed during the war."

In short, "no proof has been afforded to Congress of a constituency in any one of the so-called Confederate States, unless we except the State of Tennessee, qualified to elect senators and representatives in Congress." For this reason, "the so-called Confederate States are not, at present, entitled to representation in the Congress of the United States." To allow them to reenter Congress before giving "adequate security for future peace and safety" would mean that "[t]reason, defeated in the field, has only to take possession of Congress and the Cabinet."

The report had its effect during the fall elections, as a statement of the congressional theory. It had another effect as well: the strain of writing it knocked the recovering Fessenden off his feet once again. Once more his thoughts turned with morbid satisfaction to death. "The time I looked forward to, of 'Come, Daddy, supper's ready,' seems to be fast approaching," he wrote home. Wanting nothing more than to go home to Portland and smell the roses, he nonetheless chose to stay for the debate, apparently fearing to leave New England primarily represented by Sumner. But he asked a colleague on the joint committee, Jacob M. Howard, to take on the job of shepherding the proposed amendment through the Senate.

"Honest Jake" Howard was sixty-one years old, another New England Yankee who had lit out for the territory at an early age. Born in Vermont and educated at Williams, he had moved to Detroit in 1833, when the future Motor City was a village of fewer than five thousand souls. As a firebrand antislavery lawyer, he had predicted as early as 1850 that the overweening grasp of the slavocracy, as embodied in the Fugitive Slave Act, would lead the country to violent civil war. His friends liked to claim that, four years later, he had suggested that the first national convention of the new antislavery party adopt the name "Republican." (Like many lawyers then as now, he fancied himself as a man of letters as well as a public servant; he had, in 1848, translated for publication the mildly scandalous *Historical and Secret Memoirs of the Empress Josephine*.) Even Howard's admirers admitted that his oratorical style could be a bit heavy, and they often remarked on the pungent smell of his hair pomade; but he was respected for his constitutional knowledge.

But Howard did not command the kind of obedience from senators that Stevens could gain from the House. And the weeks before debate opened were filled with informal consultations on how to salvage the draft amendment. No conclusions had been reached by the time Howard opened debate on May 23, though most people expected the third section to be changed.

Howard explained the committee's draft section by section. Remarkably enough, he noted, to this point in American history there was no clear legal definition of "citizens of the United States." As for citizens' "privileges and immunities," he said they included "the personal rights guaranteed and secured by the first eight amendments of the Constitution; such as the freedom of speech and of the press; the right of the people peaceably to assemble and petition the Government for a redress of grievances, a right appertaining to each and all the people; the right to keep and bear arms; the right to be exempted from the quartering of soldiers in a house without the consent of the owner; the right to be exempt from unreasonable searches and seizures, and from any search or seizure except by virtue of a warrant issued upon a formal oath or affidavit; the right of an accused person to be informed of the nature of the accusation against him, and his right to be tried by an impartial jury of the vicinage; and also the right to be secure against excessive bail and against cruel and unusual punishments."

Beyond extending the Bill of Rights to the states, Howard said, "The last two clauses of the first section of the amendment disable a state from depriving not merely a citizen of the United States, but any person, whoever he may be, of life, liberty, or property without due process of law, or from denying to him the equal protection of the laws of the state. This abolishes all class legislation and does away with the injustice of subjecting one caste of persons to a code not applicable to another."

The first section, in effect, was designed to make every state live by the basic rules of republicanism. And the fifth section completed the change by permitting Congress to enforce its view of free and equal government. "I look upon the first section, taken in connection with the fifth, as very important," Howard said. "It will, if adopted by the States, forever disable every one of them from passing laws trenching upon those fundamental rights and privileges which pertain to citizens of the United States, and to all persons who may happen to be within their jurisdiction. It establishes equality before the law, and it gives to the humblest, the poorest, the most despised of the race the same rights and the same protection before the law as it gives to the most powerful, the most wealthy, or the most haughty. That, sir, is republican government, as I understand it, and the only one which can claim the praise of a just Government."

Speaking for himself, Howard said he favored black voting "to some extent at least, for I am opposed to the exclusion and proscription of an entire race." But the committee did not believe a suffrage amendment could be ratified. So the second section "is so drawn as to make it the political interest of the once slaveholding States to admit their colored population to the right of suffrage." It would operate whether the Southern states drew a racial line to exclude freed slaves from voting or used a formally nonracial category like a literacy test, he said.

Howard was somewhat cavalier about Sections 3 and 4—the disfranchisement and debt-repudiation provisions—as if embarrassed by them. Section 3, as written, was "not of any practical benefit to the country," he said. Section 4 might not be urgently needed. But there were still creditors hoping for repayment of the Confederate debt, and "if suffered to remain in quasi existence it can only be left in that condition as a subject of political squabbling and party wrangling."

Again, Howard emphasized the importance of the fifth section empowering Congress. "It casts upon Congress the responsibility of seeing to it, for the future, that all the sections of the amendment are carried out in good faith, and that no State infringes the rights of persons or property," he said. "It enables Congress, in case the States shall enact laws in conflict with the principles of the amendment, to correct that legislation by a formal congressional enactment."

It was a stirring defense of the Bingham sections of the amendment, and a rather halfhearted defense of the rest. The real legislative action, meanwhile, was taking place behind the scenes, where a series of closed party caucuses were meeting to consider how to salvage the committee's work. By Tuesday, May 29, the process was complete and Howard rose to offer a remodeled amendment to the Senate and the nation. To begin with, the Senate unanimously struck out Section 3, which would have disfranchised former Confederates from voting until 1870. Then Howard proposed adding a new sentence to Section 1: "All persons born in the United States and subject to the jurisdiction thereof are citizens of the United States and of the States wherein they reside." He also proposed changing the representation section to make clear that states would lose power in the House for excluding any male "inhabitants, being citizens of the United States"—thus making clear that states could not avoid the penalty by claiming that some people within their borders were American citizens but *not* state citizens. Next, Howard brought forward a new disfranchisement section, far more lenient than the House version: it did not limit ex-Confederates' right to vote, but only excluded a small group from holding office: those who had "previously taken an oath" to support the U.S. Constitution and then had afterward participated in the Confederate cause. And finally he proposed a new Section 4, requiring that the national debt "incurred in suppressing insurrection, or in defense of the Union . . . shall remain inviolate."

Debate on the proposed changes began in earnest on May 30, after the new language had been printed and circulated nationwide. Howard introduced the new citizenship language as "simply declaratory of what I regard as the law of the land already" and valuable because it "removes all doubt as to what persons are or are not citizens of the United States."

Nearly a century and a half later, the citizenship language seems almost obvious. But in 1866, the idea of a preeminent national citizenship was a radical repudiation of the "state sovereignty" theory, which held that each state had a right to define its own qualifications for citizenship, and that Americans were state citizens first, and only secondarily citizens of the Union. Edgar Cowan of Pennsylvania spoke for the Democrats in repudiating the radical implications of the new language, which would make both the nation and each state within it into multiracial republics, in which equality was a birthright and not a gift of the majority. The language, he said in horror, would make citizens of even the most undesirable nomads: "Sir, I trust I am as liberal as anybody toward the rights of all people," he began, "but I am unwilling, on the part of my State, to give up the right that she claims, and that she may exercise, and exercise before very long, of expelling a certain number of people who invade her borders; who owe to her no allegiance; who pretend to owe none; who recognize no authority in her government; who have a distinct, independent government of their own—an *imperium in imperio;* who pay no taxes; who never perform military service; who do nothing, in fact, which becomes the citizen, and perform none of the duties which devolve upon him, but, on the other hand, have no homes, pretend to own no land, live nowhere, settle as trespassers wherever they go, and whose sole merit is a universal swindle; who delight in it, who boast of it, and whose adroitness and cunning is of such a transcendent character that no skill can serve to correct it or punish it; I mean the Gypsies."

And the danger of nonwhite citizenship lay not only in the tiny Gypsy bands living in the United States. Opening citizenship to nonwhites would result in the annexation of California by the emperor of China: "[T]here is a race in contact with this country which, in all characteristic except that of simply making fierce war, is not only our equal, but perhaps our superior. I mean the yellow race; the Mongol race. They outnumber us largely. Of their industry, their skill, and their pertinacity in all worldly affairs, nobody can doubt. . . . They may pour in their millions upon our Pacific coast in a very short time. Are the States to lose control over this immigration? Is the United States to determine that they are to be citizens?"

John Conness of California assured Cowan that only "children begotten of Chinese parents in California" would be covered by the amendment. But he did ask when Gypsies had become an urgent threat to the nation. "I have lived in the United States now for many a year, and really I have heard more about Gypsies within the last two or three months than I have heard before in my life."

Wisconsin's James Doolittle, almost the last Republican supporter of Johnson, then suggested that the inclusion of the citizenship language represented a concession that the civil rights bill as passed was unconstitutional—a misapprehension that has persisted for years. "The committee of fifteen, fearing that this declaration by Congress was without validity unless a constitutional amendment should be brought forward to enforce his, have thought proper to report this amendment," Doolittle said.

Wearily Fessenden got to his feet to tell Doolittle that "[t]here is not one word of correctness in all that he is saying, not a particle, not a scintilla, not the beginning of truth." The citizenship language had not even come from the joint committee, he pointed out. Ah, yes, Doolittle replied—but Bingham, a member of the committee, had introduced similar language in the House. True, Fessenden responded—but "he brought it forward some time before the civil rights bill was considered at all." The committee's discussion of citizenship had focused around Bingham's ideas, not Trumbull's Civil Rights Bill. "It was placed upon entirely different grounds."

The Republican majority had little difficulty repulsing dissension within its own ranks; the language had been agreed to in caucus. Pro-Johnson Republicans were by now a spent force in the party and the nation; indeed, the Wisconsin legislature had a few weeks earlier specifically repudiated Doolittle and called on him to resign. After Johnson's denunciations of their leaders, rank-and-file Republicans retained little affection for the president.

The Democrats were another matter. In practical terms, they could slow but not stop the legislative juggernaut. But they could, and did, make an appeal to the country during the coming election, and the prospective debate over ratification of the new amendment. Thomas Hendricks of Indiana took up the challenge on June 4. The new citizenship language would make white Americans hold the title citizen "in common with the negroes, the coolies, and the Indians."

But his worst opprobrium he saved for the section giving Congress power to pass "appropriate legislation" to enforce the new amendment. "When these words were used in the amendment abolishing slavery they were thought to be harmless," he said. "[B]ut during this session there has been claimed for them such force and scope of meaning as that Congress might invade the jurisdiction of the States, rob them of their reserved rights, and crown the Federal Government with absolute and despotic power."

The Democrats charged that Republicans hoped to keep the country divided—in effect to prolong the war in order to maintain themselves in power. Republicans, however, responded that they were the party that was seeking a true Union—not a confederation of states any longer, but a real nation, with one social and economic system based on free labor and legal equality. Luke Poland of Vermont explained that, under the amendment, the South "will be opened and expanded by the influence of free labor and free institutions. . . . All causes of discord between North and South being over, we shall become a homogeneous nation of free men, dwelling together in peace and unity."

And here was where the issue was joined by the Democrats. What business of the nation was it whether a state had free labor and free institutions? Pennsylvania's Edgar Cowan asked. "What conceivable difference can it make to a citizen of Pennsylvania as to how Ohio distributes her political power?" he asked. "[T]o touch, to venture upon that ground is to revolutionize the whole frame and texture of the system of our Government."

The next day, June 7, was given over to a four-hour harangue by Garrett Davis of Kentucky, the most vehement and verbose border-state senator. "During most of that time," historian Horace Flack records, "less than ten members were in the chamber, and not over a score of spectators sat in the galleries." The next day, the floor was crowded again as the Senate adopted the language changes proposed by the caucus and rejected a series of amendments designed to weaken the amendment. Democrats tried to delay the vote, but senators began to shout, "Let us vote." At 5:15 P.M., the roll call began; the galleries were jammed, and nearly two dozen House members had crowded onto the senate floor. The vote was 33 to 11—three more than needed to make a two-thirds majority.

For the House, there remained the formality of acceding to the Senate's changes. On June 13, the members gathered for pro forma speeches: Andrew Rogers protested against the change in the right of each state "to have control of its own local affairs." Aaron Harding of Kentucky warned that the new amendment "at once transfers all powers from the state governments over the citizens of a State to Congress."

But the debate was perfunctory; everyone knew that Stevens had his troops in hand. Each time that Johnson roared defiance and scorned compromise, he had made Stevens stronger politically. The old man's political strength, however, did not translate into physical vigor. *The Nation* noted the signs of decay as Stevens grimly struggled to his feet to close debate. And though Stevens himself was far from resigned—even to the moment of his death, a little more than two years later, he was scheming to achieve his lifelong goal of a seat in the Senate—it is easy to read into his speech some awareness of mortality, and more than a suspicion that the work done that day in the House would, for better or worse, form his epitaph. He said:

> In my youth, in my manhood, in my old age, I had fondly dreamed that when any fortunate chance should have broken up for awhile the foundation of our institutions, and released us from obligations the most tyrannical that ever man imposed in the name of freedom, that the intelligent, pure and just men of this Republic, true to their professions and their consciences, would have so remodeled all our institutions as to have freed them from every vestige of human oppression, of inequality of rights, of the recognized degradation of the poor and the superior caste of the rich. In short, that no distinction would be tolerated in this purified Republic but what arose from merit and conduct. This bright dream has vanished "like the baseless fabric of a vision." I find that we shall be obliged to be content with patching up the worst portions of the ancient edifice, and leaving it, in

many of its parts, to be swept through by the tempests, the frosts, and the storms of despotism.

Do you inquire why, holding these views and possessing some will of my own, I accept so imperfect a proposition? I answer, because I live among men and not among angels; among men as intelligent, as determined, and as independent as myself, who, not agreeing with me, do not choose to yield their opinions to mine. Mutual concession, therefore, is our only resort, or mutual hostilities.

He continued mournfully:

You perceive that while I see much good in the proposition I do not pretend to be satisfied with it. And yet I am anxious for its speedy adoption, for I dread delay. The danger is that before any constitutional guards shall have been adopted Congress will be flooded by rebels and rebel sympathizers. . . . Hence, I say, let us no longer delay; take what we can get now, and hope for better things in further legislation; in enabling acts or other provisions.

I now, sir, ask for the question.

That, then, was the end. The roll was called at 4 P.M. The spectators were too numbed even to applaud. The final vote was 120 to 32. No Democrat voted for it; no Republican voted against it.

Congress would remain in session through the growing heat of the Washington summer, and would not adjourn until July 28. But its great work for the future of the Constitution was done; now the verdict lay with the country.

A UNION OF TRULY
DEMOCRATIC STATES

The white South had a way of upstaging Washington. The Memphis rioters had overshadowed the debate over final passage of the proposed amendment. When Congress adjourned at the end of July, an even bloodier massacre quickly framed the debate over what the Republican majority had done.

The tortured story of the ratification of the Fourteenth Amendment can only be understood against the backdrop of what seemed like a dangerous and revolutionary situation. In the North, there had been whispers all along that Johnson would step in to dismiss Congress and summon a new one made up of Democrats and his Southern allies. And in the South, the Johnson provisional governments had not been firmly established by congressional recognition; the political winds might blow them away, replacing them with military rule or a regime dominated by the Slave Power's enemies: former slaves, white Southern dissenters, and Unionist immigrants. It was this fear of "revolution" that sparked the New Orleans massacre.

The issue of black voting hung in the humid air over New Orleans during that hot summer. Former Confederates dominated the state legislature. The provisional governor, James Madison Wells, was a genuine Unionist who had lost almost all his wealth during the war and had had to spend part of that time hiding in a patch of woods called Bear Wallow. But General Phil Sheridan in 1864 had compared Wells to a twisting and slithering snake for his ability to change course depending on the directions of the political winds; after Johnson began signaling his support for restored white rule in the South, Wells had courted the former rebels—dismissing Unionist and Republican state officials—in order to win office. He and the Confederate legislature had ended the legislative session at swords' points, however; Wells had underestimated the determination of former Confederates to forge total political victory. Even though he had endorsed a conservative platform opposing black suffrage and proclaiming that Louisiana's blacks were not American citizens, Wells had fought for the Union, and his old rebel "allies" could never forgive him. By early 1865, Wells realized that his political career would shortly be over if he depended on the conservatives he had done so much to rehabilitate. Now Wells was trying to build a new power base by opening the ballot to black voters.

Louisiana, of all places in the South, might have seemed like a place where biracial politics were possible. Even during French and Spanish rule, New Orleans was the home to a significant and prosperous class of "free people of color"—many of them of mixed black and white ancestry. This mixed-race elite was highly educated, and for years before Fort Sumter enjoyed civil rights far beyond those extended to free blacks elsewhere in the slave South. In fact, a number of them had been slave owners themselves, and a few even served briefly in the Confederate army. They would form the core of the state's black political leadership during Reconstruction, and were distinctly unthreatening to white interests on most issues. Beyond that, New Orleans had fallen to the Union in 1862, meaning that by 1866 the people had had four years to adjust to living under the Union and had had little time to forge a loyalty to the "Lost Cause."

But ex-Confederates were determined to maintain political power exclusively in white hands. And the fear and uncertainty that hovered over state and national politics made whites even more suspicious of any moves to change political arrangements in the state. Disillusioned with the white legislature, Governor Wells and the state's Radicals and Unionists had decided to make an end run around them. In 1864, a constitutional convention had met to frame the state's Reconstruction charter. Though the convention had adjourned, it had never voted to dissolve itself. Accordingly, the convention's chair called for it to reassemble on July 30 at the Mechanics' Institute on Dryades Street. This building, only a few blocks from Jackson Square, was the temporary state capitol of Lousiana's reconstructed government. The agenda would be to amend the constitution to provide for black voting, exclude some former Confederates from the polls, and perhaps establish a new state government.

That morning, only twenty-five white delegates came to the hall—far less than a quorum. Those present authorized the sergeant at arms to search the city for missing members, and then recessed. The hall was surrounded by hostile whites, and New Orleans police were nearby. Usually only armed with clubs, the officers had loaded revolvers; many of them had also covered the badge numbers they wore on their hatbands. Though there were no blacks in the convention, a group of black Union veterans led a procession from the city's Third District to the west of Jackson Square, in support of black voting. Whites and blacks scuffled repeatedly, and a few shots were fired on both sides. Finally, the white mob rushed the blacks in a mass attack. The white police had been waiting for this; they attacked as well. The police openly targeted blacks for murder, and they accepted the help of the whites. When black supporters came out of the convention hall, police and rioters shot them as well and left them bleeding in the street. Other police entered the building, ran to the convention hall, and began systematically shooting at the delegates, who were crying "For God's sake don't shoot us . . . we are peaceable." A police officer agreed to accept the peaceable surrender of the delegates; but when they admitted police to the room, the police began firing again. One prominent Radical, the Reverend Jotham Warren Horton, came out of the building carrying a flag of truce; police shot him and then arrested him. On the way to jail, one of his captors crushed his skull with a brick or a club. He died a week later. A. P. Dostie, another nationally known Republican figure, was shot by the mob while police held him by the arms. When he was loaded into a cart full of corpses, a police officer took Dostie's hat and waved it in the air to the cheers of the crowd.

By the time federal troops restored order, three whites and thirty-four blacks were dead. General Sheridan, in a report to Congress, called what happened "an absolute massacre." A contemporary historian, James G. Hollandsworth Jr., wrote recently that the riot marked the beginning of the Southern white counterattack against the idea of black equality. It was "to the second phase of the Civil War what Fort Sumter was to the first"—with the major difference being that this time the South won, and suppressed its black population for the next century.

The violence was far worse than the atrocity at Memphis. Even more disturbing was the involvement of the government and the administration. Reports soon surfaced that the slaughter had been planned by the mayor of New Orleans. Beyond that, Johnson had made his sympathies pretty clear during the days before the riot; indeed, even after the riot had begun, he ordered the military not to separate the two sides or prevent all violence, but to "sustain the civil authority in suppressing all illegal or unlawful assemblies who usurp or assume to exercise any power or authority without first having obtained the consent of the people of the State"—suggesting that the convention delegates, not the white mob, were the instigators of the lawlessness.

In fact, there was one more casualty of New Orleans—Andrew Johnson. It is impossible to study Andrew Johnson without marveling at his willingness—indeed, his determination—to throw away any chance for success and reconciliation. And once again, in his response to the riots and his response to the proposed Fourteenth Amendment, this proud, doomed man embodied poignantly the human traits Shakespeare mocked in *Measure for Measure:*

> *man, proud man*
> *Drest in a little brief authority,*
> *Most ignorant of what he's most assured,*
> *His glassy essence, like an angry ape,*
> *Plays such fantastic tricks before high heaven*
> *As make the angels weep.*

A bit harsh, perhaps—the handsome Johnson was angry but not apelike. But if any angels were hovering over America in 1866, they must surely have shed tears as Johnson systematically spurned every chance to salvage his position. Even as late as the summer of 1866, he could probably have found his way back onto firm political ground and forced Congress to accept a compromise that would have left him politically strong as the nation headed into off-year elections. Johnson raced headlong to his own destruction; and he was dashed to pieces on the rock of the Fourteenth Amendment.

From the standpoint of the Republican Party, the proposed amendment was an extremely moderate measure—so respectful of public opinion about black voting that the most famous abolitionists scorned it publicly. In July, Frederick Douglass fumed that "to tell me that I am an equal American citizen, and, in the same breath, tell me that my right to vote may be constitutionally taken from me by some other equal citizen or citizens, is to tell me that my citizenship is but an empty name." A few months later, Wendell Phillips proclaimed the amendment "a swindle" that sacrificed the freed slaves "between the upper and nether millstones of Rebeldom."

For another, many people North and South believed that Congress had written the amendment to fail. The section barring former Confederates from office, it was said, was what today would be called a "poison pill" and would lead the South to reject it. (There's no evidence to support the idea that the provision was put in for conspiratorial motives, but there's also no question that the white leadership of the former Confederate states found it hard to swallow.)

What this means is that Johnson could have stepped into the breach with an alternative amendment, seemingly more moderate.

Much later, when all was lost for him, he actually pondered supporting an amendment that omitted the exclusion section but included
every other feature of Congress's proposal. What if Johnson had proposed that compromise in the summer of 1866, rather than after he
had been beaten at the polls? He could have added a provision that
any Southern state ratifying it would have its congressional seats
immediately restored. (Congress had been deliberately ambiguous
about whether ratification would be enough to win restoration.)

This would have put Congress immediately on the defensive. In
the nation as a whole there was a hunger for the war to be over, and
this urge for reconciliation was at war with the Republicans' need to
cripple the Slave Power before restoring the South.

But Andrew Johnson would have none of it. There was to be no
compromise. He was right, the people would support him, and his
enemies must be not only defeated but destroyed. Welles, his faithful alter ego, made clear that, in June when moderation might have
done Johnson some good, the White House would not consider anything that would placate "such a reckless body" as Congress or compromise with a measure that would "ruin the country." Johnson's
friends might try to smooth over the quarrel, but Welles interpreted
their efforts as deliberate treason—"a systematic plan to absorb the
President, or to destroy him." Instead, Johnson immediately began
planning for a mammoth "National Union" convention that would
endorse his policy and begin the process of creating a new fusion
party to nominate him for president in 1868. He could not veto the
amendment, because the Constitution provides no role for the president in the amendment process; nonetheless, he seems to have considered preventing his secretary of state, Seward, from sending the
proposal to the states for ratification. (Seward, who also opposed the
amendment, seems to have realized that adopting such a lawless
course would be suicidal; he sent the measure out without consulting
Johnson.)

On June 22, though, Johnson sent Congress a special message to
make clear his opposition to any amendment at all. Seward's trans-
mission of the measure was "purely ministerial," he said, "in no

sense whatever committing the Executive to an approval or a recommendation of the Amendment." In fact, "a proper appreciation of the letter and spirit of the Constitution, as well as of the interests of national order, harmony, and union . . . may at this time well suggest a doubt whether any amendment to the Constitution ought to be proposed by Congress" until the Southern states were represented.

Johnson's stance was a signal to the Southern state governments to reject the amendment. Tennessee, the first state to consider the amendment, did ratify—but only because its governor, the radical W. G. "Parson" Brownlow, was Andrew Johnson's mortal enemy. Pro-Johnson legislators almost blocked the plan by hiding to prevent a quorum; the majority had two of the fugitives arrested and held them under guard while the House passed the measure. Brownlow cabled John Bingham the news: "Battle fought and won. The Amendment was ratified in the House today by 43 to 11. . . . Give my compliments to the dirty dog in the White House." The Republicans in Congress immediately voted to seat Tennessee's members.

But though Republican-controlled states in the North ratified the amendment throughout the summer, the other Southern states rejected the proposal, usually by unanimous legislative votes. The Southern legislators made clear that no change in the old antebellum Constitution was acceptable to the white South. A committee in the Texas House said that the amendment "proposes to deprive the States of the right . . . to determine what shall constitute citizenship of a State" and to "transfer, as far as crafty and iniquitous legislation can effect the object, the government, the civilization of these States from the white race to the negroes." Georgia's governor objected to the choice between "the extension of the elective franchise to persons of African descent (nearly all of whom are notoriously unqualified for it), or a further diminution of the already relatively small weight of the Southern States in the administration of the Government." An Arkansas Senate report recommended rejection because the amendment would "take from the States all control over their local and domestic concerns." North Carolina's joint committee said the representation provisions were "inconsistent with the theory of our political system." Florida's governor, David Walker, urged rejection because the amendment would "give Congress the power to legislate in all cases touching the citizenship, life, liberty or property of every individual in the Union, of whatever race or color, and leave no further use for the State governments."

The Southern legislators had many reasons to reject the amendment. For one thing, as historian Michael Perman has shown, the ex-Confederates who ran the provisional governments were determined to prevent the emergence of an opposition party in the South. The disqualification clause would open political office to Unionists and newcomers; the conservatives decided that no representation at all was preferable to allowing their political foes to take power. Beyond that, of course, was the political calculation that Andrew Johnson would find a way to restore them without any more compromise at all.

This turned out to be a miscalculation. Johnson, in the fall of 1866, was now completing the process of snatching defeat—ignominious rout—from the jaws of victory. The events of the summer and fall handed him one setback after another. Meanwhile, the president's allies did not fare well, caught between a leader who would never compromise and a party and a voting public that was increasingly furious at his obduracy. Shortly before Congress opened in December, Johnson had lost a key ally when Preston King, collector of customs for the Port of New York, jumped from a ferry boat and drowned in the Hudson River. Suicide has complex causes, but King's death was seen at the time as at least partly stemming from Johnson's orders to purge King's allies in the Republican Party from their patronage positions with the port. After Congress adjourned, another key Johnson ally shot himself, at least partly in despair over public reaction to his vote to sustain Johnson's veto of the Civil Rights Act. Senator James H. Lane of Kansas, "the Liberator of Kansas," was an old antislavery warhorse who had stuck with Johnson in a desperate attempt to forge a compromise. Immediately after the vote, Lane realized that, like all those who imagined Andrew Johnson moderating any of his positions, he had made a mistake that would probably be fatal, politically at least. "The mistake has been made," he told a friend just after the vote. "I would give all I possess if it were undone." Lane sensed that his reputation and popularity would never recover. Indeed, Republican papers were soon printing hints that Lane had accepted bribes from government contractors, a charge that seems to have been baseless but that stung the old soldier deeply. On July 11, 1866, at the age of fifty-one, Lane was riding on a Kansas country road with two old friends. When they descended to open a gate, Lane pulled a pistol from his pocket and shot himself fatally.

Johnson's National Union Convention had met in Philadelphia on August 14. It quickly became known as "the arm-in-arm convention" because of the moving sight, during the opening session, of the delegates from abolitionist Massachusetts and secessionist South Carolina entering the "Wigwam" arm in arm. It was a potent symbol of the yearning, North and South, for an end to estrangement. The idea behind the convention was to spark the beginning of a new political movement. "National Union" was the nom de guerre Lincoln had given the Republican Party in 1864; now Johnson proposed to steal the name for a new coalition of Democrats and a very few conservative Republicans like Seward and Henry Raymond. But in fact such an alignment would not work in the long run. Welles in his diary traces the compromises that had to be made to keep the two factions together. "The proposed convention has no basis of principles," he wrote on June 21. "It will be denounced as a mere union with Rebels."

But bad as things were by August, Johnson could not resist making them worse. Citizens of Chicago were erecting a monument to Stephen Douglas, Lincoln's longtime opponent. They invited Johnson to come to the cornerstone-laying ceremony. The president got the idea of barnstorming the country—with the Cabinet and General Grant at his side—between Washington and Illinois, a political tour that came to be known as "the swing around the circle." He would explain himself to the people, and they would rally to his cause.

It was a miscalculation of the worst sort. To begin with, in 1866 the idea of an incumbent president touring the country and making stump speeches was unfamiliar and offensive to most Americans. Even presidential candidates, by and large, "campaigned" for office from their homes, writing discreet letters and granting selected interviews. Stephen Douglas, in 1860, had been the first candidate to break the mold by traveling the country, but Douglas had not been president and he had lost.

Beyond that was the brute fact that, as Rutherford B. Hayes warned a Southern relative, "Andy Johnson...don't know the Northern people." Johnson's interior mythology had crowned him the tribune of the people and their chosen savior; Southern sycophancy had strengthened this self-concept until he was unable to shake it. But in fact, the people of the North had never known Johnson before he took office, and much of what he had shown them over the past year they hadn't liked. And when Johnson ran into hostility, his fatal proclivity to impromptu oratory proved his undoing.

The "swing" started well enough, with a parade in New York and a testimonial dinner at Delmonico's. Afterward, there was a procession through Central Park in a pair of carriages drawn by magnificent horses. Ulysses Grant drove one equipage, carrying General George G. Meade, Colonel George Armstrong Custer, and Admiral David Farragut; Abram Hewitt, the iron magnate and munitions maker, drove the second, carrying the president, Seward, and others. Grant and Hewitt agreed to a race through the park, which Grant won. Johnson was "exhilarated," the press reported.

But once the party started west, things quickly went downhill. In Cleveland, Johnson first met a hostile crowd—the kind of situation he could not resist. He would persist in his policy "though the powers of hell and Thad. Stevens and his gang were by," he shouted at the hecklers. In St. Louis he faced a crowd that shouted "New Orleans," and he replied that "the riot at New Orleans was substantially planned," apparently by members of Congress. "I have been traduced, I have been slandered, I have been maligned," he went on. "I have been called Judas Iscariot and all that. . . . If I have played the Judas, who has been my Christ that I have played the Judas with?

Was it Thad. Stevens? Was it Wendell Phillips? Was it Charles Sumner?" (In the kind of headline politicians dread, the *New York Tribune* proclaimed that Johnson "Denies That He is Judas Iscariot.") By time the "swing" reached Indianapolis, the crowds had grown so hostile that Johnson could not even be heard.

What few Northern friends Johnson still had were mortified. Grant was so embarrassed by the spectacle that he stopped appearing with Johnson and finally left the tour. "I have never been so tired of anything before as I have been with the political stump speeches of Mr. Johnson," Grant wrote to his wife. "I look upon them as a National disgrace." The *Chicago Tribune* called the "Judas" speech the "crowning disgrace of a disreputable series." Mary Todd Lincoln, commenting on Johnson's visit to her husband's tomb, sniffed that he had "encountered much that would humiliate any other than himself, possessing such inordinate vanity and presumption as he does." Even the loyal Welles wrote, "I would rather the Chief Magistrate would be more reserved."

The Republicans countered Johnson's convention with one of their own and mounted a ferocious effort to get out the vote. "More than anything else," writes historian Eric Foner, "the election became a referendum on the Fourteenth Amendment. Seldom, declared the *New York Times*, had a political contest been conducted 'with so exclusive reference to a single issue.'" Carl Schurz rallied to the Republican colors. Even though he had lived several lifetimes, he was still only thirty-seven, and he flung himself into the battle like the warhorse in the book of Job, who "saith among the trumpets, Ha ha." As he had in 1860 and 1864, Schurz barnstormed the North, urging Republican voters to stay with the party and resist the president's plan of restoration on Southern terms. At a rally in Philadelphia in September 1866, Schurz summed up the Republican position in a speech as revealing, in its way, as "True Americanism" had been in 1859.

He admitted that the new amendment was a cautious measure, even somewhat less than what he would have favored; but "What objection can there be to it? Is it wrong that the civil rights of American citizens should be placed directly under the shield of the

National Constitution?" To Johnson's call for a restored Union, he replied, "We offer it to you—a Union based upon universal liberty, impartial justice and equal rights, upon sacred pledges faithfully fulfilled, upon the faith of the Nation nobly vindicated; a Union without a slave and without a tyrant; a Union of truly democratic States; a Union capable of ripening to full maturity all that is great and hopeful in the mind and heart of the American people; a Union on every square foot of which free thought may shine out in free utterance . . . in one word, a Union between the true men of the North and the true men of the South."

Johnson, by contrast, offered the blighted past of oligarchy and dictatorship: "a Union in a part of which the rules of speech will be prescribed by the terrorism of the mob, and free thought silenced by the policeman's club and the knife of the assassin; . . . a Union between the fighting traitors of the South and the scheming traitors of the North." The political general and boy revolutionary summoned the party of Union for one final test. "Forward into line, Republicans! This is to be the final battle of the war. Let it be the greatest victory of right and justice."

Among the Republicans not called forward into the line, however, was Frederick Douglass. Throughout the campaign, the party sought desperately to quell Democratic charges that the Fourteenth Amendment and the rest of the Republican platform was a disguised agenda for "social equality" between black and white. When the Republicans called a "Loyalists' Convention" to combat Johnson's "arm-in-arm" gathering, Rochester Republicans nominated Douglass as a delegate. At once party elders rushed to prevent the inflammatory image of a black American—even one as distinguished and loyal as Douglass—marching side by side with white Republicans. Thaddeus Stevens scorned the idea that equality was a fearsome prospect. "The doctrine [Negro rights] may be unpopular with besotted ignorance," he wrote in 1866. "But popular or unpopular, I shall stand by it until I am relieved of the unprofitable labors of earth." Behind the scenes, however, even Stevens urged Rochester's Republicans to select an all-white delegation. When they refused his advice, the party elders asked Douglass voluntarily to withdraw; needless to say, this proud, principled man refused. When the convention's delegates paraded in Philadelphia, only Theodore Tilton, the feminist editor of *The Independent,* would submit to march beside him. Yet the parade was, from Douglass's point of view, a triumph. Not only did he become the first black man to serve as a delegate to a national convention, but during the parade he was greeted effusively from the sidewalk by Amanda Auld Sears, daughter of the old mistress who had begun his education by teaching him his ABC's. She had traveled from her home in Maryland specifically to see him in glory; for the moment, the injuries and resentments of slavery were submerged in a wave of emotional reconciliation.

In the end, the congressional elections boosted the power of Congress and left the president all but irrelevant to the future course of Reconstruction. Republican strength in the House went from 136 to 173, and in the Senate from 39 to 57. (Because some states were readmitted, the total membership of both houses increased.) In the Senate, the number of Democrats fell from 11 to 9, while the new House had 9 more Democrats—well below one-third of the total. Johnson had finally destroyed himself; he would never recover. By the next year, Congress had taken control of Reconstruction, dissolved the provisional governments, and instituted direct military government in the old Confederate states. The Republican majority also impeached Johnson and came within one vote of removing him from office. Under the new rules of Reconstruction, Southern states could not even apply for restoration until they had ratified the Fourteenth Amendment.

One by one, the Southern states gave up the fight; they formed new biracial governments, wrote constitutions opening political rights to all, and ratified the Fourteenth Amendment. But even as they did so, some Northern states were feeling buyer's remorse. For the first time in American history, the amendment was writing the word *equal* into fundamental American law. Some in the North objected to allowing black Americans access to civil rights. Oregon,

Ohio, and New Jersey tried to "rescind" their ratification; Congress was forced to pass a law proclaiming that, once a state had ratified an amendment by the rules, its consent could not be snatched away (which remains the rule today). So confused was the situation that Secretary of State Seward would not proclaim the amendment adopted, as he had done with the Thirteenth; it was left for Congress to do that, on July 18, 1868; afterward, Seward belatedly certified it.

By the time the Fourteenth Amendment was certified, the revolutionary struggle had moved into a more radical phase. In 1869, Congress proposed the Fifteenth Amendment, which states, "The right of citizens of the United States to vote shall not be denied or abridged by the United States or by any State on account of race, color, or previous condition of servitude." A firm foundation had been laid, it seemed, for full biracial democracy in the unified nation.

But a revolutionary moment is fleeting. Much of the energy that could have been used to reform the slave South instead went into a fierce struggle between Congress and Andrew Johnson, which culminated in his impeachment by the House of Representatives on February 25, 1868. After a dramatic trial, the president was acquitted by one vote in the Senate the following May.

The impeachment of Johnson forms a lingering puzzle for historians. Politically, the president seemed like a spent force, with only a year of lame-duck service left to him. Many of the most fervent impeachers were figures far more radical than the framers of the Fourteenth Amendment, and their hints that Johnson somehow plotted the assassination of Lincoln seemed then, and seem now, at best fanciful and at worst crazy. The actual charge on which the House voted impeachment is all but incomprehensible today—that the president had fired a member of the Cabinet without the consent of Congress. Most constitutional scholars today believe that the president has the power to fire any Cabinet member at any time for any reason.

Yet there was a real issue lurking behind the verbiage. As long as Johnson remained in office, he had the power to obstruct the military reconstruction of the South; and he did so as best he could, replacing local commanders who were too assiduous in protecting the rights of freed slaves and white Unionists, and encouraging white supremacists to fight against the new biracial political institutions Congress was seeking to create. Pro-Union Southerners, white and black, flooded Republican members of Congress with desperate letters; unless Johnson was removed, they argued, their own lives would not be safe from the violent gangs of former Rebels who were working to maintain white control of the region. By surviving impeachment, Johnson helped keep alive the vision of the South as "a country for white men." As his biographer, Hans Trefousse, notes, Johnson by 1869 could view his administration as having "not been unsuccessful, at least not from his own point of view. His policies had so strengthened the Southern conservatives that he had greatly complicated the task of integrating the freedmen into [Southern] society, if he had not made it impossible at that time."

It is fascinating to imagine, too, what the nation would look like today if Johnson had been removed. The charges against him, despite their criminal disguise, were really political; he had, the impeachers were trying to argue, defied the will of the people and the legislature and betrayed the policy of the nation. In any European country, then or now, an executive who forfeited the confidence of the legislature would be required to resign. Johnson was the first modern president, holding the power of life and death over his fellow citizens; Republicans in the House, perhaps unconsciously longing for the antebellum days of congressional supremacy, were trying to wreck the powerful new office Lincoln had forged and replace it with something much more like a British prime minister. But the Constitution, by specifying "high crimes and misdemeanors" as the standard for impeachment and removal, seemed to say that only criminal conduct, not political malfeasance, was needed. Many Republicans could not convince themselves that the inept, arrogant Johnson was a lawbreaker. The failure to turn impeachment into a political remedy meant that the executive would continue, crisis by crisis, to gather power to itself; and so it has proved since.

Johnson himself continued to insist that he was only upholding the Constitution of 1787 against radicals and advocates of "negro domination." After he left office in 1869, he energetically sought vindication from the people of his home state. After running losing campaigns both for the Senate and the House, he finally in 1875 was elected by the state legislature to return to the Senate, where he was received by old friends and foes alike with tributes for his resilience. After serving one session, he returned to Tennessee for the recess; he collapsed and died in July 1875.

Even before Johnson's death, the Republican foot soldiers who had written the new vision of republicanism and equal protection into the Constitution also began to disappear from the scene, or to turn their attention to other matters. The links of comradeship were shattered by politics, death, old age, and the growing cynicism of the Gilded Age. On February 24, 1868, Thaddeus Stevens closed out debate on the House impeachment of Johnson. His strength failing, he gave his remarks to his former pupil and constant ally, Edward McPherson, to read aloud. The speech prophesied that the impeachment would determine whether "this whole continent shall be filled with a free and untrammeled people or shall be a nest of shrinking, cowardly slaves." Less than six months later, Stevens died, tended to the end by the faithful Lydia Smith.

Not long before his death, he was visited by Robert Dale Owen, who had used the spiritual telegraph to canvass the views of leaders like Daniel Webster and Stephen A. Douglas. "[P]resent my compliments to Douglas," Stevens said drily, "and tell him I think he was the greatest political humbug on the face of the earth." When another visitor complimented his appearance, Stevens responded, "[I]t is not my appearance, but my disappearance, that troubles me." Faced with the end of his career, he told a newspaper editor, "My life-long regret is that I have lived so long and so uselessly."

Ten minutes before his death, Stevens accepted the sacrament of baptism from two nuns who had devoted themselves to work with freed slaves. In his will, he left a conditional bequest to fund an orphanage that would be open to black and white alike. And he left instructions that he should be buried in a cemetery near Lancaster that accepted both white and black corpses. His headstone reads:

> *I repose in this quiet and secluded spot,*
> *Not from any natural preference for solitude*
> *But, finding other Cemeteries limited as to Race by Charter Rules,*
> *I have chosen this that I might illustrate in my death*
> *The principles which I advocated Through a long life:*
> *EQUALITY OF MAN BEFORE HIS CREATOR.*

Stevens's ambiguous alliance with Pitt Fessenden had foundered forever on the rock of impeachment. The final vote, in May 1868, was 35 for removal and 19 against—just one vote shy of the needed two-thirds majority. The most important of the "no" votes was Fessenden's. This most respected of Republican moderates had opposed impeachment from the beginning and repulsed a constituent who solicited his vote against Johnson. "[I]f I followed your advice," Fessenden wrote, "I could not look an honest man in the face." If Maine voters sought as their senator "a man who will commit perjury at their bidding," he said, he would cheerfully retire. The next year, 1869, he began an uphill battle for reelection; but on August 31, after an evening of whist in his beloved Portland home, he suffered an intestinal rupture. Ten days later, the death he had so often said he would welcome found him at last. He was sixty-two. His father, mentor, and best friend, General Samuel Fessenden, had died less than seven months before, at the age of eighty-four.

Perhaps fittingly, Robert Dale Owen's effort on behalf of spiritualism was the last crusade of the wonderful wizard's long and eventful life. In 1874 he published his autobiography, *Threading My Way*. In June 1877, at a séance in Brooklyn, he summoned the spirit of an old friend from his days in Naples. "You have sailed a good ship, you have kept a straight course," the spirit kindly told the seventy-five-year-old author. "[Y]ou will soon come to anchor." Owen died within the month, surrounded by family.

Charles Sumner's life ended in the kind of glorious wreck that often awaits those who love all mankind too much and understand individual human beings not quite enough. In October 1866, the fifty-four-year-old senator married Alice Mason Hooper, an aristocratic Massachusetts widow nearly thirty years younger than he. The marriage was a glittering one; Alice Hooper was the belle of Washington society, beautiful and vivacious (Fessenden had been briefly smitten by her charms, but retired from the field in recognition of the age difference); Sumner was, as his biographer David Donald notes, "the most conspicuous, and still the most handsome, member of the Senate."

Little is known for certain of Sumner's sexuality, but he had shown strikingly little interest in the opposite sex throughout his life, and a very short time revealed that he had no ability to change his confirmed bachelor ways to satisfy a lively young woman. Within a year, their marriage was the subject of open gossip. Democrat James Brooks, his political career at an end, popped up as editor of the *New York Express*, which alleged that Alice was having an affair with Baron Friedrich von Holstein of Prussia. She had spent the summer away from Washington and then left for Europe in the fall without seeing Sumner. Soon "Madame Rumor" was saying that he "could not perform the functions of a husband" and his political foes had dubbed him "The Great Impotent." Sumner now turned on Alice as bitterly as if she had been a defective Reconstruction bill. "[T]here cannot be two sides to the question," he wrote a friend who had offended him by saying that he was only right "in the main." Alice returned to Europe, and the two were divorced in 1873.

Sumner spent his remaining years crusading against new forms of segregation that were slowly appearing in the South. He sought a new civil rights bill that would guarantee black Americans equal access to transportation, lodging, schools, and even churches. In March 1874, he collapsed at his desk in his study, suffering an apparent heart attack. Friends and well-wishers thronged his bedside; one of his last visitors was Frederick Douglass. In the very early morning of March 11, he turned to his friend, Rockwood Hoar, and said, "Judge, tell Emerson how much I love and revere him." He died soon after. Two days later, a funeral procession formed to carry his body to the Capitol. Members of Congress had assigned themselves the lead position in the procession; but in a remarkable episode, those who had loved Sumner most—ordinary black citizens of Washington—silently pushed their way to the front of the line and led him on his last visit to the house where he had spoken so long and so proudly for the equality of all.

Frederick Douglass never held elective office. President Hayes named him U.S. Marshal for the District of Columbia, and in 1889 he became American consul general to Haiti—the first citizen of black America and the envoy to the world's first black republic. Anna died in 1882, the same year Douglass published an autobiography (his third). Two years later, after a secret courtship, Douglass remarried; his wife, Helen Pitts, was—like all the women we can be sure Douglass loved—a white feminist. The marriage subjected him to a public outcry; Helen's father, an abolitionist before the war, refused to visit the couple. The news also did not sit well with Ottilia Assing, the German-born woman who had been Douglass's companion during the prewar years. Not long after the news reached her in Paris, Assing strolled into the Bois de Boulogne and drank a fatal dose of poison. In her will, she left $13,000 in trust for Douglass and orders that all their letters should be destroyed.

For the rest of their years together, Frederick and Helen traveled the world. In 1895, he was an honored guest at a women's rights rally. His old friend Susan B. Anthony was among those who escorted him to the platform. Afterward, he met and plainly charmed a British delegate to the meeting with his passion and his physical magnetism. At home for supper, he amused Helen by parodying one of the feminist speakers. In an apparent mockery of the heroic orator, Douglass threw himself to his knees. He never rose again; he died instantly of a massive heart attack.

Five years later, John Bingham, eighty-five, died peacefully at his old home in Cadiz, Ohio. He had served in the House until 1872 and had been one of the managers of Andrew Johnson's impeachment trial. His party denied him renomination in 1872, but President Grant had named him American minister to Japan, an office he had held for twelve years. After returning home, he had retired to the family home in Cadiz, where he lived with his daughters. To the end of his life, Bingham would from time to time issue dark hints that he knew more about the Lincoln plot than he could tell because the true dimensions of the conspiracy would wreak havoc on the nation. His family reported that his last words were, "God, the United States, Franklin College."

Carl Schurz sailed on and on into the gaudy unfamiliar America of the Gilded Age. In 1885, he once again undertook a tour of the South. But the gray eminence who went South that year was much changed from the young, rather ragged Radical who had sailed on the *Arago* in 1865. Now Schurz was a former senator from Missouri (as the voice of Abraham had prophesied) and a former secretary of the interior. At fifty-six, he was no longer a Radical, or even a Republican; Schurz had been appalled by the naked spoilsmanship of the Grant administration. In 1872, he had broken with the Republican Party, and now he was known as one of the most important Independents ("Mugwumps," their political enemies called them, because they had their "mugs" on one side of the political fence and their "wumps" on the other). By 1885, Schurz was known chiefly for his efforts at sound money, conservation and, most important, civil service reform—worthy causes all, but nonetheless rather thin gruel after the revolution of 1848 and the battle for "the republic of equal rights."

The South through which he traveled was a different place as well. It had rebounded sharply from the devastation of the war; everywhere he went, the distinguished statesman was greeted by deferential, smiling white men who proclaimed their devotion to the cause of Union. In his essay, "The New South," Schurz concluded from his talks with these white leaders, so eager to please an eminent Northerner, that the difference between North and South had all but disappeared. True, Southern whites kept up the cult of Robert E.

Lee, Jefferson Davis, and Stonewall Jackson, but they had assured him that these were meaningless civic rituals that betokened no hostility either to the North or to Southern blacks. There *was* a bit of harshness toward blacks in the South, Schurz said. "We hear, from time to time, of inoffensive colored people being brutally ejected from public places and means of conveyance, and such stories come unquestionably oftener from the South than from the North."

His smiling hosts assured him, however, that these regrettable episodes betokened no general hostility toward the Southern blacks. Schurz, sounding for all the world like the "white-washing report" by Grant that Sumner had denounced in 1865, assured his readers that "as the negroes become better educated . . . their civil rights will, even without further legal machinery, find fully as much protection in the South as in the North, and perhaps more."

One of the penalties of early and prolonged success, however, is to see one's prophecies come to naught not once, but over and over. Seemingly indestructible, Schurz sailed on into the 1890s and then into a new century, a journalist of note even in his seventies. The rise of American imperialism appalled him. He bitterly opposed the annexation of Hawaii, the war with Spain, and the counterinsurgency that followed in the Philippines. It pained him, he wrote, to see his "beloved Republic in the clutches of sinister powers which seduce and betray it into an abandonment of its most sacred principles and traditions."

Imperialism (and its inevitable corollary, racism), Schurz warned, was a danger to republican liberty and equality at home. And one of the first groups to feel the chill wind was the black population of the old South. By 1904 Schurz, now a grizzled seventy-six, realized that his optimism of 1885 had been badly misplaced. The new generation of Southern whites was imposing a savage system of "segregation" on the South: blacks were to be excluded from all areas where they might mingle with whites, they were to be denied all but the most rudimentary education, and they were to lose their votes to a series of ruses—literacy tests and poll taxes, for example—that violated both the spirit and the letter of the Fourteenth and Fifteenth Amendments. In 1904,

Schurz wrote that "race-antagonism presents a problem more complicated and perplexing than most others, because it is apt to be unreasoning."

In addition, the South was once again a region where free speech and open political debate were forbidden. "The race-antipathy now heating the Southern mind threatens again to curtail the freedom of inquiry and discussion there," he said. The new radical segregationists "are striving again to burden the Southern people with another 'peculiar institution,' closely akin to its predecessor in character, as it will be in its inevitable effects if fully adopted by the Southern people."

Carl Schurz was by then one of the last survivors of his political generation, one of the few Americans living who could recognize the shrouded shape of the specter that had appeared over the post-Reconstruction South. The "New South" was not new at all; it was a continuation of the antebellum white oligarchy, with planter rule enforced by repressive laws and covert violence. Before he died in 1906, he may have wondered why no one else could recognize the ghost who had wandered into the center of American life at the dawn of a new century. Whether called "Jim Crow" or "segregation," the white South had turned back the clock. Once again, it was ruled by Schurz's old enemy, the Slave Power.

THE SECOND CONSTITUTION

The Fourteenth Amendment slumbered in the Constitution for more than half a century without beginning to bear out the hopes of its framers. It did not turn Southern states into the "model republics" Thaddeus Stevens yearned for; it did not bring the "final triumph of the right" that John Bingham foresaw; it did not establish, once and for all, Carl Schurz's "republic of equal rights."

By the first decade of the twentieth century, Southern white supremacists had found dozens of ways to lock black Southerners, and their white allies, out of political power. They had begun to rebuild the "intellectual blockade," enforcing ideological unity on the region. And they were beginning to use their control over undemocratic state governments to gain unwarranted influence in the nation as a whole.

Congress, which many Framers expected to be the key institution in preserving and extending civil and political rights, had become passive in the face of local authoritarianism. The Republican antislavery crusaders of the 1850s became, step by step, the crass spoilsmen of the 1870s, far more concerned with profit and patronage than with free labor and equality. By 1876, the Republican Party was willing to strike a bargain with the white South. Rutherford B. Hayes (known thereafter as "His Fraudulency") would be given the White House after a dubious recount; in exchange for retaining their control over federal jobs and spending, the Republicans would withdraw federal troops from the South and end enforcement of the laws passed to protect freed slaves and Unionists.

Meanwhile, the federal courts, which were to be the backstop for Congress, had refused even to try to make the states live by Republican rules. In 1873, the Supreme Court declared—in the tones of *Casablanca*'s Captain Reynaud, who was "shocked, shocked to find that gambling" was going on in Rick's Café—that it simply could not *possibly* have been the intention of the Fourteenth Amendment's framers "to bring within the power of Congress the entire domain of civil right heretofore belonging exclusively to the States," or to "fetter and degrade the State governments by subjecting them to the control of Congress." A few years later, the court struck down federal laws intended to protect black Southerners from private political and racial violence. In 1883, it invalidated the Civil Rights Act of 1875, which banned discrimination in public accommodations and transportation. Neither the Thirteenth nor the Fourteenth Amendment, the court said, allowed Congress to "step into the domain of local jurisprudence, and lay down rules for the conduct of individuals in society towards each other."

Finally, in 1896, the court completed what historian Rayford W. Logan called "the betrayal of the negro"; in *Plessy v. Ferguson*, it held that Southern states could segregate public places and mass transit by law. If black people did not like it, the court suggestion, they should just get over it: "We consider the underlying fallacy of the plaintiff's argument to consist in the assumption that the enforced separation of the two races stamps the colored race with a badge of inferiority," Justice Henry Billings Brown wrote for the majority. "If this be so, it is not by reason of anything found in the act, but solely because the colored race chooses to put that construction on it." The court made use of the Fourteenth Amendment during this time, to be sure: but almost invariably, it interpreted it as a charter of protection for business owners and corporations against such oppressive threats as health, safety, and minimum-wage laws.

In fact, in the years between the Civil War and World War I, the nation as a whole turned its back on both racial justice and "the republic of equal rights." Amid the cynical corporate splendor of the Gilded Age, small-*r* republicanism—the egalitarian ethos that had produced a small-town lawyer like Lincoln—began to seem quaint and absurd. The reasons for this cultural turn are complex. But a few are clear. For one thing, in the case of the Civil War, Americans found the pain of the slaughter so great that it all but eclipsed the reasons for the conflict. After the guns fell silent, the yearning for reconciliation was so great that many Northern whites wanted to forget the Slave Power and the danger they had seen in it, and even began to resent black Americans as if they had been the cause of the war.

For another, the year 1859 had brought an important phenomenon to American shores: Charles Darwin's *The Origin of Species* was published that year, and Darwin's idea of "natural selection"—the brute competition of individual and species for survival at all costs—began to replace the idea of divinely ordained progress as America's model of history. Natural selection in biology suggested that progress would be made by similar competition in the social sphere. Herbert Spencer and other "social Darwinists" began to argue that the goal of society was not the protection of the helpless but the ruthless elimination of the weak. Laws that protected minorities did no good, the social Darwinists argued, and in the long run they harmed society by slowing the extermination of the unfit. The courts began following the pseudo-Darwinist creed, until Justice Oliver Wendell Holmes Jr. sarcastically argued in 1905 that "[t]he Fourteenth Amendment does not enact Mr. Herbert Spencer's *Social Statics*." True enough; but it took another three decades before a majority of the Court agreed.

And finally, and probably most important, by the end of the nineteenth century, the United States was pursuing, for the first time, a world empire in Cuba and in the Pacific. As Americans have recently been reminded, empire requires silence, cunning, and ruthless violence—qualities that, then as now, render a society less, not more, hospitable to ideas like human equality and the rule of law. "As America shouldered the White Man's Burden, she took up at the same time many Southern attitudes on the subject of race," writes historian C. Vann Woodward. He quotes the editor of *The Atlantic Monthly*, who wrote that year, "If the stronger and cleverer race is free to impose its will upon 'new-caught sullen peoples' on the other side of the globe, why not in South Carolina and Mississippi?"

Like dark sorcerers in a fairy tale, the rulers of the white South were biding their time. The white Southern historian Ulrich B. Phillips wrote early in the twentieth century that the "central theme of Southern history" was the resolve of these white men that the South "shall be and remain a white man's country." Like water slowly wearing on stone, the determination of the planter elite and its allies etched away the national commitment to formal equality, to free speech, and to "truly democratic states." And finally, a half-century after Appomattox, the South rode back to power with the inauguration of the first Southern-born president since the Civil War. In an essay called "The Triumph of the South," one reporter matter-of-factly announced that the South had "come back to rule the Union." Not only a Southern president, but a Southern-dominated Cabinet and Congress took office in 1912.

Though his political career was in Yankee New Jersey, Woodrow Wilson had been born in Staunton, Virginia. Despite this, Wilson brought to the White House modern progressive ideas about economic regulation—and distinctly old-fashioned Southern ideas about race. The federal civil service, which had remained biracial, was now formally segregated. Federal facilities open to the public were also subjected to the color bar. Any pretense of federal enforcement of civil rights in the South was dropped. And in 1913, when Wilson went to Gettysburg to address a celebration to honor both Union and Confederate veterans, he spoke to a lily-white audience. Half a century after Lincoln went to Gettysburg to proclaim "a new birth of freedom," Wilson told the assembled veterans that it would be an "impertinence" to speak at the site of this great battle about "what it signified." The significance was obscured even more by the decision of the War Department that this reunion would be for whites only. Historian David W. Blight writes that "the 1913 'Peace Jubilee' [at Gettysburg] . . . was a Jim Crow reunion, and white supremacy might be said to have been the silent, invisible master of ceremonies."

In the "new South" of the twentieth century, one-party rule was the norm, and blacks were kept away from the polls by trickery and intimidation. "We have been very careful to obey the letter of the Federal Constitution," said Senator Walter F. George of Georgia. "[B]ut we have been very diligent in violating the spirit of such amendments and such statutes as would have a Negro to believe himself the equal of a white man."

It was the period African American historians call "the nadir." Historian George Tyndall quotes one Southern black newspaper as lamenting, "Any Negro who says that he is satisfied to be let alone with his broken political power, his miserable Jim Crow restrictions, his un-American segregation, his pinched and emasculated democracy, and his blood-curdling inquisition of lynching simply lies." And worse was yet to come: when black Americans answered Wilson's call to arms against Germany, they served in segregated units—and returned to widespread lynching and rioting designed to make clear to them that they had still not earned equal citizenship.

A new generation of historians began to explain that slavery had not been the cause of the Civil War, and began to construct the picture of the beleaguered and mistreated agrarian South, a victim not of its own arrogance and rigidity but of Northern aggression. Abolitionists and antislavery charlatans had brought on the war. Mostly Southern born, these sons and grandsons of Rebel soldiers won in the silence and safety of library stacks a nobility for the "lost cause" that ignored the brutality and exploitation of the Old South. The words *Slave Power* faded from the public discourse. The ghost of Thad Stevens or Carl Schurz, if either could see what had become of the "purified republic," might have begun to think the sacrifice of the war and Reconstruction as in vain.

And yet, ideas are stubborn—as stubborn, in their way, as facts. In 1776, Thomas Jefferson had written "all men are created equal" into the very birth certificate of the United States; and though it took nearly a century, those words in the end produced an Abraham Lincoln, a Frederick Douglass, a John Bingham, an Elizabeth Cady Stanton, and a Susan B. Anthony. In the end, those words brought slavery down and proclaimed liberty to the captives. Just so, during the dark years of segregation and empire, words like *due process* and *equal protection* reminded a complacent nation of promises it had made to history long before. Like yeast in a heavy mass of bread dough, the Fourteenth Amendment began slowly to transform the Constitution.

As late as 1922, the Supreme Court could offhandedly state that "neither the fourteenth Amendment nor any other provision of the constitution of the United States imposes upon the States any restrictions about 'freedom of speech.'" But only three years later, the Court backtracked and admitted that "freedom of speech and of the press . . . are among the fundamental personal rights and liberties protected by the due process clause from impairment by the States." Six years later, the Court said "it is no longer open to doubt" that freedom of the press was protected by the amendment; shortly after came freedom of assembly and petition, then free exercise of religion—one by one during the years between the wars, the Court "found" in the due process clause most of the key personal freedoms that John Bingham would have prized.

Meanwhile the idea of equal protection ate away at Southern segregation. Told by the Court that they could be confined to "separate but equal" spheres of society, black Americans began demanding that the Court take the "equal" prong seriously. Over and over they went to court to point out that Jim Crow schools were not physically or educationally equal to those provided for whites. Finally, in 1954, they had educated the Supreme Court to a belated realization that "in the field of public education the doctrine of 'separate but equal' has no place. Separate educational facilities are inherently unequal."

Those words heartened black Americans, who had known since Emancipation that legal separation was a tool of stigma and oppression. In 1956, at the onset of the Montgomery bus boycott, Martin

Luther King Jr. addressed the Montgomery Improvement Association in words that would have warmed John Bingham's rock-ribbed
Buckeye antislavery heart: "If we are wrong, the Supreme Court of
this nation is wrong. If we are wrong, the Constitution of the United
States is wrong. If we are wrong, God Almighty is wrong." Nearly a
century late, the equality genie was out of the bottle, and since then
our Congress, our courts, and our people have grappled with what it
truly means to have what Bingham called "one people, one
Constitution, and one country."

Answering that call, the sons and daughters and grandchildren of
the people who had saved the Union—the ordinary black folk of the
South—stepped forward to liberate their country once more. Prodded
by their courage, Congress outlawed the Jim Crow state. And the
Supreme Court held that "equal protection" required fair election
systems, where (at last, more than 150 years after the three-fifths
compromise created the Slave Power) each citizen's vote must count
the same as every other.

Today, we live in a nation that, at least in terms of individual liberties, is one of the most democratic in history. And Americans know
that they have rights. But too few understand that the source of our
rights is not Philadelphia 1787 but Washington 1866. The Fourteenth
Amendment has been called the "second Constitution"; in length
and number of subjects touched, it is by far the most sweeping and
complex change ever made in the original Constitution. Many literate
Americans understand the original Framers and their world, but know
virtually nothing of the second founders, or of their notions of free
labor, republicanism, and equal rights. That ignorance impoverishes
our public discourse—and it extends to far too many of our judges as
well. Too many of them appear to believe, in the words of *The Nation*
in 1866, that "the local majority is absolute," or, like John C. Calhoun,
that state interests are to be given primacy over those of the nation as
a whole. Too many believe that the ghost of state "sovereignty" lives
on, permitting states to slow or block the national march to equality.
At the dawn of a new millennium, the eminent historian David Brion

Davis wrote in the *New York Times* that "the United States is only now beginning to recover from the Confederacy's ideological victory following the Civil War."

Nowhere has that victory been more sweeping or regrettable than in the federal courts. In 1997, for example, the Rehnquist Court invalidated an important congressional civil rights statute, the Religious Freedom Restoration Act. Relying almost entirely on segregation-era analyses of the Fourteenth Amendment, the Court held that it, not Congress, had "primary authority" for determining how to protect minority rights in the states. It dismissed John Bingham's ideas as irrelevant to the final structure of the amendment. In 2000, the Court held that the Fourteenth Amendment did not authorize Congress to allow federal lawsuits by women victimized by gender-based violence, despite evidence of "pervasive bias" against female victims by local law enforcement authorities. "[T]he language and purpose of the Fourteenth Amendment place certain limitations on the manner in which Congress may attack discriminatory conduct," Chief Justice William H. Rehnquist wrote for the Court. "These limitations are necessary to prevent the Fourteenth Amendment from obliterating the Framers' carefully crafted balance of power between the States and the National Government"—for all the world as if the amendment had not been enacted to shift that "carefully crafted balance" sharply toward the federal side. And in 2004, the Court held that there is no constitutional problem when state legislatures deliberately redraw election districts to make sure that voters have no genuine choice of candidates—that, in other words, "the local majority" in a state can simply change the rules to ensure it will remain in power forever. "Fairness," sniffed Justice Antonin Scalia for a plurality, "does not seem to us a judicially manageable standard."

What is distressing in cases like these is not the specific result, though often it seems grievously wrong. More troubling is the failure of memory, the inability of contemporary Americans to grasp that their Constitution was changed by the second founders, that their eighteenth-century charter of limited government now contains the nineteenth-century values of equality, openness, and rule of law for all. Judges, politicians, and scholars solemnly echo Jefferson and Calhoun on the role of the states. "State sovereignty" and "states' rights," ideas that by rights were buried at Gettysburg, still rule us from their graves.

The American Constitution is not a fixed set of rules; it is an invitation to a national dialogue about concepts like due process, federalism, and equal protection. The voices of the second founders should be heard in that contemporary dialogue more clearly than they are. We can't summon their ghosts as guides, nor should we imagine that somehow we can divine their "original intent"—the intentions of the dead are and always remain one of earth's greatest mysteries. But to paraphrase Lincoln at Gettysburg, it is for us the living to dedicate ourselves to understanding and finishing the work they began. The words of the Second Constitution may not always be clear; nonetheless, they—like America itself—are a kind of prophecy, or a promise to history. Today, as in 1868, Americans often hesitate in front of claims of true equality. And yet that idea, and its corollary, a union of truly democratic states, was written in the sky by the second founders. More than a century later, it still goes before us, a cloud by day, a pillar of fire by night.

The melancholy lesson of history is that there will never come the "final triumph of the right." But it teaches another lesson as well: that prophecies and promises bear fruit over decades and centuries. We the people set out our path nearly a century and a half ago; in seasonable time, we will follow it.

UNITED STATES CONSTITUTION
AMENDMENT XIV

SECTION 1. All persons born or naturalized in the United States, and subject to the jurisdiction thereof, are citizens of the United States and of the state wherein they reside. No state shall make or enforce any law which shall abridge the privileges or immunities of citizens of the United States; nor shall any state deprive any person of life, liberty, or property, without due process of law; nor deny to any person within its jurisdiction the equal protection of the laws.

SECTION 2. Representatives shall be apportioned among the several states according to their respective numbers, counting the whole number of persons in each state, excluding Indians not taxed. But when the right to vote at any election for the choice of electors for President and Vice President of the United States, Representatives in Congress, the executive and judicial officers of a state, or the members of the legislature thereof, is denied to any of the male inhabitants of such state, being twenty-one years of age, and citizens of the United States, or in any way abridged, except for participation in rebellion, or other crime, the basis of representation therein shall be reduced in the proportion which the number of such male citizens shall bear to the whole number of male citizens twenty-one years of age in such state.

SECTION 3. No person shall be a Senator or Representative in Congress, or elector of President and Vice President, or hold any office, civil or military, under the United States, or under any state, who, having previously taken an oath, as a member of Congress, or as an officer of the United States, or as a member of any state legislature, or as an executive or judicial officer of any state, to support the Constitution of the United States, shall have engaged in insurrection or rebellion against the same, or given aid or comfort to the enemies thereof. But Congress may by a vote of two-thirds of each House, remove such disability.

SECTION 4. The validity of the public debt of the United States, authorized by law, including debts incurred for payment of pensions and bounties for services in suppressing insurrection or rebellion, shall not be questioned. But neither the United States nor any state shall assume or pay any debt or obligation incurred in aid of insurrection or rebellion against the United States, or any claim for the loss or emancipation of any slave; but all such debts, obligations and claims shall be held illegal and void.

SECTION 5. The Congress shall have power to enforce, by appropriate legislation, the provisions of this article.

· NOTES ·

Prologue. Philadelphia 1787: Red Sky at Morning

PAGE

1 *"an assembly of demi-gods":* Max Farrand, *The Framing of the Constitution of the United States,* p. 39.

2 *"negative all laws passed by the several States":* James Madison, *Notes of Debates in the Federal Convention of 1787 reported by James Madison,* p. 31.

3 *"monarchy, or a tyrannical aristocracy":* Ibid., p. 651.

3 *"a bill might be prepared in a few hours":* Ibid., p. 630.

4 *"between the Northern and the Southern . . .":* Ibid., p. 224. For an excellent discussion of this regional split, see Paul Finkelman, "Slavery and the Constitutional Convention: Making a Covenant with Death," in Richard Beeman, Stephen Botein, and Edward C. Carter II, eds., *Beyond Confederation: Origins of the Constitution and American National Identity,* pp. 199–200.

4 *twenty thousand of them in New York alone:* William Howard Adams, *Gouverneur Morris: An Independent Life,* p. 81.

5 *"Georgia cannot do without slaves:"* Madison, *Notes of Debates,* p. 505.

5 *"will finish the work of the sword":* Madison, *Notes of Debates,* p. 241.

7 *him "the Tall Boy":* Adams, *Morris,* p. 120.

7 *"the rake who wrote the Constitution":* Richard Brookhiser, *Gentleman Revolutionary: Gouverneur Morris, The Rake Who Wrote the Constitution.*

8 *"there are no fine Women here":* Adams, *Morris,* p. 96.

8 *"Government that power without which Government is but a Name":* Ibid., p. 138.

8 *"so nefarious a practice":* Madison, *Notes of Debates,* p. 411.

9   *"than saddle posterity with such a Constitution":* Ibid., pp. 411–12.

9   *"if the occasion were a proper one":* Ibid., p. 412.

9   *"it is a rising and not a setting Sun":* Ibid., p. 659.

10 *"the 'brilliant solution'":* Carol Berkin, *A Brilliant Solution: Inventing the American Constitution.*

10 *"the miracle at Philadelphia":* Catherine Drinker Bowen, *Miracle at Philadelphia: The Story of the Constitutional Convention May to September 1787.*

10 *"split the atom of sovereignty":* U.S. Term Limits, Inc. v. Thornton, 514 U.S. 779, 838 (1995) (Kennedy, J., concurring).

Chapter 1. The Brave Tailor

13 *what remained of the mighty armies that had saved the Union:* Jack Rudolph, "The Grand Review," *Civil War Times Illustrated* 19, no. 7 (November 1980), pp. 34–35.

14 *marched unseen by their side:* Shelby Foote, *The Civil War: A Narrative*, vol. 3, *Red River to Appomattox*, p. 1017.

14 *"bayou in July":* Margaret K. Leech, *Reveille in Washington, 1860–1865*, p. 278.

14 *"of a deserted Syrian city":* Henry Adams, *The Education of Henry Adams*, p. 44.

15 *before leading his division past the president:* Rudolph, "The Grand Review," p. 38.

16 *the regularity of a pendulum:* Foote, *The Civil War: A Narrative*, vol. 3, p. 1016.

16 *would by itself heal the country:* David S. Reynolds, *Walt Whitman's America: A Cultural Biography*, p. 309.

17 *while the steps keep time:* Walt Whitman, *Complete Poetry and Selected Prose*, p. 231.

17 *"to say nothing of all the Forts & Ships, &c., &c":* Walt Whitman to Louisa Van Velsor Whitman, May 25, 1865, in Walt Whitman, *The Correspondence*, vol. 1, pp. 260–61; see also Reynolds, *Walt Whitman's America*, pp. 448–49.

19 *"that Congress would readily ratify them":* Message to Congress in Special Session, July 4, 1861, in *Abraham Lincoln: Speeches and Writings, 1859–1865*, pp. 246–52.

19 *beginning of time:* James M. McPherson, *Battle Cry of Freedom: The Civil War Era*, p. 854. Gary W. Gallagher, *The Confederate War*, pp. 160, 162.

20 *who made more than $10,000: Encyclopedia of the American Civil War* (David S. Heidler and Jeanne T. Heidler, eds.), p. 694.

20 *a whopping 35.7 million: Historical Statistics of the United States, Colonial Times to 1970*, pp. 1090–91.

20 *20 percent of the Army's total strength for those four terrible years: Encyclopedia of the American Civil War*, vol. 2, pp. 1027–28; *Encyclopedia of American Immigration* (James Ciment, ed.), vol. 1, p. 83.

20 *one active-duty American soldier in every four:* Ibid., vol. 1, pp. 6, 85.

21 *bank porter and roustabout:* Hans L. Trefousse, *Andrew Johnson: A Biography*, pp. 18–19.

23   *then turned his attention to politics:* George Fort Milton, *The Age of Hate: Andrew Johnson and the Radicals*, pp. 59–72.

23   *"I want it, by God, for a calf pasture":* David Warren Bowen, *Andrew Johnson and the Negro*, pp. 30–31.

24   *"it shall be a government for white men":* Trefousse, *Andrew Johnson*, pp. 58, 236.

24   *as far as the eye could see:* Frank Moore, ed., *Life and Speeches of Andrew Johnson*, pp. xxxv–xxxvii.

24   *"every man in Tennessee!":* Ibid., p. xxxvii.

25   *"liberty and peace":* Ibid., pp. 251–52.

26   *another glass:* Trefousse, *Andrew Johnson*, pp. 188–89; see also Benjamin Perley Poore, *Perley's Reminiscences*, vol. 2, pp. 159–60.

26   *"I would say, you derive your power from the people":* Trefousse, *Andrew Johnson*, pp. 188–89.

26   *"dropped through it out of sight":* Ibid., p. 190.

26   *"was inebriated in public only once":* Ibid., p. 191.

28   *"any share of the credit in the suppression of the Rebellion":* James G. Blaine, *Twenty Years of Congress: From Lincoln to Garfield, with a Review of the Events Which Led to the Political Revolution of 1860*, vol. 2, p. 9.

28   *"that traitors must be punished and impoverished":* Edward McPherson, *The Political History of the United States of America during the Period of Reconstruction*, p. 45.

28   *"embarked on a course of amazing leniency":* Eric Foner, *Reconstruction: America's Unfinished Revolution*, p. 190.

29   *"old & young, men & women":* Whitman to Byron Sutherland, August 26, 1865, in Walt Whitman, *The Correspondence*, vol. 1, p. 266.

30   *"they were all loyal now":* Whitelaw Reid, *After the War*, pp. 304–5.

30   *"watched by a young Major in uniform":* Ibid., p. 306.

30   *"for the next Presidency":* Ibid., p. 305.

32   *"which his own hand earns":* "First Debate: Lincoln's Reply," August 21, 1858, in *Lincoln: Speeches and Writings, 1832–1858*, p. 512.

33   *"he has earned the right to citizenship":* McPherson, *Battle Cry*, p. 564.

33   *"the very intelligent [black men], and those who have fought":* Lincoln to Michael Hahn, in *Abraham Lincoln: Speeches and Writings, 1859–1865*, p. 579.

33   *"morbid distress and feeling against the negroes":* Eric Foner, *Reconstruction: America's Unfinished Revolution, 1863–1877*, pp. 179–81.

34   *indeed, in Congress itself:* Ibid., p. 179.

34   *galvanized this powerful voting bloc with his speeches:* Oswald Garrison Villard, "Carl Schurz," in *The Dictionary of American Biography*, vol. 16, pp. 466–70.

34   *Schurz escaped to France:* Carl Schurz, *The Reminiscences of Carl Schurz*, vol. 1, pp. 138, 217–21.

35   *embarking for the freedom of America in 1852:* Villard, "Carl Schurz," p. 466.

35   *"incorporates the vigorous elements of all civilized nations on earth":* Carl Schurz, *Speeches, Correspondence and Political Papers of Carl Schurz*, vol. 1, p. 54.

35   *"the title to citizenship":* Ibid., p. 57.

35   *"like a liquid poison":* Ibid., pp. 59–60.

36   *"feeling serious pangs of conscience":* Ibid., pp. 69–70.

36 *decisive in his victory that year:* Hans L. Trefousse, *Carl Schurz: A Biography*, pp. 93–94.

36 *widely publicized speeches in Philadelphia, New York, and Milwaukee:* Ibid., pp. 145–47.

36 *return to talk to him about the matter:* Ibid., pp. 150–54.

36 *to return to see him:* Ibid., p. 153.

37 *the thrilling pastime that was sweeping the country:* Ibid., pp. 46, 119. See also Schurz, *Reminiscences*, vol. 3, pp. 154–56.

37 *Schurz had seldom even visited:* Ibid., vol. 3, p. 154.

37 *"the anatomist chemist astronomer geologist phrenologist spiritualist mathematician historian and lexicographer":* Reynolds, *Walt Whitman's America*, p. 262. Walt Whitman, *Complete Poetry and Selected Prose*, p. 15.

37 *"recorded by physicians and psychologists of continental Europe":* Robert Dale Owen, *Footfalls on the Boundary of Another World with Narrative Illustrations*, p. 25.

37 *as many as eight séances in the White House itself:* Jean H. Banker, *Mary Todd Lincoln: A Biography*, pp. 218–20.

38 *"the sort of thing they would like":* Carl Sandburg, *Abraham Lincoln: The War Years*, vol. 2, p. 336.

38 *"with safety to the Union men and to the emancipated slaves":* Schurz, *Reminiscences*, vol. 3, pp. 157–58.

38 *how he found conditions there?:* Foner, *Reconstruction*, p. 179.

Chapter 2. Dark Wisdom

39 *freedom would have nothing to do with emancipation:* William C. Allen, *History of the United States Capitol: A Chronicle of Design, Construction, and Politics*, p. 255.

40 *without formal charges, for months or years at a time:* Margaret Leech, *Reveille in Washington*, p. 134.

40 *was carried onto the floor in a chair:* William H. Barnes, *A History of the Thirty-ninth Congress of the United States*, pp. 16–17.

40 *four strong men:* Walter Isaacson, *Benjamin Franklin: An American Life*, p. 446.

41 *grimly wagering for small stakes at faro:* Fawn Brodie, *Thaddeus Stevens: Scourge of the South*, p. 189.

41 *hacked it to death:* Ibid., p. 28.

41 *"surround him still":* Ibid., p. 20.

42 *"it won't bite!":* Ibid., pp. 25–26.

43 *respectfully called her "madam":* Hans L. Trefousse, *Thaddeus Stevens: Nineteenth-century Egalitarian*, p. 70.

43 *"than has been realized":* Brodie, *Thaddeus Stevens*, p. 87.

43 *that "it is impossible either to prove or to disprove" Brodie's conclusion:* Trefousse, *Thaddeus Stevens*, p. 71.

43 *had raised two children from the alliance:* Brodie, *Thaddeus Stevens*, pp. 90–91.

43 *"marginal politician":* Eric L. McKitrick, *Andrew Johnson and Reconstruction*, p. 260.

44 *for the slave owner, who regained his "property":* Brodie, *Thaddeus Stevens*, p. 33.

44 *"but . . . make them of everliving mind!":* Ibid., pp. 59–62.

45 *only $5 for each free black he ordered freed:* Don E. Fehrenbacher, *The Slaveholding Republic: An Account of the United States Government's Relations to Slavery,* pp. 231–32.

45 *in exchange for support in Congress and national elections:* Leonard L. Richards, *The Slave Power: The Free North and Southern Domination, 1780–1860,* pp. 86–87.

45 *rifles, knives, axes, and other farm weaponry:* James M. McPherson, *Battle Cry of Freedom: The Civil War Era,* pp. 84-85; Brodie, *Thaddeus Stevens,* pp. 116–18.

46 *four others—two black, two white—were less seriously hurt:* McPherson, *Battle Cry,* pp. 84–85; Brodie, *Thaddeus Stevens,* pp. 116–17.

46 *state's best-known antislavery lawyer, Thaddeus Stevens:* McPherson, *Battle Cry,* p. 85; Brodie, *Thaddeus Stevens,* p. 117.

46 *dropped the indictments against the remaining prisoners:* McPherson, *Battle Cry,* p. 85; Brodie, *Thaddeus Stevens,* p. 117.

48 *the spirit of Thaddeus Stevens limped by their sides:* McPherson, *Battle Cry,* pp. 353–56, 499–502; Brodie, *Thaddeus Stevens,* p. 155.

49 *"damned rebel provinces to pick one up?":* Alexander K. McClure, *Abraham Lincoln and Men of War-Times: Some Personal Recollections of War and Politics during the Lincoln Administration,* p. 282.

49 *created by the only real "sovereign" in a free republic: the people:* James Madison, "Report on the Alien and Sedition Acts," in James Madison, *Writings,* pp. 608–10.

49 *"by the powers vested in the Marshals by law":* "Proclamation Calling Militia and Convening Congress, April 15, 1861," in *Abraham Lincoln: Speeches and Writings, 1859–1865,* pp. 232–33.

49 *"The Union as it was . . .":* James Albert Woodburn, "The Attitude of Thaddeus Stevens toward the Conduct of the Civil War," p. 577.

50 *"without a slave upon its soil":* Brodie, *Thaddeus Stevens,* p. 166.

52 *horsewhipped by Southern bravos:* Clement Eaton, *The Freedom-of-Thought Struggle in the Old South,* pp. 335–52.

52 *"no regard for constitutions, no deference to courts":* *Congressional Globe* (hereafter *CG*), 36th Congress, 1st Session, p. 1872, reprinted in Michael Kent Curtis, *Free Speech: "The People's Darling Privilege": Struggles for Freedom of Expression in American History,* p. 285.

53 *"borrow it for a while":* Gerald S. Prokopowicz, "Military Fantasies," in Gabor S. Boritt, *The Lincoln Enigma: The Changing Faces of an American Icon,* p. 58.

54 *"to those pure or unmixed":* David E. Long, *The Jewel of Liberty: Abraham Lincoln's Re-Election and the End of Slavery,* pp. 153–65.

54 *"Miscegenation!":* Ibid., p. 161.

54 *"maid-servant":* "The Lincoln Catechism (New York, 1864)," in *History of American Presidential Elections,* pp. 1214–44.

55 *by August 1864:* David Herbert Donald, *Lincoln,* p. 529.

56 *They were a group that would provide little support for the Republican Party. . . . :* Edward McPherson, *The Political History of the United States of America during the Period of Reconstruction, 1865–1870,* pp. 107–9.

57 *if the Southerners were seated, they would not:* Joseph B. James, *The Framing of the Fourteenth Amendment, Illinois Studies in the Social Sciences,* p. 23.

58   *just enough, that is, to give control of the House to the antiemancipation forces:* Herman Belz, "The Etheridge Conspiracy of 1863: A Projected Conservative Coup," pp. 549–67.

59   *with their credentials in order:* Ibid.

59   *Etheridge's scheme failed:* Ibid.

59   *"let our men organize the House":* Ibid.

60   *was Edward J. McPherson:* Brodie, *Thaddeus Stevens,* p. 45.

60   *district neighboring Stevens's:* "Edward J. McPherson," C. Mildred Thompson, in *The Dictionary of American Biography,* vol. 12, pp. 159–60.

61   *now McPherson would use it to preserve the victory:* Brodie, *Thaddeus Stevens,* p. 241.

64   *left by its demise: CG,* pp. 2–5.

Chapter 3. Turns in the South

65   *"fiery whiskers, and an asserting nose with the blooded race-horse thinness of nostril":* Whitelaw Reid, *After the War: A Tour of Southern States, 1865–1866,* p. 436.

65   *Where was the Schurz report?: CG,* p. 30.

66   *"almost like a newly-discovered country":* "Our Artists in the South," *Harper's Weekly,* April 28, 1866, p. 259.

67   *slavish obedience to the Slave Power agenda:* Leonard L. Richards, *The Slave Power: The Free North and Southern Domination, 1780–1860,* p. 2.

67   *"the South Carolina hotspur James Henry Hammond":* Ibid., pp. 1–2.

68   *"enduring forces in the American Government":* David Herbert Donald, *Charles Sumner,* vol. 1, p. iii.

68   *Sumner attacked American racism as an attempt to fasten onto the country a caste system:* Ibid., pp. 180–81.

68   *Mongolians:* Ibid., vol. 2, p. 9.

69   *"the harlot, Slavery":* Ibid., p. 285.

70   *Sumner's pristine silk hat:* Ibid., pp. 237–38.

70   *urged Schurz not to bother writing one:* Hans L. Trefousse, *Carl Schurz: A Biography,* p. 158.

71   *were anything but obsequious:* Jean Edward Smith, *Grant,* p. 421.

71   *the report supported Johnson's policies nicely: CG,* p. 78.

73   *"If the youngest of you lives to my age even, you will not see another musket shouldered in the South against the Union":* Sidney Andrews, *The South since the War: As Shown by Fourteen Weeks of Travel and Observations in Georgia and the Carolinas,* p. 95.

73   *turkey buzzards massed on the roofs of the warehouses and fashionable homes:* Carl Schurz, *The Reminiscences of Carl Schurz,* vol. 3, p. 165.

73   *"a wealth of offal and garbage and beef-bones":* Andrews, *The South since the War,* p. 10.

74   *"seventy-five cents for a cobbler (wine punch)":* Reid, *After the War,* p. 66.

74   *"the effects of intense heat":* John Richard Dennett, *The South as It Is, 1865–1866,* p. 8.

74   *"smashed and torn by missiles":* John Townsend Trowbridge, *The Desolate South 1865–1866: A Picture of the Battlefields and of the Devastated Confederacy,* p. 114.

74 *"the agencies which they used"*: Andrews, *The South since the War,* p. 33.

74 *The rest, Sherman said, was "simple waste and destruction"*: Shelby Foote, *The Civil War: A Narrative,* vol. 3, pp. 644–45.

74 *"mass of blackened chimneys and crumbling walls"*: Andrews, *The South since the War,* pp. 29–33.

75 *"the debris of burnt buildings"*: Reid, *After the War,* p. 360.

75 *from overturning the rig*: Dennett, *The South as It Is,* pp. 38–39, 234.

76 *"in which a piece of cloth is plunged for a wick"*: Ibid., p. 224.

76 *"and 'sweet bread' (a name given to a plain sort of cake)"*: Trowbridge, *The Desolate South,* p. 166.

76 *"Won't be worth a copper in two years"*: Dennett, *The South as It Is,* p. 232.

77 *"'I'd know you just de same. . . .'"*: Reid, *After the War,* p. 185.

77 *business with Northern speculators*: Reid, *After the War,* pp. 402–3.

77 *"trading and swift fortune-making"*: Andrews, *The South since the War,* p. 340.

77 *men loved not the Union more . . . but Jeff. Davis less"*: Reid, *After the War,* pp. 184–85.

77 *"a cheat, a will-o'-the-wisp, and any man who trusts it will meet with overthrow"*: Andrews, *The South since the War,* p. 391.

78 *"supremacy of the State over the general government"*: Ibid., pp. 283, 333–58.

78 *compromise their state's prerogatives*: Carl Schurz, *Report on the Condition of the South,* p. 35.

78 *"to demand our rights!"*: Andrews, *The South since the War,* p. 320.

78 *"what more can the General Government have to do with the matter?"*: Reid, *After the War,* p. 264.

79 *"Then we'll show you who's going to govern this country"*: Ibid., p. 404.

79 *"I reckon they've not changed very much yet"*: Andrews, *The South since the War,* pp. 232–33, 355, 391.

79 *"meddlesome interference with his policy!"*: Reid, *After the War,* pp. 318–19, 393, 567.

80 *"we must unite with them"*: Dennett, *The South as It Is,* p. 351.

80 *"very unpopular in the South"*: Schurz, *Condition of the South,* p. 14.

80 *"'I reckon not!'"*: Andrews, *The South since the War,* p. 219.

80 *"less than twelve months"*: Dennett, *The South as It Is,* p. 91.

80 *"What's fair for one is fair for the other"*: Reid, *After the War,* pp. 352–58.

81 *"resume the debt"*: Andrews, *The South since the War,* pp. 260–61, 266.

81 *"Congress, will be almost a unit"*: Schurz, *Condition of the South,* p. 14.

81 *"gov'ment is bound to pay for them"*: Andrews, *The South since the War,* p. 218.

82 *"nothing but misrepresent and slander"*: Reid, *After the War,* pp. 71, 375.

82 *"in the way of progress"*: Schurz, *Condition of the South,* pp. 40–41.

82 *into silence or exile*: Clement Eaton, *The Freedom-of-Thought-Struggle in the Old South,* pp. 198, 376–78.

82 *SPECIAL COMMITTEE*: Dennett, *The South as It Is,* pp. 300, 344.

83 *"political theories and opinions of his neighbors"*: Dennett, *The South as It Is,* p. 273.

83 *had to slink out of town*: Andrews, *The South since the War,* pp. 294–300.

83 *"it ends with Sambo"*: Ibid., p. 22.

83 *"the blacks at large belong to the whites at large"*: Schurz, *Reminiscences,* vol. 3, p. 189.

83 *"but, after all, an animal"*: Andrews, *The South since the War,* p. 87.

84 *go to the children's former "owners"*: On the "black codes" and their relationship

to the antebellum status of "free blacks," see Theodore Brantner Wilson, *The Black Codes of the South.*

84   *"we can tell better when the next Congress meets and after the Supreme Court has decided":* Dennett, *The South as It Is,* p. 90.

84   *"more nearly related to the former than to the latter":* Schurz, *Condition of the South,* pp. 17, 32.

84   *"but it won't differ much from slavery":* Andrews, *The South since the War,* pp. 323–24, 371.

85   *"That's what free niggers come to!":* Trowbridge, *The Desolate South,* p. 225.

85   *"would not work without compulsion?":* Schurz, *Reminiscences,* vol. 3, p. 160.

85   *"among the southern people":* Schurz, *Condition of the South,* p. 16.

85   *"except under the lash":* Reid, *After the War,* p. 34.

85   *led only to fines for whites:* Wilson, *The Black Codes of the South,* pp. 30, 72.

86   *had been a domestic animal:* Andrews, *The South since the War,* p. 100.

86   *"be sworn to give his evidence!":* Dennett, *The South as It Is,* p. 75.

86   *"the old masters will still control him":* Reid, *After the War,* p. 84.

86   *"when we passed our free-suffrage law":* Andrews, *The South since the War,* p. 41.

87   *"to promote the interest of both races":* Dennett, *The South as It Is,* p. 76.

87   *"they must be colonized":* Reid, *After the War,* p. 163.

87   *"just like the Indians":* Trowbridge, *The Desolate South,* p. 47.

87   *"the extermination of the freedmen":* Dennett, *The South as It Is,* p. 191.

87   *affected not to see them:* Trowbridge, *The Desolate South,* pp. 177–78.

88   *"obligations of the national debt":* Andrews, *The South since the War,* p. 394.

88   *"fundamental principles of our political system":* Schurz, *Condition of the South,* p. 46.

88   *"and losses occasioned by the war":* Trowbridge, *The Desolate South,* pp. 316–17.

88   *"and the North does not dispute it":* "News from Washington," *Richmond Examiner,* January 9, 1866.

Chapter 4. The Mighty Heart of the World

90   *where it remains today:* San Mateo County v. Southern Pacific Railway Co., 116 U.S. 138 (1885).

90   *direct rule from Washington indefinitely:* David Herbert Donald, *Charles Sumner,* vol. 2, pp. 239–41.

91   *it was the proposer:* Ibid., pp. 240–41.

92   *"that vile ingredient, called conservatism":* Brodie, *Thaddeus Stevens,* p. 196.

93   *"Do not delay it on my account":* Charles A. Jellison, *Fessenden of Maine: Civil War Senator,* p. 77.

94   *"the candidate of my party":* Ibid., p. 111.

94   *referred privately to Sumner as a "dirty dog":* Ibid., p. 178.

95   *"of the word reform":* Alan Peskin, "Roscoe Conkling," in John A. Garaty and Mark C. Carnes (eds.), *American National Biography,* vol. 5, pp. 332–33.

95   *"man in the House":* Whitelaw Reid, *After the War: A Tour of the Southern States, 1865–1866,* p. 431.

96   "*its sure foundation and defense*": Michael Kent Curtis, "John A. Bingham and the Story of American Liberty: The Lost Cause and the Lost Clause."

96   "*one Constitution, and one country!*": Jacobus TenBroek, *Equal under Law*, pp. 331, 339–40.

97   "*in precisely the same channel*": Erving E. Beauregard, *Bingham of the Hills: Politician and Diplomat Extraordinary*, p. 47.

97   "*powerful, steady, pealing blast*": Ibid., p. 66.

97   *States with His kingdom on earth*: Mark A. Noll, *A History of Christianity in the United States and Canada*, pp. 115–19; Sydney A. Ahlstrom, *A Religious History of the American People*, pp. 277–78.

97   "*foretold in prophecy and invoked in song*": Beauregard, *Bingham*, p. 39.

98   "*freedom and free labor in the Territories*": *CG*, 36th Cong., 1st Sess., at 1840, c. 2–3. Bingham's speech is quoted in Curtis, "John A. Bingham," p. 617.

98   *lifelong friends and correspondents*: Beauregard, *Bingham*, pp. 11, 30.

98   "*into a horrid charter of wrong*": *CG*, 37th Cong., 3rd Sess., p. 266.

98   "*which are the gift of God*": John Bingham, "Argument in Reply to the Several Arguments in Defense of Mary E. Surratt," in Edward Steers Jr., ed., *The Trial: The Assassination of President Lincoln and the Trial of the Conspirators*, pp. 361, 363.

99   "*alike sacred before the sublime majesty of its laws*": *CG*, 37th Cong., 3rd Sess., Jan. 9, 1863, p. 266.

100   "*read it to suit yourself*": Bernard C. Steiner, *The Life of Reverdy Johnson*, pp. 6, 15, 18, 42, n. 50.

100   "*let our patriotism run wild*": Ibid., pp. 68, 115–16.

101   "*than had been done for the present*": Benjamin B. Kendrick, *The Journal of the Joint Committee of Fifteen on Reconstruction, Thirty-ninth Congress, 1865–1867*, pp. 40–41.

101   *and on the Thirty-ninth Congress*: Stevens's speech is set out in *CG*, pp. 72–75. All the quotes that follow are found there.

106   *New England states losing votes to the western states*: Joseph B. James, *The Framing of the Fourteenth Amendment, Illinois Studies in the Social Sciences*, p. 56; *CG*, p. 141.

107   "*excluded from the basis of representation*": Kendrick, *Journal*, p. 53.

107   "*not the language of the Constitution*": *CG*, appendix, p. 1.

109   "*We are ready!*": Ibid., p. 351.

109   "*a perfect equality with the white citizen*": Ibid., pp. 353–54.

110   "*to legislate for white people*": Ibid., p. 356.

110   "*no provision was made for it*": Ibid., pp. 356–57.

110   "*government at all*": Ibid., p. 357.

110   "*they are fit only for beasts of burden*": Ibid., p. 359.

111   "*as free negroes the right of representation?*": Ibid., p. 379.

111   "*of the ground of sex*": Ibid., p. 380.

111   "*women of my country to the negro*": Ibid., p. 380.

112   "*This country is the refuge of and is maintained for the white race*": Ibid., p. 382.

112   "*coming round there to make political speeches*": Francis Brown, *Raymond of the Times*, p. 15.

113 *"before the going down of the sun!"*: *CG*, pp. 490.

113 *"freely and without coercion"*: Ibid., pp. 491–92.

113 *force its adoption by 120 to 46*: Ibid., pp. 508, 535–38.

114 *"a covenant with Death and an agreement with Hell"*: Lindsay Swift, *William Lloyd Garrison*, p. 307.

114 *"State to the contrary notwithstanding"*: *CG*, p. 674.

115 *"Caste, Oligarchy, and Monopoly, on account of color"*: Ibid., p. 686.

115 *"the qualifications requisite for electors"*: S.R. No. 1, 39th Cong., 1st Sess., December 4, 1865.

116 *assault the joint committee*: Donald, *Charles Sumner*, vol. 2, pp. 244–45.

116 *"why every female that is taxed ought not to vote"*: *CG*, p. 704.

116 *distinctions of race or color*: Ibid., p. 704.

116 *"What can pass?"*: Ibid., p. 704.

117 *"in exact proportion to your action in the right direction?"*: Ibid., pp. 705–6.

117 *"consisting of words alone!"*: Ibid., pp. 707–8.

118 *"exclusion? Certainly not"*: Ibid., pp. 768–69.

118 *"They do not put them in command of the Army"*: Ibid., p. 769.

118 *"ground of race or color for any consideration whatever"*: Ibid., p. 849; Frederick Douglass, *Autobiographies*, p. 823.

119 *"the fate of the black man"*: *CG*, pp. 833, 880.

119 *"very Koh-i-Noor of blackness"*: Ibid., p. 1225.

119 *"that noses have been counted"*: Ibid., p. 1277.

120 *"perhaps it is of little value"*: Ibid., p. 1275.

120 *"to see what company they had fallen into?"*: Ibid., p. 1281.

Chapter 5. This Good Right Hand

121 *"The affair passed off very well"*: Gideon Welles, *The Diary of Gideon Welles*, vol. 2, p. 408; Hans L. Trefousse, *Andrew Johnson*, pp. 239–40.

122 *"following the return of Congress in January 1866"*: Trefousse, *Andrew Johnson*, p. 241.

122 *threatened the rights of Northern States*: William E. Gienapp, *The Origins of the Republican Party, 1852–1856*, p. 276, n. 10.

123 *Congress might also hold honest convictions*: Welles, *Diary*, pp. 410, 421–22, 432, 434, 435, 438.

123 *"their most vulnerable ground: Negro suffrage"*: Albert E. Castel, *The Presidency of Andrew Johnson*, p. 63.

124 *"continued to expand in the North until the Civil War"*: Paul Finkelman, "Prelude to the Fourteenth Amendment: Black Legal Rights in the Antebellum North," pp. 415, 420.

125 *between Johnson and Congress*: Constance McLaughlin Green, *The Secret City: A History of Race Relations in the Nation's Capital*, p. 77.

126 *"countenances me"*: Ralph Joseph Roske, *His Own Counsel: The Life and Times of Lyman Trumbull*, p. 8.

126 *bridesmaid*: Ibid., pp. 8, 40.

126 *bridal attendant*: Mark M. Krug, *Lyman Trumbull: Conservative Radical*, p. 43.

126 *freeing their descendants as well:* Krug, *Lyman Trumbull,* pp. 63–64.

127 *spectators howled:* Roske, *His Own Counsel,* pp. 40–41.

127 *never forgave Julia Jayne Trumbull:* Krug, *Trumbull,* p. 99–100.

127 *"no other way":* Ibid., p. 201.

128 *"to adopt it":* Ibid., p. 219.

128 *"this good right hand wrote this amendment to the constitution":* Roske, *His Own Counsel,* p. 109.

128 *rather than to the French regicides:* Michael Vorenberg, *Final Freedom: The Civil War, the Abolition of Slavery, and the Thirteenth Amendment,* pp. 49–66.

128 *"develop their powers":* Krug, *Trumbull,* p. 152.

130 *"familiar phrase, 'a fair chance' ":* James M. McPherson, *The Struggle for Equality: Abolitionists and the Negro in the Civil War and Reconstruction,* p. 186. For a general account of the agitation to create the bureau, see pp. 178–91.

130 *"confidence of [the] Christian public":* John Cox and LaWanda Cox, "General O. O. Howard and the 'Misrepresented Bureau,'" pp. 110–11.

130 *order the plantations restored to pardoned rebels:* Eric Foner, *Reconstruction: America's Unfinished Revolution,* pp. 142–70.

131 *a year in prison, a $1,000 fine, or both:* S. 60, 39th Cong., 1st Sess.

131 *It provided the tools to revolutionize Southern society:* Foner, *Reconstruction,* p. 244.

132 *"become the purchasers of homes for them?":* CG, p. 317.

132 *"so that it be a means to accomplish the end":* CG, p. 322.

132 *"wish of those who invent them and give them currency":* Ibid., p. 366.

133 *on January 25 the measure passed, 37 to 10:* Ibid., pp. 365, 366, 420.

133 *"of the world going on everywhere around us":* Ibid., p. 586.

134 *"The rebel States are not sovereign States":* Ibid., appendix, pp. 64–65.

134 *"distinguished senator":* Trefousse, *Andrew Johnson,* p. 241.

134 *cost him his head:* CG, p. 688; Eric L. McKitrick, *Andrew Johnson and Reconstruction,* p. 283; Edward McPherson, *The Political History of the United States during the Period of Reconstruction, 1865–1870,* pp. 51–52.

135 *Johnson claimed to represent:* McPherson, *The Political History,* p. 52 ff.

135 *"keep the mind of the freedman in a state of uncertain expectation and restlessness":* Ibid., pp. 68–72.

135 *"war not less than others":* Ibid.

136 *"or to overcome obstructions to the laws":* Ibid.

136 *postponement until 1 P.M. the next day:* CG, p. 917–18.

137 *"have escaped entirely the observation of the President":* Ibid., p. 941.

137 *until they were restored by congressional vote:* CG, pp. 941–42.

137 *"the representative of those eleven states than I am":* Ibid., pp. 942–43.

137 *"to the decision of the Senate":* Ibid., p. 943.

138 *Again, the galleries exploded:* Ibid., p. 943.

139 *"wasn't a nigger present":* Boston Daily Advertiser, February 23, 1866.

139 *It was a vintage Johnson speech:* The text of the speech is set out in McPherson, *Political History,* pp. 58–63.

139 *no fewer than 210 times:* McKitrick, *Andrew Johnson and Reconstruction,* p. 293, n. 46.

140 *"impertinent questions":* Welles, *Diary,* p. 439.

141 *"then they have made out their case":* CG, p. 1308.

Chapter 6. Birth of a Nation

142 *a common African surname:* William S. McFeely, *Frederick Douglass,* p. 5.

143 *oldest communities of free blacks in America:* Ibid., p. 74.

143 *"A man! a man!" roared the crowd":* Ibid., p. 88.

143 *"listeners never forgot":* Ibid., pp. 124–25.

145 *"origin, or of my unpopular color":* Frederick Douglass, *Life and Times of Frederick Douglass,* in Frederick Douglass, *Autobiographies,* p. 797.

145 *"but it was too late":* Douglass, *Life and Times,* in *Autobiographies,* p. 802.

146 *equal terms with whites:* Leslie H. Fishel, "Downing, George Thomas." In *American National Biography,* vol. 6, edited by John A. Garaty and Mark C. Carnes.

146 *African Methodist Episcopal Church:* Dictionary of American Biography, vol. 3, p. 138.

146 *Illinois's anti-black statutes:* W. Augustus Low and Virgil A. Clift, *Encyclopedia of Black America,* p. 66.

146 *another veteran of the Underground Railroad:* Jack Saltzman et al., *Encyclopedia of African-American Culture and History,* vol. 5, p. 2817.

146 *"the privileges of this condition":* Edward McPherson, *The Political History of the United States of America during the Period of Reconstruction, 1865–1870,* p. 52.

146 *"instead of their being mine":* Ibid., p. 53.

147 *more than, the black slaves:* Ibid., p. 53.

148 *"I believe they will do what is right":* Ibid., pp. 54–55.

148 *"cut a white man's throat than not":* Hans L. Trefousse, *Andrew Johnson: A Biography,* p. 242.

149 *"having been freed from their chains":* McPherson, *Political History,* p. 56.

150 *"deprivation of their rights":* Frederick Douglass, "What the Black Man Wants: Speech at the Annual Meeting of the Massachusetts Anti-Slavery Society at Boston, April 1865," in Philip S. Foner, ed., *The Life and Writings of Frederick Douglass,* vol. 4, pp. 158–59.

151 *"in the Negroes of the South?":* Ibid., p. 160.

151 *"a wall of fire for [every loyal citizen's] protection":* Douglass, "Reconstruction," *The Atlantic Monthly,* December 1866, in Foner, ed., *Life and Writings,* vol. 4, p. 199.

151 *"among which they live":* Frederick Douglass, "The Issues of the Day: An Address Delivered in Washington, D.C., on 10 March 1866," in *The Frederick Douglass Papers, Series One: Speeches, Debates and Interviews,* vol. 4, p. 120.

151 *"any State or States such power":* Douglass, *Life and Times,* in *Autobiographies,* p. 823.

151 *the symbolic name she assumed in 1843:* Nell Irvin Painter, *Sojourner Truth: A Life, a Symbol,* p. 73.

152 *and Rochester, New York:* Carleton Mabee, with Susan Mabee Newhouse. *Sojourner Truth: Slave, Prophet, Legend,* pp. 145–46.

152 *throw her off in 1865:* Painter, *Sojourner Truth,* p. 211.

152 *was up and running:* Russell Duncan, *Freedom's Shore: Tunis Campbell and the Georgia Freedmen,* pp. 22–23.

153 *"You say you will not fight"*: James M. McPherson, *Battle Cry of Freedom: The Civil War*, p. 687.

153 *"Some of them seem willing to fight for you"*: McPherson, *Battle Cry*, p. 687.

154 *"into the armed service of the United States"*: Abraham Lincoln, Proclamation No. 17, Statutes at Large, vol. 12, pp. 1268–69 (January 1, 1863).

154 *should fight for their own freedom*: McPherson, *Battle Cry*, p. 563.

154 *"participated in combat action"*: Leon Litwack, *Been in the Storm So Long: The Aftermath of Slavery*, p. 70.

154 *"Aye, indeed for a lifetime"*: Ibid., p. 77.

155 *the black sacrifice for the Union*: James M. McPherson, *Battle Cry of Freedom: The Civil War Era*, p. 686.

155 *sometimes put Confederate detachments to flight*: Dudley Taylor Cornish, *The Sable Arm: Black Troops in the Union Army, 1861–1865*, pp. 142–47.

155 *"cannot cope with Southerners"*: Ibid., p. 173.

155 *"they are hell in fighting"*: Ibid., p. 147.

156 *"on the move," Litwack writes*: Litwack, *Been in the Storm So Long*, p. 305.

156 *shipped away from home*: Ibid., pp. 229–32.

156 *"too affecting to describe," he wrote*: McFeely, *Frederick Douglass*, p. 259.

156 *often in mass ceremonies*: Litwack, *Been in the Storm So Long*, p. 240.

156 *"a charge on the Bureau"*: Ibid., p. 242.

156 *required black children to be "apprenticed" to whites*: Eric Foner, *Reconstruction: America's Unfinished Revolution*, p. 366.

157 *"as was the case in the days of slavery"*: Ibid., p. 103.

158 *"conception of themselves"*: Ibid., p. 109.

158 *leaving their slaves behind*: James M. McPherson, *The Negro's Civil War: How American Blacks Felt and Acted during the War for the Union*, p. 57.

158 *to cultivate for food*: Edwin D. Hoffman, "From Slavery to Self-Reliance: The Record of Achievement of the Freedmen of the Sea Island Region," pp. 8–42, 14–15.

158 *no time for them to graze*: Oliver Otis Howard, *Autobiography of Oliver Otis Howard: Major General United States Army*, p. 68.

159 *Congress decided the final ownership of the conquered lands*: McPherson, *Battle Cry of Freedom*, p. 841.

159 *"such title as it could convey"*: LaWanda Cox, "The Promise of Land for the Freedmen," p. 413.

159 *10 percent of the eligible Southern land*: Eric Foner, "Thaddeus Stevens, Confiscation, and Reconstruction," in Foner, *Politics and Ideology in the Age of the Civil War*, p. 135.

160 *"those that they can control"*: Ibid., p. 133.

160 *restored to its former owners*: Ibid., p. 138.

160 *"general murmur of dissatisfaction"*: Hoffman, "From Slavery to Self-Reliance," p. 23.

160 *"a quieting effect on the audience"*: Howard, *Autobiography*, pp. 238–39.

160 *as the song went up*: Hoffman, "From Slavery to Self-Reliance," pp. 23–24.

161 *caught in corrupt dealings*: Paul A. Cimbala, *Under the Guardianship of the Nation: The Freedmen's Bureau and the Reconstruction of Georgia, 1865–1870*, p. 181.

161 *"likely candidate for a race riot"*: Litwack, *Been in the Storm So Long*, p. 313.

161 *as the fact of emancipation sank in:* Foner, *Reconstruction*, p. 95.
161 *black political elite:* Ibid., pp. 111–13.
162 *"someday cast would be safe":* Litwack, *Been in the Storm So Long*, p. 286.
162 *"THE WHITE RACE in this Republic":* William Peirce Randel, *The Ku Klux Klan: A Century of Infamy*, pp. 15–16.
162 *eagerly accepted:* Ibid., p. 16.

Chapter 7. The Jeweled Word

165 *neither house would act alone:* CG, pp. 981–82.
165 *"I decline to give my assent to any such proposition":* Ibid., pp. 985–86.
166 *"the Country's worst enemies—Northern Copperheads":* Eric L. McKitrick, *Andrew Johnson and Reconstruction*, p. 297, n. 51.
166 *improve their numerical position:* For party affiliation and biography of each member, see William H. Barnes, *A History of the Thirty-ninth Congress of the United States* at 577–624.
166 *"the constitutional powers of the courts of the United States and of the States":* Edward McPherson, *The Political History of the United States of America during the Period of Reconstruction, 1865–1870*, pp. 68, 70.
167 *"'all Privileges and Immunities of Citizens in the several States'":* CG, 35th Cong., 2d Sess. at 984; see also Michael Kent Curtis, "John A. Bingham and the Story of American Liberty: The Lost Clause."
167 *which states could not legally abridge:* CG, 35th Cong., 2d Sess., p. 982.
167 *"States have no inherent rights; they have only derivative or delegated rights":* Erving E. Beauregard, *Bingham of the Hills: Politician and Diplomat Extraordinary*, p. 26.
168 *"due protection in the enjoyment thereof by law":* John Bingham, "The Constitution of the United States and the Proslavery Provisions of the 1857 Oregon Constitution," in Jacobus TenBroek, *Equal under Law*, pp. 321, 336.
168 *the assassination along with John Wilkes Booth:* Beauregard, *Bingham of the Hills*, p. 77.
169 *"were better it were well done":* Thomas Reed Turner, *Beware the People Weeping: Public Opinion and the Assassination of Abraham Lincoln*, p. 94.
169 *"Jefferson Davis is as clearly guilty of this conspiracy as is John Wilkes Booth":* Edward Steers Jr., ed., *The Trial: The Assassination of President Lincoln and the Trial of the Conspirators*. Page v provides a timeline of the prosecution; for Bingham quote in court, see p. 380.
169 *"perpetuate the devilish slavocracy":* Erving E. Beauregard, *Bingham of the Hills*, p. 93.
169 *"The truth must remain sealed":* Ibid., p. 88.
170 *the committee voted to send it to the full Congress:* CG, pp. 26–35 (December 6, 1865); Benjamin B. Kendrick, *The Journal of the Joint Committee of Fifteen on Reconstruction, Thirty-ninth Congress, 1865–1867*, pp. 46–47, 62–63.
171 *snips and snaps of the original Constitution:* See, for example, Charles Fairman, "Does the Fourteenth Amendment Incorporate the Bill of Rights? The Original Understanding," p. 26.
171 *"as it stands in the Constitution today:* CG, p. 1088.

171 *"or the copper blood of the Indian"*: Ibid., appendix, pp. 133–34.

172 *"they do not propagate in our country"*: Ibid., pp. 1054, 1056.

172 *"govern and be uniform throughout this Union"*: Ibid., p. 1095.

172 *of his amendment until April 2:* Ibid.

173 *"the due execution of this act"*: S.B. 61, 39th Cong., 1st Sess.

174 *"hereby declared to be citizens of the United States"*: CG, p. 474.

174 *"by the Constitution, is prohibited"*: Ibid.

174 *"body when you pass these laws"*: Ibid., pp. 477–79.

175 *"Not to vote"*: Ibid., pp. 529–30.

175 *"It only comes back to this, that a nigger is a nigger"*: Ibid., pp. 529–30.

175 *"changed the fundamental principles of our Government in some respects?"*: Ibid., p. 570.

175 *"It is to be executed through the courts, and in no other way"*: Ibid., p. 605.

176 *without being accused of hostility toward the freed slaves:* Mark M. Krug, *Lyman Trumbull: Conservative Radical*, p. 240.

176 *"Congress must be with the Administration or against it"*: Gideon Welles, *Diary of Gideon Welles*, vol. 2, p. 443 (March 3, 1866).

176 *Stockton then won the seat on a party-line vote:* Anne M. Butler and Wendy Wolff, *United States Senate Election, Expulsion and Censure Cases, 1793–1990*, p. 127.

177 *"that their children shall attend the same schools"*: CG., 1866, p. 1117.

177 *"to protect and enforce those which already belong to every citizen"*: Ibid.

177 *"the proud character of American citizenship"*: Ibid., pp. 1119.

178 *"Sir, that is forbidden by the Constitution of your country"*: Ibid., p. 1292.

178 *the bill was quickly passed, 111 to 38:* Ibid., p. 1367.

178 *"laugh and grow fat upon the public treasury"*: "The Civil Rights Bill—Its Probable Approval by the President," *New York Herald*, March 17, 1866, p. 4; on other magazines, see McKitrick, *Andrew Johnson*, p. 311, n. 80.

178 *"Alien and Sedition"*: Welles, *Diary*, p. 461 (March 23, 1866).

179 *"who is opposed to you or your policy"*: McKitrick, *Andrew Johnson*, pp. 313–14.

179 *alarming:* William Dudley Foulke, *Life of Oliver P. Morton*, vol. 1, pp. 466–67.

179 *"adhere to it"*: McKitrick, *Andrew Johnson*, p. 314.

179 *rumors of an impending veto:* Welles, *Diary*, p. 463.

179 *to the Adamses:* Sylvia B. Larson, "Stockton, John Potter"; www.anb.org/articles/04/04-00959.html; *American National Biography Online*, February 2000.

180 *to win with only a plurality:* U.S. Constitution, Article I, section 1, cl. 1.

180 *a group of opponents together got 41:* Butler and Wolff, *United States Senate Election*, p. 127.

180 *not legal:* CG, pp. 1565–67.

180 *procedure:* Ibid., pp. 1567–68.

181 *"each branch"*: McKitrick, *Andrew Johnson*, p. 323.

181 *"be called"*: CG, 1866, p. 1602.

182 *"Mr. Stockton"*: Ibid., 1866, p. 1635.

182 *hapless Stockton:* CG, p. 1677.

182 *"patriotic foreigners"*: Edward McPherson, *Political History of the United States during the Period of Reconstruction*, pp. 74–75.

182 *discriminatory state laws:* Ibid., pp. 75–76.

183 *"rights of the states"*: Ibid., pp. 77–78.

183   *"revolutionists in Congress"*: "Anxiety of the Politicians," *New York Herald*, March 30, 1866, p. 1.

183   *33 to 15: CG*, p. 1809.

183   *141 to 22:* Ibid., p. 1861.

183   *lost control of events and would never get it back:* McKitrick, *Andrew Johnson*, p. 324.

Chapter 8. The Ugliest American

185   *"and then the other":* Walt Whitman, *The Correspondence*, vol. 1, pp. 277–79.

185   *provide a political alternative to Johnson:* Quoted in Eric L. McKitrick, *Andrew Johnson and Reconstruction*, pp. 344–45.

185   *"became, to borrow the Quaker term, greatly exercised in regard to this matter":* Robert Dale Owen, "Political Results from the Varioloid," p. 662.

187   *she would marry no one at all:* Robert W. Leopold, *Robert Dale Owen: A Biography*, p. 108.

187   *"the rights of the Negro":* Ibid., p. vii.

187   *"as utterly divested":* Ibid., p. 111.

188   *"perfected as he might be":* Robert Dale Owen, "Moral Physiology, or, A Short and Plain Treatise on the Population Question," in *Birth Control and Morality in Nineteenth-Century America: Two Discussions*, pp. 21–22.

188   *"happier than the last":* Leopold, *Robert Dale Owen*, p. 111.

188   *to become a U.S. citizen:* Ibid., p. 25.

188   *"the lost world of Thomas Jefferson":* Daniel J. Boorstin, *The Lost World of Thomas Jefferson*.

188   *the great man's granddaughter:* Willard Carl Klunder, "Trist, Nicholas Philip." In *American National Biography*, vol. 20, edited by John A. Garaty and Mark C. Carnes.

189   *and Over the World:* Leopold, *Robert Dale Owen*, p. 217.

189   *a capacity audience in the House of Representatives chamber in 1825:* Ibid., p. 22.

189   *by doing good:* Ibid., p. 14.

189   *for unpaid debts:* Ibid., pp. 29–44.

190   *and divorce:* Ibid., p. 39.

190   *History of Woman Suffrage.* Lori D. Ginzberg, "'The Hearts of Your Readers Will Shudder': Fanny Wright, Infidelity, and American Freethought," p. 209.

190   *"The Great Red Harlot of Infidelity":* Donna Grear Parker, "Wright, Frances." In *American National Biography*, vol. 24, edited by John A. Garaty and Mark C. Carnes.

191   *followed Fanny for the rest of her life:* Celia Morris Eckhardt, *Fanny Wright: Rebel in America*, pp. 72–76.

191   *unheard of in the manly age of Andrew Jackson:* Ginzberg, "'The Hearts of Your Readers Will Shudder,'" p. 210 and n. 39.

191   *and to both partners:* Ibid., p. 217.

191   *"moral and physical well-being":* Frances Wright, "Explanatory Notes, Respecting the Nature and Objects of the Institution of Nashoba, and of the

Principles upon Which It Is Founded," *The New Harmony Gazette*, January 30, 1828, p. 124 ff., February 6, 1828, p. 132.

191   *"affection and kindness":* Leopold, *Robert Dale Owen*, p. 52.

192   *social upheaval:* Ibid., pp. 47–48.

192   *resettled in Haiti:* Eckhardt, *Fanny Wright*, p. 104.

192   *including free love between the sexes and the races:* Ibid., pp. 142–43.

192   *made them both infamous:* Ibid., pp. 56–62.

192   the Enquirer's *copy:* Leonard W. Levy, "Satan's Last Apostle in Massachusetts," pp. 16–30.

192   *"in all cases, effectual":* Owen, "Moral Physiology," p. 36.

193   *April 12, 1832:* Leopold, *Robert Dale Owen*, p. 110.

193   *opulent Palazzo Valli:* Ibid., p. 316.

194   *"around Walden Pond":* R. Laurence Moore, "Spiritualism and Science: Reflections on the First Decade of the Spirit Rappings," p. 476.

195   *Charleston Harbor that April day:* Leopold, *Robert Dale Owen*, pp. 345–50.

195   *campaigning for an immediate decree of emancipation:* Leopold, *Robert Dale Owen*, pp. 354–56.

196   *self-supporting members of the American nation:* Ibid., pp. 362–63.

196   *tolerates it:* Robert Dale Owen, *The Wrong of Slavery, the Right of Emancipation, and the Future of the African Race in the United States*, p. 117.

196   *"concurrent sentiment of citizenship":* Ibid., p. 179.

196   *"a ready tool for the political demagogue":* Ibid., p. 201.

196   *"the sovereign in person":* Ibid., p. 175.

197   *"because of color":* Ibid., pp. 197–98.

197   *"Blueprint for Radical Reconstruction":* John G. Sproat, "Blueprint for Radical Reconstruction," pp. 25–44.

197   *who was a soldier:* Leopold, *Robert Dale Owen*, p. 365.

198   *"voters of another section":* "Letter from Robert Dale Owen: Negro Suffrage and Representative Population," *New York Tribune*, June 24, 1865, p. 8.

198   *discrimination of color:* Leopold, *Robert Dale Owen*, p. 366.

198   *brick house on B Street:* Hans L. Trefousse, *Thaddeus Stevens: Nineteenth-century Egalitarian*, p. 128.

198   *"the poor and the oppressed":* Owen, "Political Results from the Varioloid," p. 664.

198   *for the time being:* Owen, "Political Results from the Varioloid," pp. 661–62.

199   *"by appropriate legislation":* The full text of the Owen plan is set out in Benjamin B. Kendrick, *The Journal of the Joint Committee of Fifteen on Reconstruction, Thirty-ninth Congress, 1865–1867*, pp. 296–97.

199   *"Take your own time":* Owen, "Political Results from the Varioloid," p. 662.

199   *"my best to put it through":* Ibid., pp. 662–63.

199   *treaty of peace:* The phrase itself is from David A. Strauss, "The Irrelevance of Constitutional Amendments," p. 1479.

200   *"such easy terms":* Owen, "Political Results from the Varioloid," p. 664.

200   *"happen to be ultra secessionists":* Ibid., p. 664.

200   *"the civil rights which we proposed to assure":* Ibid., p. 664.

201   *but not his common sense:* Ibid., pp. 664–65.

201 *April 21:* Kendrick, *Journal of the Joint Committee,* p. 82.
202 *adjourned until April 23:* Ibid., pp. 82–89.
202 *plans at every step:* Joseph B. James, *The Framing of the Fourteenth Amendment, Illinois Studies in the Social Sciences,* p. 107.
202 *the "leakiness" of the proceedings:* Ibid., p. 108.
202 *plan basically intact:* Kendrick, *Journal of the Joint Committee,* pp. 97–99.
202 *different from the Owen proposal:* Ibid., pp. 115–20.
203 *"whole policy of the country":* Owen, "Political Results from the Varioloid," p. 664.
203 *the committee vote was 12 to 2:* Kendrick, *Journal of the Joint Committee,* p. 101.

Chapter 9. The Prospect of a Good Long Life

206 *"adornment in dress":* New York Herald, Friday, May 11, 1866, p. 4.
206 *hear without being seen:* Henry Mayer, *All on Fire: William Lloyd Garrison and the Abolition of Slavery,* p. 288.
207 *"such an angelic, holy-looking face":* Ibid., pp. 290–91.
207 *"from this World's Anti-Slavery Convention":* Elizabeth Cady Stanton, Susan B. Anthony, Joslyn Gage, *History of Woman Suffrage,* vol. 1, pp. 61–62.
207 *determined, though moderate, abolitionist:* Eleanor Flexner and Ellen Fitzpatrick, *Century of Struggle: The Woman's Rights Movement in the United States,* pp. 68–69.
208 *"or find teachers at home":* Elizabeth Cady Stanton, *Eighty Years and More: Reminiscences, 1815–1897,* p. 145.
208 *all men and women are created equal:* Stanton et al., *Woman Suffrage,* vol. 1, pp. 70–71 (emphasis added).
208 *"tall and dignified, in Quaker costume" as the chair:* Ibid., p. 69.
209 *the great quest of the rest of her life:* Stanton, *Eighty Years and More,* p. 155.
210 *"we shall be good for twenty years at least":* Flexner and Fitzpatrick, *Century of Struggle,* p. 84.
210 *"and she fired them":* Stanton, *Eighty Years and More,* p. 165.
211 *"the united product of our two brains":* Ibid., p. 166.
211 *"separate action in legal matters":* Edward D. Mansfield, *The Legal Rights, Liabilities and Duties of Women; with an Introductory History of Their Legal Condition in the Hebrew, Roman and Feudal Civil Systems,* pp. 272–73.
212 *working in factories were female:* Catherine Clinton and Christine Lunardini, *The Columbia Guide to American Women in the Nineteenth Century,* p. 30.
212 *"they have a superior influence":* David Brion Davis, ed., *Antebellum American Culture: An Interpretive Anthology,* p. 16.
213 *"and the wife the breeches":* Flexner and Fitzpatrick, *Century of Struggle,* pp. 82–83.
214 *"made this great war":* James M. McPherson, *Battle Cry of Freedom: The Civil War Era,* p. 90.
214 *on behalf of any cause:* Judith E. Harper, *Susan B. Anthony: A Biographical Companion,* p. 258.
214 *two strong black men had to carry it:* Flexner and Fitzpatrick, *Century of Struggle,* p. 105.

214   *in time, the Thirteenth Amendment:* Michael Vorenberg, *Final Freedom: The Civil War, the Abolition of Slavery, and the Thirteenth Amendment,* pp. 38–39.

214   *after the Union was saved:* Eleanor Clift, *Founding Sisters and the Nineteenth Amendment,* p. 38.

214   *the first serious quarrel between the two friends:* Elisabeth Griffith, *In Her Own Right: The Life of Elizabeth Cady Stanton,* pp. 110–11.

215   *"the wish and will of our best friends":* Kathleen Barry, *Susan B. Anthony: A Biography of a Singular Feminist,* p. 149.

215   *"beloved Susan's judgment against the world":* Stanton, *Eighty Years and More,* p. 254.

215   *"in her own hand for protection":* Stanton et al., *History of Woman Suffrage,* vol. 1, pp. 747–48.

215   *"the Republican party can stand":* Ibid., vol. 2, p. 91.

216   *"the right of petition":* Ibid., p. 92 n.

216   *"but it could not be done":* Ibid., p. 91.

216   *"word 'male' into the Federal Constitution":* Ibid., p. 152.

216   *"principle of equal rights to all":* Ibid., p. 153.

216   "that the black man should vote": Ibid., p. 159.

216   *"cruel injustice to the women of the nation":* Ibid., p. 154.

216   *"alike needing only the ballot":* Ibid., p. 171.

217   *"wielding all her power":* James Brewer Stewart, *Wendell Phillips: Liberty's Hero,* p. 282.

217   *female voting for a hundred years:* Flexner and Fitzpatrick, *Century of Struggle,* p. 137.

217   *"a degraded, ignorant black one":* Stanton et al., *History of Woman Suffrage,* vol. 2, p. 94.

218   *"equal to our own":* Ibid., p. 382.

218   *"to have precedence":* Ibid., p. 178.

219   *"an enfranchised race now before Congress":* Ibid., p. 100.

219   *"abeyance to all orders and classes of men":* Ibid., p. 320.

219   *a delegate to the Democratic National Convention:* Ibid., p. 340.

219   *"treachery of Republicans":* Ibid, p. 322.

219   *Membership would be all-female:* Flexner and Fitzpatrick, *Century of Struggle,* p. 145.

220   *"the conservator of public morals":* Stanton et al., *History of Woman Suffrage,* vol. 2, p. 384.

220   *she cast a vote in the 1920 presidential election:* Flexner and Fitzpatrick, *Century of Struggle,* pp. 71–72.

Chapter 10. Not Among Angels

223   *and the all-white Memphis police:* "Reports of Outrages, Riots and Murders, Jan. 15, 1866–Aug. 12, 1868" [hereinafter, *Freedmen's Bureau Report*].

223   *a chance collision between two cabs:* Eric Foner, *Reconstruction: America's Unfinished Revolution,* pp. 261–62.

223   *as many as twenty thousand:* James Gilbert Ryan, "The Memphis Riots of 1866: Terror in a Black Community during Reconstruction," p. 244.

223   *"it is a nigger":* Theodore Brantner Wilson, *The Black Codes of the South*, p. 111.

223   *mostly Irish and Irish American:* Foner, *Reconstruction*, p. 262.

223   *the antiblack violence in Memphis:* "The Moral of the Memphis Riots," *The Nation*, May 15, 1866, pp. 616–17.

223   *on the street and in their houses:* "The Memphis Riots," *Harper's Weekly*, May 26, 1866, pp. 321–22.

223   *"kill the last dam[n]ed one of the nigger race":* Ryan, "The Memphis Riots," p. 250.

223   *handed out weapons to the crowd:* Ibid., p. 251.

223   *"responsible functions of his office":* Freedmen's Bureau Report.

224   *declaring martial law:* Ryan, "The Memphis Riots," pp. 251–52.

224   *"placed the damage at over $100,000":* Ibid., p. 243.

224   *"they are appointed":* "The Moral of the Memphis Riots," *The Nation*, May 15, 1866, p. 616.

224   *"foes of the unhappy negroes":* "The Memphis Riots," *New York Times*, May 10, 1866, p. 4.

225   *Republican radicals counted as one of their own:* Gideon Welles, *The Diary of Gideon Welles*, pp. 495–97.

225   *"supported the committee's amendment":* Eric L. McKitrick, *Andrew Johnson and Reconstruction*, p. 351.

225   *"ruled it for so many years":* CG, p. 2403.

226   *"of eternal justice":* Ibid., p. 2459.

226   *"the present state of public opinion":* Ibid., p. 2459.

226   *"it will be repealed":* Ibid., p. 2459.

226   *"who is not himself a rebel":* Ibid., p. 2460.

227   *"and that without remedy":* Ibid., pp. 254–2.

227   *"supplied by the first section of this amendment":* Ibid., p. 2543.

227   *"in this land which was once the land of freedom":* Ibid., p. 2538.

228   *"side by side with the negro!":* Ibid., p. 2538.

228   *"groans of the dying victims at Memphis":* Ibid., p. 2544.

229   *"'insult the spectators":* Ibid., p. 2545.

229   *insisted on opposing him:* The Nation, April 19, 1866, p. 481.

229   *"time, in which I should have rested":* Francis Fessenden, *Life and Public Services of William Pitt Fessenden*, vol. 2, p. 62.

230   *"continue the desperate struggle":* Report of the Joint Committee on Reconstruction, pp. ix–xi.

230   *"and lead to a similar result":* Ibid., p. xiii.

230   *"without distinction of color or race":* Ibid., p. xiii.

230   *"the prospects are far from encouraging":* Ibid., pp. xiv–xv.

231   *"and property destroyed during the war":* Ibid., p. xvii.

231   *"[t]reason, defeated in the field, has only to take possession of Congress and the Cabinet":* Ibid., pp. ix–xi.

231   *he wrote home:* Fessenden, *Life and Public Services of Fessenden*, vol. 2, p. 62.

232   *respected for his constitutional knowledge:* Silvana Siddali, "Howard, Jacob Merritt." In *American National Biography*, vol. 11, edited by John A. Garaty and Mark C. Carnes.

232   "and unusual punishments": CG, p. 2765.
232   "applicable to another": Ibid., p. 2766.
233   "a just Government": Ibid., p. 2766.
233   literacy test, he said: Ibid., pp. 2766–67.
233   "and party wrangling": Ibid., p. 2768.
233   "formal congressional enactment": Ibid., p. 2768.
234   "wherein they reside": Ibid., p. 2869.
234   afterward participated in the Confederate cause: Ibid.
234   "shall remain inviolate": Ibid.
234   not citizens of the United States: Ibid., p. 2890.
235   "I mean the Gypsies": Ibid., p. 2891.
235   "they are to be citizens?": Ibid., p. 2891.
236   "heard before in my life": Ibid., pp. 2891–92.
236   "report this amendment": Ibid., p. 2896.
236   "entirely different grounds": Ibid., p. 2896.
236   on him to resign: The Nation, April 19, 1866, p. 482.
236   "the negroes, the coolies, and the Indians": CG, pp. 2939–40.
237   "absolute and despotic power": Ibid., p. 2940.
237   "dwelling together in peace and unity": Ibid., pp. 296–4.
237   "system of our Government": Ibid., p. 2987.
238   to make a two-thirds majority: Horace E. Flack, The Adoption of the Fourteenth
         Amendment, p. 149.
238   "to have control of its own local affairs": CG, appendix, p. 231.
238   "the citizens of a State to Congress": ibid., pp. 3145–47.
239   "or mutual hostilities": Ibid., p. 3148.
239   "I now, sir, ask for the question": Ibid., p. 3148.

Chapter 11. A Union of Truly Democratic States

241   twisting and slithering snake: Joseph G. Tregle Jr., "Thomas J. Durant, Utopian
         Socialism, and the Failure of Presidential Reconstruction in Louisiana," p. 496.
241   so much to rehabilitate: Walter McGehee Lowrey, "The Political Career of
         James Madison Wells," p. 1076.
241   a number of them had been slave owners themselves: David C. Rankin, "The Origins
         of Black Leadership in New Orleans during Reconstruction," pp. 420–21.
242   perhaps establish a new state government: Eric Foner, Reconstruction: America's
         Unfinished Revolution, p. 263.
242   "we are peaceable": James G. Hollandsworth Jr., An Absolute Massacre: The New
         Orleans Race Riot of July 30, 1866, pp. 109, 116, 130.
243   "an absolute massacre": Foner, Reconstruction, p. 263.
243   "what Fort Sumter was to the first": Hollandsworth, Absolute Massacre, p. 3.
244   "As make the angels weep": Measure for Measure, act 2, scene 2, line 180.
245   every other feature of Congress's proposal: Joseph B. James, The Ratification of the
         Fourteenth Amendment, pp. 139–40.
245   "to absorb the President, or to destroy him": Gideon Welles, The Diary of Gideon
         Welles, vol. 2, pp. 526–27.

245   *out without consulting Johnson:* Glyndon G. Van Deusen, *William Henry Seward,* p. 451.

246   *until the Southern states were represented:* Edward McPherson, *The Political History of the United States of America during the Period of Reconstruction, 1865–1870,* p. 83.

246   *"the dirty dog in the White House":* James, *Ratification,* p. 23.

246   *"white race to the negroes":* Ibid., p. 59.

246   *"in the administration of the Government":* Ibid., p. 91.

246   *"control over their local and domestic concerns":* Ibid., pp. 98–99.

246   *"the theory of our political system":* Ibid., p. 106.

247   *"leave no further use for the State governments":* Ibid., pp. 110–11.

247   *without any more compromise at all:* Michael Perman, *Reunion without Compromise: The South and Reconstruction, 1865–1868,* pp. 156–57, 169–70.

248   *"I would give all I possess if it were undone":* James G. Blaine, *Twenty Years of Congress: From Lincoln to Garfield, with a Review of the Events Which Led to the Political Revolution of 1860,* vol. 2, p. 185.

248   *shot himself fatally:* John Speer, *The Life of Gen. James H. Lane, "The Liberator of Kansas," with Corroborative Incidents of Pioneer History,* pp. 313–16.

248   *entering the "Wigwam" arm in arm:* Hans L. Trefousse, *Andrew Johnson: A Biography,* p. 261; Welles, *Diary,* vol. 2, p. 535.

248   *known as "the swing around the circle":* Trefousse, *Andrew Johnson,* p. 262.

249   *Douglas had not been president:* James M. McPherson, *Battle Cry of Freedom: The Civil War Era,* pp. 223–24.

249   *"don't know the Northern people":* Rutherford B. Hayes, *Diary and Letters of Rutherford B. Hayes, Nineteenth President of the United States,* letter of October 1 to S. Birchard, vol. 3, p. 33.

249   *"exhilarated," the press reported:* Jean Edward Smith, *Grant,* pp. 425–26.

250   *Johnson could not even be heard:* Trefousse, *Andrew Johnson,* pp. 263–66.

250   *"as a National disgrace":* Smith, *Grant,* p. 427.

250   *"disgrace of a disreputable series":* Trefousse, *Andrew Johnson,* p. 265.

250   *"vanity and presumption as he does":* Ibid., p. 264.

250   *"would be more reserved":* Welles, *Diary,* vol. 2, pp. 593–94.

250   *"'so exclusive reference to a single issue'":* Foner, *Reconstruction,* p. 267.

251   *"the greatest victory of right and justice":* Carl Schurz, *Speeches, Correspondence and Political Papers of Carl Schurz,* vol. 1, pp. 404, 412–13, 416.

251   *"of the unprofitable labors of earth":* Fawn Brodie, *Thaddeus Stevens: Scourge of the South,* p. 288.

252   *in a wave of emotional reconciliation:* William S. McFeely, *Frederick Douglass,* pp. 250–51; Frederick Douglass, *Autobiographies,* p. 829.

253   *belatedly certified it:* James, *Ratification of the Fourteenth Amendment,* pp. 294–98.

254   *"impossible at that time":* Trefousse, *Andrew Johnson,* p. 350.

255   *"shrinking, cowardly slaves":* Brodie, *Stevens,* pp. 335–36.

255   *"lived so long and so uselessly":* Ibid., pp. 362–66.

256   *"EQUALITY OF MAN BEFORE HIS CREATOR":* Ibid., p. 366.

256   *"perjury at their bidding":* Francis Fessenden, *Life and Public Services of William Pitt Fessenden,* vol. 2, p. 220.

256   *month, surrounded by family:* Robert Leopold, *Robert Dale Owen,* pp. 513–24.

257 *"the most conspicuous, and still the most handsome, member of the Senate"*: David Herbert Donald, *Charles Sumner*, vol. 2, p. 273.

257 *him "The Great Impotent"*: Ibid., p. 314.

257 *"two sides to the question"*: Ibid., p. 319.

257 *and even churches*: Ibid., p. 531.

258 *died soon after*: Ibid., p. 587.

258 *led him on his last visit*: Ibid., p. 4.

258 *should be destroyed*: McFeely, *Frederick Douglass*, pp. 321–22.

258 *died instantly of a massive heart attack*: Ibid., p. 381.

259 *"God, the United States, Franklin College"*: Erving E. Beauregard, *Bingham of the Hills: Politician and Diplomat Extraordinary*, p. 190.

260 *"oftener from the South than from the North"*: Schurz, *Speeches*, vol. 4, p. 391.

260 *"as much protection in the South as in the North, and perhaps more"*: Ibid., p. 393.

260 *"sacred principles and traditions"*: Hans L. Trefousse, *Carl Schurz: A Biography*, p. 289.

261 *"be unreasoning"*: Carl Schurz, "Can the South Solve the Negro Problem?" p. 269.

261 *"inquiry and discussion there"*: Ibid., p. 270.

261 *"fully adopted by the Southern people"*: Ibid., p. 271.

Afterword. The Second Constitution

263 *"them to the control of Congress"*: The Slaughter-House Cases, 83 U.S. 36, 77–79 (1873).

263 *"in society towards each other"*: The Civil Rights Cases, 109 U.S. 3 (1993).

263 *"race chooses to put that construction on it"*: Plessy v. Ferguson, 163 U.S. 537 (1896).

264 *"Mr. Herbert Spencer's Social Statics"*: Lochner v. New York, 198 U.S. 45, 75 (1905) (Holmes, J., dissenting).

265 *"why not in South Carolina and Mississippi?"*: C. Vann Woodward, *The Strange Career of Jim Crow*, p. 54.

265 *"shall be and remain a white man's country"*: Ulrich B. Phillips, "The Central Theme of Southern History," p. 31.

265 *"come back to rule the Union"*: Judson C. Welliver, "The Triumph of the South," quoted in George B. Tindall, *The Emergence of the New South, 1913–1945*, p. 2.

266 *"silent, invisible master of ceremonies"*: David W. Blight, *Race and Reunion: The Civil War in American Memory*, p. 9.

266 *"such statutes as would have a Negro to believe himself the equal of a white man"*: Tindall, *Emergence of the New South*, p. 161.

266 *"inquisition of lynching simply lies"*: Ibid., p. 156.

267 *"States any restrictions about 'freedom of speech'"*: Prudential Insurance Co. v. Cheek, 259 U.S. 530, 543 (1922).

267 *"from impairment by the States"*: Gitlow v. New York, 268 U.S. 652, 666 (1925).

267 *"it is no longer open to doubt"*: Near v. Minnesota, 283 U.S. 697, 707 (1931).

267 *"separate educational facilities are inherently unequal"*: Brown v. Board of Education, 347 U.S. 483, 495 (1954).

268   *"God Almighty is wrong"*: Herbert Shapiro, *White Violence and Black Response: From Reconstruction to Montgomery*, p. 435.

268   *"second Constitution"*: James E. Bond, "The Original Understanding of the Fourteenth Amendment in Illinois, Ohio, and Pennsylvania," p. 435.

268   *"the local majority is absolute"*: "The Latest Version of the New Orleans Affair," *The Nation*, August 30, 1866, pp. 172–73.

269   *"ideological victory following the Civil War"*: David Brion Davis, "Free at Last: The Enduring Significance of the South's Civil War Victory," *New York Times*, "Week in Review," August 26, 2001, p. 1.

269   *"primary authority" for determining how to protect minority rights in the states: City of Boerne v. Flores*, 521 U.S. 507, 524 (1997).

269   *"carefully crafted balance of power between the States and the National Government": United States v. Morrison*, 529 U.S. 598, 620 (2000).

269   *"a judicially manageable standard": Vieth v. Jubilirer*, 544 U.S. 267, 291 (2004).

· BIBLIOGRAPHY ·

The *Congressional Globe* was the official report of Congressional debates, published daily and then collected into multivolume sets for each session of Congress. It is abbreviated here *CG*. Unless otherwise noted, *CG* means "*Congressional Globe*, 39th Congress, 1st Session, 1865–66."

Newspapers and Periodicals

Boston Daily Advertiser
The Congressional Globe
Harper's Weekly
The Nation
New York Herald
New York Times
New York Tribune
Richmond Examiner

Journal Articles

Abrams, Paul R. "The Assault upon Josiah B. Grinnell by Lovell H. Rousseau." *Iowa Journal of History and Politics* 10 (1912): 383–402.
Aron, Cindy S. "'To Barter Their Souls for Gold': Female Clerks in Federal Government Offices, 1862–1890." *The Journal of American History* 67, no. 4 (1981): 835–53.

Aynes, Richard L. "The Antislavery and Abolitionist Background of John A. Bingham." *Catholic University Law Review* 37 (1988): 881–932.

———. "The Continuing Importance of Congressman John Bingham and the Fourteenth Amendment." *Akron Law Review* 36, no. 4 (2003): 589–615.

———. "On Misreading John Bingham and the Fourteenth Amendment." *Yale Law Journal* 103 (1993): 57–103.

Baker, Jean H. "Protection of Personal Liberty in Republican Emancipation Legislation of 1862." *The Journal of Southern History* 42, no. 3 (1976): 385–400.

Beauregard, Erving E. "The John A. Bingham–Thaddeus Stevens Feud." *The Lincoln Herald* 93, no. 2 (1991): 50–60.

———. "Secretary Stanton and Congressman Bingham." *The Lincoln Herald* 91, no. 4 (1989): 141–50.

Belz, Herman. "The Etheridge Conspiracy of 1863: A Projected Conservative Coup." *The Journal of Southern History* 36, no. 4 (1970): 549–67.

Betts, John R. "Mind and Body in Early American Thought." *The Journal of American History* 54, no. 4 (1968): 787–805.

Bond, James E. "The Original Understanding of the Fourteenth Amendment in Illinois, Ohio, and Pennsylvania." *Akron Law Review* 18, no. 3 (1985): 435–67.

Carter, Dan T. "The Anatomy of Fear: The Christmas Day Insurrection Scare of 1865." *The Journal of Southern History* 42, no. 3 (1976): 346–64.

Cimbala, Paul A. "The Freedmen's Bureau, the Freedmen, and Sherman's Grant in Reconstruction Georgia, 1865–1867." *The Journal of American History* 55, no. 4 (1989): 597–632.

Clancy, John J., Jr. "A Mugwump on Minorities." *The Journal of Negro History* 51, no. 3 (1966): 174–92.

Cox, John, and LaWanda Cox. "Andrew Johnson and His Ghost Writers: An Analysis of the Freedmen's Bureau and Civil Rights Veto Messages." *The Mississippi Valley Historical Review* 48, no. 3 (1961): 460–79.

Cox, LaWanda. "The Promise of Land for the Freedmen." *The Mississippi Valley Historical Review* 45, no. 3 (1958): 413–40.

Curti, Merle. "The American Exploration of Dreams and Dreamers." *Journal of the History of Ideas* 27, no. 3 (1966): 391–416.

Curtis, Michael Kent. "John A. Bingham and the Story of American Liberty: The Lost Cause Meets the Lost Clause." *Akron Law Review* 36 (2003): 617–69.

Dellinger, Walter E. "1787: The Constitution and 'The Curse of Heaven.'" *William and Mary Law Review* 29 (1987): 145–61.

Di Nunzio, Mario. "Secession Winter: Lyman Trumbull and the Crisis in Congress." *Capitol Studies* 1 (Fall 1972): 29–39.

Dorris, J. T. "Pardoning the Leaders of the Confederacy." *The Mississippi Valley Historical Review* 15, no. 1 (1928): 3–21.

DuBois, Ellen Carol. "Outgrowing the Compact of the Fathers: Equal Rights, Woman Suffrage, and the United States Constitution, 1820–1878." *The Journal of American History* 74, no. 3 (1987): 836–62.

Durden, Robert F. "Book Review: *Fessenden of Maine: Civil War Senator*." *The Journal of Southern History* 42, no. 4 (1962): 491–93.

Ehrlich, Walter. "Was the Dred Scott Case Valid?" *The Journal of American History* 55, no. 2 (1968): 256–65.

Fairman, Charles. "Does the Fourteenth Amendment Incorporate the Bill of Rights? The Original Understanding." *Stanford Law Review* 2, no. 1 (1949): 5–139.

Farber, Daniel, and John Muench. "The Ideological Origins of the Fourteenth Amendment." *Constitutional Commentary* 1, no. 2 (1984): 235–80.

Finkelman, Paul. "The Historical Context of the Fourteenth Amendment." *Temple Political and Civil Rights Law Review* 13 (2004): 389–409.

———. "Prelude to the Fourteenth Amendment: Black Legal Rights in the Antebellum North." *Rutgers Law Journal* 17 (Spring–Summer 1986): 415–82.

Foner, Eric. "Andrew Johnson and Reconstruction: A British View." *The Journal of Southern History* 41, no. 3 (1975): 381–90.

Gates, Paul Wallace. "Federal Land Policy in the South 1866–1888." *The Journal of Southern History* 6, no. 3 (1940): 303–30.

Ginzberg, Lori D. "'The Hearts of Your Readers Will Shudder': Fanny Wright, Infidelity, and American Freethought." *American Quarterly* 46, no. 2 (1994): 195–226.

———. "'Moral Suasion Is Moral Balderdash': Women, Politics, and Social Activism in the 1850s." *The Journal of American History* 73, no. 3 (1986): 601–22.

Goldhaber, Michael. "A Mission Unfulfilled: Freedmen's Education in North Carolina, 1865–1870." *Journal of Negro History* 77, no. 4 (1992): 199–210.

Goldman, Eric. "Importing a Historian: Von Holst and American Universities." *The Mississippi Valley Historical Review* 27, no. 2 (1940): 267–74.

Hobbs, Steven. "From the Shoulders of Houston: A Vision for Social and Economic Justice." *Howard Law Journal* 32 (1989): 505–47.

Hoffman, Edwin D. "From Slavery to Self-Reliance: The Record of Achievement of the Freedmen of the Sea Island Region." *The Journal of Negro History* 41, no. 1 (1956): 8–42.

James, Joseph B. "Southern Reaction to the Proposal of the Fourteenth Amendment." *The Journal of Southern History* 22, no. 4 (1956): 477–97.

Kaczorowski, Robert J. "To Begin the Nation Anew: Congress, Citizenship, and Civil Rights after the Civil War." *The American Historical Review* 92, no. 1 (1987 suppl): 45–68.

Kutler, Stanley I. "Ex parte McCardle: Judicial Impotency? The Supreme Court and Reconstruction Revisited." *The American Historical Review* 72, no. 3 (1967): 835–51.

Les Benedict, Michael. "Preserving the Constitution: The Conservative Basis of Radical Reconstruction." *The Journal of American History* 61, no. 1 (1974): 65–90.

Levy, Leonard W. "Satan's Last Apostle in Massachusetts." *American Quarterly* 5, no. 1 (1953): 16–30.

Low, W. A. "The Freedmen's Bureau and Civil Rights in Maryland." *The Journal of Negro History* 37, no. 3 (1952): 221–47.

Lowrey, Walter McGehee. "The Political Career of James Madison Wells." *The Louisiana Historical Quarterly* 31, no. 4 (1948): 995–1123.

Luti, Anthony Ngula. "When a Door Closes, a Window Opens: Do Today's Historically Black Colleges and Universities Run Afoul of Conventional Equal Protection Analysis?" *Howard Law Journal* 42 (1999): 469–504.

Lynd, Staughton. "Rethinking Slavery and Reconstruction." *The Journal of Negro History* 50, no. 3 (1965): 198–209.

Moore, Frederick W. "Representation in the National Congress from the Seceding States, 1861–1865." *The American Historical Review* 2, no. 2 (1897): 279–93.

Moore, R. Laurence. "Spiritualism and Science: Reflections on the First Decade of the Spirit Rappings." *American Quarterly* 24, no. 4 (1972): 474–500.

Nichols, Roy Franklin. "United States v. Jefferson Davis, 1865–1869." *The American Historical Review* 31, no. 2 (1926): 266–84.

Owen, Robert Dale. "Political Results from the Varioloid." *The Atlantic Monthly* 35, no. 212 (June 1875): 660–70.

Pease, William H. "Organized Negro Communities: A North American Experiment." *The Journal of Negro History* 47, no. 1 (1962): 19–34.

Phillips, Ulrich B. "The Central Theme of Southern History." *The American Historical Review* 34, no. 1 (1928): 30–43.

Quarles, Benjamin, ed. "Frederick Douglass and the Women's Movement." *Journal of Negro History* 25, no. 1 (1940): 35–44.

Randall, James G. "Some Legal Aspects of the Confiscation Acts of the Civil War." *The American Historical Review* 18, no. 1 (1912): 79–96.

Rankin, David C. "The Origins of Black Leadership in New Orleans during Reconstruction." *The Journal of Southern History* 40, no. 3 (1974): 417–40.

Rudolph, Jack. "The Grand Review." *Civil War Times Illustrated* 19, no. 7 (November 1980): 34–43.

Russ, William A., Jr. "Was There Danger of a Second Civil War during Reconstruction?" *The Mississippi Valley Historical Review* 25, no. 1 (1938): 39–58.

Ryan, James Gilbert. "The Memphis Riots of 1866: Terror in a Black Community during Reconstruction." *The Journal of Negro History* 62, no. 3 (1977): 243–57.

Schurz, Carl. "Can the South Solve the Negro Problem?" *McClure's Magazine* (1904): 258–75.

Simms, Henry H. "The Controversy over the Admission of the State of Oregon." *The Mississippi Valley Historical Review* 32, no. 3 (1945): 355–74.

Sioussat, St. George L. "Notes of Colonel W. G. Moore, Private Secretary to President Johnson, 1866–1868." *The American Historical Review* 19, no. 1 (1913): 98–132.

Somers, Dale. "Black and White in New Orleans: A Study in Urban Race Relations, 1865–1900." *The Journal of Southern History* 40, no. 1 (1974): 19–42.

Sproat, John G. "Blueprint for Radical Reconstruction." *The Journal of Southern History* 23, no. 1 (1957): 25–44.

Strauss, David A. "The Irrelevance of Constitutional Amendments." *Harvard Law Review* 114 (2001): 1457–505.

Tregle, Joseph G., Jr. "Thomas J. Durant, Utopian Socialism, and the Failure of Presidential Reconstruction in Louisiana." *The Journal of Southern History* 45, no. 4 (1979): 485–512.

Vorenberg, Michael. "Imagining a Different Reconstruction Constitution." *Civil War History* 51, no. 5 (2005): 416–26.

Walters, Ronald G. "The Erotic South: Civilization and Sexuality in American Abolitionism." *American Quarterly* 25, no. 2 (1973): 177–201.

Williams, Lorraine A. "Northern Intellectual Reaction to the Policy of Emancipation." *The Journal of Negro History* 46, no. 3 (1961): 174–88.

Woodburn, James Albert. "The Attitude of Thaddeus Stevens toward the Conduct of the Civil War." *The American Historical Review* 12, no. 3 (1907): 567–83.

Young, James Harvey. "Anna Elizabeth Dickinson and the Civil War: For and Against Lincoln." *The Mississippi Valley Historical Review* 31, no. 1 (1944): 59–80.

Books

Adams, Henry. *The Education of Henry Adams.* Edited by Ernest Samuels. Boston, Mass.: Houghton Mifflin, 1974.

Adams, William Howard. *Gouverneur Morris: An Independent Life.* New Haven, Conn.: Yale University Press, 2003.

Ahlstrom, Sydney A. *A Religious History of the American People.* New Haven, Conn.: Yale University Press, 1972.

Allen, William C. *History of the United States Capitol: A Chronicle of Design, Construction, and Politics.* Washington, D.C.: Government Printing Office, 2001.

Altschuler, Glenn C., and Stuart M. Blumin. *Rude Republic: Americans and Their Politics in the Nineteenth Century.* Princeton, N.J.: Princeton University Press, 2000.

The American Annual Cyclopedia and Register of Important Events of the Year 1865. Vol. 5. New York: D. Appleton & Co., 1869.

The American Council of Learned Societies. *Dictionary of American Biography.* New York: Charles Scribner's Sons, 1928–1958.

Anderson, Eric, and Alfred A. Moss Jr. *The Facts of Reconstruction: Essays in Honor of John Hope Franklin.* Baton Rouge: Louisiana State University Press, 1991.

Andrews, Sidney. *The South since the War: As Shown by Fourteen Weeks of Travel and Observations in Georgia and the Carolinas.* New York: Arno Press, 1969.

Ash, Stephen V. *When the Yankees Came: Conflict and Chaos in the Occupied South, 1861–1865.* Chapel Hill: University of North Carolina Press, 1995.

———. *A Year in the South: Four Lives in 1865.* New York: Palgrave Macmillan, 2002.

Baker, Jean H. *Mary Todd Lincoln: A Biography.* New York: W. W. Norton, 1987.

Barlett, Irving H. *The American Mind in the Mid-Nineteenth Century.* Edited by John Hope Franklin and A. S. Eisenstadt. 2d ed., *The American History Series.* Wheeling, Ill.: Harlan Davidson, 1982.

Barnes, William H. *A History of the Thirty-ninth Congress of the United States.* New York: Negro Universities Press, 1969.

Barry, Kathleen. *Susan B. Anthony: A Biography of a Singular Feminist.* New York: New York University Press, 1988.

Beauregard, Erving E. *Bingham of the Hills: Politician and Diplomat Extraordinary.* Vol. 68, *American University Studies IX, History.* New York: Peter Lang, 1989.

Belz, Herman. *Abraham Lincoln, Constitutionalism, and Equal Rights in the Civil War Era.* Vol. 2, *The North's Civil War.* New York: Fordham University Press, 1998.

Berkin, Carol. *A Brilliant Solution: Inventing the American Constitution.* New York: Harcourt, Brace, 2002.

Berlin, Ira. *Slaves without Masters: The Free Negro in the Antebellum North.* New York: Oxford University Press, 1974.

Berlin, Ira, et al., eds. *Free at Last: A Documentary History of Slavery, Freedom and the Civil War.* New York: The New Press, 1992.

Blaine, James G. *Twenty Years of Congress: From Lincoln to Garfield, with a Review of the*

Events which Led to the Political Revolution of 1860. 2 vols. Norwich, Conn.: Henry Hill, 1893.

Blight, David W. *Race and Reunion: The Civil War in American Memory.* Cambridge, Mass.: Harvard University Press, 2001.

Bond, James E. *No Easy Walk to Freedom: Reconstruction and the Ratification of the Fourteenth Amendment.* Westport, Conn.: Praeger, 1997.

Boorstin, Daniel J. *The Lost World of Thomas Jefferson.* New York: Henry Holt, 1948.

Boritt, Gabor S., ed. *Why the Civil War Came.* New York: Oxford University Press, 1996.

Bowen, Catherine Drinker. *Miracle at Philadelphia: The Story of the Constitutional Convention, May to September, 1787.* Boston, Mass.: Little, Brown, 1966.

Bowen, David Warren. *Andrew Johnson and the Negro.* Nashville: University of Tennessee Press, 1989.

Brichford, Maynard. "The Life of John A. Bingham." (1951) (unpublished M.S. thesis, University of Wisconsin).

Brodie, Fawn. *Thaddeus Stevens: Scourge of the South.* New York: W. W. Norton, 1959.

Brookhiser, Richard. *Gentleman Revolutionary: Gouverneur Morris, the Rake Who Wrote the Constitution.* New York: The Free Press, 2003.

Brown, Francis. *Raymond of the Times.* New York: W. W. Norton, 1951.

Brown, Thomas H. *George S. Boutwell: Human Rights Advocate.* Groton, Mass.: Groton Historical Society, 1989.

Burton, Theodore. *John Sherman.* Boston, Mass.: Houghton Mifflin, 1906.

Butler, Anne M., and Wendy Wolff. *United States Senate Election, Expulsion and Censure Cases, 1793–1990.* Washington, D.C.: Government Printing Office, 1995.

Cairnes, John E. *The Slave Power: Its Character, Career, and Probable Designs: Being an Attempt to Explain the Real Issues Involved in the American Contest.* Edited and with an introduction by Harold D. Woodman. New York: Harper & Row, 1969.

Carter, Dan T. *When the War Was Over: The Failure of Self-Reconstruction in the South.* Baton Rouge: Louisiana State University Press, 1985.

Castel, Albert E. *The Presidency of Andrew Johnson, American Presidency Series.* Lawrence, Kan.: Regents Press of Kansas, 1979.

Catt, Carrie Chapman, and Nettie Rogers Shuler. *Woman Suffrage and Politics: The Inner Story of the Suffrage Movement.* New York: Charles Scribner's Sons, 1923.

Chinard, Gilbert. *The Life and Letters of Lafayette and Jefferson.* Baltimore, Md.: The Johns Hopkins University Press, 1929.

Cimbala, Paul A. *Under the Guardianship of the Nation: The Freedmen's Bureau and the Reconstruction of Georgia, 1865–1870.* Athens: University of Georgia Press, 1997.

Cimbala, Paul A., and Randall M. Miller, eds. *The Freedmen's Bureau and Reconstruction: Reconsiderations.* New York: Fordham University Press, 1999.

Ciment, James, ed. *Encyclopedia of American Immigration.* 4 vols. Armonk, N.Y.: M. E. Sharpe, 2001.

Clarke, Grace J. *George W. Julian.* Indianapolis: Indiana Historical Commission, 1923.

Clift, Eleanor. *Founding Sisters and the Nineteenth Amendment.* Hoboken, N.J.: John Wiley & Sons, 2003.

Clinton, Catherine. *Harriet Tubman: The Road to Freedom.* Boston: Little, Brown, 2004.

———. *The Other Civil War: American Women in the Nineteenth Century.* Rev. ed. New York: Hill & Wang, 1999.

Clinton, Catherine, and Christine Lunardini. *The Columbia Guide to American Women in the Nineteenth Century.* New York: Columbia University Press, 2000.

Cochran, Thomas C. "Did the Civil War Retard Industrialization?" In *United States Economic History: Selected Readings,* edited by Harry N. Schreiber. New York: Alfred A. Knopf, 1964.

Cornish, Dudley Taylor. *The Sable Arm: Black Troops in the Union Army, 1861–1865.* Lawrence: University Press of Kansas, 1956.

Cox, John, and LaWanda Cox. "General O. O. Howard and the 'Misrepresented Bureau.'" In *The Freedmen's Bureau and Black Freedom,* edited by Donald G. Nieman. New York: Garland, 1994.

Cox, LaWanda, and John Cox. *Politics, Principle and Prejudice, 1865–1866: Dilemma of Reconstruction America.* New York: Free Press of Glencoe, 1963.

Crawford, Mark. *Encyclopedia of the Mexican-American War.* Consulting eds. David S. Heidler and Jeanne T. Heidler. Santa Barbara, Calif.: ABC–CLIO, 1999.

Current, Richard N., ed. *Reconstruction, 1865–1877.* Englewood Cliffs, N.J.: Prentice-Hall, 1965.

Curtis, Michael Kent. *Free Speech: "The People's Darling Privilege": Struggles for Freedom of Expression in American History.* Durham, N.C.: Duke University Press, 2000.

Davis, David Brion, ed. *Antebellum American Culture: An Interpretive Anthology.* University Park: Pennsylvania State University Press, 1997.

Davis, William C. *An Honorable Defeat: The Last Days of the Confederate Government.* New York: Harcourt, Brace, 2001.

Dennett, John Richard. *The South as It Is, 1865–1866.* Edited and with an introduction by Henry M. Christman. Athens: University of Georgia Press, 1986.

Dickinson, Emily. *The Poems of Emily Dickinson.* Edited by R. W. Franklin. Reading edition. Cambridge, Mass.: The Belknap Press of Harvard University Press, 1999.

Diedrich, Maria. *Love across Color Lines: Ottilie Assing and Frederick Douglass.* New York: Hill & Wang, 1999.

Donald, David Herbert. *Charles Sumner.* 2 vols. New York: Da Capo Press, 1996.

———. *Liberty and Union.* Lexington, Mass.: D. C. Heath, 1978.

———. *Lincoln.* New York: Simon & Schuster, 1995.

———. *Lincoln Reconsidered: Essays on the Civil War Era.* New York: Vintage Books, 1989.

———. *The Politics of Reconstruction, 1863–1867.* Repr. ed. Cambridge, Mass.: Harvard University Press, 1984.

———. *Why the North Won the Civil War.* New York: Simon & Schuster, 1996.

Douglass, Frederick. *Autobiographies.* Library of America College ed. New York: Library of America, 1996.

———. *The Frederick Douglass Papers, Series One.* Edited by John W. Blassingame and John R. McKivigan. Vol. 4. New Haven, Conn.: Yale University Press, 1991.

———. *The Frederick Douglass Papers, Series One: Speeches, Debates and Interviews.* 5 vols. Edited by John W. Blassingame and John R. McKivigan. New Haven, Conn.: Yale University Press, 1979.

———. *The Life and Writings of Frederick Douglass.* Edited by Philip S. Foner. Vol. 4. New York: International Publishers, 1955.

DuBois, Ellen Carol. *Woman Suffrage and Women's Rights*. New York: New York University Press, 1998.

DuBois, W. E. B. *Black Reconstruction*. New York: Harcourt, Brace, 1935.

Duncan, Russell. *Freedom's Shore: Tunis Campbell and the Georgia Freedmen*. Athens: University of Georgia Press, 1986.

Easum, Chester Verne. *The Americanization of Carl Schurz*. Chicago, Ill.: University of Chicago Press, 1929.

Eaton, Clement. *The Freedom-of-Thought Struggle in the Old South*. Rev. and enl. ed. New York: Harper & Row, 1964.

Eckhardt, Celia Morris. *Fanny Wright: Rebel in America*. Cambridge, Mass.: Harvard University Press, 1984.

Emerson, Ralph Waldo. *Emerson's Antislavery Writings*. Edited by Len Gougeon and Joel Myerson. New Haven, Conn.: Yale University Press, 1995.

———. *Essays and Lectures*. Edited by Joel Porte. New York: Library of America, 1983.

Ericson, David F. *The Debate over Slavery: Antislavery and Proslavery Liberalism in Antebellum America*. New York: New York University Press, 2000.

Farber, Daniel. *Lincoln's Constitution*. Chicago, Ill.: University of Chicago Press, 2003.

Fehrenbacher, Don E. *The Dred Scott Case: Its Significance in American Law and Politics*. New York: Oxford University Press, 1978.

———. *The Slaveholding Republic: An Account of the United States Government's Relations to Slavery*. Completed and edited by Ward M. McAfee. New York: Oxford University Press, 2001.

Ferrand, Max. *The Framing of the Constitution of the United States*. New Haven, Conn.: Yale University Press, 1990.

Fessenden, Francis. *Life and Public Services of William Pitt Fessenden*. 2 vols. Boston, Mass.: Houghton Mifflin, 1907.

Finkelman, Paul. *An Imperfect Union: Slavery, Federalism, and Comity, Studies in Legal History*. Chapel Hill: University of North Carolina Press, 1981.

———. "Slavery and the Constitutional Convention: Making a Covenant with Death." In *Beyond Confederation: Origins of the Constitution and American National Identity*, edited by Richard Beeman, Stephen Botein, and Edward C. Carter II, 189–225. Chapel Hill: University of North Carolina Press, 1987.

Flack, Horace E. *The Adoption of the Fourteenth Amendment*. Baltimore, Md.: Johns Hopkins University Press, 1908.

Flexner, Eleanor, and Ellen Fitzpatrick. *Century of Struggle: The Woman's Rights Movement in the United States*. Enl. ed. Cambridge, Mass.: Harvard University Press, 1996.

Foner, Eric. *Free Soil, Free Labor, Free Men: The Ideology of the Republican Party before the Civil War*. 2d ed. New York: Oxford University Press, 1995.

———. *Politics and Ideology in the Age of the Civil War*. New York: Oxford University Press, 1980.

———. *Reconstruction: America's Unfinished Revolution, 1863–1877*. New York: Harper & Row, 1988.

Foner, Philip S., ed. *The Life and Writings of Frederick Douglass*. 4 vols. New York: International Publishers, 1950.

Foote, Shelby. *The Civil War: A Narrative. Vol. 3, Red River to Appomattox*. New York: Random House, 1958.

Foulke, William Dudley. *Life of Oliver P. Morton*. 2 vols. Indianapolis, Ind.: The Bowen-Merrill Co., 1899.

Franklin, John Hope. *The Emancipation Proclamation*. Garden City, N.Y.: Doubleday, 1963.

———. *The Militant South, 1800–1861*. Cambridge, Mass.: Harvard University Press, 1956.

———. *Reconstruction after the Civil War*. 2d ed. Chicago, Ill.: University of Chicago Press, 1994.

Franklin, John Hope, and Alfred A. Moss Jr. *From Slavery to Freedom: A History of African Americans*. 8th ed. New York: Alfred A. Knopf, 2000.

Frederickson, George M. *The Inner Civil War: Northern Intellectuals and the Crisis of the Union*. New York: Harper & Row, 1965.

Freehling, William W. *The Reintegration of American History*. New York: Oxford University Press, 1994.

Freidel, Frank. *Francis Lieber: Nineteenth-Century Liberal*. Baton Rouge: Louisiana State University Press, 1947.

Furgurson, Ernest B. *Ashes of Glory: Richmond at War*. New York: Alfred A. Knopf, 1996.

Gallagher, Gary W. *The Confederate War*. Cambridge, Mass.: Harvard University Press, 1997.

Garaty, John A., and Mark C. Carnes, eds. *American National Biography*. New York: Oxford University Press, 1999.

Gienapp, William E. *The Origins of the Republican Party, 1852–1856*. New York: Oxford University Press, 1987.

Goldsmith, Barbara. *Other Powers: The Age of Suffrage, Spiritualism, and the Scandalous Victoria Woodhull*. New York: Alfred A. Knopf, 1998.

Goodwin, Jason. *Greenback: The Almighty Dollar and the Invention of America*. New York: Henry Holt, 2003.

Gossett, Thomas F. *Race: The History of an Idea in America*. Dallas, Tex.: Southern Methodist University Press, 1963.

Green, Constance McLaughlin. *The Secret City: A History of Race Relations in the Nation's Capital*. Princeton, N.J.: Princeton University Press, 1967.

Griffith, Elizabeth. *In Her Own Right: The Life of Elizabeth Cady Stanton*. New York: Oxford University Press, 1984.

Grinnell, Josiah Bushnell. *Men and Events of Forty Years*. Boston, Mass.: D. Lothrop, 1891.

Habegger, Alfred. *My Wars Are Laid Away in Books: The Life of Emily Dickinson*. New York: Random House, 2001.

Hanchett, William. *The Lincoln Murder Conspiracies: Being an Account of the Hatred Felt by Many Americans for President Abraham Lincoln during the Civil War and the First Complete Examination and Refutation of the Many Theories, Hypotheses, and Speculations Put Forward since 1865 Concerning Those Presumed to Have Aided, Abetted, Controlled, or Directed the Murderous Act of John Wilkes Booth in Ford's Theater the Night of April 14*. Urbana: University of Illinois Press, 1983.

Harper, Judith E. *Susan B. Anthony: A Biographical Companion.* Santa Barbara, Calif.: ABC–CLIO, 1998.

Hay, John. *Inside Lincoln's White House: The Complete Civil War Diary of John Hay.* Carbondale: Southern Illinois University Press, 1997.

Hayes, Rutherford B. *Diary and Letters of Rutherford B. Hayes, Nineteenth President of the United States.* 5 vols. Columbus: The Ohio State Archaeological and Historical Society, 1922–26.

Heidler, David Stephen, and Jeanne T. Heidler, eds. *Encyclopedia of the American Civil War: A Political, Social, and Military History.* Associate editor David W. Coles. 5 vols. Santa Barbara, Calif.: ABC–CLIO, 2000.

Hickey, Donald R. *The War of 1812: A Short History.* Urbana: University of Illinois Press, 1995.

Hollandsworth, James G., Jr. *An Absolute Massacre: The New Orleans Race Riot of July 30, 1866.* Baton Rouge: Louisiana State University Press, 2001.

Holt, Michael F. *The Rise and Fall of the American Whig Party: Jacksonian Politics and the Onset of the Civil War.* New York: Oxford University Press, 1999.

Holzer, Harold, ed. *The Lincoln-Douglas Debates: The First Complete, Unexpurgated Text.* New York: HarperCollins, 1993.

Hopkins, Donald R. *Princes and Peasants: Smallpox in History.* Chicago, Ill.: University of Chicago Press, 1983.

Howard, Oliver Otis. *Autobiography of Oliver Otis Howard: Major General United States Army.* 2 vols. New York: Baker & Taylor, 1907.

Hummell, Jeffrey Rogers. *Emancipating Slaves, Enslaving Free Men: A History of the American Civil War.* Chicago, Ill.: Open Court Press, 1996.

Huston, James L. *The Panic of 1857 and the Coming of the Civil War.* Baton Rouge: Louisiana State University Press, 1987.

Hyman, Harold M. *A More Perfect Union: The Impact of the Civil War and Reconstruction on the Constitution.* New York: Alfred A. Knopf, 1973.

Hyman, Harold M., ed. *The Radical Republicans and Reconstruction, 1861–1870.* Edited by Leonard W. Levy and Alfred Young, *The American Heritage Series.* Indianapolis, Ind.: Bobbs-Merrill, 1967.

Hyman, Harold M., and William M. Wiecek. *Equal Justice under Law: Constitutional Development, 1835–1875.* Edited by Henry Steele Commager and Richard B. Morris, *The New American Nation Series.* New York: Harper & Row, 1982.

Isaacson, Walter. *Benjamin Franklin: An American Life.* New York: Simon & Schuster, 2003.

James, Joseph B. *The Framing of the Fourteenth Amendment, Illinois Studies in the Social Sciences.* Urbana: University of Illinois Press, 1956.

———. *The Ratification of the Fourteenth Amendment.* Macon, Ga.: Mercer University Press, 1984.

Jellison, Charles A. *Fessenden of Maine: Civil War Senator.* Syracuse, N.Y.: Syracuse University Press, 1962.

Johnson, Andrew. *The Papers of Andrew Johnson.* Edited by Leroy P. Graf and Ralph W. Haskins. 10 vols. Knoxville: University of Tennessee Press, 1967–2000.

Johnson, Daniel M., and Rex R. Campbell. *Black Migration in America: A Social Demographic History.* Durham, N.C.: Duke University Press, 1981.

Jordan, David. *Roscoe Conkling of New York: Voice in the Senate.* Ithaca, N.Y.: Cornell University Press, 1971.

Kendrick, Benjamin B. *The Journal of the Joint Committee of Fifteen on Reconstruction, Thirty-ninth Congress, 1865–1867.* New York: Negro Universities Press, 1969.

Keyssar, Alexander. *The Right to Vote: The Contested History of Democracy in the United States.* New York: Basic Books, 2000.

Kramer, Lloyd. *Lafayette in Two Worlds: Public Cultures and Personal Identities in an Age of Revolutions.* Chapel Hill: University of North Carolina Press, 1996.

Krug, Mark M. *Lyman Trumbull: Conservative Radical.* New York: A. S. Barnes, 1965.

Kyvig, Donald. *Explicit and Authentic Acts: Amending the U.S. Constitution, 1776–1995.* Lawrence: The University Press of Kansas, 1996.

Lawson, Melinda. *Patriot Fires: Forging a New American Nationalism in the Civil War North.* Edited by William Carey and Lance Banning McWilliams, *American Political Thought.* Lawrence: University Press of Kansas, 2002.

Leech, Margaret. *Reveille in Washington.* Edited by James M. McPherson. New York: Carroll & Graf, 1991.

Leiber, Francis. *Amendments of the Constitution Submitted to the Consideration of the American People.* Vol. 83. New York: Loyal Publication Society, 1865.

Leopold, Robert. *Robert Dale Owen: A Biography.* New York: Farrar, Straus & Giroux, 1969.

Les Benedict, Michael. *A Compromise of Principle: Congressional Republicans and Reconstruction, 1863–1869.* New York: W.W. Norton, 1974.

Levine, Bruce. *Half Slave and Half Free: The Roots of Civil War.* New York: Hill & Wang, 1992.

Lincoln, Abraham. *Abraham Lincoln: Speeches and Writings, 1832–1865.* Edited by Don E. Fehrenbacher. 2 vols. New York: Library of America, 1989.

Linden, Glenn M., and Thomas J. Pressly, eds. *Voices from the House Divided: The United States Civil War as Personal Experience.* New York: McGraw-Hill, 1995.

Litwack, Leon F. *Been in the Storm So Long: The Aftermath of Slavery.* New York: Alfred A. Knopf, 1979.

Lloyd, Lewis. *The Assassination of Lincoln: History and Myth.* New York: Harcourt, Brace, 1929.

Long, David E. *The Jewel of Liberty: Abraham Lincoln's Re-election and the End of Slavery.* Mechanicsburg, Penn.: Stackpole Books, 1994.

Loth, David. *Lafayette.* London: Cassell, 1952.

Low, W. Augustus, ed., and Virgil A. Clift, assoc. ed. *Encyclopedia of Black America.* New York: McGraw-Hill, 1981.

Lowance, Mason, ed. *Against Slavery: An Abolitionist Reader.* New York: Penguin Books, 2000.

Mabee, Carleton, with Susan Mabee Newhouse. *Sojourner Truth: Slave, Prophet, Legend.* New York: New York University Press, 1993.

McClure, Alexander K. *Abraham Lincoln and Men of War-Times: Some Personal Recollections of War and Politics during the Lincoln Administration.* 4th ed. Edited by James A. Rawley. Lincoln: University of Nebraska Press, 1997.

McFeely, William S. *Frederick Douglass.* New York: W. W. Norton, 1991.

McKitrick, Eric L. *Andrew Johnson and Reconstruction.* Chicago, Ill.: University of Chicago Press, 1960.

McManus, Edgar J. *A History of Negro Slavery in New York.* Syracuse, N.Y.: Syracuse University Press, 1966.

McPherson, Edward. *The Political History of the United States of America during the Period of Reconstruction, (from April 15, 1865, to July 15, 1870,) Including a Classified Summary of the Legislation of the Thirty-Ninth, Fortieth, and Forty-First Congresses.* Washington, D.C.: Philp & Solomons, 1871.

McPherson, James M. *Abraham Lincoln and the Second American Revolution.* New York: Oxford University Press, 1990.

————. *Battle Cry of Freedom: The Civil War Era.* New York: Oxford University Press, 1988.

————. *The Negro's Civil War: How American Blacks Felt and Acted During the War for the Union.* 2d ed. New York: Vintage, 1991.

————. *The Struggle for Equality: Abolitionists and the Negro in the Civil War and Reconstruction.* 2d ed. Princeton, N.J.: Princeton University Press, 1995.

McPherson, James M., ed. *"We Cannot Escape History": Lincoln and the Last Best Hope of Earth.* Urbana: University of Illinois Press, 1995.

McPherson, James M., and William J. Cooper Jr., eds. *Writing the Civil War: The Quest to Understand.* Columbia: University of South Carolina Press, 1998.

Maddex, Jack P., Jr. "The Reconstruction of Edward A. Pollard: A Rebel's Conversion to Postbellum Unionism." In *The James Sprunt Studies in History and Political Science*, Vol. 54, edited by J. Carlyle Sitterson et al. Chapel Hill: University of North Carolina Press, 1974.

Madison, James. *Notes of Debates in the Federal Convention of 1787 Reported by James Madison.* Edited by Adrienne Koch. New York: W. W. Norton, 1966.

Maltz, Earl. *Civil Rights, The Constitution, and Congress, 1863–1869.* Lawrence: University Press of Kansas, 1990.

Mansfield, Edward D. *The Legal Rights, Liabilities and Duties of Women: With an Introductory History of Their Legal Condition in the Hebrew, Roman and Feudal Civil Systems: Including the Law of Marriage and Divorce, the Social Relations of Husband and Wife, Parent and Child, of Guardian and Ward, and of Employer and Employed.* Salem, Mass.: John P. Jewett, 1845.

Maverick, Augustus. *Henry J. Raymond and the New York Press, for Thirty Years: Progress of American Journalism from 1840 to 1870.* Hartford, Conn.: A. S. Hale, 1870.

Mayer, Henry. *All on Fire: William Lloyd Garrison and the Abolition of Slavery.* New York: St. Martin's Griffin, 1998.

Miller, William Lee. *Arguing about Slavery: The Great Battle in the United States Congress.* New York: Alfred A. Knopf, 1996.

Milton, George Fort. *The Age of Hate: Andrew Johnson and the Radicals.* New York: Coward-McCann, 1930.

Momeni, Jamshid A. *Demography of the Black Population in the United States.* Westport, Conn.: Greenwood Press, 1983.

Moore, Frank, ed. *Life and Speeches of Andrew Johnson.* Boston, Mass.: Little, Brown, 1865.

Morris, Roy, Jr. *The Better Angel: Walt Whitman in the Civil War.* New York: Oxford University Press, 2000.

Neely, Mark E., Jr. *The Fate of Liberty: Abraham Lincoln and Civil Liberties.* New York: Oxford University Press, 1991.

————. *The Union Divided: Party Conflict in the Civil War North.* Cambridge, Mass.: Harvard University Press, 2002.

Neely, Sylvia. *Lafayette and the Liberal Ideal, 1814–1824: Politics and Conspiracy in an Age of Reaction.* Carbondale: Southern Illinois University Press, 1991.

Nelson, William E. *The Fourteenth Amendment: From Political Principle to Judicial Doctrine.* Cambridge, Mass.: Harvard University Press, 1988.

Nichols, Roy Franklin. *The Disruption of American Democracy.* New York: Macmillan, 1948.

————. *The Stakes of Power, 1841–1877.* New York: Hill & Wang, 1961.

Niven, John. *Gideon Welles: Lincoln's Secretary of the Navy.* New York: Oxford University Press, 1973.

————. *Salmon P. Chase: A Biography.* New York: Oxford University Press, 1995.

Noll, Mark A. *A History of Christianity in the United States and Canada.* Grand Rapids, Mich.: William B. Eerdmans, 1992.

Oates, Stephen B. *To Purge This Land with Blood: A Biography of John Brown.* 2d ed. Amherst: University of Massachusetts Press, 1984.

Olmsted, Frederick Law. *The Cotton Kingdom: A Traveller's Observations on Cotton and Slavery in the American Slave States, 1853–1861.* Edited and with an introduction by Arthur M. Schlesinger. New York: Alfred A. Knopf, 1953.

Owen, Robert Dale. *Footfalls on the Boundary of Another World, with Narrative Illustrations.* Philadelphia, Penn.: J. B. Lippincott, 1860.

————. "Moral Physiology, or, A Short and Plain Treatise on the Population Question." In *Birth Control and Morality in Nineteenth-Century America: Two Discussions,* edited by David J. Rothman and Sheila M. Rothman. New York: Arno Press and The New York Times, 1972.

————. *The Wrong of Slavery, the Right of Emancipation, and the Future of the African Race in the United States.* Rep. ed. New York: Krause Reprint Co. ed. Philadelphia, Penn.: J. B. Lippincott, 1864.

Painter, Nell Irvin. *Sojourner Truth: A Life, a Symbol.* New York: W. W. Norton, 1996.

Payne, Charles E. "Josiah Bushnell Grinnell." In *Iowa Biographical Series,* edited by Benjamin F. Shambaugh. Iowa City, Iowa: The State Historical Society of Iowa, 1938.

Pease, William H., and Jane H. Pease. "The Anti-Slavery Argument." In *The American Heritage Series,* edited by Leonard Levy and Alfred Young. Indianapolis, Ind.: Bobbs-Merrill, 1965.

Perman, Michael. *Reunion without Compromise: The South and Reconstruction, 1865–1868.* Cambridge: Cambridge University Press, 1973.

Perry, Lewis. *Boats against the Current: American Culture between Revolution and Modernity, 1820–1860.* New York: Oxford University Press, 1993.

Peskin, Alan. "Roscoe Conkling." In *American National Biography,* edited by John A. Garaty and Mark C. Carnes. New York: Oxford University Press, 1999.

Peterson, Merrill D. *John Brown: The Legend Revisited.* Charlottesville: University Press of Virginia, 2002.

Poore, Benjamin Perley. *Perley's Reminiscences of Sixty Years in the National Metropolis.* 2 vols. New York: AMS Press, 1886.

Potter, David M., with Don E. Fehrenbacher. *The Impending Crisis, 1848–1861.*

Edited by Henry Steele Commager and Richard B. Morris, *The New American Nation Series*. New York: Harper & Row, 1976.

Pressly, Thomas J. *Americans Interpret Their Civil War*. Princeton, N.J.: Princeton University Press, 1962.

Prokopowicz, Gerald J. "Military Fantasies." In *The Lincoln Enigma: The Changing Faces of an American Icon*, edited by Gabor S. Boritt. New York: Oxford University Press, 2001.

Quarles, Benjamin, ed. *Frederick Douglass, Great Lives Observed*. Englewood Cliffs, N.J.: Prentice-Hall, 1968.

Randel, William Peirce. *The Ku Klux Klan: A Century of Infamy*. Philadelphia, Penn.: Chilton Books, 1965.

Rawley, James A. *The Politics of Union: Northern Politics during the Civil War*. Lincoln: University of Nebraska Press, 1974.

Reid, Whitelaw. *After the War: A Tour of the Southern States, 1865–1866*. Edited by C. Vann Woodward. New York: Harper & Row, 1965.

Reynolds, David S. *Walt Whitman's America: A Cultural Biography*. New York: Alfred A. Knopf, 1995.

Richards, Leonard L. *The Slave Power: The Free North and Southern Domination, 1780–1860*. Baton Rouge: Louisiana State University Press, 2000.

Richardson, Heather Cox. *The Death of Reconstruction: Race, Labor and Politics in the Post–Civil War North, 1865–1901*. Cambridge, Mass.: Harvard University Press, 2001.

Richardson, Robert D., Jr. *Emerson: The Mind on Fire*. Berkeley: University of California Press, 1995.

Riddle, A. G. *The Life of Benjamin F. Wade*. Cleveland, Ohio: William W. Williams, 1886.

Riddleberger, Patrick W. *1866: The Critical Year Revisited*. Carbondale: Southern Illinois University Press, 1979.

Riggs, C. Russell. "The Ante-Bellum Career of John A. Bingham: A Case Study in the Coming of the Civil War." (1958) (unpublished Ph.D. dissertation, New York University).

Rodell, Fred. *Fifty-Five Men*. Harrisburg, Penn.: The Telegraph Press, 1936.

Roske, Ralph Joseph. "His Own Counsel: The Life and Times of Lyman Trumbull." In *Nevada Studies in History and Political Science*, No. 14, edited by Wilbur S. Shepperson. Reno: University of Nevada Press, 1979.

Rossiter, Clinton. *1787: The Grand Convention*. New York: Macmillan, 1966.

Salter, William. *The Life of James W. Grimes*. New York: D. Appleton, 1876.

Saltzman, Jack, David Lionel Smith, and Cornel West, eds. *Encyclopedia of African-American Culture and History*. Vol. 5. New York: Macmillan Library Reference, 1996.

Sandburg, Carl. *Abraham Lincoln: The Prairie Years*. 2 vols. New York: Charles Scribner's Sons, 1942.

———. *Abraham Lincoln: The War Years*. 4 vols. New York: Charles Scribner's Sons, 1942.

Schlesinger, Arthur M. *History of American Presidential Elections, 1789–1968*. New York: Chelsea House, 1971.

Schurz, Carl. *The Reminiscences of Carl Schurz*. 3 vols. New York: The McClure Co., 1907–08.

————. *Report on the Condition of the South*. New York: Arno Press, 1969.

————. *Speeches, Correspondence and Political Papers of Carl Schurz*. Edited by Frederic Bancroft. 6 vols. New York: G. P. Putnam's Sons, 1913.

Sewell, Richard H. *Ballots for Freedom: Antislavery Politics in the United States, 1837–1860*. New York: Oxford University Press, 1976.

————. *A House Divided: Sectionalism and the Civil War, 1848–1865*. Baltimore, Md.: Johns Hopkins University Press, 1988.

Shakespeare, William. *Measure for Measure*. London: Cambridge University Press, 1969.

Shapiro, Herbert. *White Violence and Black Response: From Reconstruction to Montgomery*. Amherst: University of Massachusetts Press, 1988.

Sherman, John. *John Sherman's Recollections of Forty Years in the House, Senate, and Cabinet*. 2 vols. New York: Werner, 1895.

Silbey, Joel H. *A Respectable Minority: The Democratic Party in the Civil War Era, 1860–1868*. New York: W. W. Norton, 1977.

Silbey, Joel H., ed. *The American Party Battle: Election Campaign Pamphlets, 1828–1876*. Vol. 2. Cambridge, Mass.: Harvard University Press, 1999.

Smith, Jean Edward. *Grant*. New York: Touchstone, 2001.

Sneed, Joseph T., III. *Footprints on the Rocks of the Mountain: An Account of the Enactment of the Fourteenth Amendment*. San Francisco, Calif.: TYSAM Press, 1997.

Solomon, Martha M., ed. "A Voice of Their Own: The Woman Suffrage Press, 1840–1910." In *Studies in Rhetoric and Communication*, edited by E. Culpepper Clark, Raymie E. McKerrow, and David Zarefsky. Tuscaloosa: The University of Alabama Press, 1991.

Speer, John. *The Life of Gen. James H. Lane, "The Liberator of Kansas," with Corroborative Incidents of Pioneer History*. Garden City, Kan.: John Speer, 1897.

Stampp, Kenneth M. *The Era of Reconstruction, 1865–1877*. New York: Alfred A. Knopf, 1965.

Stampp, Kenneth M., ed. *The Causes of the Civil War*. 3d ed. New York: Simon & Schuster, 1991.

Stampp, Kenneth M., and Leon F. Litwack. *Reconstruction: An Anthology of Revisionist Writings*. Baton Rouge: Louisiana State University Press, 1969.

Stanton, Elizabeth Cady. *Eighty Years and More: Reminiscences, 1815–1897*. New York: Schocken Books, 1971.

Stanton, Elizabeth Cady, Susan B. Anthony, and Matilda Joslyn Gage, eds. *History of Woman Suffrage*. 2d ed. 6 vols. Rochester, N.Y.: Susan B. Anthony, 1889.

Steers, Edward, Jr., ed. *The Trial: The Assassination of President Lincoln and the Trial of the Conspirators*. Lexington: The University Press of Kentucky, 2003.

Steiner, Bernard C. *The Life of Reverdy Johnson*. Baltimore, Md.: The Norman, Remington Co., 1914.

Stewart, James Brewer. *Wendell Phillips: Liberty's Hero*. Baton Rouge: Louisiana State University Press, 1986.

Swift, Lindsay. *William Lloyd Garrison*. Philadelphia, Penn.: G. W. Jacobs, 1911.

Syrett, John. "John Armour Bingham and Reconstruction." (1956) (unpublished M.S. thesis, University of Wisconsin).

Taylor, John M. *William Henry Seward: Lincoln's Right Hand*. New York: HarperCollins, 1991.

TenBroek, Jacobus. *Equal under Law.* Rev. ed. New York: Collier Books, 1965.

Thornbrough, Emma Lou, ed. *Black Reconstructionists, Great Lives Observed.* Englewood Cliffs, N.J.: Prentice-Hall, 1972.

Thorndike, Rachel S., ed. *The Sherman Letters: Correspondence between General and Senator Sherman from 1837 to 1891.* New York: Charles Scribner's Sons, 1894.

Tidwell, William, et al. *Come Retribution: The Confederate Secret Service and the Assassination of Lincoln.* Jackson: University of Mississippi Press, 1988.

Tindall, George Brown. *The Emergence of the New South, 1913–1945,* vol. 10, *A History of the South,* Wendell Holmes Stephenson and E. Merton Coulter, editors. Baton Rouge: Louisiana State University Press, 1967.

Tourgee, Albion W. *A Fool's Errand.* Edited by John Hope Franklin. Cambridge, Mass.: Belknap Press of Harvard University Press, 1961.

Trefousse, Hans L. *Andrew Johnson: A Biography.* New York: W. W. Norton, 1989.

———. *Benjamin Franklin Wade: Radical Republican from Ohio.* New York: Twayne Publishers, 1963.

———. *Carl Schurz: A Biography.* Knoxville: University of Tennessee Press, 1982.

———. *The Radical Republicans: Lincoln's Vanguard for Racial Justice.* New York: Alfred A. Knopf, 1969.

———. *Thaddeus Stevens: Nineteenth-century Egalitarian.* Chapel Hill: University of North Carolina Press, 1997.

Trefousse, Hans, ed. *Background for Radical Reconstruction: Testimony Taken from the Hearings of the Joint Committee on Reconstruction, the Select Committee on the Memphis Riots and Massacres, and the Select Committee on the New Orleans Riots, 1866 and 1867.* Edited by John A. Garraty, *Testimony of the Times: Selections from Congressional Hearings.* Boston: Little, Brown, 1970.

Trowbridge, John Townsend. *The Desolate South 1865–1866: A Picture of the Battlefields and of the Devastated Confederacy.* Edited by Gordon Carroll. New York: Duell, Sloan and Pearce, 1956.

Turner, Thomas Reed. *Beware the People Weeping: Public Opinion and the Assassination of Abraham Lincoln.* Baton Rouge: Louisiana State University Press, 1982.

United States Bureau of Refugees, Freedmen, and Abandoned Lands, 1865–1869. "Reports of Outrages, Riots and Murders, Jan. 15, 1866–Aug. 12, 1868." In *Records of the Assistant Commissioner for the State of Tennessee.* 1866. http:// freedmensbureau.com/tennessee/index.htm.

United States Census Bureau. *Historical Census Statistics on Population Totals by Race, 1790 to 1990, and by Hispanic Origin, 1970 to 1990, for the United States, Regions, Divisions, and States.* Compiled by Campbell Gibson and Kay Jung, 2002. www.census.gov/population/www/documentation/twps0056.html.

United States Congress. Joint Committee on Reconstruction. *Report of the Joint Committee on Reconstruction at the First Session, Thirty-Ninth Congress.* Washington, D.C.: Government Printing Office, 1866.

United States Congress. Senate. *Senate Election, Expulsion and Censure Cases from 1793 to 1972.* Compiled by Richard D. Hupman. Washington, D.C.: Government Printing Office, 1972.

United States War Department. *Annual Report of the Secretary of War [1864].* Washington, D.C.: Government Printing Office, 1865.

Urofsky, Melvin I., and Paul Finkelman. *A March of Liberty: A Constitutional History of the United States*. 2 vols. New York: Oxford University Press, 2002.

Van Deusen, Glyndon G. *William Henry Seward*. New York: Oxford University Press, 1967.

Vandal, Gilles. *The New Orleans Riot of 1866: Anatomy of a Tragedy*. Lafayette: The Center for Louisiana Studies, University of Southwestern Louisiana, 1983.

Vander Velde, Lewis G. *The Presbyterian Churches and the Federal Union, 1861–1869*. Vol. 33, *Harvard Historical Studies*. Cambridge, Mass.: Harvard University Press, 1932.

Vorenberg, Michael. *Final Freedom: The Civil War, the Abolition of Slavery, and the Thirteenth Amendment*. New York: Cambridge University Press, 2001.

Walters, Ronald G. *American Reformers, 1815–1860*. Rev. ed. New York: Hill & Wang, 1997.

Waterman, William Randall. *Frances Wright, Studies in History, Economics and Public Law*. New York: Columbia University Press, 1924.

Watkins, Charles L., and Floyd M. Riddick. *Senate Procedure: Precedents and Practices*. Washington, D.C.: Government Printing Office, 1958.

Waugh, John C. *Reelecting Lincoln: The Battle for the 1864 Presidency*. New York: Crown, 1997.

Welles, Gideon. *The Diary of Gideon Welles*. Edited by Howard K. Beale. 3 vols. New York: W. W. Norton, 1911.

Welter, Rush. *The Mind of America, 1820–1860*. New York: Columbia University Press, 1975.

Wheeler, Leslie, ed. *Loving Warriors: Selected Letters of Lucy Stone and Henry B. Blackwell, 1853 to 1893*. New York: The Dial Press, 1981.

Wheeler, Marjorie Spruill, ed. *Votes for Women! The Woman Suffrage Movement in Tennessee, the South, and the Nation*. Knoxville: The University of Tennessee Press, 1995.

White, Horace. *The Life of Lyman Trumbull*. Boston, Mass.: Houghton Mifflin, 1913.

Whitman, Walt. *Complete Poetry and Selected Prose*. New York: Library of America, 1982.

———. *The Correspondence*. Edited by Edward Haviland Miller. 6 vols. *The Collected Writings of Walt Whitman*. New York: New York University Press, 1961–1977.

———. *Walt Whitman's Civil War*. Edited by Walter Lowenfels. New York: Alfred A. Knopf, 1961.

Whyte, James H. *The Uncivil War: Washington during the Reconstruction, 1865–1878*. New York: Twayne Publishers, 1958.

Wiebe, Robert H. *Self-Rule: A Cultural History of American Democracy*. Chicago, Ill.: The University of Chicago Press, 1995.

Wilson, Henry W. *The Rise and Fall of the Slave Power in America*. 3 vols. Boston, Mass.: Houghton Mifflin, 1872–77.

Wilson, Theodore Brantner. *The Black Codes of the South*. Tuscaloosa: University of Alabama Press, 1965.

Wish, Harvey, ed. *Reconstruction in the South, 1865–1877: First-Hand Accounts of the American Southland after the Civil War, by Northerners and Southerners*. New York: Farrar, Straus & Giroux, 1965.

Woldman, Albert A. *Lawyer Lincoln*. Boston, Mass.: Houghton Mifflin, 1936.

Woodward, C. Vann. *Origins of the New South, 1877–1913*. Vol. 9, *A History of the South*, Wendell Holmes Stephenson and E. Merton Coulter, eds. Baton Rouge: Louisiana State University Press, 1951.

———. *The Strange Career of Jim Crow*. New York: Oxford University Press, 1955.

Wright, Frances. *Life, Letters and Lectures, 1834–1844*. Edited by Annette K. Baxter and Leon Stein, *American Women: Images and Realities*. New York: Arno Press, 1972.

Chapters in Books, Other Miscellaneous Sources

Bingham, John. "Argument in Reply to the Several Arguments in Defense of Mary E. Surratt." In *The Trial: The Assassination of President Lincoln and the Trial of the Conspirators*, edited by Edward Steers Jr. Lexington: The University Press of Kentucky, 2003.

———. "The Constitution of the United States and the Proslavery Provisions of the 1857 Oregon Constitution." In *Equal under Law*, by Jacobus TenBroek. New York: Collier Books, 1965.

Douglass, Frederick. "The Issues of the Day: An Address Delivered in Washington, D.C., on 10 March 1866." In *The Frederick Douglass Papers, Series One: Speeches, Debates and Interviews*, edited by John W. Blassingame and John R. McKivigan. New Haven, Conn.: Yale University Press, 1979.

———. "Life and Times of Frederick Douglass." In *Autobiographies*. New York: Library of America, 1996.

———. "What the Black Man Wants: Speech at the Annual Meeting of the Massachusettts Anti-Slavery Society at Boston, April 1865." In *The Life and Writings of Frederick Douglass*, vol. 4, edited by Philip S. Foner. New York: International Publishers, 1955.

Fishel, Leslie H. "Downing, George Thomas." In *American National Biography*, vol. 6, edited by John A. Garaty and Mark C. Carnes. New York: Oxford University Press, 1999.

Foner, Eric. "Thaddeus Stevens, Confiscation, and Reconstruction." In *Politics and Ideology in the Age of Civil War*, by Eric Foner. New York: Oxford University Press, 1980.

Hayes, Rutherford B. "Letter of October 1 to S. Bichard." In *The Diary and Letters of Rutherford B. Hayes, Nineteenth President of the United States*. Vol. 3, edited by Charles Richard Williams. Columbus: Ohio State Archeological and Historical Society, 1922.

Klunder, Willard Carl. "Trist, Nicholas Philip." In *American National Biography*, vol. 21, edited by John A. Garaty and Mark C. Carnes. New York: Oxford University Press, 1999.

Larson, Sylvia B. "Stockton, John Potter." In *American National Biography*, vol. 20, edited by John A. Garaty and Mark C. Carnes. New York: Oxford University Press, 1999.

Lincoln, Abraham. "First Debate: Lincoln's Reply, August 21, 1858." In *Abraham*

Lincoln: Speeches and Writings, 1832–1858, edited by Don E. Fehrenbacher. New York: Library of America, 1961–1977.

———. "Lincoln to Michael Hahn, March 13, 1864." In *Abraham Lincoln: Speeches and Writings, 1859–1865: Speeches, Letters and Miscellaneous Writings, Presidential Messages and Proclamations*, edited by Don E. Fehrenbacher. New York: Library of America, 1961–1977.

———. "Message to Congress in Special Session, July 4, 1861." In *Abraham Lincoln: Speeches and Writings, 1859–1865: Speeches, Letters and Miscellaneous Writings, Presidential Messages and Proclamations*, edited by Don E. Fehrenbacher, pp. 246–61. New York: Library of America, 1961–1977.

———. "Proclamation Calling Militia and Convening Congress, April 15, 1861." In *Abraham Lincoln: Speeches and Writings, 1859–1865: Speeches, Letters and Miscellaneous Writings, Presidential Messages and Proclamations*, edited by Don E. Fehrenbacher. New York: Library of America, 1961–1977.

———. "Proclamation No. 17, January 1, 1863." In *United States Statutes at Large*, vol. 12. Boston: Little, Brown & Co., 1863.

"The Lincoln Catechism Wherein the Eccentricities & Beauties of Despotism are Fully Set Forth: A Guide to the Presidential Election of 1864." In *History of American Presidential Elections 1789–1968*, edited by Arthur M. Schlesinger. New York: Chelsea House, 1971.

Madison, James. "Report on the Alien and Sedition Acts." In *Writings*. New York: Library of America, 1999.

Parker, Donna Grear. "Wright, Frances." In *American National Biography*, vol. 24, edited by John A. Garaty and Mark C. Carnes. New York: Oxford University Press, 1999.

Peskin, Alan. "Conkling, Roscoe." In *American National Biography*, vol. 5, edited by John A. Garaty and Mark C. Carnes. New York: Oxford University Press, 1999.

Siddali, Silvana. "Howard, Jacob Merritt." In *American National Biography*, vol. 11, edited by John A. Garaty and Mark C. Carnes. New York: Oxford University Press, 1999.

Thompson, C. Mildred. "McPherson, Edward J." In *Dictionary of American Biography*, vol. 12, compiled by the American Council of Learned Society. New York: Charles Scribner's Sons, 1943.

Villard, Oswald Garrison. "Schurz, Carl." In *Dictionary of American Biography*, vol. 16, compiled by the American Council of Learned Society. New York: Charles Scribner's Sons, 1943.

Welliver, Judson C. "The Triumph of the South." In *The Emergence of the New South, 1913–1945: A History of the South*, by George B. Tindall. Baton Rouge: Louisiana State University Press, 1967.

Whitman, Walt. "Walt Whitman to Byron Sutherland, August 26, 1865." In *Walt Whitman: The Correspondence, vol. 1, 1842–1867*, edited by Edwin Haviland Miller. New York: New York University Press, 1961–1977.

———. "Walt Whitman to Louisa Van Velsor Whitman, May 25, 1865." In *Walt Whitman, The Correspondence, vol. 1, 1842–1867*, edited by Edwin Haviland Miller. New York: New York University Press, 1961–1977.

Cases

Brown v. Board of Education, 347 U.S. 483 (1954).
City of Boerne v. Flores, 521 U.S. 507 (1997).
The Civil Rights Cases, 109 U.S. 3 (1883).
Gitlow v. New York, 268 U.S. 652 (1925).
Lochner v. New York, 198 U.S. 45 (1905).
Near v. Minnesota, 283 U.S. 697 (1931).
Plessy v. Ferguson, 163 U.S. 537 (1896).
Prudential Insurance Co. v. Cheek, 259 U.S. 530 (1922).
San Mateo County v. Southern Pacific Railway Co., 116 U.S. 138 (1885).
The Slaughter-House Cases, 83 U.S. 36 (1873).
United States v. Morrison, 529 U.S. 598 (2000).
United States v. Virginia, 518 U.S. 515 (1996).
U.S. Term Limits, Inc. v. Thornton, 514 U.S. 779 (1995).
Vieth v. Jubilirer, 544 U.S. 267 (2004).

· ACKNOWLEDGMENTS ·

First thanks first: in early 2002, before I had written a word, I told
the story of this book to an old friend. She smiled.

I hope the finished book makes her smile again.

Beyond that, the book has had a dozen mothers and as many
fathers, and I hope I remember to thank them all. First, the
University of Oregon provided generous support with two summer
grants from the Luvaas Faculty Fellowship Endowment fund. My
teachers, and later colleagues, at Duke University Law School—
Walter Dellinger, Paul Haagen, Robert Mosteller, H. Jefferson
Powell, Christopher Schroeder, and William Van Alstyne—gave
encouragement and counsel at key moments. The staff of the Duke
library system, and particularly Professor Richard Danner of the
Duke Law Library, were also crucial in helping me access rare mate-
rials and documents. The Pence Law Library at the Washington
College of Law and the American University Library provided crucial help in filling last-minute holes in the book. Angus Nesbit, Mary
Ann Hyatt, and the staff of the University of Oregon Law Library
were also helpful. The Houghton Library at Harvard University gave

me a chance to examine the records of the American Freedmen's Inquiry Commission.

Many of my Oregon colleagues provided encouragement, including Rennard Strickland, and Robert Tsai; Maurice J. Holland, Professor Jack P. Maddex of the History Department, went far beyond the call of duty in attempting to dissuade me from various historical errors. If any persist, they are there in spite of, not because of, his generous help. David Bradley, a friend of thirty years, also was lavish with time and suggestions. My assistants, Debbie Warren, Jill Forcier, and Julie Seiwell, worked skillfully to incorporate changes in multiple drafts. I was also blessed with excellent research assistants: Patricia Bradwell, Anne Cohen, William Dickens, Jessica Freeman, Alyssa Gibson, Wendy Huang, Lydia Lawless, Brian Millington, Eric Mitton, Ann Mortland, Emmet Soper, and Joe Torregrossa. Students in my seminar at Oregon, "The Framing of the Fourteenth Amendment," produced very interesting research papers and gave excellent suggestions. Joan Mathys provided superb photo research.

Scholars on other campuses were of great assistance. They include Jane Harris Aiken, Richard H. Aynes, Mary Sarah Bilder, David Butleritchie, Michael Kent Curtis, Adrienne Davis, Lynda G. Dodd, Paul Finkelman, William Forbath, John Hope Franklin, Jason Gillmer, Frederick Dennis Greene, Lewis Grossman, Phoebe Haddon, Stewart L. Harris, Darren Hutchinson, David Kairys, Sanford J. Levinson, Earl H. Maltz, Ward McAfee, James McGrath, James M. McPherson, Elliott Millstein, Reginald Oh, Jamin J. Raskin, Judith Resnik, Leonard L. Richards, Herman Schwartz, Ann Shalleck, Gerald Torres, Michael Vorenberg, and Peter Wood. Michael Kent Curtis and Richard Aynes, experts in the field, were generous and helpful indeed. I profited from the opportunity to address faculty colloquia at the Appalachian Law School, the Marshall-Wythe School of Law at the College of William and Mary, the University of North Carolina School of Law, the T. C. Williams School of Law of the University of Richmond, the University of Texas School of Law, and the Washington College of Law at the American University.

Wendy Weil, my agent of nearly four decades, supported the project with time and counsel. I forgive her for remaining young while the rest of us get older. Jack Macrae of Henry Holt is a literate and wise editor. I hope to be like him when I grow up. Supurna Banerjee was brilliant and calm. My son, Daniel, and my daughter, Maggie, were useful sounding boards. Spencie Love is always my inspiration as a historian, and she, too, is on every page. Rozanne Epps, the feared and admired Rosie Right, remains an acute copy editor sixty years after leaving *Pathfinder*. David Ignatius, my dear friend and newspaper comrade, remains an ideal writing buddy. *Here's to ourselves, old friend; so many beautiful things.* Laura Anne Fine gave me a snowy owl to watch over me, and it helped.

Toward the end, I lost my way in a dark forest, and four fierce friends walked with me toward morning: Lynn Darling, my oldest friend and my most valued counselor; Katherine Fulton and Katherine Kunst, my models of happiness; and Ann Hubbard, my colleague and comrade. No one has ever been blessed with more love or better advice than these four gave me when I was in terrible need. I will always owe them more than I can ever repay.

· INDEX ·

· ABOUT THE AUTHOR ·

GARRETT EPPS teaches constitutional law at the University of Oregon. A former reporter for *The Washington Post*, he is the author of two novels, *The Shad Treatment* and *The Floating Island: A Tale of Washington*. His most recent book is *To an Unknown God: Religious Freedom on Trial*.